Clement of Alexandria

Patrick, John

BIBLIOLIFE

The Croall Lecture for 1899-1900

Clement of Alexandria

BY

JOHN PATRICK, D.D.

PROFESSOR OF BIBLICAL CRITICISM AND BIBLICAL ANTIQUITIES,
UNIVERSITY OF EDINBURGH

William Blackwood and Sons
Edinburgh and London
1914

To the Memory of

WILLIAM PATRICK, D.D.,

PRINCIPAL OF MANITOBA COLLEGE,

1900-1911.

PREFACE.

THE Lectures on which the present volume is based were delivered in 1899-1900, and their publication is long overdue. The delay has been caused by impaired health, which compelled me for many years to confine myself to the work of my Chair. I have to thank the Croall Trustees for their courtesy and forbearance.

Since the delivery of the Lectures there has appeared the edition of the works of Clement by O. Stählin, the three volumes of which were published respectively in 1905, 1906, 1909. In preparing the Lectures for publication I have used his text throughout. It is impossible to exaggerate the services of Stahlin in the elucidation of the text and sources of Clement. I have also consulted the relative literature that has appeared since the Lectures were written, as well as other earlier writings on the subject, to which I had not access at the time. This has led to the reconsideration of some questions touched upon in the Lectures and to the consideration of others not then discussed. For these reasons the work in its present form differs in many respects from the Lectures as delivered, though the general plan and order of treatment have been preserved.

I desire to acknowledge my obligations to the Rev. Dr Gardiner of Kirknewton for the great care which he has bestowed on the revision of the proofs.

CONTENTS.

———

Clement of Alexandria.

—◆—

LECTURE I.

CLEMENT AND HIS WRITINGS.

ALEXANDRIA occupies an important place in the intellectual and spiritual history of the world. Founded by
Alexander the Great in 332 B.C., with the view of binding the East with Greece not only in an external
political union but in the bond of a common intellectual culture, it amply fulfilled, under the Ptolemies,
the end for which it had been established. From its
geographical position in relation to Greece, Asia Minor,
and Syria, it was a natural centre for the commerce
of the world; and in the realm of thought in like
manner it became a centre of intellectual activity, a bridge
between East and West, Greek and barbarian, the gods
of Greece and the gods of Egypt. On the institution
of the Museum, scholars from Greece of all schools
flocked to it, some to study, some to lecture on criticism,
or history, or rhetoric, or philosophy. Its two great
libraries furnished abundant materials for work in every
department of science and scholarship—for the philological criticism which sometimes degenerated into pedantic

A

trifling, for the laborious commentaries which took
the place of original work, for the dilettantism and endless controversies of the cloistered literati which called forth
the gibes of the satirist.[1]   Some half a century before
Clement began his activity there, the Emperor Hadrian
visited Alexandria, and in a letter of his which has been
preserved we have a vivid, if one-sided and unsympathetic,
picture of the restless life, religious and commercial, of
the community.   "I have now gained full knowledge,"
he writes, "of that Egypt whose praises you were wont
to sing. I have found the people vain and fickle, shift-
ing with every breath of popular opinion.   Those who
worship Serapis are in fact Christians; and those who
call themselves Christian bishops are devotees of Serapis.
There is no head of a Jewish synagogue, no Samaritan,
no Christian presbyter, who is not an astrologer, a
fortune-teller, or a conjurer. . . . The populace are sedi-
tious and turbulent to a degree.   The city is rich and
opulent; in it no one lives at leisure. . . . They have but
one god—money; him Christians, him Jews, him all the
peoples adore."[2]   The picture, in part, no doubt, owes its
malicious touches to the irritation felt by Hadrian at the
rejection by the Alexandrians of his minion Antinous; but
it contains sufficient truth to point the sting, and in some
of its features it is confirmed by many details in the
writings of Clement.   To an observer of a different order,
the greatness of the city seemed to contend with its
beauty, and the people to be rivals of the city.[3]   To
Hadrian, the syncretism of various forms of religious thought
might well seem an amalgam of contradictory elements, a
confusion of antagonistic systems in which everything that

---

[1] Cf. Athenæus, i. 41 (Meineke)

[2] Flavius Vopiscus Saturninus, c. 8—'Scriptores Historiæ Augustæ,' vol. ii. p.
209 (Hermann Peter).   [3] Achil. Tat., v. i.

was most distinctive of each had been toned down and effaced. So with the material luxury. Even if all allowance be made for the tendency of all moralists in their eagerness to discourage every form of vice or moral weakness to exaggerate its extent, and to ascribe to one city or age the collective vices of all cities and ages, there remains enough in Clement's allusions to show that in spite of its intellectualism the population of Alexandria was passionately devoted to all forms of luxury and enervating pleasure.[1] The religious syncretism was in harmony with the aim of its founder. In the centuries that had intervened between its foundation and the Christian era, Alexandria had become a rendezvous of all creeds, all languages, all nationalities, a veritable cosmopolis of intellectual and religious movements, a nursery of all forms of eclecticism. Like as the founder himself had built temples to Isis as well as to the gods of Olympus, so there had been effected there a fusion of forms of thought and belief which elsewhere existed in sharp antagonism to each other. Partly from an apologetic motive, partly in harmony with the tendency to syncretism in its environment, Jewish writers before the Christian era sought to show that the great thinkers of Greece were indebted to the Hebrews for their deepest speculations, and, not out of harmony with some aspects in the literary activity of the period, even fabricated and adulterated writings to prove their thesis. The translation of the Old Testament into Greek not only enabled the Jews of Alexandria to read their sacred books in their own tongue, but excited a measure of interest in Greek-speaking peoples of other nationalities, though mainly an interest of antagonism called forth by what seemed to them the preposterous claims put forth on behalf of the religious literature of a despised

[1] See Glaser, 'Zeitbilder aus Alexandrien nach dem Paedagogus des C. A.,' 1905.

section of the community. In the early years of the Christian era, Philo, while not ignoring the hypothesis of dependence, took a loftier view of the relation between the Greek philosophy and Mosaism, and by means of the allegorical method of exegesis read speculative forms and conceptions into the Pentateuch. A like syncretistic tendency was exhibited in Gnosticism, which found in Alexandria its most brilliant representatives. This intellectual and religious ferment was at once a danger and a stimulus to the exponent of the Christain faith. Such syncretism led to indifference to, or toleration of, all manifestations of the religious spirit; but Christianity by its very constitution could not but be intolerant of any form of polytheism. It furnished an interested audience; for if in Alexandria there was no great eagerness in the attainment of truth, there was keen interest in discussions about it. Into this soil in which so many diverse seeds had been sown the Gospel of Christ had been cast; it had a fierce struggle for mere existence, a still fiercer struggle before it if it were to gain the mastery. It was compelled to face new problems, to define its attitude to various forces and movements with which elsewhere it had not been brought into such immediate contact. Was it to stand aside as if these forces were of no interest to it, to leave its adherents in an intellectual atmosphere without intellectual armoury? Was it to strive to bring all that was best in them into relation to itself, or to act as if they were absolutely out of relation to it? To show the method that was adopted in the solution of such problems by the first great Alexandrian thinker whose works have come down to us, in what spirit he confronted Greek philosophy and culture, what conceptions of God, of Christ, of the Christian ideal, of Scripture, he presented to his students and fellow-disciples, is the purpose of the present course of Lectures.

From an early date, according to Eusebius, there had

existed at Alexandria a school of sacred learning.[1] The assumption of some of the older writers on the subject that it stood in a close relation to the Museum has no validity. That its teachers must in some measure have felt the academic influence, that the teaching would have reference direct and indirect to the intellectual needs and characteristics necessarily arising from its environment, may be assumed; but of any official or actual relationship between it and the Museum there is no trace. Of the origin of this Christian School nothing definite is known. A gnostic origin has been assigned to it.[2] This would no doubt account for the jealousy which it created in some quarters; but on other grounds it is improbable. Eusebius speaks of it in varying terms. Sometimes he speaks of it as a school of catechesis, sometimes as a school of sacred learning.[3] From this it may be inferred that it was a school of catechesis that had developed into a school of sacred learning. It derived its origin from the necessity of giving special instruction to catechumens in the elements of the Christian faith; but it was compelled from its surroundings to extend the sphere of its operations and give instruction in all branches of learning. Whether from the first it was dependent on the local bishop is doubtful. That it was so by the time of Origen we see from a statement of Eusebius;[4] that it may have been so at an earlier date may be conjectured from the fact that both Pantænus and Clement were presbyters of the Church. Like the Missionary Colleges in India in our own time, it was probably attended by non-Christian students as well as by Christians. But we must dismiss any idea of a separate

---

[1] Ἐξ ἀρχαίου ἔθους διδασκαλείου τῶν ἱερῶν λόγων παρ' αὐτοῖς συνεστῶτος (Eus., H. E., v. 10).

[2] Loofs, 'Leitfaden . . . Dogmengeschichte,' p. 106.

[3] . . . τοῦ τῆς κατηχήσεως . . . διδασκαλείου (vi. 3). . . . τῆς τοῦ κατηχεῖν διατριβῆς (ib.) . . . τῆς τῶν πιστῶν . . . διατριβῆς (v. 10).

[4] H. E., vi. 3.

building as such an analogy would suggest. The language of Eusebius with regard to Origen rather suggests that he taught in his own house.[1] The picture presented by Gregory Thaumaturgus[2] of the school under the guidance of Origen may be regarded as exhibiting the general lines on which it was working from the third quarter of the second century. Christianity was set forth as the crown of all learning, and all liberal arts were represented as its handmaids. The scholars were carefully trained in the art of detecting sophisms and fallacies. They were encouraged to read everything that had been written by poets and philosophers of old, with the exception of the works of atheists. They were trained in natural science, especially in astronomy and geometry, in ethics, and in the discussion of philosophical problems; but in all these not for their own sakes, but as a means to an end, as aids to the interpretation and defence of the Scriptures. In this lay the essential difference between it and the Stoic and Platonic schools of the Imperial era, though otherwise it ran on parallel lines[3] In this respect, too, it had analogies with the Missionary Colleges of to-day.

According to a statement of Philip of Side, the first head of the Catechetical School was Athenagoras. But in view of the notorious inaccuracy of the writer, and especially of his reversal of the relation of Pantænus and Clement, no weight can be attached to the tradition. The first teacher whose name is definitely known to us, who prescribed the range of its work, and from whom it received the impetus that made it famous and influential in the history of the Church, was Pantænus. Probably not later than the year 180 he became the head of the school. Of the ecclesiastical traditions concerning him the one statement that may be admitted without controversy is that, before his con-

---

[1] H. E., vi. 3.   [2] Paneg. in Orig , vi.-xiv.
[3] Cf. 'Rheinische Museum für Philologie,' vol. lvi. p. 56

version, he had belonged to the school of the Stoics.[1] By
his teaching he attracted many scholars, and among others
Clement. According to Jerome,[2] Pantænus wrote commentaries on many books of Scripture. The accuracy
of the assertion is disputed;[3] in any case, with the exception of one or two passages or allusions, which may have
been derived from oral tradition, they have perished; but
his teaching, his methods, his principles, in all likelihood
even many of the details of his system, survive in the works
of his disciple.

Titus Flavius Clemens was born in all probability in
Athens,[4] and of heathen parentage, about the middle of
the second century. He was endowed by nature with a
deeply religious temperament and a burning thirst for
knowledge. His religious yearnings he seems to have
sought to satisfy by initiation into the mysteries;[5] he
evinced his love of learning by the passionate pursuit of
all branches of science and philosophy. The same religious
earnestness that had created in his spirit dissatisfaction
with heathenism drove him to seek for fuller knowledge
and deeper insight into the mysteries of the Christian
religion. In many lands—in Greece, Italy, Syria, Palestine
—and under many teachers, he studied zealously, but found
no lasting satisfaction for his spirit till he came to Egypt.
Of the "truly blessed and memorable men" whom he was

[1] Eus., H. E., v. 10.　　　　　　[2] De Vir. Ill., c 36.
[3] Cf. Ec. Pr., 27 : οὐκ ἔγραφον δὲ οἱ πρεσβύτεροι.
[4] Epiph. Hær., xxxii. 6. Κλήμης τε ὅν φασί τινες Ἀλεξανδρέα, ἕτεροι δὲ
Ἀθηναῖον. Greece was the starting-point of his search for truth (Str , i 1 [1])　In
Prot., ii.[20], referring to the prevalence of the legend concerning Demeter, he
says : ὅπου γε Ἀθηναίοις καὶ τῇ ἄλλῃ Ἑλλάδι, αἰδοῦμαι καὶ λέγειν　His sen-
sitiveness on the point suggests that he was a Greek and an Athenian. He is not
sensitive as to the details.
[5] This is an inference from the knowledge which he displays of the details of
the mysteries　Cf Eus., Præp Evang., ii. 2, p. 61. It is not regarded as
cogent by Bratke　'Die Stellung des Cl. Al zum antiken Mysterienwesen'
(St. u. Kr., 1887, p. 656). Cf. St. u. Kr., 1894.

privileged to hear, and of their "convincing and living
words," he writes as follows: "Of these, one was in Greece,
an Ionian. Others were in Magna Græcia, one from Cœle-
Syria, the other from Egypt. There were others in the
East, one of whom was of the Assyrians, and the other in
Palestine, a Hebrew by origin. When I fell in with the last
of my teachers (he was the first in power), having hunted
him out as he lay concealed in Egypt, I came to rest. He
was in truth a Sicilian bee who culled the flowers of the
prophetic and apostolic meadow, and begot in the souls of
his hearers an unsullied store of knowledge. These men,
preserving the true tradition of the blessed teaching directly
from Peter, James, John, and Paul, the holy apostles, the
son receiving it from the father (but few are like their
fathers), came with God's blessing also to us to deposit
these ancestral and apostolic seeds."[1] That these were
Christian teachers is manifest; they were six in number.
Who the others were is disputed or unknown: some have
identified the Ionian with Athenagoras, the Assyrian with
Tatian; but that the last was Pantænus there can be no
doubt. The words of Clement show his eagerness in the
search for a solution of the problems that had created unrest and his complete satisfaction with the solution. He
became a presbyter of the Church,[2] and for a period of more
than twenty years he wrought and taught in Alexandria,
first as coadjutor of Pantænus, and afterwards as his successor. In the year 202 the persecution of Severus broke
out, and in accordance with his own teaching on martyrdom, as professedly based on the injunction of Christ, he
left Alexandria that he might serve the Church of Christ
elsewhere.[3] Of his subsequent career little is known. We
catch a final glimpse of his activity in the year 211, in a

[1] Str., i. 1 [1].   [2] Pæd., i. 6 [37].
[3] Matt. x. 23. Cf. Str., iv. 4 [14-17]; Stah., vol. iii. p. 226, fr. 56.

letter of Alexander, then bishop of Cappadocia, who had
been a fellow-student of Origen in the school of Clement.
In sending a letter to the Church of Antioch by the hands
of Clement, he describes him as the blessed presbyter,
a man virtuous and approved, who had confirmed and
advanced the Church of the Lord.[1] In a later letter of
Alexander to Origen, he alludes to Pantænus and Clement
as those blessed fathers who had trodden the way before
them, with whom after a little they would be.[2] He died
probably about 215.

Though the facts of his life are so meagre, the portrait
of the man himself stands out in his writings as that of
a singularly lovable personality. He gives the impression
of a certain intellectual naïveté, combined with a moral
austerity. He has a lofty conception of the function of the
teacher, as well as of the duty of the scholar. If he
demands from the student that he shall approach the
study of the Christian faith with earnest reverence and
not in the merely curious spirit with which men go to
strange cities and buildings, and if he insists that the ears
of those who seek to become partakers of the truth must
be sanctified, he demands from himself as a teacher that
he shall keep in view the varied character and temperament
of those who are under his tuition, that he shall set aside
all ignoble impulses and motives, and have for his sole
aim the salvation of his hearers.[3] What Gregory says of
his scholar Origen may be applied to his master. " He
did not merely discuss ethical matters with his scholars, but
incited them to the practice of morals, and stimulated by
what he did even more than by what he said."[4] There can
be little doubt that in the representation of the gnostic
he sets forth the ideal which was the goal of his own

[1] Eus., H. E., vi. 11.   [2] Ib., vi. 14.
[3] Str., i. 1 ⁴⁶.   [4] Paneg. in Orig., c. 9.

endeavour. "I do not know," says Maurice, "where we shall look for a purer or a truer man than this Clement of Alexandria. . . . He seems to me that one of the old fathers whom we should all have reverenced most as a teacher and loved most as a friend."[1]

Of the writings of Clement many have perished; many to which he makes allusion as in contemplation were in all probability never written. Of the writings that have survived, the most important are the Protrepticus, the Pædagogus, and the Stromateis. Till a few years ago it was universally assumed by writers on the subject that the three works were written in the order named, that though distinctive in aim they were closely and progressively related to each other and formed a series, that they were so intended by the writer himself, and, accordingly, that they may be regarded as one work in three sections, the general aim of which was to transform the Greek pagan by stages into a Christian gnostic, to initiate the reader into the ethics and philosophy of the Christian faith by setting forth different aspects of the activity of the one Logos. But the "discovery" of Wendland—to use the phrase of Harnack—has produced a complete reversal of this view, and introduced an entirely novel conception of the literary relationships of these writings. According to Wendland, the order was, Protrepticus; Stromateis, I.-IV.; Pædagogus; Stromateis, V.-VII. The hypothesis has been supported by Heussi and Harnack, and accepted by Duchesne and others The question is discussed afterwards;[2] here it may be said that, if not "ungrounded and improbable," as it is described by a patristic authority of the first rank,[3] the hypo-

---

[1] 'Ecclesiastical History of the First and Second Centuries,' p. 239. Clement has no legal right to the official designation of "saint" sometimes ascribed to him.

[2] See Appendix D.   [3] Bardenhewer.

thesis raises difficulties not less great than the traditional view which it seeks to supplant. It is not a purely literary or academic question, for in some cases the order has a direct bearing on the exposition of the teaching.

The 'Exhortation to the Greeks'[1] is the earliest extant work of Clement, and is at once a powerful exposure of the paganism from which he sought to wean them and a powerful appeal in favour of Christianity. He begins with an invitation to turn aside from heathen myths and listen to the New Song—the Word of God. He then exposes with almost superfluous fulness the corruptions of paganism, its mysteries, the legends as to the gods, the cruelty and impurity of its sacrifices, its worship of images made by men's hands. From this he passes to the imperfect views of God set forth in the works of philosophers and poets, with which he contrasts the truth of Christianity as set forth in the Scriptures. He then refutes the objection that they should not abandon ancestral customs, showing its folly and the loss which it entails. Finally, he exhibits the beneficence of God as revealed in Christianity, and urges them in the name of Christ to choose life, not death.[2] It was probably written before 195[3] — perhaps some years earlier.

With the Pædagogus or Tutor we enter upon the second stage of the work of the Word. Clement himself tells us that the aim of the writing was to set forth the way of life and training from the stage of childhood—that is, the rule of life, derived from instruction, which grows along with faith, and prepares the virtuous soul in the case of those who

---

[1] Προτρεπτικὸς πρὸς Ἕλληνας

[2] For an analysis, which, however, can give no idea of its eloquence and passionate movement, see Appendix A.

[3] Bardenhewer, Patrologie,[3] about 195; Geschichte der altkirchlichen Litt., before 199; Zahn, before 189; Harnack, in the ninth decade of the second century.

were reaching the rank of men for the reception of gnostic science.[1]   An ethical foundation had to be laid before introduction to the higher truths of Christianity, for moral health was the condition of spiritual insight.   The Tutor is the Word, the Son of God Himself, who sets forth a system of practical ethics in conformity with a Christian ideal of life.   Certain general principles are laid down.   Nothing is to be done contrary to nature.[2]   We must beware of all that is unnatural and all that is excessive.[3]   Everything is to be done in harmony with right reason.[4]   Moderation should be our aim in everything.[5]   We are not to take away what is natural to man but to impose upon it a just measure.[6]   The life of the Christian ought to be a unity.[7]   It should be a kind of organised whole of rational actions — that is, an infallible fulfilment of what is taught by the Word.[8]   He ought to live after the image of the Tutor,[9] to take on the impression of the truly saving life of the Saviour and follow in the footsteps of God.[10]   As his aim is to set forth what a Christian ought to be in every relation of life,[11] Clement gives the most minute details of guidance in everything that affects a citizen of the kingdom of God.   The extraordinary minuteness of the instruction, of which he himself at times is conscious,[12] has brought on him the charge of petty pedantry; but it is in large measure due to the fact that he has throughout the needs of the catechumens in mind; and, it may be, in part due to the fact that he is following the methods of some Stoic teachers,[13] possibly of Pantænus himself, who gave to their disciples similarly detailed prescriptions.   The dominating ethical ideal in Alexandria was non-Christian; and the emphasising of a negative to it at all

[1] Str , vi 1[1].   [2] Pæd , ii. 13[129].   [3] Ib , ii. 11[114].   [4] Ib , ii. 2[29].

[5] Ib , iii. 10[61].   [6] Ib., ii. 5[46].   [7] Ib., iii. 1[1].   [8] Ib , i. 13[102].

[9] Ib., i. 12[100].   [10] Ib , i. 12[95].   [11] Ib., ii. 1[1].   [12] Ib., ii. 1[7].

[13] Cf. Zeller, 'Eclecticism,' p 253 (Eng. trans.)

points was imperative; and this involved in the circumstances not merely the inculcation of general principles but
definite instruction by way of guidance. As they had to
adjust the new force to their intellectual environment, they
had also to adjust it to the manifold relations of everyday
life. Many of the precepts which seem to us trifling or
superfluous were no doubt called forth by antagonism to the
immorality or irreligion with which they were associated.
If any justification for his procedure is necessary, it is
justified by the consideration that the strength of paganism,
from the glamour of which the converts were only just
emancipated, lay not so much in its religious conceptions,
which could easily be overthrown by arguments, as in the
social customs which were an inseparable element in it. In
this way things in themselves morally indifferent might
acquire a moral stamp or stigma for the time. A code of
practical ethics, with suggestions, so to speak, on Christian
etiquette, was a necessary part of the equipment of the
Greek who had entered upon the career of a Christian
citizen. From the nature of the case it was inevitable that
emphasis should be placed on the restrictions imposed by
their Christian profession, rather than on its liberties.
Clement certainly did not err in insisting on the necessary
relation between the dogmatic and the ethical side of
Christianity, or in making the attainment of truth in its
highest form depend on the realisation of the moral ideal in
every relation of life as its essential prerequisite. It is
significant that the first systematic teacher of Christian
doctrine, the foremost champion of liberal culture in the
Church, should at the same time be the most eloquent
exponent in that age, and for many ages that followed, of
Christianity in common life.

The treatise was divided by the writer himself into Three
Books. In the First Book Clement explains who the Tutor

is, who His pupils are, and what has been and is His method
of education.   The Tutor is the Word; babes in Christ are
His pupils; He adopts all methods of training—including
punishment, which is consistent with, nay, is a proof of,
love—to secure the moral salvation of those under His
tuition.   In the Second Book he enters into details.   Under
the subject of the relation of the Christian to the body, he
touches on the proper use of food, of drink, of gold and
silver vessels, of music, of jesting, condemns all manner of
filthy speaking and frivolous talk, the use of floral crowns,
and indicates the limits to be placed on the use of ointments
and sleep.   He sets forth the Christian view of marriage,
reprobates all manner of impurity, luxury in clothing, and
the use of precious stones in place of cultivating true beauty.
In the Third Book he continues the same subject, censures
the love of finery in women, as well as effeminacy in men and
extravagance in the number of slaves, prescribes the proper
use of the public baths, of wealth, of physical exercises,
condemns the use of false hair, all forms of gambling, the
visiting of racecourses and theatres.   He exhibits the duty
of the Christian in business, gives counsel as to his conduct
on the way to church, in church, and out of it.   He concludes with some suggestions, based on the words of
Scripture, on prayer, civil government, and kindred matters.
A prayer to the Tutor brings the work to a close.   Two
hymns are adjoined to the treatise.   The first may have
been written by Clement; the second certainly is not by
him.   The work was written before the Stromateis.   The
date is put by Zahn about 190, and by Bardenhewer soon
after the Protrepticus;[1] by Harnack, in accordance with
his hypothesis of the relative order of composition of the
great writings, in the first decade of the second century.[2]

[1] Patrologie[2].   [2] See Analysis, Appendix B.

The third and highest stage of discipleship is set forth in the Stromateis, or 'Gnostic notes according to the true Philosophy,' as he designates its contents.[1] "A 'stromateus' was a long bag of striped canvas in which bedclothes were rolled up."[2] From a statement of his own we see that it was the custom to give fancy designations, such as 'Meadow,' 'Helicon,' 'Honeycomb,' 'Robe,' and the like, to works of a miscellaneous order.[3] As applied to a literary work, it was not invented by Clement,[4] though it was afterwards so associated with his name that he is often described as the Stromatist.[5] The title was meant to suggest freedom of movement and artful disorder. He speaks of it as if it were only the reproduction of the teaching which he had received from "blessed and truly memorable men"; and, if this is not to be taken literally, it may contain a larger measure of truth than is sometimes supposed.[6] He tells us that his writing is not to be compared to trim pleasure-grounds, but rather to a dense and umbrageous wood, where all kinds of trees, fruit-bearing and others, are intentionally mingled;[7] to a meadow, in which the flowers blossom promiscuously, where things are scattered advisedly without regard to order or style;[8] to the "herbage of all kinds," of which the Scripture speaks.[9] One reason for this disorder is the desire to stimulate the reader and encourage the earnest searcher after truth, by making it more precious in his eyes when hunted out instead of making it too easy of access; to indicate the path to the reader, instead of accompanying him the whole

---

[1] Τῶν κατὰ τὴν ἀληθῆ φιλοσοφίαν γνωστικῶν ὑπομνημάτων στρωματεύς (Str., iii. 18 [101]).

[2] Hort.

[3] Str , vi. 1 [2].

[4] Cf Aulus Gellius, Praef., 6-8

[5] Cf. Frag. 48, Stah., vol. iii. p. 224.

[6] Str., i. 1 [11].

[7] Ib., vii. 18 [111].

[8] Ib , vi. 1 [2].

[9] Ib., iv. 2 [6]; Job v. 25.

way.[1] Another reason adduced is the necessity of concealing truth or expressing it in obscure symbol.[2] This is hard
to account for, unless it be the fruit of an unconscious
apologetic impulse, or a concession to the Greek catechumens whom he has in view at every stage of his work.
He has little interest in, and makes no appeal to, the Jews
in Alexandria. To his desire to confirm his hold on the
Greeks is due the display, often irrelevant, of his curious
scientific, medical,[3] philosophical, philological, and religious lore, the digressions, the numerous quotations from,
and allusions to, Greek poets and thinkers, and the superfluous fulness with which he enters into details even when
the enumeration brings him into formal antagonism to his
own standpoint.[4] The result of his method is that "readers
of the present day are often puzzled to know what he is
driving at."[5] And as with the lack of order, so with the
style. He tells us that he does not make any special effort
at writing pure Greek, as he who cares for truth will not
study phraseology.[6] As the Christian must cultivate a
simple way of living, so he must cultivate a style severely
simple and artless, with more nourishment in it than sauce.
Style is but the vesture of thought, and clothing should not
take precedence of the body.[7]

Perhaps by way of reaction against the fashionable
rhetoric of the day, to write well seemed to him a mark
of frivolity.[8] As a consequence, he is sometimes at once

[1] Str , i. 2²¹; iv. 2⁴.   [2] Ib., v. 8⁵⁴; vi. 1¹²

[3] Cf. Harnack, 'Medizinisches aus der altesten Kirchengeschichte,' T. u. U., 1892.

[4] Cf., e.g., Pæd., ii. 8⁶⁹, and Str., i. 16¹⁷⁶

[5] Mayor, 'Clement of Alexandria' (Hort and Mayor), p. xiv.

[6] Str., ii. 1³. "His language swarms with grammatical errors : he lacks discrimination in the use of the negatives οὐ and μή, of the pronouns ὅς and ὅστις,
and the different forms of hypothetical sentences" (W Christ., Phil. Stud. zum
C. A , p 13).

[7] Str., i. 10⁴⁸.

[8] Cf. Croiset, 'Histoire de la Littérature grecque,' vol. v. p. 752.

both obscure and diffuse, and adds analogy to analogy and epithet to epithet without adding to the thought or sharpening its definiteness. At times it may be that the Stromateis may be compared to a "confused causerie";[1] but it is improperly described as "Miscellanies," if by that is meant a series of disconnected essays. For, while there is a lack of order in details, there is no confusion as to the principles which are fundamental in his thought, which are in no way affected by disorder or irregularity of form.

In its extant form the Stromateis contains Seven Books and a fragment of an Eighth.[2] The general aim of the First Book is to represent Christianity as the true and final philosophy, and to exhibit the place of Greek philosophy in this connection. He condemns those who attacked philosophy, exhibits its usefulness, and marks it off from the sophistry which has usurped the name. He sets forth the succession of philosophers among the Greeks, with the aim of showing that it was inferior to the Christian truth both in respect of antiquity and of its secondary origin. To a like end he extols the work of Moses, defends the principles of his legislation, and maintains that, as compared with the Christian philosophy, the Greeks were no better than children, and that their science had no claim to the veneration due to age.

The Second Book begins with a statement of the plan which he proposed to follow. It then enters on a discussion as to the knowledge of God, emphasising in this matter the function of faith. It proceeds to set aside erroneous views as to the nature of faith, and exhibits its true nature as the foundation of the highest knowledge and truth. It goes on to discuss the place of fear as a

---

[1] Croiset, ib "Causerie confuse, ou se mêlent tous les tons, ou manquent l'ordre, la lumière, le bon goût même."

[2] The first leaf of the MS. is lost.

motive to Christian duty, the relation of the virtues to one another, and, in particular, the nature of penitence. It touches on the anthropomorphic expressions in Scripture, claims a Mosaic origin for the Greek conceptions of virtue, and defends the beneficent character of the Mosaic economy. It then exhibits the attitude of the Christian to pleasure and the passions, discusses various theories as to the highest good, and some aspects of the question of marriage.

The Third Book continues the discussion on marriage, and is mainly taken up with the refutation of heretical doctrines on the subject. In particular, the teaching of the school of Carpocrates with its glorification of lust is condemned, and the teaching of Marcion with its false and impious conception of continence. The position of those who taught that all actions were morally indifferent is examined. The scriptural arguments, for the most part taken from the Epistles of St Paul, are adduced in support of his refutation of the false and his exhibition of the true teaching as to continence and marriage in relation to the Christian ideal of life.

In the Fourth Book, after a detailed statement of his proposed order of treatment, he proceeds to consider the distinctive excellence of man, the nature of true martyrdom, its motive and end, the attitude of the Christian to persecution, and the grounds on which this is permitted by God and held to be reconcilable with His power and righteousness. He represents the ideal of gnostic love and its reward as equally attainable by women and men, indicates the difference between legal and gnostic perfection, and exhibits the pre-eminence of the knowledge of God, which was only possible through the Son, by faith in whom our life is unified. The true nature of the body and its relation to the soul in the Christian economy is then set forth.

The Fifth Book opens with a discussion on the nature

of faith and its relation to knowledge, and touches on the nature of hope and its place among the Christian virtues. He proceeds to show that in expressing the deepest mysteries in symbolic guise the Scriptures had followed a method universal in religion as well as in poetry and philosophy. He then explains the anthropomorphic language of the Scriptures, points out some analogies between the grades in the mysteries, beginning with purification and ending in contemplation, and the Christian stages towards the knowledge of God; shows how logical demonstration is from the nature of the case impossible in the case of God, and that, accordingly, He can only be apprehended through grace by faith in the Son as revealed in Scripture. Whatever measure of truth the Greeks possessed had been taken from this source. Though men everywhere had a certain knowledge of God, even when this had reached its highest as among the Greeks, it was imperfect in its range and saving power.

The Sixth Book opens with a renewed statement of his plan of writing, touching on the relation of the Stromateis to the Pædagogus in this connection. He confirms his thesis of the theft of the Greeks from the Scriptures by seeking to prove that they stole from each other *en masse*. The Greeks had but a limited grasp of the truth; whereas the Jews required only the addition of faith, the Greeks had further to abandon idolatry. He then discusses the nature of true wisdom, and its pre-eminence as having been derived from the Wisdom of God. The gnostic is then delineated in his relation to philosophic culture, to his own body, to the world and its duties, to God and fellowship with Him, to his moral ideals and the method of their realisation, to his fellow-men, to the Scriptures and their interpretation. He gives an exposition of the Decalogue as a specimen of gnostic insight. He again touches on the divine origin of philosophy, while showing that it lacked the divine signs that accredited Christianity, as well as its universality, and its power to rise above the forces that threatened to crush it.

To show that the gnostic is truly pious is declared to be the purpose of the Seventh Book. This piety is portrayed in manifold aspects, alike on the divine and the human sides, which are not to be separated. His devoutness is set forth in relation to God, in his knowledge of the things of God, in his worship free from superstition and all ignoble elements, in his prayer, in his goal of unending contemplation. God accepts service of men as service of Him. So the gnostic is characterised by teaching, by beneficence, by self-sacrifice, by forgiveness of wrong, by striving after Christian perfection in love. In the closing section of the book Clement examines at length the objection that the Christian faith should not be embraced because of its divisions, and demonstrates that such a position was untenable save on grounds which were not in harmony with the real facts as to Christian truth and its heretical caricature.[1]

The Eighth Book on the face of it does not seem to have any close connection with the previous discussions, and might be a fragment of a logical treatise. It touches on such topics as the necessity of exact definition, the nature and method of demonstrative proof, genera and species. It is a matter of controversy whether it was originally a part of the Stromateis.[2] It does not deal specifically with any of the questions suggested in his various programmes. But, on the other hand, he seems to indicate at the close of the Seventh Book that he was about to pass to another subject of inquiry.[3]

The whole work is unfinished; many topics which formed

---

[1] See Appendix C.   [2] Cf Zahn, Supplem. Clem., p. 114 et seq.
[3] Str., vii. 18 [111].

part of his plan were never touched upon : whether he abandoned his task, as Overbeck suggests, because he despaired of being able to finish a subject that had proved so unwieldy, or, as others think, died before he had completed his task, it is impossible to say. Zahn puts the work at 202-203; Bardenhewer substantially agrees; Harnack puts the earlier portion at a similar period, and the later books after his departure from Alexandria.[1]

The only other work of Clement that has survived is the tractate entitled " Who is the Rich Man that is being Saved ? "[2] This is an exposition of the narrative in the Gospel of the rich young man,[3] with a discussion on the problem therein suggested—the possibility of salvation in the Christian sense for the rich. The solution of Clement is that wealth is in itself a thing neither good nor bad, that its moral character is determined by its use or misuse, and that it may be so used as to be a stepping-stone towards spiritual progress and final salvation. The question of date turns mainly on the meaning that is to be attached to a phrase in the Homily itself: " As to the mystery of the Saviour, you may learn from my Exposition concerning First Principles and Theology."[4] In the Stromateis reference is made to this treatise or section as in contemplation, but it is doubtful whether it was ever carried out. If, as is maintained by Zahn,[5] the reference suggests a work already written, then the " Quis Dives " must have been written after the Stromateis ; if, as is held by others,[6] it only refers

[1] All the chronological data are brought down to the death of Commodus. Str., i. 21.
[2] Τίς ὁ Σῳζόμενος Πλούσιος (Quis Dives Salvetur)
[3] Mark x. 17-31 ; Matt. xix. 16-30 ; Luke xviii. 18-30.
[4] Ὅπερ ἐν τῇ περὶ ἀρχῶν καὶ θεολογίας ἐξηγήσει μυστήριον τοῦ Σωτῆρος ὑπάρχει μαθεῖν. Q D., p. 26.
[5] Zahn, op. cit , p 39. Barnard agrees with Zahn. See Q. D., p. 44, 'Cambridge Texts and Studies,' 1897.
[6] v. Arnim, de Faye, Harnack.

to a work contemplated, it may have been written before the
Stromateis. There is nothing distinctive in its teaching in
its bearing on the question of date, and it may be well with
Krüger and Ehrhard [1] to hold that the date of composition
cannot be definitely determined. [2]

In the only manuscript in which the Stromateis have been
preserved, after the fragment of the Eighth Book are found
two series of extracts. The first has the title, "Summaries
from Theodotus and the so-called Anatolic School in the
Times of Valentinus." [3] These contain quotations from a
Gnostic writer, with comments by Clement, and it is often
difficult to tell whether we are reading the commentary
or the original. Even a scholar like Zahn, who made an
exhaustive study of this, as of all other Clementine problems,
in his 'Supplementum Clementinum,' published in 1884,
altered his opinion in regard to the apportioning of the
fragments to their separate sources in a further study of the
subject, published in 1892. [4] In view of this difficulty of
severing the wheat from the tares, in an exposition of the
teaching of Clement, they must be used with reserve, and
are of no value as an independent source. They can only
be used with confidence when they find complete or partial
confirmation in the undoubted writings. Even when there
is little doubt that the words are those of Clement, we have
to be on our guard, for the simple reason that they are
excerpts, and that we are ignorant of the context as well

[1] Kruger, 'Early Christian Literature,' p. 170; Ehrhard, 'Die altchristliche
Litteratur,' p. 303
[2] The main points in the Homily are noted in Lecture V.
[3] Ἐκ τῶν Θεοδότου καὶ τῆς ἀνατολικῆς καλουμένης διδασκαλίας κατὰ τοὺς
Οὐαλεντίνου χρόνους Ἐπιτομαί.
[4] Clem. Supp., p. 126. Zahn assigned the Fragments to Clement thus: Sections 8-15 with certainty, 18-20, 27, 66-74, 81-86, with more or less definiteness;
perhaps also 4, 5. In his 'Geschichte d. ntl. K.,' vol. ii pp. 961-964, he regards
as Clementine 4, 5, some sentences in 7, 8-15, 17ᵇ.20, 27; and regards the whole
sections 66-86 as Valentinian.

as of the methods and grounds on which the epitomist proceeded.

The second series of Extracts bears the title "Selections from the Prophets."[1] The contents are varied in character, the most connected and complete section being a characteristic exposition of the nineteenth psalm. They were probably taken from the same source as the "Excerpts from Theodotus." But as to what that source was there is divergence of opinion. Westcott thinks that there "can be no reasonable doubt" that they were taken from the 'Hypotyposes.'[2] Zahn holds that, like the extant fragment, they were taken from the Eighth Book of the Stromateis.[3] This hypothesis was accepted by Harnack in the first volume of his 'History of Early Christian Literature,' published in 1893, but rejected as "highly improbable" in a later volume of the same work.[4] By v. Arnim the suggestion was made that both series of extracts were made by Clement from Gnostic writings, with comments added by himself, as preparatory sketches for a further treatise.[5] This conflict and fluctuation of opinion emphasise the lesson already noted as to the limitation to be exercised in the use of materials of such uncertain origin.

Of the lost writings of Clement, the most important is the 'Hypotyposes' or 'Outlines.' From the statements of Eusebius and Photius, as well as from the fragments that survive, it would seem that it contained a running commentary, with notes as to date and authorship, on the

---

[1] 'Εκ τῶν προφητῶν 'Εκλογαί.   [2] D. C. B., vol. i. p. 564.

[3] Op. cit., pp. 117-129.

[4] 'Geschichte der altchristlichen Litteratur,' vol. i. p. 181. So Preuschen, p. 315. In vol. ii. p. 18 (1904), he expresses approval of the hypothesis of v. Arnim. "Ich weiss nichts gegen sie einzuwenden" (p. 18, n. 3).

[5] 'De Octavo Clementis Stromateorum Libro,' 1894. Cf. Ehrhard, op. cit., p. 311.

books of Scripture. Eusebius and Photius give conflicting statements as to its extent. Eusebius says that it
embraced abridged explanations of all the Canonical
Scripture, not passing by the disputed books — that is,
Jude and the rest of the Catholic Epistles, and Barnabas,
and the so - called Apocalypse of Peter.[1] Photius says
that the 'Outlines' contained a brief explanation and interpretation of some passages of the Old and the New
Scripture. After condemning the impious blasphemies
with which, according to him, it abounded, he says that
the whole aim was to give interpretations, as it were, of
Genesis, Exodus, the Psalms, the Epistles of the divine
Paul, the Catholic Epistles, and Ecclesiastes.[2] If the
statement of Eusebius be accurate, Photius must have had
an imperfect copy before him, as in his sweeping condemnation of the errors of Clement he would hardly have
refrained from adding Clement's use of Apocryphal writings.
A fragment of the section of the 'Outlines' dealing with
the First Epistle of Peter, the Epistle of Jude, the First
and Second Epistles of John, survives in a Latin version
made by Cassiodorus, or at his instance.[3] Cassiodorus so
far supports the statement of Photius as to its heretical
contents, for he says that Clement spoke some things
with rashness, and that in translating them into Latin he
had purged the teaching from the offending matters [4] The
more weighty of the heresies charged against Clement—
those touching the Person and nature of Christ—will be
noted afterwards.[5] Here I only touch on the question of
his heterodoxy in its bearing on the date of the work.

---

[1] Eus , vi. 14 · . . . πάσης τῆς ἐνδιαθήκου γραφῆς ἐπιτετμημένας πεποίηται διηγήσεις, μηδὲ τὰς ἀντιλεγομένας παρελθών. . . .

[2] Phot., cod. 109 · ὁ δὲ ὅλος σκοπὸς ὡσανεὶ ἑρμηνεῖαι τυγχάνουσι τῆς Γενέσεως, τῆς Ἐξόδου, τῶν Ψαλμῶν, τοῦ θείου Παύλου τῶν ἐπιστολῶν καὶ τῶν καθολικῶν καὶ τοῦ Ἐκκλησιαστοῦ

[3] Stäh , vol. iii. pp. 203-215.   [4] Quoted by Zahn, p. 134.   [5] See Lecture IV.

According to Zahn, the 'Hypotyposes' was written after his flight from Alexandria, and is to be regarded as the latest of his important writings.[1] The same view is taken by Westcott and Chapman.[2] On the other hand, v. Arnim,[3] de Faye,[4] and Harnack[5] criticise adversely this hypothesis, mainly on the ground that the incomplete form of the Stromateis shows that it was his latest work. On the assumption that the 'Outlines' were more heterodox in character than the Stromateis, Harnack makes the interesting suggestion that it is not probable that Clement grew more heterodox in course of time, and that, especially in view of the manner in which docetic and gnostic elements were gradually crushed out of the Church, it is not probable that Clement, who was a presbyter, should have so developed. The latter consideration is, perhaps, more weighty than the former. For, apart from the fact that in the sphere of doctrine and criticism — as in other spheres — a development from a more conservative to a more radical standpoint is not unknown, in the case of Clement, who was apt to be influenced by his temporary aim and mood, an argument on *a priori* grounds is precarious. But the latter consideration is weighty. It is altogether inconsistent with the esteem in which he was held by Alexander, and with the services which he rendered to the Church in his later years, to suppose that there was an increased divergence from the ecclesiastical norm, and not a progressive movement towards it. Harnack regards it as overwhelmingly probable that it was written considerably earlier than the earliest portion of the Stromateis.[6]

---

[1] *Op. cit.*, p. 176.   [2] Rev. Bened., vol xxi. p. 369. Cf. Mayor, *op. cit.*, p. xix.
[3] *Op. cit*, pp 14, 15.   [4] Clément d'Alexandrie, 1898, pp. 110, 111.
[5] *Op. cit*, pp 19, 20.
[6] Chapman regards the 'Muratorian Fragment' as taken from the 'Hypotyposes,' and supports the date of Zahn. He finds in the criticism passed there

The writings of Clement are characterised by an appearance of enormous and varied erudition. They were so regarded by Jerome, Eusebius, Cyril of Alexandria, and Theodoret in the early centuries.[1] They were so regarded by his editors and historians generally till a recent date. From this point of view one of his early editors speaks of him as a Christian Plutarch or Athenæus, and says that he quotes more than three hundred authors of whom otherwise we know not the names, and adds that for this reason he is a treasure-house not only for theologians but for grammarians, historians, and philosophers, even for jurists and physicians.[2] Within recent years, however, from a minute study of the sources, many endeavours have been made to reduce this erudition to very meagre dimensions. His show of learning, it is averred, is an illusion, if not a fraud. He belongs to the mosaic type of writers, and understands thoroughly how to simulate a profound learning while concealing the very trivial handbooks from which it is really derived.[3] He has borrowed many sections from Aristotle.[4] He has transcribed whole sections from Musonius, and though he has inserted words and phrases to give them a Christian

on the 'Pastor' of Hermas and the denial of its canonicity a retractation of the earlier view implied in the Stromateis.

The 'Hypotyposes' contained eight books. The contents, as suggested by Zahn, were as follows: I.-III., Genesis, Exodus, Psalms, Ecclesiastes (?), (Gospels); IV., (Romans), 1 and 2 Corinthians; V., Hebrews (?), Galatians, (1 and 2 Thessalonians, Ephesians, Philippians, Colossians); VI., (Gospels, see I.-III.); VII., James (?), 1 Peter, Jude, i., ii. (iii), John, 1 and 2 Timothy, (Titus, Philemon); VIII , Barnabas (?), 2 Peter (?), Apocalypse of Peter (?), (Apocalypse of John). There is no clear evidence that the works in brackets were commented on in the 'Hypotyposes.' (Zahn, *op. cit.*, p. 156)

[1] See "Testimonia Veterum" in Dindorf, vol. i. pp. lv-lxiv; Harnack, *op. cit.*, vol. i. p. 296.

[2] Sylburg in Potter, vol. ii. p. 1038.   [3] Wilamowitz, Eur. Her., vol. i. p 171.

[4] Bernays, 'zu Aristoteles et Clemens, Symbola. Philol. . . .,' 1864, vol. i p 301 *et seq.*

colouring, by the elimination of the Christian interpolations we can reproduce the original text.[1] Much in his
writings — even that dealing with the literature and
antiquities of Greece — is taken from Aristobulus[2] or
from the Universal History of Favorinus.[3] He is indebted to Philo not only for his theory of Scripture but
for the application of it to details, and often gives no
indication of his indebtedness.[4] There are clear reminiscences of Plutarch.[5] His knowledge, especially of the
later Greek thinkers, has been derived in part, if not
wholly, from the works of the "doxographers," whose
compilations formed a store-house for many inquirers.[6]
Now, that there is a large measure of truth in these
statements has been proved beyond the possibility of
doubt. His indebtedness to Musonius, or to some one
dependent on Musonius, has been proved to a demonstration. The same may be said of his obligations to
Philo. The sources of many of the sections that seem
most erudite can be traced with confidence. But, from
such admitted facts, an entirely erroneous conception of
the genius, even of the knowledge, of Clement may be
drawn. Even if it were true to the letter, if Clement
were only a piecer together of the phrases and thoughts
of others, he would be none the less important as a witness

---

[1] Wendland, 'Quæstiones Musonianæ,' p. 61 Cf C. P. Parker, 'Harvard
Studies,' vol xii, 1901 The editor of the 'Reliquiæ Musonii' (O. Hense),
1895 attaches little value to this method of reconstructing the text of Musonius.

[2] Scheck, 'De Fontibus Cl Al.,' 1889

[3] Gabrielssen, 'Über die quelle des Cl. Al.,' 1906, 1909. In vol. ii. pp.
441-482 he replies to his critics

[4] Siegfried, 'Philo von Alexandria . .,' p 343; Wendland, Hermes, vol.
xxxi p. 435; Heinisch, 'Die Einfluss Philos auf die alteste christliche Exegese,'
1908.

[5] A mistake similar to that of Plutarch in a quotation from Heraclitus shows that
Clement "had read his Plutarch" (Burnet, 'Early Greek Philosophy,' p. 139)

[6] Cf. Diels, 'Doxographi Gr.,' p. 129, &c.

to the development of Christian thought; for in that case
he would represent the detailed views of a previous generation or generations, and his appropriation of ideas from
without would be an indication of the assimilative force
of Christianity. But a consideration of what he certainly
did know tends to indicate that we must be on our guard
against an exaggerated conclusion.[1] It is certain that he
knew the Septuagint and the New Testament with aston-
ishing width and accuracy. With regard to Philo, it is
probable that the Philonic theory and methods of exegesis
had become the common property of the Alexandrian
School; and in the case of the Old Testament, the acceptance of the method involved the acceptance of much traditional exposition—for it was probably the results that in his
eyes justified the method; at any rate, the two were indissolubly related. One thing is certain : the inexhaustible
fertility with which he can suggest possible interpretations
of passages in the New Testament shows conclusively that
when he borrowed, it was not from intellectual or imagin-
ative poverty. With regard to his knowledge of Greek
philosophy one general consideration may be adduced.
Clement attached great value to erudition as a charm to
win Greek adherents to Christianity. Would a mere show
or parade of learning, a use of a learned cyclopædia, have
served his purpose, or the use of writings to which scholar
and teacher alike had ready access? But, waiving that, it
is certain that he had a first-hand knowledge of the works
of Plato. This is proved not only by his detailed references
to passages in various treatises, even by his erroneous
references, paradoxical though it may seem, but by suggestions and reminiscences, constantly recurring, of Platonic
metaphors, allusions, and individual words. " Such remin-

---

[1] Cf. Harnack, *op. cit.*, vol. ii. p. 16.

iscences are characteristic rather of the lover of Plato, who
has an intimate knowledge of his favourite author, than
the skimmer of florilegia."[1]   His knowledge of Homer,
Hesiod, and the great Greek dramatists could only have
come from first-hand.   It is hard to conceive of any handbooks which could have contained so many and so varied
quotations as are adduced.   But his free use of other
materials is not thereby explained.   No doubt it was the
fashion of his age not to be rigorous in regard to the owner-
ship of intellectual toil.   As Clement borrowed from his predecessors, so he in turn formed a quarry for his successors.[2]
But by his own criticism Clement has made it difficult to
develop for him this line of defence or explanation.   For
a considerable section of his work is occupied with
endeavouring to prove that the Greeks plagiarised whole-
sale from the Old Testament, and he even lays it down
as a thesis that this was a universal and ingrained trait
of Greek writers; and it is hardly consistent with the
transparent sincerity that breaks through every page of
his writings to suppose that his attack on plagiarism
was itself a conscious plagiarism.   Something may be due
to the literary fashion of the age, something may be due
to the unconscious reproduction of a tenacious memory,[3]
something to his method of literary work, something to
the hypothesis of theft, which might enable him to regard
the abstraction of the writing of others as a mere restoration of stolen materials; but when all allowance has been
made, there remains a psychological and ethical problem,
which must be explained in a way consistent with the

[1] F. S. Clark, 'American Philological Association,' 1902, pp. xiii, xiv.   See
the notes in Stahlin *passim*.

[2] Rohricht, 'De Clemente Alex. Arnobii . . . Auctore,' 1893.

[3] *E.g*, he often quotes passages of Scripture with perfect accuracy, even when
he reverses the order of the verses.

moral elevation of the man and the far-reaching conceptions of the writer. For the greatness and originality and
richness of his central thoughts disprove the idea that he had
been "at a great feast of languages and stolen the scraps,"
that he was a mere sewer together of shreds and patches.
For if everything were eliminated that he can be proved
to have borrowed, it might reduce to small compass his
independent knowledge of some departments of Greek
literature, but it would otherwise make little difference
to his place in the history of Christian thought. After
all, the method which he adopted was less important than
his aim; the passages which he quoted or appropriated
were not taken for the mere sake of quotation, but in
order to give weight to his general design.

The problem which Clement raised and endeavoured to
solve in his writings has been characterised by Overbeck [1]
in a masterly study as perhaps the most daring literary
undertaking in the history of the Church. Clement was
well aware of the novelty of the task which he had under-
taken, and of the suspicion which it was certain to create,
apart altogether from the method of solution which he
adopted. That he found it necessary to defend the composition of books at all, is a significant fact.[2] He makes
no such apology in the Protrepticus or in the Pædagogus;
and it could hardly be the reception of these works that
inspired his defence. No one could take exception to the
former work, for it was a powerful attack upon heathen
polytheism; few could take exception to the practical ethics
of the Pædagogus, at least on principle. Had he restricted
himself to a refutation of the teaching of the heretics, his
Christian contemporaries would have thanked him. But,
without any external stimulus, to formulate and co-ordinate
Christian truths in relation to each other as well as in

---

[1] Hist. Zeitschrift N. F., vol. xii. (1882), pp. 417-472.   [2] Str., i. 1.

relation to philosophy seemed to many a superfluous as well as a dangerous task, an imperilling of the unique dignity and claims of the Christian faith by bringing it into the light of common day. To substitute a Christian gnosis for a heretical gnosis might seem to some an indirect recognition of a movement with which there could be no compromise: the transformation of a heretical watchword, which had become an orthodox byword, into a designation for the highest Christian ideal, might seem a superfluous and confusing concession to the spirit of the age. In carrying out his task he does not lose sight of the controversies within the Church, but his aim in dealing with them is not mainly polemical, but rather to bring out the truth of which the controverted views were an exaggeration or a caricature. It is in accordance with his early training, as well with his desire to come into *rapprochement* with Greek converts, that, like Justin Martyr, his ruling thought is not that of a Christian theology but of a Christian philosophy. But it is only a philosophy in the sense of being a philosophy of life. The originality of Clement does not lie in the details or illustrations which he unhesitatingly borrowed, but in the formulating of the unifying conception which bound the scattered elements together, and in the width of outlook which enabled him to co-ordinate all the materials. That unifying principle he found in the doctrine of the Word by whom the universe was brought into order, whose inspiration was the key to a true philosophy of history, in whose Incarnation men could see the ideal of humanity, and who, by becoming incarnate, had not only revealed the close relation of the divine and the human, but had made possible the deifying of all humanity. The peculiar distinction of Clement, in a word, is not that he gave a final solution of the problem which he raised, but his clear recognition of the fact that there was a problem to be solved, that in that place and at that stage in the development of Christianity it was imperative for the Church to realise the relation in which it stood to the intellectual and moral forces that had hitherto been the most powerful factors in moulding the intellectual life of nations and individuals, if it were to escape the certain danger of being stranded or submerged. It was, indeed, a proceeding not without danger; but not to recognise the necessity of it would have been a still greater danger; for it would have extinguished Christianity in Alexandria, or reduced it to a mere official ritual, neither influencing its environment nor being influenced by it, or would have left the gnostic misrepresentation of Christianity in undisputed possession of the field. Clement was the first to see the necessity of formulating a Christian theory of the universe, a Christian philosophy of history, a Christian code of ethics. It was, of course, inevitable that his attempt should be marred by the defects of his age; that he accepted the current critical theories and literary presuppositions of his time without scrutiny, and was satisfied with seeking only to illustrate them; that he was fettered both in the exposition of principles and details by the consciousness of discouragement, if not of opposition, in his enterprise; that from a scientific point of view his work was hampered by the nature of the instruments with which he had to work; that, generally, it bears the stamp of the pioneer who is groping in an untried and unexplored province. His principles are not always co-ordinated, but sometimes lie side by side without any attempt to bring them into harmony with one another, or even without any apparent consciousness of the necessity of such co-ordination. The conception was greater than the execution; "the artist fell short of the thinker;" [1]

[1] Cf. de Faye, p. 113.

but the greatness of the conception abides. Nothing can take from Clement the glory of having been the first Christian teacher to find a place in his system of thought for all forms of truth; of bringing Christianity into the line of historical development without surrendering its absolute uniqueness; of laying down principles which, when stripped of their temporary cerements, are not dead, but as vital to a true Christian philosophy and apologetic to - day as they were in the closing years of the second century. He neither ignored the rights of the past nor the claims of the future, but sought to assign to each its due place and proportion. " Large portions of his field of thought," says Hort, " remained for long ages unworked, or even remain unworked still. But what he at once humbly and bravely attempted under great disadvantages at the beginning of the third century will have to be attempted afresh with the added experience and knowledge of seventeen centuries more, if the Christian faith is to hold its ground among men; and when the attempt is made, not a few of his thoughts and words will shine out with new force, full of light for dealing with new problems." [1]

[1] Ante-Nicene Lectures, pp. 90, 91.

c

LECTURE II.

THE RELATION OF CHRISTIANITY TO HELLENIC CULTURE AND PHILOSOPHY.

EVERY advance of the kingdom of God, every victory of the Gospel, gave rise to new problems. When men of philosophic culture became adherents of the Christian faith, the Church had to decide what was to be its general attitude towards that new force with which it had hitherto for the most part been in conflict. All men of culture, Christian and non-Christian alike, found in philosophy a common ground. The immediate effect of the admission of the new ally was such as to create suspicion. It sought to be a master, not a servant, in the house of God, to assimilate Christianity to itself rather than to assimilate itself to Christianity, and thus created heresies that threatened to break up the unity of the Church. The natural consequence was that widely antagonistic views were adopted with regard to the relation of the Church to philosophic culture generally. The one view is represented by Tatian and Tertullian; the other by Justin Martyr and Clement. Tatian scoffs at Hellenic culture, recounts with almost savage glee the fables as to the life and death of the Greek philosophers, and abjures altogether any contact with the wisdom of the Greeks. "We have," he says, "bidden farewell to your wisdom."[1] In like manner Tertullian

[1] Orat. ad Græc., c. 1.

branded philosophy generally as the fountain of all heresies, and maintained that the Church had nothing to do with it save to disown all intercourse with it.[1] The influence which it had exercised on the Christian faith made this a natural attitude; and it required men of no ordinary courage and insight to rise above the temptation to attack or belittle a force with associations so sinister. Such were Justin and Clement. Justin, whose intellectual and spiritual life to a certain extent had proceeded on parallel lines to that of Clement, takes up substantially the same attitude as he did. In becoming a Christian, he did not cease to be a philosopher, for he regarded Christianity as the only true and useful philosophy. Like Clement, he supports the hypothesis of theft as a solution of the analogies between Christianity and the philosophy of the Greeks, reads Christian teaching into Plato, and claims all that was akin to Christianity in Greek philosophy as his own.[2] At the same time that Tertullian in Carthage was abjuring all contact with philosophy, Clement in Alexandria was exhibiting and defending Greek philosophy as virtually on a level with Judaism as a preliminary discipline for Christianity. It was not to be regarded merely as an unconscious negative preparation for the Gospel, testifying by its very failure to the necessity of something higher than itself; it had played a positive part, a divinely appointed part, in the history of humanity. What the Law of Moses was to the Jew, philosophy was to the Greek. It was a tutor to the Greeks, just as the law was to the Hebrews.[3] It was as a covenant peculiar to them, like a stepping-stone to the philosophy which is according to Christ.[4] As God gave prophets to

---

[1] Præsc. adv. Hæret., c. 7.

[2] ii. Apol , 13. ὅσα οὖν παρὰ πᾶσι καλῶς εἴρηται ἡμῶν τῶν χριστιανῶν ἐστι.

[3] Str., i. 5 ²⁸.

[4] Ib., vi. 8 ⁶⁷. τὴν δὲ φιλοσοφίαν καὶ μᾶλλον "Ελλησιν, οἷον διαθήκην οἰκείαν αὐτοῖς.

the Jews, so He raised up men of the highest repute among
the Greeks, their own prophets in their own tongue, so far
as they were able to receive the beneficence of God, and
thus marked them off from the great mass of men.[1] The
Mosaic Law and Greek philosophy alike had each its own
place in the divine economy; each came like the Gospel in
its own God-appointed time; each was designed to prepare
men for the reception of the truth of Christ.[2]

Clement assigned this lofty function to philosophy on a
variety of grounds. He based it on statements in Scripture,
on the unity of truth, on the universality of inspiration, on
the nature of philosophy itself, above all, on the nature
of God, whose Providence was not to be regarded as local
or national. According to the Scriptures, men among the
Gentiles are sons in God's sight.[3] The statement of the
Psalmist that " God had not dealt so with any nation" as with
Israel, implies that though God's relation to the Gentiles
was not so intimate as that which He occupied to the Jews,
He had a certain relation.[4] The quaintness of the exegesis
is at least convincing proof of the strength of his conviction on the matter. When David speaks of the Gentiles
" forgetting God," he implies a former remembrance, and
that there was a dim knowledge of God among the Gentiles.[5] The five barley loaves in the miracle are a figure
of the law; the two fishes are a figure of the Greek philosophy which was begotten and carried about in the Gentile
waves. The quotation from Aratus by St Paul shows that
he approved of what was well said among the Greeks.[6]
The way of truth is one, but into it as into an ever-flowing
river various streams flow, some from this side, some from

---

[1] Str., vi. 5 [42].
[2] Ib., i. 5 [28] , vi. 6 [47]; vi. 13 [106] ; vi. 17 [159] ; vii. 2 [11].
[3] Pæd., i. 5 [14].   [4] Str , vi. 8 [63]; Psa. 147. 20.
[5] Ib., vi. 8 [64]; Psa. 9. 17.   [6] Ib., i. 19 [91].

that.[1] The law of nature and the law of the divine education are from God, and one.[2] Injunctions of righteousness
pronounced by those who pursue the wisdom of the world
are not to be despised. Sayings such as that of Hesiod
were spoken by the God of all, even though they were
spoken by way of conjecture, not by way of apprehension.[3]
All apprehension of God is due to His inspiration.[4] Clement
starts with the assumption, based on his own experience,
that philosophy in itself was a good thing. The source
from which it drew its inspiration was sufficiently proved
by its results; it made men virtuous, and was accorded
only to the best among the Greeks.[5] To suppose that so
powerful a factor in thought and life had come into the
world without a direct divine impulse was to put a limit
and a dishonour on the omniscience, the beneficence, and
the omnipotence of God. It is really a clear image of
truth, a divine gift to the Greeks.[6] By a different process of advancement, He led both Greek and barbarian
to the perfection which is through faith.[7] If the very
hairs of our head are numbered, shall philosophy not be
taken into account?[8] If philosophy were discovered by the
Greeks by the mere exercise of human understanding, yet,
according to the Scriptures, understanding is from God.[9]
Many things the fruit of human reasoning derived from
Him their primal spark.[10] He is even the source of every
artistic device.[11] If, according to Solomon, it was wisdom
as artificer that framed the ship, were it not irrational to
regard philosophy as inferior to shipbuilding?[12] To deny
that philosophy came from God was to run the risk of
saying that it was impossible for Him to know all things

[1] Str., i. 5 [29].   [2] Ib., i. 29 [182].   [3] Ib., i. 29 [181].
[4] Prot., vi. [71].   [5] Str., vi. 17 [159].   [6] Ib., i 2 [20]
[7] Ib., vii 2 [11].   [8] Ib., vi. 17 [153].   [9] Ib., vi. 8 [62].
[10] Ib., vi. 17 [157]. [11] Ib., i. 4 [25].   [12] Ib., vi. 11 [93], [94].

individually, and that He is not the cause of all good things.[1] To ascribe philosophy to the devil was to forget that evil had an evil nature, and never could be the source of anything good; nay, it was virtually to make the devil more beneficent than the Providence of God.[2] If the devil be "transformed into an angel of light," that can only be when he prophesies that which is true.[3] Even if the devil had stolen it, the gift was not an injurious one, and therefore not such as to call forth the intervention of God.[4] But what necessity, it might be objected, was there for assigning the introduction of philosophy to any divine intervention? Why not regard it simply as the fruit of human reasoning? Even so, it was from God, the source of reason. Nothing could have existed at all unless God had so willed. That philosophy did exist, shows that He willed it to exist, and that it existed for the sake of those who would not have abstained from evil save by its means. Did the thinkers of Greece utter some truth by accident? It was the accident due to the administration of God. Did they do so by mere coincidence? The coincidence had been divinely foreseen. Was it by a so-called natural conception? God, and not man, was the creator of that natural conception.[5]

To what philosophy or philosopher did Clement specially assign this work of preparation for Christianity? What did he mean by the word itself? "By philosophy," he says, "I do not mean the Stoic, nor the Platonic, nor the Epicurean, nor the Aristotelian, but whatsoever things have been spoken in each of these sects well, giving thorough instruction in righteousness along with a knowledge inspired by piety, all this eclectic matter I call philosophy. But whatsoever things of human reasonings they have appropriated and put

---

[1] Str , vi. 17 156.   [2] Ib., vi. 17 159.   [3] Ib., vi. 8 66.
          [4] Ib., i. 17 83.   [5] Ib., i. 19 84.

a false stamp on, that I would never call divine."[1] Again,
"By philosophy we do not propose to discuss that way of life
which obtains in each sect, but that which is really philosophy, strictly technical wisdom,[2]—which furnishes experience of the things that pertain to life. And we say that
wisdom is the steadfast knowledge of things divine and
human, an apprehension firm and unalterable, embracing
the things which are, and the things which have been, and
the things which shall be. . . . Philosophy, then, would be
the uncontroverted dogmas in each of the sects—philosophical sects, I mean—gathered into one selection, and accompanied by a way of life correspondent."[3] Philosophy, then,
is the apprehension of truth,—in particular, the truth about
God, and the attainment of a way of life correspondent to
the truth apprehended. Its goal is rectitude of reason and
purity of life.[4] This view of philosophy explains, on the
one hand, his admiration for Plato,[5] and on the other, his
detestation both of the theology and the moral teaching of
Epicurus. He explains away the teaching of Plato in the
Republic as to the community of women, and holds that
Marcion found support for his heresies only by a misuse of
the Platonic principles at once thankless and ignorant.[6] He
is in sympathy with all that is best in Stoicism, and has
transferred to his own way of thinking many of its technical
terms and formulas; but he is so far from being blind to its
defects that he describes its conception of the Divinity per-
vading all matter as a clumsy degradation of philosophy.[7]
He can be fair even to Epicureanism. While he regards

---

[1] Str , i. 7 [37] φιλοσοφίαν δὲ οὐ τὴν Στωικὴν λέγω οὐδὲ τὴν Πλατωνικὴν ἢ τὴν
Ἐπικούρειόν τε καὶ Ἀριστοτελικήν, ἀλλ' ὅσα εἴρηται παρ' ἑκάστῃ τῶν αἱρέσεων
τούτων καλῶς, δικαιοσύνην μετὰ εὐσεβοῦς ἐπιστήμης ἐκδιδάσκοντα, τοῦτο σύμπαν
τὸ ἐκλεκτικὸν φιλοσοφίαν φημί.
[2] Stahlin suspects a corruption in the text here.   [3] Str., vi. 7 [54], [55].
[4] Ib., vi. 7 [55].   [5] Ib., v. 10 [66], &c.   [6] Ib., iii. 2 [10], iii. 3 [21].
[7] Prot., v [66]; Str., i. 11 [51].

St Paul's condemnation of philosophy in the Epistle to the
Colossians as a condemnation of the Epicureanism which
abolishes Providence and deifies pleasure,[1] and compares
it to tares sown in the Hellenic philosophy,[2] characteris-
ing its doctrines as doctrines of darkness,[3] he quotes with
approval a letter of Epicurus himself,[4] and even does not
hesitate to say, in harmony with his eclectic principles,
that Metrodorus, Epicurean though he was, spoke some
things under inspiration.[5] He lays down the sound principle that we are not to condemn what is said because
of the speaker, but examine it to see whether it adheres
to the truth.[6] An intellectual force which, in the judgment of Clement, had played so important a part as
philosophy in the development of life and thought of the
past, must still have a part assigned to it by God in the
sphere of Christianity. In its past function was to be
found the key to its present function. It purges the soul,
and prepares it for the reception of the faith, on which
foundation the truth builds up the edifice of knowledge.[7]
It serves as a first or second stair to one going to the upper
room, as grammar serves philosophy.[8] It is an intellectual
gymnastic, necessary for the attainment of the highest degree
of goodness.[9] As the husbandman waters the soil before
casting in the seed, so he, as a teacher, waters, so to speak,
the souls of his hearers with the discourses of the Greeks,
that they may be fitted to receive the spiritual seed when it
is cast down.[10] So far from dragging men away from the
faith, philosophy provides a conjoint discipline which serves
to demonstrate the truth of the faith.[11] It co-operates in
discussions about the truth ; it is a co-worker in the appre-

---

[1] Str., i. 11 50.   [2] Ib., vi. 8 67.   [3] Ib., iv. 22 144.
[4] Ib, iv. 8 69.   [5] Ib, v. 14 138.   [6] Ib, vi. 8 66.
[7] Ib., vii 3 20   [8] Ib., i. 19 99.   [9] Ib., vi 11 91; i. 3 22.
[10] Ib , i. 1 17.   [11] Ib., i. 2 20.

hension of the truth.[1] With philosophy as a copestone,
wisdom is unassailable by sophists.[2] By it we may buffet
the heretical sects.[3] Hence in the Stromateis he does not
hesitate to use what is best in philosophy and other preliminary discipline.[4] It is plain from many allusions in his
writings that this sane and liberal attitude was received by
many of his contemporaries with suspicion and antagonism.
Some regarded philosophy as useless, some as a source of
danger, some adduced the authority of Scripture against it.[5]
He speaks of the chattering of some who, in their ignorance,
were frightened at every noise, who said that we should
restrict ourselves to things which were most essential and
which contained the faith, and pass by things external
and superfluous, which contributed nothing to the main
end.[6] He alludes to the many who were frightened at the
Hellenic philosophy like children at masks,[7] to some who in
their conceit refused to touch philosophy or dialectics and
insisted on bare faith alone,[8] who asked triumphantly what
use there was in knowing the causes of the movements of
the stars, or in meditating on the theories of geometry or
other branches of learning, since such studies were of no
service in the discharge of duty, and the Hellenic philosophy
was only the fruit of human understanding, and was not
taught by the truth?[9] Clement admits that there was a
possibility of the faith of some being submerged by the
perusal of Hellenic literature, unless the principles which he
laid down were taken as a guide,[10] and even brings it as a
charge against some that they preferred to remain ignorant
lest, after giving their ears to Hellenic instruction, they might
not be able to find their way back.[11] He denies the right
of any one to condemn the philosophy of the Greeks who

[1] Str., vi. 11 [91]; i. 20 [97].   [2] Ib., i. 5 [28].   [3] Ib., i. 19 [95].   [4] Ib., i. 1 [15].
[5] Ib., i. 17 [81].   [6] Ib., i. 1 [18].   [7] Ib., vi. 10 [80].   [8] Ib., i. 9 [42].
[9] Ib. vi. 11 [98].   [10] Ib., v. 14 [140].   [11] Ib., vi. 11 [89].

knew nothing but the bare letter, and argues that we must
philosophise even in order to decide that we should not;
that even if philosophy were useless, it would be useful to
demonstrate its own uselessness. He defends his procedure
on the ground that the display of varied learning acts as
an art of enchantment on scholars, and serves as a letter
of commendation to the truth.[1] He claims to have in his
method the support of the example and teaching of St Paul.
It would appear that his opponents had adduced passages
to the contrary.[2] In writing to Titus, St Paul had made
a quotation from the Cretan Epimenides, and in the Epistle
to the Corinthians he had quoted a line from some Greek
poet,[3] and in that sense had become all things to all men.
All things were God's—therefore, what belonged to the
Greeks was ours; and the natural way to bring the Greeks
to faith in the truth was, in the first place, to appeal to what
was cognate, and to find a middle point of transition in
their own intellectual possessions.[4] It was possible, no
doubt, to live rightly in poverty; but it was also possible
to do so in superfluity. Virtue was not unattainable without preliminary instruction, but it was attained more easily
and quickly with it.[5] To insist on bare faith alone was,
in contradiction to the teaching of the Lord, to expect at
the very outset to take clusters of grapes without having
taken any care of the vine. From every science, every
branch of culture, something might be plucked that was
helpful in making the truth unassailable. The study of
ambiguous words and synonyms in the two Covenants was
important. If the Lord by an ambiguous phrase eluded the
devil at the temptation, could the devil be the author of
philosophy and dialectic?[6] How can he be an "approved

---

[1] Str., i. 2[19], [20].
[2] Col. ii. 4, 8 ; 1 Cor. i. 19.
[3] Str., i. 14[59]; Tit. i. 12 ; 1 Cor. xv. 33.
[4] Ib., v. 3[18]; v. 4[19].
[5] Ib , i. 6[38].
[6] Ib., i. 9[43], [44].

money-changer," who is not able offhand to distinguish
the pure coin from the spurious?[1] Do not the so-called
orthodox apply themselves to good works not knowing
what they do?[2] Clement had sympathy with the weak
brother in ethical and practical matters, but not so much
in intellectual matters; though only once does a touch of
the arrogance of philosophical culture escape him. Irritated
by the charge of dangerous methods that had obviously
been brought against him, he breaks out: "But if this
faith of theirs—for I cannot call it knowledge—be such
that it can be dissolved by plausible speech, let it be by all
means dissolved, and let them confess that they will not
have the truth."[3] But this temporary outburst is altogether foreign to his usual mode of thought. In general
he seeks rather to win adherents than to refute opponents.

Along with this lofty estimate of the function of philosophy Clement is inspired with a keen sense of the newness of Christianity, and the consequent limitations of
philosophic culture. Christ is the "New Song" by which
the Greek legends have been antiquated and fulfilled.
Christians are a new people. So full is he of this idea
of the newness of Christianity that he speaks of the
manifestation of Christ as if it were a thing of
yesterday.[4] The newness of humanity in Christ he
finds revealed in unexpected phrases.[5] "I make things
new," the Word says. "With a new eye, a new ear,
a new heart, the disciples of the Lord speak, hear,
and do in spiritual wise whatsoever things are seen
and heard and apprehended through faith and understanding."[6] "In contradiction to the older people we
are the new people, having learned the new blessings. To

---

[1] Str , vi 10[81].   [2] Ib., 1 9[45]: οἱ ὀρθοδοξασταὶ καλούμενοι.
[3] Ib., vi 10[81].   [4] Pæd., i 5[20].
[5] Ib , 1. 5[15]. Cf Zech. ix. 9   [6] Str , 11. 4[15].

us belongs the rich prime of our years, this youth which
knows no age, in which we are always vigorous in thought,
always young, and always gentle, and always new; for
those who are partakers of the new Word should themselves be new.   And that which partakes of eternity is
wont to be assimilated to that which is incorruptible, so
that the age of our boyhood may be named a spring-time
of all our life, because old age never falls upon the truth
in us and our way of life, which is saturated with the truth.
For wisdom is ever-blooming, always the same and un-
changing."[1]   This conception of the newness of Christianity
shows that the function of philosophy in the Christian
economy is not absolute, but is to be restricted in a variety
of ways.   In no sense does Clement admit that Christianity
depends on Greek philosophy.   The teaching according to
the Saviour is self-effective and in need of nothing; and
Greek philosophy by coming over to its side does not add
to the potency of the truth, but reduces to impotence the
sophistical attacks against it.   Though it were absent, no
defect would take place in the absolute Word, nor would
the truth be destroyed; just as the senses contribute to
truth, but the intellect is the natural organ for knowing it.[2]
Philosophy is a co-worker for the apprehension of the truth;
but although a joint cause, it is not the efficient cause, as
if apart from philosophy truth did not exist; for many without philosophy or any academic training, or even without
knowledge of letters, have accepted the word about God
through faith, instructed by self-working wisdom.   Philosophy by itself is powerless to energise; it is only a cause
when acting in unison with another.[3]   Nor is it to be used
indiscriminately.   No time must be occupied with the discussion of useless and irrelevant matters, no heed paid to
wrangling sophisms, or to the mere pursuit of the shadow of

[1] Pæd., i. 5 [20].   [2] Str., i. 20 [99], [100]   [3] Ib.

words.[1] All sophistical arts must be set aside, as making the worse appear the better reason.[2] Proficiency in philosophy and the curriculum of studies is not a principal but a secondary end, to be used incidentally. It is of the nature of an intellectual dessert, a relish not bread to the spirit.[3] It is not essential to the apprehension of truth by the individual. The Christian philosophy has no barriers save moral barriers at the entrance; it is open to the attainment of barbarian and Greek, slave and aged, child and woman.[4] If any of the Greeks, dispensing with the preliminary guidance of the Hellenic philosophy, proceeds straight to the true teaching, he outdistances others, though an unlettered man, by choosing the short cut to perfection—namely, that of salvation through faith.[5] So in his earliest writing he had held that for him who had come to the school of Christ, academic learning was a superfluity. " Since the Word has come to us from heaven, we need not go to the teaching of men in our search after learning, to Athens, or the rest of Greece, or Ionia. For if we have as our Teacher Him who filled the universe with His holy energies in creation, salvation, beneficence, legislation, prophecy, teaching, we have the Teacher from whom all instruction comes ; and the whole world with Athens and Greece has come under the sway of the Word." [6] When St Paul describes Hellenic philosophy as " the rudiments of the world," he hints that it was essentially rudimentary, and that it was unworthy of the man who had attained to the height of the gnostic to run back to it.[7] Moreover, in respect of its origin, philosophy was inferior to Christianity; nay, all that was best in it was taken from the Hebrew Scriptures.[8] Before the advent of Christianity, Greek philosophers took fragments of truth

[1] Str , vi. 10 [82].   [2] Ib., i. 8 [39].   [3] Ib , i. 20 [100].
[4] Ib., iv. 8 [58].   [5] Ib., vii. 2 [11]   [6] Prot., xi. [112].
              [7] Str., vi. 8 [62].   [8] Ib., i. 17 [87] ; i. 20 [100].

from the Hebrew prophets, but not with the insight of knowledge, and appropriated them, falsifying some things and
ignorantly explaining others in over-subtlety.[1]   Clement
endeavours to demonstrate that what he calls the philosophy according to the Hebrews—that is, the religious and
moral conceptions in the books of Scripture, along with
philosophic ideas read into the Pentateuch by allegorical
exegesis—is the most ancient of all forms of wisdom;[2] that
Moses flourished long before the date at which, according
to Greek mythology, the race of men had sprung into being;[3]
that philosophy and other arts flourished among the barbarians long before they appeared among the Greeks.[4]   He
finds in the higher aspects of the legislation of Numa a
reflection of the teaching of Moses;[5] in the cosmogony of
Homer, as set forth in the shield of Vulcan, an imitation
of the Mosaic cosmogony, even in minute details;[6] thinks
that, by a happy divination, Homer seems to speak of the
Father and the Son;[7] and that Euripides unconsciously
refers to the Saviour Himself.[8]   Some of the distinctive
tenets of the Stoics[9]—in some cases based on misinterpre-
tations of passages in Scripture,—the esoteric principles of
the Pythagoreans expressed in symbol and proverb,[10] the
doctrines of the Peripatetic philosophy generally and even
some minute points in it,[11] all the ethical commonplaces of
the Greeks, come from the same source.[12]   From the
Hebrew Scriptures Greek generals, like Miltiades, derived
their military stratagem;[13] Hellenic legends are based on
the facts of Scripture;[14] the marvels of Greek mythology
are imitations of the marvels recorded in Scripture.[15]   In
particular, the Greeks imitated the symbolic and enigmatic

[1] Str., i. 17[87].   [2] Ib., i. 21[101].   [3] Ib., i. 21[106].   [4] Ib., i. 16[74].
[5] Ib., i. 15[71].   [6] Ib., v. 14[101].   [7] Ib., v. 14[116].   [8] Ib., v. 11[70].
[9] Ib., v. 14[97].   [10] Ib., v. 5[30].   [11] Ib., v. 14[90].   [12] Ib., ii. 18[78].
[13] Ib., i. 24[162].   [14] Ib., vi. 3[28].   [15] Ib., i. 24[170].

part of the barbarian philosophy, as that which was most essential to the knowledge of the truth.[1] The Hellenic philosophy is like the torch which men kindle, stealing the light artfully from the sun.[2] The influence of the Holy Scriptures is particularly conspicuous in Plato.[3] Clement quotes many analogies between Plato and the Scriptures— though in some cases the resemblance may only have been a coincidence, the happy conjecture of a great nature,[4]—maintains that Plato himself acknowledged his dependence,[5] that his doctrine of creation was taken from Moses,[6] that he exhibits the life of a Christian in the 'Theætetus,'[7] that he seems to have divined the Lord's day,[8] that he had a perception of the Holy Trinity,[9] that he all but prophesied the economy of salvation.[10] From a reference to diverse interpretations of a passage in the ' Republic,' it would seem that Christian exegesis had already been applied by several to Plato.[11] He quotes with approval the saying of Numenius the Pythagorean, " What is Plato but Moses atticising ? "[12] and he himself apostrophises Plato thus : " Whence, O Plato, is that hint of thine of the truth ? I know thy teachers, even if thou wouldst conceal them. For your laws that are consistent with truth, and your opinions concerning God, you are indebted to the Hebrews."[13] Clement speaks in wavering terms about the agency by which the Hebrew teaching came to the knowledge of the thinkers and poets of Greece. Sometimes it is represented as a case of pure theft; in one case he attributes it to the fallen angels, who revealed the secrets to the women after whom they lusted, instead of reserving the knowledge to the advent of Christ.[14] Elsewhere, in accordance with later Jewish thought, as

[1] Str., ii. 1[1], [2].   [2] Ib., v. 5[29].   [3] Ib., i. 1[10]; i 25[165].
[4] Ib., ii. 19[100].   [5] Ib., i. 15[69].   [6] Ib., v. 14[92].
[7] Ib., v. 14[95].   [8] Ib., v. 14[106].   [9] Ib., v. 14[106].
[10] Ib., v. 14[108].   [11] Ib., v. 14[98]; Rep., iii. 415 A.
[12] Ib., i. 22[150].   [13] Prot., vi.[70].   [14] Str., i. 17[81]; v. 1[10].

based on a passage in Deuteronomy, he ascribes it to the inferior angels to whom the nations were assigned.[1]   In confirmation of his theory of theft, he adduces the alleged fact that the Greek poets, philosophers, and historians stole from one another, and argues that those who stole from one another would hardly refrain from touching what belonged to Christians.[2]   Of this hypothesis, which seems to have been started by Aristobulus, an Alexandrian Jew, in the third century before Christ in all probability from apologetic motives,[3] maintained by Tatian, Justin, and Theophilus, exhibited by Clement with great ingenuity and wealth of illustration, repeated by Eusebius in the fourth century, almost in the matter and form of Clement, and supported here and there by individual writers in subsequent ages, any discussion is superfluous, for it is entirely destitute of historical and literary foundation.   From the elaborate treatment of it by Clement, it is plain that many before his time must have been at work in the search after analogies between the Scriptures and the literature of Greece; and it was probably part of the traditional apologetic and exegesis of the Alexandrian School.   One is tempted for a moment to suppose that Clement's defence of it was a mere *tour de force*, or that it was a concession to his opponents.   But on the latter supposition it would have been futile; for why should they concern themselves about what had been stolen when they had the original treasury?   It was not at all necessary to his argument, but rather out of harmony with his higher view of the relation between the Christian faith and Hellenic philosophy; yet it occurs so frequently in an incidental way, and is, moreover, developed so elaborately, that there can be no doubt of his acceptance of it.   From a passage

[1] Str, vii. 2⁶; Deut. xxxii. 8   [2] Ib., vi. 2⁴.
[3] For a criticism of some modern views regarding Aristobulus, see Schurer, 'Geschichte des Judischen Volkes,' vol. iii.³ p. 388.

quoted by him, it would appear that the idea was held by heterodox and orthodox alike.[1] The only original contribution by Clement to it is that though the truth was stolen, it was none the less true, a real possession however acquired.[2] He did not invent the hypothesis, but he found in it a weapon at once to disarm the opposition of the narrower section in the Church, and a means of constructing a bridge between Greek thought and Christian truth. Apart from the fantastic theories noted above, he makes no attempt to show that direct historical contact between the Hebrew Scriptures and Greek thought can be demonstrated, or in what way the transition of analogous facts or conceptions from the one sphere into the other took place or was possible. But when we call to mind the manner in which the hypothesis of literary dependence has been exaggerated as a solvent for the problems of the New Testament by the extreme Dutch school, or even how the argument from analogy has been pushed by the more extravagant adherents of the school of Gunkel, we shall wonder less at the uncritical attitude of Clement in the second century. The main difference, so far as their attitude to Christianity is concerned, is that Clement, starting from the conception of the absolute originality of Christianity, regarded all other truth as secondary and derivative : the modern representatives of the theory of analogy regard Christian truth as derivative and secondary, without re-cognising any truth as absolute or uniquely divine.

Apart from this relation of dependence on the Hebrew Scriptures, the philosophy of the Greeks was in some im-portant respects inferior to Christianity. Its relation was that of Hagar to Sarah, of a maid to a mistress.[3] It had not led to the abandonment of idolatry.[4] Many of

---

[1] Str., vi. 6 53.   [2] Ib., i 20 100.
[3] Ib., i. 5 32, from Philo.   [4] Ib., vi. 6 44.

D

its teachers had imperfect conceptions of God, and paid
honour to the elements: at best, they knew Him as
Creator, not as Father in the Christian sense.[1] Both
philosophy and Christianity come from God, the one
source of all good things; but the former had only come
from Him in the way of natural sequence, not as a principal end, though to the Greeks before the Advent it may
have been given as a principal end.[2] Like the good land,
philosophy shares in the rain from heaven, but the result is
not the same.[3] It may be compared to nuts, the whole of
which is not eatable.[4] It is by no means to be regarded as
a substitute for Christianity. On the contrary, philosophers
are but children, unless they have become mature men
through Christ.[5] Though men have studied the Greek
philosophy, they must learn the truth of Christ in order
to be saved.[6] To act or speak without the word of truth
is as if a man tried to walk without feet.[7] Christian
piety is a kind of science, and as such has distinctive
principles of its own. As well try to become a rhetorician
by taking up the principles of medicine, or a physician
by taking up the principles of rhetoric, as try to become
a Christian by other than Christian principles.[8] The
difference between Christianity and philosophy is thorough-
going and far-reaching. Philosophy at best contains but
a fragment of the truth of which Christianity contains
the whole.[9] "Like as the Bacchæ tore to pieces the
limbs of Pentheus, so have the sects of philosophy, both
barbarian and Greek, done with truth, each claiming as
the whole the portion that has fallen to it." [10] The difference between philosophy and Christianity is a difference

[1] Str., i. 11 [60]; v. 14 [136].   [2] Ib., i. 7 [87]; i. 5 [28].   [3] Ib, i. 7 [37].
[4] Ib., i. 1 [7].   [5] Ib., i. 11 [53].   [6] Ib, v. 13 [87].
[7] Prot., vii [75].   [8] Stah , vol. iii. p. 229, fr. 68.
[9] Prot., vii. [74]; Str., vi. 17 [160].   [10] Str , i, 13 [87].

between names and things, between the probable and the true,[1] between truth and guessing at truth,[2] between the particular and the universal;[3] for that which the chiefs of philosophy only guessed at, the disciples of Christ apprehend and proclaim.[4] Moreover, the truth in Greek philosophy is not only fragmentary but elementary. It is not concerned with such intellectual objects as are beyond the sphere of this world.[5] Like geometry or painting, it presents only one side of the truth which it delineates.[6] It does not embrace the majesty of the truth.[7] In the dark night of the pre-Christian era it was as the faint light of a wick whose light was taken from the sun. With the proclamation of the Word it is extinguished, as the lamp by the sun; the whole night is illumined.[8] "While truth is one, many things contribute to its investigation, but the discovery is only through the Son. . . . There is the truth of geometry and there is the truth of music, and in right philosophy there would be Hellenic truth. But the only authoritative truth is that in which we are taught by the Son of God. . . . The Greek truth has the same name as our truth, but it differs from it in respect of the grandeur of knowledge, and more authoritative process of demonstration, and divine grace, and the like."[9] It lacks the spiritual and moral force which Christianity imparts. It says that man was made for the vision of heaven, and yet worships the things that appear in the heavens.[10] Its lack of moral force is mainly due to the fact that while the self-control of the Greek philosopher is directed against ministering to lust in act, the self-control of the Christian is directed against the lusting itself.[11] The primary ground of the inferiority of philosophy is

---

[1] Str., vi. 17[149].   [2] Ib., i. 7[38].   [3] Prot., xi. [113].   [4] Ib., xi. [112].
[5] Str., vi. 15[117]; vi. 8[68].   [6] Ib., vi. 7[56].   [7] Ib., i 16[80].
[8] Ib., v. 5[29].   [9] Ib., i. 20[98].   [10] Prot., iv. [63].   [11] Str., iii. 7[57].

found in the uniquely divine origin of Christianity. His argument here, so far as it seeks to prove the truth of the Christian faith, is based mainly on a series of what he regards as necessary presuppositions. He assumes the necessity of revelation, and seeks to support it. We needed a Divine Teacher, because the soul was too feeble to apprehend things that are as they really are. Hence the Saviour was sent down.[1] Men speaking about God are not trustworthy, in so far as they are merely men. The feeble and mortal cannot speak worthily of Him who is unoriginated and incorruptible, nor can the work of Him who made it.[2] In refutation of the theory of Valentinus, that men were saved by natural constitution, he deems it sufficient to point to the fact that in that case the teaching both of the Old and the New Testament was a superfluity, and that the higher natures, apart from the advent of Christianity, would some time or another have come to the light. But if the Valentinians admitted that the sojourning of the Saviour was a necessity, then the peculiar prerogatives of nature were gone.[3] He assumes the divine origin of the Christian Scriptures. All other systems of thought depend on some teacher, who in turn depended on his predecessor, and so on in like manner in an ascending series; but Christianity is taught by Him who was taught of none, but is Himself the teacher of all created beings.[4] He adduces what he calls an unanswerable argument that it is God who speaks in detail of the matter under investigation and presents it in writing. "Who, then, is so atheistic as to disbelieve God, and to demand demonstration from God as from man?" If the followers of Pythagoras regard his *ipse dixit* as a matter of faith shall we demand from God the Saviour proof of

[1] Str , v. 1 [7].

[2] Ib , vi. 18 [16b]. Cf. ib., i. 28 [178].

[3] Ib., v. 1 [3].

[4] Ib., vi. 7 [37], [66].

what is said ?[1] Theism involves Christianity. Admit the
existence of Providence, and it would be impious to suppose that the whole of prophecy and the dispensation
in relation to it did not take place in accordance with
Providence.[2] A first principle must be assumed, for a
first principle which required the support of anything
else could not be regarded as a first principle.[3] The
demonstration which is based on opinion is human, the
demonstration of the Scripture is based on knowledge.
Scripture itself, being derived from the First Principle,
shares like characteristics. " With a view to the discovery
of realities we use Scripture as a criterion. . . . That
cannot be a first principle which needs to be judged. We,
embracing by faith the first principle without demonstration, receive demonstration concerning the first principle
from the first principle itself, and are instructed by the
voice of the Lord with a view to the knowledge of the
truth. Human testimony needs confirmation, but by the
voice of the Lord we prove that which is under inquiry, and
this is more trustworthy than any demonstration, rather is
the only real demonstration."[4] If, in the ordinary sense
of the word, demonstration of the truth of Christianity is
unnecessary or impossible, nevertheless, in the judgment
of Clement, it has a demonstration of its own. The organ
of this demonstration is faith. " Faith is a grace which
leads up from that which cannot be demonstrated to that
which is universally simple, which is neither with matter,
nor matter, nor under matter."[5] So far from being facile
or vulgar, faith is something divine. It is the foundation of
knowledge.[6] " Unless ye believe, ye will not understand."
When the Scripture says that God is faithful, it implies
that He is worthy of faith when making any assertion.[7]

---

[1] Str., ii 5 [24].   [2] Ib., v. 1 [7].   Cf ib. ii. 2 [9].   [3] Ib., vii. 16 [95].
[4] Ib.   [5] Ib., ii. 4 [14]   [6] Ib , ii. 6 [30], &c.   [7] Ib , ii. 6 [27].

From the person of the Teacher it follows that, in respect
of substance, our teaching is perfect. He who suffered
out of love to us would not have kept back anything with
a view to our instruction in knowledge.[1] In defence of
the Christian faith Clement presents some grounds of a
more definite character. " They say that a proof is either
the antecedent, or the coincident, or the consequent. The
discovery of what is sought concerning God is the teaching
through His Son ; and the proof of our Saviour being the
Son of God is the prophecies announcing Him which preceded His coming, and the testimony regarding Him which
coincided with His birth in the world ; and, in addition,
His powers proclaimed and openly shown after His ascension."[2]   " Undoubtedly of the coming of the Lord, who
was our teacher, to men there were myriad indicators,
proclaimers, precursors from the beginning, from the
foundation of the world, intimating beforehand by words
and deeds, prophesying that He would come, and when,
and where, and what should be the signs."[3]   Thus,
apparently, the argument from prophecy is the most
weighty argument, but it must be taken along with the
evidence of the working of a living Christ. The miraculous
in the sphere of knowledge impressed him more than the
miraculous in the sphere of action. He speaks of the
latter as a concession to men in a lower stage of spiritual
development. " God spake by the burning bush, for the
men of that day needed signs and wonders."[4] He admits
it as one of the methods by which God saves men.[5] This
attitude of Clement is to be explained, on the one hand,
by his faith in the power of truth, and on the other by
his insistence on the liberty of the individual. In no case
is the freedom of the individual to be forced or touched.

[1] Str., vi. 8 ^{70}.   [2] Str., vi. 15 ^{122}.   [3] Ib., vi 18 ^{166}.
        [4] Prot., i. 8.   [5] Str , vi. 3 ^{28}

In a striking fragment he says : " I regard it as a form of necessity to astonish and compel the faith of a man by that which is miraculous, seeing that God wishes a man to be saved of himself, taking only the impulse from the commandment. God does not deal in compulsion, nor would it be right that the self-determined soul should, after the fashion of lifeless images, be influenced by an external cause." [1] In view of the fact that we know nothing of the context of this passage, it may be unwise to push it too far or to its logical issue ; but it is in harmony with Clement's views on human freedom,[2] as well as with the absence in his writings of specific and definite arguments for the truth of Christianity based on the miraculous, and with his very scanty allusions to the miracles of Jesus.

As a testimony to the divinity of the Christian faith, Clement points to its universality. It is not limited as a philosophical coterie is in the character or number of its adherents. Neither poverty nor lack of reputation can stand in the way of him who is eagerly intent on the knowledge of God.[3] And as it is independent of individual limitations, so it transcends all national or racial boundaries. "The word of our teacher remained not in Judæa alone, as philosophy did in Greece, but was scattered throughout the whole world, winning whole households of Greek and barbarians at once, in nation, village, and city, and individual hearers also, and bringing to the truth not a few of the philosophers themselves." [4] The reality of Christian faith and truth was evinced by the fact of martyrdom. No doubt, there had been isolated cases of martyrdom for truth before the coming of Christianity. " But we see the spectacle every day of innu-

---

[1] Stah., vol. iii. p. 217. [2] Cf. Pæd , i. 6 [33], &c.
[3] Prot., x. [106]. [4] Str., vi. 18 [167].

merable crowds of martyrs roasted, impaled, beheaded."[1]
The whole Church was filled with those who throughout
their whole life "had made a study of death."[2] This whole-
sale martyrdom had failed in its aim, and had only proved
the impossibility of crushing Christianity by force. Persecution by the State would cause any system of Greek philosophy to disappear forthwith; but it is futile as a check to
the progress of Christianity. "Our teaching from the very
moment of its first proclamation was prohibited by kings
and tyrants together, as well as by rulers and governors in
turn, with all their mercenaries, and in addition by count-
less men warring against us, and endeavouring to the
utmost of their power to cut it down. But it flourishes
the more. For it dies not as the teaching of men, nor
fades away as a gift without strength, for no gift of God
is without strength. It remains unhindered, though it
is predicted of it that it is destined to be persecuted
to the end."[3] The rapidity of its victorious march was
all the more noteworthy. With unsurpassable celerity
the divine power had shone over the earth, and filled the
universe with the seed of salvation.[4] The divinity of
Christ had been attested by the moral and intellectual
influence which it had exercised both socially and individually. It had transfigured and ennobled all social
relations. "Those who have betaken themselves to the
Father for the sake of wisdom have proved good fathers
to their children, and those who have known the Son
have proved good parents to their sons; and those who
remember the Bridegroom good husbands to their wives;
and those who have themselves been redeemed from the
lowest slavery good masters to their servants."[5] To the
individual it contributes the greatest of blessings, "the

[1] Str., ii. 20 [125].   [2] Ib., iv. 8 [58]; Plato, Phædo, 67 E.   [3] Ib., vi. 18 [167].
[4] Prot., x. [110].   [5] Ib., x. [107].

origin of faith, eagerness for heavenly citizenship, the impulse towards truth, a spirit of inquiry, a trace of knowledge,—in brief, the means of procuring salvation.   Those
who have been really nourished on the words of truth
receive a viaticum for eternal life, and are prepared for
flight heavenwards." [1]   In the double *rôle* which Clement
had to discharge, on the one hand, to maintain the quasi-
divine character of Greek philosophy against those in the
Church who were jealous of any contact with it, and,
on the other hand, to maintain against the Greeks its
inferiority to Christianity, while recognising the divine
element in it, he wavers a little in his language while he
exaggerates now this, now that, side of his polemic ; but
his central principles do not vary.

This lofty claim on the part of Christianity did not pass
unchallenged.   Greek and Jew alike pointed scornfully to
the divisions in the Church and said, " We ought not to
believe because of the dissonance of the sects ; truth is
strained, when some put forth one opinion and some
another." [2]   The careful discussion which Clement gives
of the objection is an index of the importance which was
attached to it alike by objector and adherent.   Clement
begins by showing that the application of this principle
to other departments of work or study would lead to
paralysis of action.   Because there were various schools
of philosophy, should all study of philosophy be summarily
abandoned?   So far from being unexpected, heresies were
predicted by the Lord Himself.   The beautiful is always
followed by its caricature.   Because some have let the
truth go, shall we not believe those who have kept a firm
hold of it ?   To stand aloof from the Christian faith on
the ground of such divisions was illogical.   Because there

----

[1] Str., i. 1 [4].   [2] Ib., vii. 15 [89].

were conflicting theories of disease in the science of
medicine, would the sick man refuse to go to a physician?
Why, then, should the sick of soul put forth divisions as
a pretext for indifference or unbelief?   If fruit ripe and
real is put before us, and fruit made of wax, shall we refrain from both?   Because there are many byroads, some
of which may lead to a precipice, shall we hesitate to travel
by the one royal highway?[1]   Because grass grows among
the garden produce, does the farmer give up gardening?
Such divisions of opinion were the inevitable result of
endeavours to investigate the meaning of the truth, and
from that point of view were a stimulus to the search
after truth, and a tribute to Christianity.   The attitude of
aloofness would only be justifiable if the truth were not
to be found anywhere, if demonstration were impossible,
and if there were no criterion of truth and error.   But
truth does exist; and he who does not seek to distinguish
the incongruous and unseemly and contrary to nature
and false from their opposites, stands self-condemned.[2]
And for this there is a criterion.   That criterion is the
Scripture itself; and the true, because the traditional,
interpretation of Scripture is to be found in the ancient
Catholic Church.   The sophists tear away some fragments
of truth with a view to the injury of men and bury them
in human systems of their own devising, and pride themselves on being the head of a school rather than a church.[3]
They dare to use the Prophetic Scriptures; but they do
not use them in their entirety, or mutilate what they
use, and do not deal with them in accordance with the
analogy of Scripture, as the body and tissue of Prophecy
demand.   They pick out ambiguous sayings, glean a few
words here and there, and consider the bare letter, not

---

[1] Str., vii. 15 89, 90.   [2] Ib., vii. 15 91.   [3] Ib., vii. 15 92.

the meaning.   To find the truth we must consider what
is perfectly fitting and becoming to the Lord and the
Almighty God, and must confirm each point that is
demonstrated by the analogy of Scripture.   When the
heretics are proved to be in antagonism to the Scriptures, they either make light of the logical consistency of
their own dogmas or of prophecy itself.   They disclaim
the authority of Scripture, and prefer their own conceptions to that which was spoken by the Lord through
the prophets, and attested and confirmed by the Gospels
and also by the Apostles.   They lack understanding for
the majesty of the truth.[1]   As mischievous boys bar out
their tutor, they shut out the prophecies from their own
church.[2]   They quibble at the things handed down by
the blessed apostles and teachers which are naturally
attached to the inspired words, and oppose human teaching to divine tradition.   Marcion and Prodicus were not
wiser than the men before them, and might well have
been contented with learning the previous traditions.[3]
The heretics have only a false key.   We open the main
door and enter in through the tradition of the Lord;
they cut down a side-door and secretly dig through the
wall of the Church.   Outstepping the truth, they initiate
into the mysteries the souls of the impious.   The Catholic
Church existed prior to the gatherings of the heretics;
all heresy is innovation.   The heretics try to break up
the unity of the Church; the true, the ancient Church
is one.   This oneness it shares with God.   The pre-
eminence of the Catholic Church, like the First Principle
of its constitution, is in accordance with the Monad, surpassing all other things, and having nothing or like equal
to itself.[4]   Even when all allowance has been made for

[1] Str., vii. 16 93.97.   [2] Ib., vii. 16 99.
[3] Ib., vii. 16 103.105.   [4] Ib., vii. 17 106, 107.

the polemical note in his criticism, there remains enough
to show that while Clement claimed for himself an independent position on some matters held by some of his
contemporaries to be vital, and may be considered as a
representative of a liberal attitude in respect of doctrine,
he regarded himself as loyal to the tradition of the Church.
A traditionalist of the type of Irenæus, Clement was not;
questions of ecclesiastical organisation or ritual had little
interest for him; no emphasis is put on the office of the
bishop in relation to the Church or to the truth; but in
his conflict with heresy, the main weapon in his armoury
with which he confronts his opponents is the authoritative standard, the ecclesiastical rule, which he regards
as of apostolic origin. At the same time, it is none the
less significant that in the Protrepticus the word Church
is not mentioned save in an allusion to a passage in the
Epistle to the Hebrews,[1] that he invites the Greeks to
enter not into the fold of the Church but into the domain
of truth, that his appeal is to the Scriptures, that often
as the word "salvation" occurs, it is nowhere associated
with the Church or its ordinances. No doubt, it may be
urged that such an appeal would not have been relevant
to his immediate aim, that he sought to bring them to
the threshold of the truth, in the assurance that they
would thereafter enter within the sanctuary; and that in
emphasising the unity and catholicity of the Church in
conflict with heresy, he emphasises it precisely at the
point where it was most natural to do so.[2]

From this survey it is plain that Clement held with great
firmness that Christianity, though divine in a unique sense,

---

[1] Prot., ix.[82]; Heb. xii. 23.

[2] For a temperate statement of the position of the Roman Catholic Church, as
against Harnack and Bigg, see Batiffol, ' L'Eglise Naissante et le Catholicisme,'
pp 295-315.

was not to be regarded as an isolated fact in the history of
the world, and that with regard to other forms of truth, it
stood not in the relation of antagonism or complete independence, but rather as the absolute stands to that which is
incomplete and undeveloped. Starting from the principle
that the Providence of God had been at work in universal
history, and that all truth was from Him, he did not regard
any aspect of it with jealousy, but welcomed it so far as it
was true. To Clement a religion that appealed to the
general heart of humanity and claimed for itself universal
homage, and at the same time was unrelated to other manifestations of the spirit of man, was an absurdity; for it
would find nothing in man to appeal to, nothing to receive
the seed. The possession of partial truth was the best
preparation for the attainment of fuller truth. Clement
transferred to the world of intellect what St Paul had
affirmed of the world of nature, that God never left Himself
without witness.[1] He represents Christianity as the true
mystery of which the Greek mysteries were only a shadow,
and calls on the Greeks to embrace Christianity in the very
language of the mysteries which he urged them to abandon;[2]
but there is no evidence that he wished to modify Christian
institutions in harmony with heathen forms of worship.[3]
The ascription to theft of what was cognate to Christianity
in the great thinkers of Greece was a grotesque recognition
of the unity of truth; but it was surely wiser and more
reverent than to deny any relationship whatsoever. It has,
indeed, been averred that in seeking to bring Hellenic
thought and culture into fellowship with the Christian faith,
Clement was endeavouring to carry out an impossible, if not
a treasonable task, and that he only seemed to succeed
because he abandoned that which was most distinctive of

[1] Acts xiv. 17.   [2] Prot., xii. [118], [119].
[3] Cf. Kattenbusch, ' Das apostolische Symbol,' vol. ii. p. 109

primitive Christianity. It is said that in his conception of Christianity as having for its aim the individual perfection of man, in his presentation of the facts of salvation, in his view of Christian life as an ascent to God, in his exaggeration of the human factors of salvation in relation to the divine, Clement is more in harmony with the current of thought in our time than in accord with the early teaching of the Church.[1]   That such a charge should have been made, now on the conservative, now on the liberal side, in the eighteenth century, is intelligible,[2] but it is somewhat of an anachronism to-day.   It is plain that our view of such objections to the aim as well as to the results of his method will depend very largely on what our view of primitive Christianity is.   Unless it be illegitimate or treasonable to put things in a different perspective, unless it be held that to emphasise certain truths involves disloyalty to others, Clement is not to be blamed for bringing Christianity into the moulds of his early life and training.   What teacher, in his discrimination of what is relatively important or unimportant, is not influenced by his own intellectual or spiritual history?   To have created a new terminology would have divorced Christianity from all relation to the past — the very thing which Clement was determined to avoid.

Platonic, Stoic, Aristotelian terms, definitions, and phrases repeatedly occur.   But this power to assimilate is surely a symptom of life, the characteristic of every healthy organism. It is only when it is a question of the introduction of a foreign body, of something actually hostile to that which has assimilated it, of something in the present case that is inconsistent alike with the primitive form of the Gospel or

---

[1] Kutter, 'Schweizer Theolog. Zeit.' 1899.

[2] Cf Walch, 'Miscell. Sacr.,' vol. ii. p. 516   'De Erroribus C. A. eorumque causis.'   Semler, 'Gesch. d. christ. Glaubens,' vol. ii. p. 133.

its natural inner development, that foreign influence can be established.   The elements in the theology and ethics of Clement that may be assigned to the undue influence of Hellenic bias or culture will be noted in the course of the exposition.   This at least is certain, that Clement was him-self unconscious of any disloyalty to the teaching of the Church; and while he faced the situation of the time with intellectual courage, he did not dream of making any con-cession to the Hellenic culture around him that either trans-formed or deformed the Christian faith.   On the contrary, he maintained that his teaching derived breath and life from the Scriptures of the Lord;[1] and he believed that he was loyal to the Church when he sought to bring all truth under its shadow.   If all truth were from God, a conflict in truth was impossible.   The problem of the Church in Alexandria was to adjust itself to the intellectual impulse from which philosophy in all its schools derived its being; and Clement held that to make the Church and its doctrine a non-intellectual preserve was fatal to its usefulness, as well as to its claims to master and permeate the world.   It has often been observed that he lived in an age of transition.   It was so in regard to doctrine, the authority of the Church, and the Canon of the New Testament.   In Alexandria, in particular, it was so in regard to the relation of the Church to intellectual culture.   In such an age the attitude of a thinker is sometimes of more importance than the results which he achieves.   And the attitude of Clement was that of one who believed that a Christianity which could claim for itself all that was highest in the thought of the past could alone face the future with confidence.   The problem of the Church to-day is, in loyalty to the past, to adjust itself to the new forces in the thought of our time.   And,

[1] Str., vii. 1 [1].

surely, there can be little doubt that it will act wisely if it adopts the principles that underlie the attitude of Clement. Intellectual monasticism is as bad for the Church as moral monasticism was for the individual, and can only end in lopsidedness of development or impoverishment. In regard to other forms of religion, for example, there can be no doubt that the wise procedure is that of Clement, to recognise what in them is cognate to Christianity and work from that as relatively true; for Christianity does not call upon us to postulate the absolute falsity of other religions, but its own absolute truth. And of a like nature will be our attitude to all the intellectual forces and movements of the present. The Christian thinker who adopts the position of Clement need not regard these with any hostile or even unsympathetic eye; he can recognise in each of them a manifestation of the one Word who is "the sleepless guard of humanity,"[1] and will only be hostile when they claim to represent not one but the only aspect of truth. In this way the pre-eminence of Christianity is maintained: it is not dishonoured, though other gifts of God are honoured; for all science, all art, all philosophy, regarded in their ideal function, are the inspiration of the one God who speaks to-day as He spoke to the fathers of old, "by diverse portions and in divers manners."

[1] Pæd., iii. 8 ⁴⁴.

LECTURE III.

THE NATURE AND ATTRIBUTES OF GOD.

To have a right conception of God in Himself, and in His relation to the universe and to man, is the essential basis not only of Christian thought but of all thought whatsoever. The ethical ideal of Clement was an ever-growing likeness to God, but this was inseparably related to intellectual cognition of Him. That this knowledge was hard to realise Clement well knew. But the difficulty of the investigation furnished no ground for abandoning the inquiry, as some suggested, but rather the contrary. We must continue to inquire in order that we may say what ought to be said, and hear what ought to be heard, concerning Him. Only one limitation is necessary. All inquiry must be conditioned by the faith.[1] Here, as elsewhere, Clement remains faithful to his eclectic principles. We find in his doctrine of God clear evidence of the influence of Plato, still clearer of the influence of Philo. This eclecticism leads him into paradoxes and apparent contradictions. At times the conception of God seems to be purely philosophical, and the Christian element a mere graft, or even an accretion. At other times his presentation seems to be fundamentally Christian; and in this case a main interest of his doctrine of God does not

---

[1] Stah., vol. iii. p. 228, fr. 67.

E

lie in what he has appropriated or assimilated, but in his own point of view which made that appropriation possible.

No thinker of the early Church realised with more earnestness the necessity and the dignity of the knowledge of God. It has even been brought as a charge against him that to him Christianity is essentially a knowledge of God. "The knowledge of the truly existent God," he says, "is the immutable beginning and foundation of life: to be ignorant of Him is death, but to have full knowledge of Him and become like unto Him is the only life." [1] If it were possible to distinguish between the knowledge of God and eternal salvation, and such alternative choice were put before the ideal Christian, he would without any hesitation whatsoever choose the knowledge of God. [2] But to know Him we must first be assured of His existence. "He that cometh to God must believe that He is." This need not be demonstrated. To demand demonstration of the existence of God is to raise a question, the very putting of which deserves punishment. [3] Christianity confirms the doctrine of a Providence and presupposes it. With the abolition of theism Christianity becomes a myth. [4] But though such demonstration is superfluous, we may appeal to the testimony borne by the order of the universe, by the spirit of man, and by the universal consciousness of mankind. The Providence of God is manifest from the vision of all things that are seen, the works of skill and wisdom, both of things that come into existence in due order and of those which are made manifest in due order. [5] The voice of God—as even the philosophers have noted—may be heard by all who give earnest contemplation to the constitution of the universe, which owes its being and its unceasing subsistence to Him. [6] The wisest of the Greeks have ascribed the pre-eminence to

[1] Q. D., 7.
[2] Str., iv. 22 [146].
[3] Ib., v. 1 [6].
[4] Ib., i 11 [52].
[5] Ib, v. 1 [6].
[6] Ib, v. 14 [99]; v. 1 [6].

"the invisible, sole, most powerful, most skilful, and principal cause of all that is fairest."[1] God gave to the Gentiles
the stars for worship, that through the worship of the stars
they might rise to the Maker of them.[2] And to this conviction, which is borne in upon us by the wisdom and
order manifest in the world without, the inner voice of the
spirit of man is responsive. "Into all men whatsoever a
certain divine effluence has been instilled; wherefore, though
unwillingly, they confess that God is one, indestructible,
and unoriginated."[3] A divine power is at work in the
Providence which is exercised in relation to us. Such a
Providence is inconsistent with the hypothesis of many
gods. There is, then, only one God who truly is and
subsists.[4] This belief in the existence of God is universal,
and is essential to true life. "No race of men anywhere,
tillers of the soil, or nomads, or even dwellers in cities, can
live unless it has previously received faith in One who is
better. Every nation alike in the east and the west, the
north and the south, has one and the same conception
regarding Him who has established the hegemony."[5] In
like manner the common consciousness of mankind bears
witness by its ordinary forms of speech to the existence of
One who is Almighty.[6] If the conception of God be thus
innate and universal, how comes it that belief in Him is
not universal, that His existence is ignored or denied by
many? Such unbelief is moral rather than intellectual in
its origin, and arises in part from the apparent victory of
unrighteousness in the world and misconception as to the
true ground of that apparent victory, and in part from the
moral disorders of men themselves. Some men looking at
the existence of injustice which passes unchastened think

---

[1] Str., v 14 [134].   [2] Ib., vi. 14 [110], [111].   [3] Prot., vi. [68]. Cf. xii. [120].
[4] Ib., x. [103]; Str., v. 13 [87].   [5] Str., v 14 [133].
[6] Ib., v. 14 [135].

that there is no God. They do not observe, says Clement,
the self-determination of the soul, and that it cannot be
enslaved.   Like these in opinion are those who from in-
continence in pleasures fall into pains out of the common
course and unlooked-for accidents, and sinking under their
calamities say that there is no God, or that, if He exists,
He does not oversee all things.[1] This universal conviction,
however, did not carry with it oneness of conception. That
the conceptions of God varied with the moral character of
men and were determined thereby, and that this in turn
reacted on their moral life, is again and again emphasised.[2]
A mere belief in God, unless accompanied by a right apprehension of the God in whom we ought to believe, was
accordingly of no value.

Apart from the numerous passages where his conception
of God comes out incidentally, there are at least three occasions on which he gives a formal definition ; and though the
second is professedly based on a saying of the Lord, and
there is a scriptural phrase in the third, they are all purely
philosophical.   "In the case of God," he says, "being is
God.   The Divine being is something eternal and without
beginning and which cannot be circumscribed, and is the
cause of things that exist."[3] Again—"What is God ? God is
spirit, as also the Lord says.   Now spirit is truly essence,
bodiless, and that which cannot be circumscribed. And that
is bodiless which is not completed by means of a body, whose
existence is not in breadth, length, and depth. And that
cannot be circumscribed of which there is no place, which
is altogether in all things, and is in each whole and independently the same."[4] Again—"No one can form any conception of God according to His worth ; but to form a
conception of Him as far as it is possible, let him conceive

[1] Str., vii. 3[18].   [2] Cf. ib., vii. 3[14], vii. 4[22].
[3] Stah., vol. iii. p. 219.   [4] Ib., p. 220.

of 'light inaccessible,' great, incomprehensible, and most fair—of light, which has embraced within itself every power that is good, every gracious excellence, which cares for all, is pitiful, passionless, good, knows all things, foreknows all things, is pure, sweet, bright, unmixed."[1] The first two definitions are concerned solely with the essence — the essential nature—of God; in the third an ethical element enters into the conception. It is important to keep the first two definitions especially in mind, when we find descriptions that have caused some to claim Clement, if not as an agnostic, at least as a precursor of Hamilton and Mansel.

Clement repeatedly emphasises the transcendence of God. "The God of the universe," he says, "is above all speech, all perception, all thought."[2] "The discourse concerning God is most difficult to deal with."[3] "The subject of God embraces not one thing but ten thousand things. There is a difference between seeking God and seeking things about God. In this, as in everything else, the accidents are to be distinguished from the essence."[4] "The Governor of the universe is a Being hard to comprehend and apprehend, always receding and withdrawing from him who pursues. . . . God is not in darkness or in place, but above place and time and the property of things that have come into being. Wherefore He is never in a part, neither containing nor contained, either by way of definition, limitation, or of section."[5] A kindred thought is developed elsewhere. "How can that be expressed," he asks, "which is neither genus, nor species, nor individual, nor number,—nay more, is neither an accident nor that to which an accident happens? One cannot rightly call Him whole. For on account of His greatness He is ranked as the whole, and

---

[1] Ec. Pr , 21. Cf. Adum. in 1 Joan., p. 210. "Quia deus," inquit, "lumen est : non essentiam divinam exprimit, sed declarare volens majestatem dei."
[2] Str., v. 10[66].   [3] Ib., v. 12[81].   [4] Ib., vi. 17[150].   [5] Ib., ii. 2[5], [6].

is the Father of the universe. Nor are any parts to be predicated of Him. For the One is indivisible, wherefore, also, He is infinite, not so much because conceived as impossible to be embraced, but with reference to His being without dimensions and not having a limit. And, therefore, He is without form and name. And if we name Him, we do not do so, properly speaking, calling him either the One, or the Good, or Mind, or the Absolute, or Father, or God, or Creator, or Lord.[1] We do not speak of declaring His name; but by reason of our perplexity we use good names, so that the mind may not go astray about other names, but may be able to lean upon those. For each name by itself does not express God; but all collectively are indicative of the power of the Omnipotent. For things may be described by their attributes or mutual relations; but none of these qualities can be applied to God. Nor, again, can He be apprehended by the science of demonstration. For demonstration depends on what is anterior to, and better known than, that which is demonstrated. But nothing existed prior to the Unbegotten."[2] "Everything that falls under a name is begotten."[3] "Human speech is by nature feeble and incapable of declaring God. I do not mean declaring His name,—for to name Him is common not to philosophy only but to all poets—nor declaring His essence, for that is impossible, but declaring the power and the works of God."[4] If this be so, how is any conception of God, still less any knowledge of Him, possible? The method is that of analysis or the elimination of attributes that imply definition or limitation. "By analysis we advance to Him who is the first conception. Start-

---

[1] καλοῦντες ἤτοι ἓν, ἢ τἀγαθὸν, ἢ νοῦν, ἢ αὐτὸ τὸ ὂν, ἢ πατέρα, ἢ θεὸν, ἢ δημιουργὸν, ἢ κύριον. Str., v. 12 ⁹².

[2] Str., v. 12 ⁸¹, ⁸².   [3] Ib., v. 13 ⁸³.   [4] Ib., vi. 18 ¹⁶⁶.

ing with things which are subordinate to it, we begin
by abstracting from body its natural properties. Then we
cut off the three dimensions, length, breadth, and depth.
That which is left is a point, a unit having position, so
to speak. Take away position, and you have the conception of the unit, If, then, abstracting all that belongs to
bodies and the properties of things called incorporeal,
we cast ourselves into the greatness of Christ, and thence
go forward through holiness into immensity, we may attain
somehow to the conception of the Almighty, not knowing
what He is, but what He is not. And form, or motion, or
standing, or a throne, or place, or right hand, or left, are
not at all to be conceived as belonging to the Father of the
universe, though these things are written of Him. . . . The
First Cause is not, then, in a place, but above both place,
and time, and name, and conception."[1] " God is one, and
beyond the one, and above the monad itself."[2]

All this description of the Divine Being seems absolutely
fatal to the thought to which he has given emphatic expression, that the knowledge of God was life. What possible
knowledge of, or fellowship can there be with, One who cannot be scientifically known, because He cannot be logically
demonstrated, who is a mere metaphysical abstraction, of
whom we can predicate nothing but negations, who seems
only " the deification of zero,"[3] and whose transcendence
seems to put Him out of all possible relation to us? " A
God out of all relations," says Professor Flint, " is no God
at all."[4]

There is a sense, however, in which these sayings of
Clement are in harmony with Scripture and express a

---

[1] Str, v. 11 [71]. οὔκουν ἐν τόπῳ τὸ πρῶτον αἴτιον, ἀλλ' ὑπεράνω καὶ τόπου
καὶ χρόνου καὶ ὀνόματος καὶ νοήσεως.

[2] Pæd., i. 8 [71]. ἐν δὲ ὁ θεὸς καὶ ἐπέκεινα τοῦ ἑνὸς καὶ ὑπὲρ αὐτὴν μονάδα

[3] Mayor, p. xxxix.   [4] ' Agnosticism,' p. 521.

profound truth. That man cannot by searching find out
God, that no man hath seen God at any time, that
He alone hath immortality, dwelling in light inaccessible,
whom no man hath seen or can see, is but the expression in simple language of what Clement sought to express in the language of the schools. And if, like him,
we try to define the essence rather than the nature of
God as manifested in that which is external to Him, to
express what God is in Himself, apart from any relation
to the universe or to man, can we conceive of Him or name
Him in any other way than by denying to Him any
attributes that imply anything that is distinctive of the
finite? This is but an amplification of the thought that God
cannot be described in terms of Deductive Logic or sub-
sumed under its categories. It implies that God, the
absolutely First Principle, need not, and cannot, be demonstrated, because He is a necessary postulate of human
thought. What God is in Himself only God Himself can
fully know. "God only knows the love of God." We can
only guess at what He is in Himself by what He is to us.
It is true that no category which implies limitation can be
ascribed to God, that no name of man can describe His
essence, and that our names are only points of support
by which we may give definiteness to our conception of
Him. The language of Clement expresses a truth which
has been recognised by the highest teachers of all ages, and
which forms an essential element in all true theism—viz.,
that the essence of God must ever escape our analysis,
that we may apprehend but cannot comprehend the nature
of Deity, that He may be known to be infinite though not
known as infinite. This method of conceiving God is due
in part to the influence of Plato on his early training,
in part to the influence of Philo. But though the language is similar, Clement's motive of ascribing such

transcendence to God is different from theirs. The aim of the transcendence in Plato was to keep the Deity from contact with the world. The aim of Clement is rather, in harmony with his view of a universal providence, to maintain the unconditional freedom of God and to emphasise the necessity of revelation. We can only understand the Unknown by divine grace, and by the Word that came from Him.[1] "The same One who is very far off has come very near—an unspeakable wonder. I am a God near at hand, says the Lord. He is far off in respect of essence —for how can that which is created apprehend the Uncreated—but He is very near by His power in which all things have been embraced. Yea, the power of God is always present, laying hold of us by that power which sees, and is beneficent and disciplinary."[2] Thus the transcendence of God, in the thought of Clement, is consistent with His immanence; rather the immanence is an essential factor in his conception.

On the ground of a saying preserved by Maximus the Confessor, it has been affirmed that "Clement expressly denied to God any consciousness of the external world."[3] After having stated that Dionysius the Areopagite says that we are called "divine volitions" by the Scripture, Maximus quotes in confirmation or illustration a reply that had been given by some of the adherents of Pantænus or Clement to a question concerning the nature of the divine knowledge. Stählin assigns the saying to Clement.[4] Some who were vain of their secular culture wished to know in what way the Christians represented God's knowledge of existent things (the real). They supposed that He knew the things of sense by sensation and the things of intellect by intellection. The answer ascribed to Clement is as follows: "God does not know the things of sense by sensation, nor

[1] Str., v. 12 82.   [2] Ib., ii. 15.   [3] Bigg, p. 64.   [4] Stah., vol. iii. p. 224.

the things of intellect by intellection. For it is not possible that He who is above existent things should apprehend existent things after the manner of existent things. We say that He knows existent things as His own volitions — a reasonable argument to adduce. For if He has made the totality of things by volition—which reason will not gainsay—and if it is always right and pious to say that He knows His own volitions, and He by volition has made each of the things that have come into being, then God knows existent things as His own volitions, seeing that also by volition He has made existent things."

The aim of Clement in this answer is not to deny the divine knowledge, but rather to emphasise its nature and method in contrast with human knowledge, and so to deny anthropomorphism both in a grosser and a subtler form. Man, who is himself a part of existent things, can only know them by sense-perception, or by a process of intellection, mediate and partial, bit by bit, as it were. God, who is not a part of existent things but above them, cannot know them as such, not only because He is above them, but because of His immediate relation to them as acts of His will. His argument is: God made all things by volition. He knows His own volition. Therefore, He knows existent things as His own volitions. And His volition, in the thought of Clement, is no barren volition, but a realised volition; for His volition is work.[1] Can that be called a denial of God's consciousness of the external world? If we may judge from human analogy, there is nothing of which we have such immediate knowledge as we have of our own volitions and their realisation or embodiment. Does an artist not know that which he has willed to delineate? In a real sense does any one else know it, or does he know anything else? If any-

[1] Pæd., i. 6²⁷   τὸ θέλημα αὐτοῦ ἔργον ἐστί.

thing be denied of God's relation to the external world in this saying, would it not be more correct to say that Clement denied to God any consciousness of *an* external world, of the external world, as external ? [1]

The universe, according to Clement, owes its continual subsistence as well as its origin to God. He is as essential to the continuance of the universe as He was to its creation. The husbandman who casts in the seed is only an agent. It is God who brings about the growth and perfection of all things, and carries forward things that come into being to their natural end. To attribute growth and changes to the stars as the principal cause is to deprive the Father of the universe, so far as in them lies, of His unwearied power.[2] Things created have no power of themselves. "An axe does not operate without some one to use it. Things do not energise of themselves, but possess certain natural qualities which accomplish their distinctive work through the energy of the craftsman. So by the universal Providence of God, through the medium of proximate causes, the power to act is transmitted in succession to individual objects."[3]

From this it would seem that Clement avoided on the one hand the danger of thinking of the transcendence of God in such a way as to place Him entirely out of relation to the universe which He had formed, and on the other hand that of conceiving Him in pantheistic fashion as merged and lost in His own world. The relation of the world to God is not like that of a machine which has been set agoing and endowed with certain qualities that make it independent of the Creator. The axe of a workman has no power to act of itself, and can only realise its end when put into action by the will of man ; so no force in the universe has an independent energy,

[1] Cf. 'Church Quarterly Review,' 1904.   [2] Str., vi. 16 [148].   [3] Ib.

but has only a potentiality of energy which would cease to develop into actuality were it not for the continuous operation of the Almighty. The same thought is enforced by the illustration drawn from the tillage of the ground. The husbandman can only use the seed with the potencies with which God has endowed it, and take advantage of the laws of growth which God has ordained for its development. But every stage of that growth is not only controlled but directed by God; and were His energy to be withdrawn, these laws which are not only derived from God but administered by Him would cease to be operative. To attribute an independent energy to anything in itself, or to attribute it to any force external to the world, or to anything whatever but God Himself, is to dishonour the untiring power of the Almighty. He Himself created, sustains, and administers the universe. Is this conception of the absolute sovereignty of God in the ceaseless administration of the universe reconcilable with a dualism of original principles? If unfettered in administration, must He not have been unfettered in creation? Matter may be conceived as formless; can it be conceived as existing uncreated before God imparted to it the quality of receiving form? If it can be so conceived, must we not ascribe to matter a certain independence of God, and therewith a certain limitation of the divine power in creating and administering? But that the creative and administrative activity of God was absolutely unconditioned, Clement again and again asserts. "There is nothing which God cannot do." [1] "The universe sprang into existence at a mere act of His will." [2] "Nothing at all exists unless He had willed it to exist." [3] If, then, even essentially chaotic matter existed before God fashioned it, He must have been its Creator. In itself

[1] Pæd., i. 3 [7]   [2] Prot., iv [63].   [3] Pæd., i. 8 [62].

the doctrine of intermediaries might seem opposed to
the doctrine of immanence. But that would only be the
case if the underlying conception were that in no other
way could the gulf between matter and the transcendent
God be bridged. But this conception of immanence being
denied, the use of proximate causes is not inconsistent with
immanence : it is only a method by which the immanence
of God is effected. The employment of men as agents,
for example, is in accordance with the divine method. But
this does not mean that God can do some things but not
other things, nor that some things take place with His will
and some things against His will.[1] It is important to keep
in mind the unconditioned activity assigned to God, as we
turn to the controverted question as to the view of Clement
on the eternity of matter.

On this subject widely different views are, and have been,
held. In accordance with a statement of Photius, some have
maintained that he held a dualistic theory of the origin of
the universe. One of the heresies which Photius found in
the ' Hypotyposes ' was the eternity or timelessness of
matter.[2] Some maintain that Photius was right ; some
that he was in error, and in any case, that "timeless"
was not synonymous with "uncreated." Some have held
that in view of the conflicting statements no conclusion
can be drawn, and that the conceptions of Clement
remained in a fluid or chaotic form.

Take first the positive statements which he makes as to
his position. He avers that the Greek philosophers took
from Moses the doctrine that the world was created.[3] He
represents the conception of the creation of the world as
the teaching of Scripture. He adduces the " prophecy " in
Genesis[4] as evidence that "we may be taught that the

[1] Ec. Pr., 16   [2] Photius, Cod., 109
[3] Str., v. 14 [99].   [4] Gen. 11. 4.

world was created, and that God did not make it in time." [1]
Still more definitely, in an altogether fantastic exegesis of
the sixth commandment—which, as being read into the
commandment, all the more certainly expresses his thought
—does he make his position clear. It is true that the text
of the conclusion of the passage is uncertain, but there is
no corruption in the part of the passage to be adduced.
He holds that to maintain that the world was uncreated
was a transgression of the sixth commandment, to be put
on a level with a denial of the providential administration
of the universe. Both opinions alike are the introduction of
false and pernicious views regarding God and His eternity. [2]
Now when it is kept in mind, as we have seen, that the
denial of Providence was in his judgment not a matter for
discussion or argument, but rather only for the punishment
of the denier, there would seem to be little doubt as to
what his opinion was. So, elsewhere, he says that the
earth could not make itself, so that it could not be the
cause of itself. [3] It may at least be claimed that the other
evidence should be read in the light of these positive statements. With regard to the creation of man, he says
incidentally that God may have formed man either of that
which was absolutely non-existent or out of matter. [4] As
he expresses no preference for either opinion, all that can
be urged from the passage is that the conception—so far as
man was concerned—of a creation from the non-existent was
not altogether foreign to his thought. The terms applied
to God Himself are opposed to a dualistic view of original
principles. He is the absolutely First Principle, and He
alone is unbegotten. [5] Himself without beginning, He is
the perfect beginning of the universe, the maker of the
beginning. [6] Can there be more than one Unbegotten?

[1] Str., vi. 16[146].   [2] Ib., vi. 16[147].   [3] Ib., viii. 9[28]   [4] Ib., ii. 16[74].
[5] Ib., v. 12[81]; vi. 7[58].   [6] Ib., iv. 25[162].

Can there be two first principles? If matter were a first principle, it, too, would be unbegotten ; and the only difference between it and God would be the difference between an unconscious and a conscious first principle. But, on the contrary, Clement maintains, in spite of the maintenance of the opposite by some philosophers, that matter was not to be regarded as among first principles, as this would imply that there was more than one first principle. And he interprets a passage in the ' Timæus ' as implying that the truly existent first principle was one. Even making allowance for the polemical element, if he did not accept the hypothesis of only one first principle, why should he thus have done violence to the interpretation of Plato?[1]

In speaking of the Marcionites, he says that they taught that evil was derived from matter, which was evil.[2] Matter, in the conception of Marcion, was thus a limit to the power of the God whom he called the Creator. Clement puts off the discussion of the question until he took up the question of the First Principles. This proposed section he never reached. But elsewhere he protests against the idea that the body as such, as being formed of matter, was evil by nature;[3] and he nowhere indicates that he regarded matter as being independent of God, as from its evil nature it must have been, since God is in no way the cause of evil. It is true that he nowhere says, in opposition to Marcion, that matter was created by God, and therefore good in itself; but he denies that it had anything to do with evil. It in no way fettered the action of the Almighty; it was absolutely under His control. This does not prove that in the opinion of Clement matter owed its origin to God; but it is more in harmony with the view that matter was not eternal, and, as far as it goes, confirms the statements already adduced.

One passage, in particular, creates a difficulty, and seems

---

[1] Str., v. 14 ^{89}.   [2] Ib., iii. 3 ^{12}.   [3] Ib., iv. 25 ^{164}.

to support the affirmation of Photius. In speaking of the
" rest " of God, he says that does not mean that God ceased
from doing, for that were to cease to be God. In the case
of God, " rest " means that He has ordained that the order
of things which have come into being should be preserved
inviolably, and that each of the things created should
" rest " from the ancient disorder.[1] He says that all things
came into being together from one essence by one Power.
And then he asks, How could creation take place in time,
seeing that time also came into being along with things that
exist ?[2] On the face of it, this might seem to reduce the
work of the Creator to the Platonic *rôle* of bringing order
out of disorder, to that of organising, not of creating, the
universe. But it is quite consistent with the narrative in
Genesis, which speaks first of a creation of the universe,
and then of its ordering. And the " rest " of God refers to
the end of the ordering. Nor does the reference to time
coming into existence along with existent things involve
dualism. No one argues more powerfully against the
eternity of matter than Augustine. And yet in the very
chapter in which he affirms that those who say that the
world was eternal were raving in their impiety, he says
almost in the language of Clement, that assuredly the world
was not made in time but simultaneously with time.[3] So,
by a timeless creation Clement did not mean that matter
was eternal, but that creation, however he conceived it, was
eternal. And his ground is that God must be conceived as
having been eternally at work. From the context it is
plain that it was not the question of the relation of matter

---

[1] Cf Plato, Tim. 30 A. : εἰς τάξιν αὐτὸ ἤγαγεν ἐκ τῆς ἀταξίας

[2] Str , vi. 16[143] : πῶς δ᾽ ἂν ἐν χρόνῳ γένοιτο κτίσις, συγγενομένου τοῖς οὖσι καὶ
τοῦ χρόνου; Cf. vi. 16[145]

[3] De Civit , xi 4, 6 . " Procul dubio non est mundus factus in tempore, sed
cum tempore "

to God, nor of God's relation to matter, that was in his thought, but the nature of the Divine working; and that he declares to be eternal. The essential thing is that matter, whether conceived as created in time or not, should not have come into existence independently of God; and of his view on that point Clement leaves us in no doubt. Taking into account, then, his own positive statements, his conception of God and His relation to the world, the method of creation presented, his attitude towards the teaching of Plato and Marcion, I am of opinion that Clement did not hold a dualistic theory of the origin of the universe.

The transcendence ascribed to God by Clement was in part due to his antagonism to pantheism. It is true that in his writings there are passages which, if they stood alone, might reasonably be held to imply a pantheistic conception of the universe. " The same Being is just and good, the true God, He who is Himself all things and the same in all things, because He is Himself God, the only God."[1] But from the context it is plain that he simply meant to emphasise the fact that God was the one reality, that He was at once the origin and the goal of all things, and that nothing was unrelated to, nor independent of, Him. So the phrases in the formal definitions already quoted[2] express the same thought, and at most are but another way of putting the scriptural conception of the divine omnipresence. Quite explicitly he says that it is not as a part of God that the Spirit is in each of us.[3] That such is the force of the apparently pantheistic passage is proved by his repeated repudiation of the doctrine of the Stoics that the divine nature permeated all matter, even the vilest. " How," he asks, " can any one who has known God endure the saying that we are a part of God, and the same in essence with Him, when he has come to know his own life and the evils

---

[1] Pæd., i 9 ⁸⁸.   [2] See pp. 68, 69   [3] Str., v. 13 ⁸⁸.

F

by which we are defiled? For, in that case—which it is
not lawful to say,—God would sin in part, if the parts are
parts of the whole; and if they are not complementary,
they could not be parts." [1] To pantheism, then, in this
crude material form, Clement is opposed alike on metaphysical and ethical grounds.

The same applies to his criticism of anthropomorphism.
It is partly in antagonism to the gross anthropomorphism
of Greek mythology that he strips God of all attributes
that suggest His kinship by nature with man. " Most
men entertain the same opinion of the blessed and incorruptible God as of themselves." [2] The Greeks represent
their gods as human in passions as well as human in
form. Each nation paints the shapes of its gods after
its own likeness—" the Ethiopian, as Xenophanes says,
black and snub-nosed; the Thracians, with red hair and
blue eyes." [3] But if the divine nature were human in
form, it would need like man food and covering and a
house and all things belonging to these. [4] But God is
not like any created thing in form, and does not hunger
so as to desire food. [5] The Greek satirists themselves
represent the worshippers as supposing that they could
cheat the gods whom they professed to worship, or make
them connive at their guilt. [6] To seek to localise in a
shrine the Divine Being who cannot be circumscribed by
place is an absurdity. [7] It is superfluous to set up any
statue of Him as an object of worship, [8] still more, to
offer to Him any material sacrifice. We honour God by
prayer. [9] The only recompense that we can offer is a
thankful and submissive heart as a kind of house-rent
for our dwelling here below. [10] Not only must all gross

---

[1] Str., ii. 16 [74].   [2] Ib., v 11 [68].   [3] Ib., vii. 4 [22].   [4] Ib., vii 5 [29].
[5] Ib., vii 6 [30].   [6] Ib., vii 3 [16].   [7] Ib., vii. 5 [29].   [8] Ib., v. 11 [74].
[9] Ib., vii. 6 [31].   [10] Prot., xi. [115].

anthropomorphism be set aside, but no passion or affection of any kind must be ascribed to Him. "God is passionless, and without anger, and without desire. He is not fearless in the sense that He does not turn aside from things terrible, nor temperate in the sense that He rules over desire; for the nature of God could not fall into anything terrible; nor does He shun timidity, just as He will not even desire that He may rule over desire."[1] To desire to rule over desire would imply the possibility of being conquered by it, and such possibility would be a moral imperfection in God. For a kindred reason the forgiveness of God must not be limited by any conception of human forgiveness.[2] In his eagerness to avoid any appearance of anthropomorphism, Clement uses language which on the face of it ascribes to God an ethical transcendence parallel to the metaphysical transcendence. In formal antagonism to his own ideal of ethical assimilation to God, he energetically condemns the thesis of the Stoics, that the virtue of God and man is identical.[3] But he nowhere denies that they were related; on the contrary, he says that the mercy of God alone fulfils the ideal of mercy.[4] To this conception of a passionless God it was objected that joy and mercy are ascribed in the Scriptures to God, and that they are passions of the soul.[5] God, rejoins Clement, only rejoices in the sense in which Christ could say, "I was hungry," making the joy of men His own. But surely, we may ask, whence came the impulse to such identification, to such oneness? The language of Clement is due to his desire to keep his idea of God free from any human element—in particular, from such passions as were an essential constituent of

---

[1] Str., iv. 23[151] · θεὸs δὲ ἀπαθὴs, ἄθυμόs τε καὶ ἀνεπιθύμητοs
[2] Ib., iv. 24[153].   [3] Ib., vi. 14[114], vii. 14[88].
[4] Ib., ii. 16[79].   [5] Ib., ii. 16[72].

human nature, and to represent Him as "alone in and unto Himself, not standing in need of any creatures which He hath made."[1]   But do we not read in Scripture of the hand and feet and mouth and eyes of God, of His going out and His coming in, of His anger and threatening?[2]   Such expressions, he answers, are to be interpreted allegorically, or to be regarded as a concession to human weakness.   It was not possible for the Divine nature to be described as it is, but only in so far as it was possible for men fettered by sense to hear.[3]   In brief, God spake to men as they were able to hear it; alike in form and substance His revelation of Himself was affected by the material embodiment; the measure of His power to unveil Himself was determined by the capacity of man to receive.

God is omniscient.   He does not, like man, judge the soul from external movement nor from the result.[4]   He hears not only the voice but the thought.   He is "all ear, all eye," if we may use such an expression.[5]   He knows all things,—not merely the things which are but those which shall be, and how they shall be.   He sees the soul naked within.   As in an amphitheatre He sees the whole and each thing at a glance.[6]   The Pythagorean saying, "Pray with the voice," did not mean that God did not hear those who speak in silence; but that our prayer should be such as no one would be ashamed to offer, though many were to hear it.[7]   The power of God, like light, instantly sees through the whole soul.[8]

God is omnipotent.   He is the universal King and Almighty Father, the Creator of all things.[9]   There is nothing which God cannot do.[10]   That God is "consuming fire" is to be interpreted of His power.   As fire is

---

[1] Westminster Confession, c. ii. 2.   [2] Str., v. 11 [68].   [3] Ib., ii. 16 [72].
[4] Ib., vi. 12 [101].   [5] Ib., vii. 7 [37].   [6] Ib , vi. 17 [156].   [7] Ib., iv. 26 [171].
[8] Ib., vii. 7 [37].   [9] Ib., vii. 3 [16].   Pæd., i. 3 [7].

the most powerful of the elements, and gains mastery of all things, so also God is all-powerful. As fire is superior to the elements, so is the Almighty to the gods, and powers, and principalities. He is a power strong and irresistible, to which nothing is impossible.[1]

Clement exhibits with great emphasis the absolute goodness of God. This goodness is based by him on the nature of God Himself, on the nature of the Good, with which God is identified, and on the teaching of Scripture. God does good, He does all good, and that voluntarily and designedly. He did not begin at some period to be Lord and good, being always what He is. His goodness is an essential constituent of His nature. Hence He will never cease to do good.[2] If he were to cease to do good, He would cease to be good.[3] For what is the use of Good that does not operate?[4] All benefits belonging to life in its highest sense proceed from the sovereign God. He does good in a manner peculiarly His own. He is occupied with unceasing acts of beneficence, and remains unalterably in the same condition of goodness.[5] But this goodness is not to be conceived as akin to any physical attribute; it is no mechanical goodness, but the goodness of a loving personality. Goodness, no doubt, is as natural to God as warmth to fire—but with an important difference. Unlike the fire, He is not involuntarily good.[6] He does not do good by necessity, but of His free choice He benefits those who of themselves turn to Him.[7] He is the adversary of no one, and the enemy of no one.[8] His goodness is seen in His providential care, which is at once supreme and good, universal and individual.[9] It is ever at work, and is like the care of a shepherd for

---

[1] Ec. Pr., 26.   [2] Str., v. 14 [141].   [3] Ib , vi. 16 [141].
[4] Ib., vi. 12 [104].   [5] Ib.   [6] Ib., vii. 7 [42].
[7] Ib.   [8] Ib., vii. 12 [69].   [9] Ib., i. 27 [173] ; i. 11 [52].

his sheep or a king for his subjects.[1] All things are
arranged by the Lord of the universe, both generally and
particularly, with a view to the safety of the universe.[2]
The goal of the ineffable Goodness is always as far as
possible to bring the nature of existing things up to that
which is better.[3] He loves everything that exists; in
particular does He love man, the noblest of created
objects.[4] The argument from the nature of the good is
to the following effect. That which does service to
another is better than that which does not do service.
But nothing is better than the good; therefore, the good
does service. God, therefore, as the Good, does all possible service to man. Now, that which does service of
set purpose is better than that which does not do service
of set purpose. But nothing is better than God. Therefore, God does service of set purpose to man,—that is,
He is concerned for him, has a care of him. He has
proved it by giving to him as Tutor the Word, the fellow-
worker of the love of God to man.[5] That the God and
Father of our Lord Jesus is good, is expressly declared
by the Word. "He is kind to the unthankful and the
evil." "Be merciful, as your Father is merciful." "None
is good but my Father in heaven." "My Father makes
His sun to shine upon all." "My Father sends rain on the
just and on the unjust."[6] In view of his conception of the
goodness of God, Clement held that no one could be condemned for disobedience to the Gospel who had not had
an opportunity of hearing the call of the Gospel; that, if
this were not so, the goodness of God was impugned; and
that the will of God, which was disciplinary and operative, would save all, whether they lived before the advent
or not, who turned to Him.[7] The world, then, is the

[1] Str., vi. 17 [137], [138].   [2] Ib. vii. 2 [12].   [3] Ib., vi. 17 [154].   [4] Pæd., i. 8 [63].
[5] Ib., i. 8 [62], [63].   [6] Ib., i. 8 [72].   [7] Str., vi. 6 [51], [52].

best of all possible worlds. "There could not be any better government of man, nor one more in harmony with the nature of God, than that which has been ordained." [1] To the obstacles that stood in the way of the accept-ance of this conception of the absolute goodness of God, Clement was not blind. Two problems were thrust upon him. How explain the existence of evil in a world governed by absolute goodness associated with unlimited power, where nothing takes place without the will of the Lord of the universe? [2] How explain the seeming in-difference of God to the practical working of evil as exhibited in the temptations to which Christians are exposed, and, above all, in the apparent triumph of un-righteousness in the persecution and death of the followers of Christ?

To begin with, in its essential nature evil has no relation to God. It has no independent existence or reality apart from the activity of some doer of evil; it has no objective basis in matter.[3] "But, by not preventing it, does He not cause it?" No, argues Clement, that is a mistaken con-ception of the nature of causality. Causality is not a nega-tive but a positive concept—it implies activity. Accord-ingly, that which prevents is a cause, but that which does not prevent is not a cause. A cause is only a cause when conceived in relation to an effect. Where there is no effect there is no cause at work. That which does not prevent produces no effect, therefore it is not a cause. To these logical principles, laid down in the last book of the Stromateis,[4] he has given application in an earlier dis-cussion of the relation of God to evil. To those who kept declaring that that which does not prevent is a cause,—that, for example, he who did not quench a fire at the outset was responsible for the subsequent conflagration, and was

[1] Str., vii. 2 ⁸.   [2] Ib., iv. 12 ⁸⁶.   [3] Ib., iv. 13 ⁹³, ⁹⁴.   [4] Ib., viii. 9 ⁹⁷, ⁹⁹.

punished by the law accordingly,—Clement replies in accordance with the above principles that the notion of causality is in doing, energising, and acting; that that which does not prevent is inoperative and stands in no logical relation to that which comes into being. As well say that the wound was not caused by the dart but by the shield which did not prevent its entrance. To prevent is a causal relation; not to prevent is not a causal conception.[1] "The responsibility lies with him who makes choice: God is not responsible." This saying of Plato,[2] repeated more than once by Clement,[3] had already been applied by Justin in elucidation of the same problem, and had virtually become a watchword in early Apologetics. In a like spirit Basilides had declared, " I will affirm anything rather than affirm that Providence is evil." So far Clement would have agreed with him. But his solution that individual punishment must always be held to imply individual sin, and that men were punished here for sins which they had committed in a previous state of existence, is set aside by Clement as no solution. It only pushes the question of the relation of Providence to evil a stage backwards, and is entirely opposed to the fact that it is wholly within our power to say whether we shall confess by martyrdom or not; and on such a hypothesis there is no place for faith in God or love to man, nor for moral praise or censure.[4] The question was forced on Clement, not in a theoretical but in a practical form, partly in its bearing on the inner life of the individual Christian, partly in its bearing on the question of persecution. When it is said in Scripture that " God tried them," all that is meant is that, in order to test them and to put the tempter to shame, He permitted them to be tried. He permits temptation, because we must be saved

---

[1] Str., i. 17 [81], [84].
[2] Plato, Rep., x. 617 E.
[3] Str., i 1 [4]; iv 23 [180], &c.
[4] Ib., iv. 12 [82-88].

of ourselves, in order to put to confusion him who has
tempted and failed, to confirm those within the Church,
and to have regard to the conscience of those who admire
our endurance.[1] "If God cares for you," was the retort
of the heathen persecutors, "why are you persecuted and
slain?" This was a problem that was not new in a sense,
but was specially insistent, when the Christian conception
of an Almighty and All-holy God was promulgated and
maintained. Hence its recurrence in Psalmist and Prophet.[2]
It was no problem to polytheism or pantheism or to a
monotheism which was not rooted in Christian ground. To
the Christian consciousness, is the virtual reply of Clement,
there is nothing arbitrary in the persecution, so far as God
is concerned. It is in accordance with the prediction of
the Lord Himself, who by such prediction trained us to
fortitude. To say that evil-doers justly undergo punishment is an involuntary tribute to Christians who are
punished for the sake of righteousness. Moreover, it is
no hardship for us to be set free by death and go to the
Lord, always provided that our witness by martyrdom is
grounded on love.[3] As for the injustice of the judge,
that in no way touches the Providence of God. There
must be no interference with his freedom of action. He
must not be reduced to a mere puppet, like a lifeless instrument, receiving impulses from an external cause.[4] In
harmony with his views on causality, Clement solves this
problem in the same way as the general question. Such
persecution takes place without the prevention of God.
For the fact of non-prevention, thus interpreted, saves both
His providence and His goodness.[5] We may not say that
the activity of God produces afflictions, but we may fitly

[1] Str., iv. 12 [85]   [2] Ps. 76, &c.; Mal. iii.
[3] Str., iv. 11 [50].   [4] Ib., iv. 11 [78], [79].
[5] Ib., iv. 12 [86]. τοῦτο γὰρ μόνον σῴζει καὶ τὴν πρόνοιαν καὶ τὴν ἀγαθότητα τοῦ θεοῦ.

be persuaded that He does not prevent those who cause
afflictions, and that He transforms the daring deeds of His
enemies into good.[1]   In brief, the force of the reply of
Clement may be put thus: Postulate freedom on the part
of man, and the possibility of the misuse of freedom, and
therefore the possibility of evil, at once emerges.   Freedom
to disobey is the necessary correlate of freedom to obey;
and the choice lies between a mechanical goodness without
freedom and freedom with the possibility of disobedience.
The latter alternative is alone worthy of God and man.   By
bestowing freedom on man, God voluntarily, so far as man
is concerned, put a limit on His own omnipotence; and He
can only show that evil is not independent of Him nor
indifferent to Him, by transforming it into good.

With this essential goodness of God all the other attributes and actions of God are in harmony.   The controversy
raised by Marcion led Clement to touch specially on the
relation of the Divine justice to the Divine goodness.
Marcion had sought to explain the difference between the
representation of God in the Old Testament and that in
the New Testament by ascribing the origin of the Old
Testament to a subordinate God whose essential nature
was justice, and the New Testament to the Supreme God
whose essential nature was goodness.   He assumed, therefore, that justice and goodness were irreconcilable attributes.   "The economy of God," says Clement, "is just."[2]
Punishment by God does not arise from anger.   Its goal
is justice.   It is not expedient that justice should be ignored
for our sake.[3]   The same Lord who in the Gospel speaks of
His Father as alone good, addresses Him in prayer as the
"just Father."[4]   He who is truly God is just and good.
The justice of God in His censure of evil does not create
the transgression, any more than the physician is the cause

[1] Str., iv. 12 [87].   [2] Ib., iv. 6 [29].   [3] Pæd., i. 8 [71].   [4] John xvii. 25.

of the fever which he points out; it only acts like a mirror
which reveals to an ugly man the fact and the measure
of his ugliness. God is good for His own sake, and just
also for our sakes, and that because He is good.[1] The
justice of God is good, and His goodness is just.[2] The
Incarnation, which is the measure of the love of God to
man, is at the same time an exhibition of His justice.[3]

From the fact that Clement regards justice as indissolubly related to goodness, it follows that he regards all
punishment of men by God as disciplinary and remedial.
God corrects men as a teacher or parent corrects his
children. In His punishment of disobedience there is no
element of vengeance, for vengeance is retaliation for evil,
sent for the advantage of him who takes the revenge;
but He corrects for the public and private good of those
who are corrected.[4] Nor is He eager to execute His
threatenings. He is not like a serpent which bites its prey
as soon as it fastens upon it.[5] He chastens for three
causes, all of which have a disciplinary end. He chastens
for the sake of the man who is chastened, that he may rise
superior to his former self; he chastens by way of example
to others, that by such admonition they may be driven back
from sin before sinning; and in the case of the man who
has suffered wrong, He chastens the wrong-doer that the
wronged person may not become an object of contempt
and a fit subject for being wronged.[6] All punishment is
medicine. If a physician who removes some disease is a
benefactor, is he not more so who removes some injustice
from the soul? If he who cuts or cauterises a diseased
part of the body is called saviour and healer, why not
the Physician of the souls of men? Whether God em-

---

[1] Pæd., i. 9 [88]; Str., vii. 12 [73].   [2] Str., vi. 14 [109].

[3] Pæd., i. 8 [62]; i. 9 [88].   [4] Str., vii. 16 [102].

[5] Pæd., i. 8 [63].   [6] Str., iv. 24 [154].

ploys mercy or reproof, His aim is the salvation of the
reproved.[1] In God the affection of anger, if it be right
to call admonition by such a name, is inspired by love to
man.   He condescends to emotion for the sake of man.[2]
Herein is the legitimate function of fear and threatening.
It is but the application of spiritual medicine to the varying temperament of His children.   The true, the ideal,
motive of Christian life is love; but there are some who
will turn to Him from fear, while they would spurn His
love.[3]

His conception of the absolute goodness of God seems
to be inconsistent, however, with the manner in which he
represents God's relation to man.   In opposition to the
teaching of the Gnostics, Clement lays down that " God has
no natural relation to man,[4] as the founders of heresy will
have it. . . . God, who is by nature rich in pity because
of His goodness, takes care of us who are neither parts of
Him nor by nature His children.   What is more—this is
the greatest index of the goodness of God, that though our
relation to Him be such, and though we are by nature
entirely estranged, He nevertheless cares for us.   Animals
have a natural affection for their offspring, and persons who
are like-minded from intercourse become friends.   But rich
is the mercy of God to us who are not related to Him in
anything—neither in our essence, I mean, nor in nature,
nor in the specific part of our essence, but only in this that
we are the work of His will; and the man who by discipline has won the knowledge of the truth He calls to the
adoption of sons, which is the greatest advance of all."[5]

[1] Pæd., i., 8 [72].

[2] Ib., i. 8 [74]: ἀλλὰ καὶ τὸ ἐμπαθὲς τῆς ὀργῆς, εἰ δὴ ὀργὴν τὴν νουθεσίαν αὐτοῦ
χρὴ καλεῖν, φιλάνθρωπόν ἐστιν εἰς πάθη καταβαίνοντος τοῦ θεοῦ διὰ τὸν ἄνθρωπον.

[4] Pæd., i 9 [86].

[4] ὁ θεὸς δὲ οὐδεμίαν ἔχει πρὸς ἡμᾶς φυσικὴν σχέσιν. Cf. Adum. in 1 John
(Stah., vol. iii, p. 213).   Str., ii. 16 [74], [75].

The apparent harshness of this passage is due in part to
its polemical tendency, in part to his desire to free his
conception of God from anything akin to pantheism, but
mainly to his purpose of emphasising the unconditional
freedom of the divine mercy. But, surely, the fact that
man is in a special sense the work of absolute goodness
creates a certain relationship. Is not he who is a son
in posse internally related *in esse*? This he affirms elsewhere.[1] "All other things were made by the word of
command alone, but man was formed by God Himself,
and He breathed into him that which was peculiar to
Himself."[2] The creation of man, of something capable of
knowledge of God, seems to be represented in a sense as
essential to the complete goodness of the Creator.[3] If the
pity of God is unconditional, it is exhibited as the only
true pity, and in a way that softens if it does not con-
tradict His own thesis. Properly speaking, the greater
pities the less; and man, as he is by nature man, cannot
be greater than a man. But God is greater than a man
in all things. If, then, the greater pities the less, God
alone will pity us.[4] "O surpassing love to man!" he
cries; "not as a teacher speaking to his scholars, not as
a master to his servants, but as a gentle father, the Lord
admonishes his sons."[5] "God of His great love to man
lays hold of him to help him, as the mother-bird flies to
one of her young when it falls out of the nest. And if a
serpent open its mouth to swallow the little one, 'the
mother flutters around, uttering cries of grief for her
little ones';[6] and God the Father seeks His creature, and
heals his transgression, and pursues the reptile, and takes
up again the young one and urges it to fly up to the
nest."[7] "His love to man is unspeakable, and His

[1] Cf. Str., v. 13 87.   [2] Pæd., i. 2 7.   [3] Ib.   [4] Str., ii. 16 73.
[5] Prot , ix. 82.   [6] Homer, Il., ii. 315.   [7] Prot., x. 91.

hatred of evil is immeasurable."[1]   The Christian heart
in Clement gained the victory over his metaphysical
abstractions.

God is conceived as a Trinity. Clement not only uses
the word, but again and again implies the doctrine,
though it is not definitely formulated by him in a developed form.   Referring to a passage in the 'Timæus'
of Plato he says, "I understand nothing other than
the Holy Trinity to be indicated."[2]   "Our treasure in
an earthen vessel is guarded by the power of God the
Father, and the blood of God the Son, and the dew of
the Holy Spirit."[3]   At the close of the Pædagogus he
prays "that all may praise with thanksgiving the alone
Father and Son, the Son who is Tutor and Teacher, together with the Holy Ghost also."[4]   Of the work of the
Spirit in the Church and in the individual believer, as
the inspirer of Holy Scripture, as the source of the higher
life, Clement often speaks; but of the Spirit in Himself,
and in relation to the Father and the Son, he says little.
In the lost or unfinished treatises on Prophecy and the
Soul he intended to discuss the question of the method
in which the Holy Spirit was distributed and His nature.
But though the doctrine of the Trinity is in the background of his thought, he nowhere, like his contemporary
Tertullian, discusses the relation of the Persons in the
Trinity to one another. Though in most cases the com-
parative absence of incidental allusions to a doctrine cannot be pressed, in the case of a writer so discursive as
Clement it is a feature that cannot be treated as without
significance; and the conclusion would seem to be that
the question in itself was of little interest to him, and
was only of importance on its speculative and practical

[1] Prot., x. 104.   [2] Str., v. 14 103; Tim., 41 A.
[3] Q. D., 34   Cf. Pæd , i. 6 42.   [4] Pæd., iii. 12 101. Cf. Ec. Pr., 13, 29.

side in its bearing on the fact and the doctrine of the Incarnation of the Word.

What is of permanent value in this doctrine of God presented by Clement with the view of winning over to the Christian faith the cultivated Greeks of Alexandria? It contains many noble elements. In representing the knowledge of God as the true life of man and the possibility of its attainment as the goal of all lofty aspiration, he lays down the basis that underlies all positive religious life. At the same time, he begets a sense of reverence within us by reminding us that, apart from the manifold revelations of the Word, the Father of the universe is an unknown God, and that even with His revelation we can but touch the hem of His garment. It gives a place to the manifestation of God in nature as well as in the universal consciousness of mankind. If in setting aside all possibility of a pantheistic conception of God, he ascribes to Him a transcendence which seems to remove Him absolutely from the range of our vision, and out of all relation to us, he at the same time represents Him as immanent, as eternally operative in His own world. Though some phrases in his writings may be interpreted as favouring a dualistic origin of the universe, the general direction of his thought is distinctly anti-dualistic; and it is possible to interpret such phrases in a way that is reconcilable with his otherwise emphatically reiterated teaching that the universe owes its existence and its continued existence to the One, Unbegotten, Almighty God. If partly under the influence of Plato, partly from a polemical interest in opposition to Gnosticism, he sometimes exaggerates the unrelatedness between the Creator and man, and seems to make the relation an external rather than an internal and moral relation, he establishes anew the natural relationship which he had seemed to disown by ascribing

to man a unique dignity among created things as alone
"made in His image," and therefore capable of appre-
hending Him. In some other aspects this theology is of
a type that we are wont to consider as primarily modern,
whereas the modern and loftier conception of the nature
and purposes of God may be said to be but a return to
an earlier position which the Church ignored, superseded,
or abandoned. In making not the sovereignty of God
but His goodness—and that a goodness that had always
been at work—as the central principle of his thought, in
leading us to think of the justice of One who is good
rather than of the goodness of One who is just, and
thus bringing the punishment of sin in immediate relation
to the goodness rather than to the sovereignty of God,
Clement is in harmony with a strong current of thought
in our own time. It may be that he is not free from
the imperfect grasp of the sin of man in relation to the
holiness of God that is sometimes associated with that
mode of thought; but what his theology loses thereby in
stately symmetry it gains in warmth and life.

LECTURE IV.

THE PERSON AND WORK OF CHRIST.

"In the beginning was the Word, and the Word was with God, and the Word was God. The same was in the beginning with God. All things were made by Him, and without Him was not anything made.[1] That which hath been made in Him was life; and the life was the light of men. . . . And the Word became flesh and tabernacled among us (and we beheld His glory, glory as of the only begotten from the Father), full of grace and truth." "No man hath seen God at any time; the only begotten God[2] who is in the bosom of the Father, He hath declared Him." "Even as Thou, Father, art in me and I in Thee." "He is the image of the invisible God, the First-born of all creation; for in Him were all things created. . . . All things have been created through Him and unto Him; and He is before all things, and in Him all things consist." "No man knoweth the Son but the Father, and no one knoweth the Father save the Son, and He to whom the Son shall have revealed Him." "God having of old time spoken to the fathers in the prophets by diverse portions and in divers manners, hath at the end of these days spoken unto us in His Son, whom

[1] So, like the Ante-Nicene fathers generally, Clement divides the sentence.
[2] So Clement reads in John i. 18.

G

He appointed heir of all things, through Whom also He made the worlds: Who being the effulgence of His glory and the impress of His substance, and upholding all things by the word of His power, when He had made purification of sins, sat down on the right hand of the Majesty on high." "That which was from the beginning, that which we have heard, that which we have seen with our eyes, that which we beheld, and our hands handled, concerning the Word of Life—and the life was manifested, and we have seen, and bear witness, and declare unto you the eternal life which was with the Father, and was manifested unto us."[1]   The Christology of Clement is an endeavour to make explicit the conceptions that underlie these state- ments.   A keen and restless spirit to whom the truth was no external possession, but a part of his very being, to whom the injunction, "Seek and ye shall find," came with special insistence, could not be satisfied without specula- tion on the meaning of the words and seeking to elaborate their contents.   And that that elaboration should have been cast in the mould of his earlier teaching, and to that extent have been modified thereby, is merely what might have been expected.   He was not called upon to discard the positions of his pre-Christian days, unless so far as they were inconsistent with the Christian standpoint.   A change of attitude involved no breach of intellectual continuity.   The only question is, Was the Christian teaching so modified in the process that it became inconsistent with the primary source or with a legitimate development of it?   To seek to bring his thought into perfect conformity with the for- mulas of a later age, or to expect that he should have an- ticipated such formulas, would be an absurd anachronism. Keeping in view his liberal attitude towards the pre-Christian

[1] John i. 1-4, 14, 18; xvii. 21.   Col. i. 15, 16, 17.   Luke x. 22   Heb. i. 1-3. I John i 1, 2.

history of mankind, the width as well as the limitations of his individuality, all that we can expect is, that he shall witness in general outlines to the teaching of the Church of his time. In view, further, of the measure in which individual expressions may have been determined in part by his polemical aim, in part by his strong bias towards eclecticism, and in view of "the mystic and turgid rhetoric"[1] to which he at times gives way, it may not be possible to obtain a presentation of his doctrine in all respects consistent and harmonious.

Clement has himself distinctly set forth the essential points in the teaching of the Church with reference to Christ and the main questions which arise in connection with it. "The whole economy which prophesied concerning the Lord appears a parable to those who have not known the truth : when one says and the rest hear, that the Son of God, the Son of Him who made the universe, assumed flesh and was conceived in the womb of the Virgin, in so far as His sensible flesh was made; and subsequently, as was the case, suffered and rose again, being to the Jews a stumbling-block and the Greeks foolishness."[2] "It has escaped their notice that we must truly believe in the Son that He is the Son, and that He came, and how, and for what, and concerning His passion ; and we must know who is the Son of God."[3] The points here detailed suggest order of treatment.

Who, then, is the Son of God? What is the teaching of Clement as to the Pre-Incarnate Word?

According to him, fatherhood is an inalienable attribute of the Divine Being. The Son must therefore have been eternally begotten, for fatherhood and sonship are correlative conceptions. "Along with the fact that God is Father, He

[1] Ritter, 'Geschichte der christlichen Philosophie,' vol. 1. p. 424

[2] Str , vi. 15 [127].   [3] Ib., v. 1 [1].

is the Father of the Son."[1] The one thing which is unoriginated is the almighty God; and there is only one First-
begotten.[2] The beginning of generation is not separated
from the beginning of the Creator. When it is said, "That
which was from the beginning," the reference is to the generation, without beginning, of the Son who co-existed with the
Father. The word "was" is indicative of His eternity
which had no beginning. So also the Word, that is the
Son, who, according to equality of substance, consists one
with the Father, is eternal and uncreate.[3] The Son is in
the Father, and the Father in the Son.[4] The creation of
the world is assigned indifferently to the Father and the
Son.[5] The essential attributes of deity are assigned to
both. As God is almighty, so is the Word.[6] As God
inspects all things, so does the Word.[7] As God is love,
that which He begat was love.[8] As the Father is perfect,
so is the Son.[9] As God is good, so of necessity the Word
must be.[10] He is a genuine Son of God.[11] Others are but
sons by adoption, and cannot be equal in point of subsistence to that which is by nature.[12] He is the true, only-
begotten, the express image of the glory of the universal
king and Almighty Father.[13] He is timeless and without
beginning, the beginning and first-fruits of existing things.[14]
Before the foundation of the World He was the Counsellor
of the Father, the Wisdom in which the Almighty God
rejoiced.[15] This Son is the Word of the Father, nay, one
with the Father.[16] He was before the morning-star.[17] He

---

[1] Str , v. 1 [1]. Cf. Adum. in 1 Joan.; Stah., vol. iii. p. 210 : "Patris appellatione
significat, quoniam et filius semper erat sine initio."

[2] Str., vi. 7 [58].   [3] Adum. in 1 Joan i. 1 ; Stah., vol iii. pp. 209, 210.

[4] Pæd , 1 7 [53].   [5] Ib., i. 8 [72], &c.   [6] Ib., iii. 7 [39].

[7] Str., iii. 10 [69]; Pæd., iii. 12 [101], 8 [44].   [8] Q. D., c. 37.

[9] Pæd , i. 5 [25].   [10] Str., i. 18 [90].   [11] Ib., v 13 [84].

[12] Ib., ii. 17 [77].   [13] Ib., vii. 3 [16].   [14] Ib., vii. 1 [2].

[15] Ib., vii. 2 [7]; Prov, viii. 30.   [16] Pæd., i. 8 [62].   [17] Prot., i. [6].

was in the beginning and before the beginning.[1] He is
the image of God.[2] He is the first principle of the universe,
and fashioned all things that came into existence after
Himself.[3] He was the Creator of the world and man,
is the leader of the universe, and the guide of all mankind.[4] He is the face of God, the Word by whom God is
manifested and made known.[5] "The best thing on earth is
the most devout man; and the best thing in heaven is the
angel who is nearest in place to God, the partaker already
in a purer way of the eternal and blessed life. But the
nature of the Son who is nearest to Him, who alone is the
Almighty One, is the most perfect, and most holy, and most
sovereign, and most princely, and most kingly, and most
beneficent. This is the highest supremacy which orders
all things in accordance with the Father's will and holds
the helm of the universe in the best possible way, perform-
ing all things with unwearied and tireless power, beholding
the secret thoughts of God through His operations. For
from His own watch-tower the Son of God never departs,
is never divided nor severed, changes not from place to
place; existing everywhere at all times, and being circumscribed nowhere; 'all mind, all eye,' all light of the Father,
seeing all things, hearing all things, knowing all things, with
power scrutinising the powers."[6] His pre-incarnate activity
was universal in its range. The progressive education of
humanity was His distinctive work. It was He who gave
philosophy to the Greeks.[7] It was He who acted as
Tutor to the people of Israel, who appeared to Abraham
and Jacob. It was He who by signs and wonders in
Egypt and in the desert incited the people to salvation.
It was He who spoke by Moses and all the prophets.[8] So

---

[1] Prot., i. 7 [1].   [2] Ib., x. [98].   [3] Str., v. 6 [38].
[4] Pæd., iii. 12 [100]; i. 7 [58]; i. 7 [56]   [5] Ib., i. 7 [77].
[6] Str., vii. 2 [5].   [7] Ib., vii. 2 [11].   [8] Pæd., i. 7 [66.68].

far, the teaching of Clement may claim to have scriptural authority for its content and form, or to be a legitimate deduction from it. But there are other elements that seem irreconcilable either with Scripture or with his own fundamental positions. In some cases he speaks of the Word in terms that suggest an attribute of God rather than a distinct personality.[1] There are passages in which the distinction of persons in the Godhead is so minimised that he can be charged with Sabellianism.[2] There are passages in which the equality of the persons is so lost sight of that he seems to favour subordinationism.[3]

These apparent waverings and inconsistencies are minor offences compared with the "altogether impious and fabulous statements" that Photius found in the 'Hypotyposes,' among which were the degradation of the Son of God to the rank of a thing created, and the hypothesis that it was not the Word of the Father but a subordinate Word that became incarnate.[4] The supposition, suggested by Photius himself and supported by some expositors of the teaching of Clement, that the writings of Clement had been interpolated in a heretical sense, may be set aside; and there can be little doubt that Photius found in the 'Hypotyposes' statements which could be interpreted in harmony with this charge. He had no bias against Clement, and speaks of his errors more in sorrow than in anger. The question is, therefore, whether Photius was right in his interpretation; and in our ignorance of all the passages but one on which he based his charge, that question must be determined by the extent to which they find complete or partial confirmation in the extant writings. The presumption that he may have erred is strengthened by the fact that he certainly misunderstood the meaning of the one passage which he quotes in sup-

[1] Str., vii. 2 [7].   [2] Pæd., i. 8 [71].   [3] Str., vii. 2 [7].   [4] Cod. 109.

port of his thesis. As to the first point. Zahn, who on this, as on the other criticisms made by Photius, supports his accuracy, calls attention to a few passages in the writings of Clement that may be adduced in support of the contention of Photius.[1] Clement repeatedly identifies the Word with the Wisdom of God, and yet he refers to Wisdom as the first-created of God;[2] while in one passage he attaches the epithet "First-created,"[3] and in another "First-begotten," to the Word.[4]   But this seems to be rather a question of language than a question of doctrine.   At a later date a sharp distinction was drawn between " first - created " and " first - born " or " first-begotten ";[5] but no such distinction was drawn in the time of Clement, who with the Septuagint rendering of a passage in Proverbs before him could have had no misgiving as to the use of these terms.[6]   "We find nothing in Clement," says Dorner, "about the subordination or creation of the Son."[7]   That is, perhaps, putting the matter too strongly.   But it may be confidently said that the evidence adduced in support of the statement of Photius is far from cogent, and in no way counterbalances the evidence of the positive statements in the writings of Clement to the opposite effect.

As to the second point.   According to Photius, Clement taught that there were two "Words," the less of whom appeared to men, or rather not even He.   In proof he quotes the following: "The Son is called the Word, being of the same name with the Word of the Father, but it is not

---

[1] Supplementum Clementinum, pp. 141-147.   [2] Str., v. 14 [89].
[3] Ex. Theod., c. 20.   [4] Str , vi. 7 [58].
[5] See Suicer's Thesaurus on πρωτόκτιστος.
[6] κύριος ἔκτισέν με ἀρχὴν ὁδῶν αὐτοῦ.   Prov. viii. 22.   Cf. Ex. Theod., 20.
τὸ γὰρ πρὸ ἑωσφόρου ἐγέννησά σε, οὕτως ἐξακούομεν ἐπὶ τοῦ πρωτοκτίστου θεοῦ
λόγου.
[7] Person of Christ, vol. i. p. 287.

this that became incarnate.　Nor, indeed, is it the Word of
the Father, but a certain power of God, an emanation, as
it were, of His Word, that has become 'nous,' and pervaded the hearts of men." [1]　If this be the correct way of
dividing the sentence,[2] there is no reference in the second
part to the Incarnation, but only to the indwelling of
"nous," conceived as an emanation of the Word, in the
hearts of men.　Both statements seem to be in answer to
the same objection, which appears to have been urged by
some one against the Incarnation of the Word, that this
would imply that God was in that case separated from, or
without, His Word (Reason).　The reply of Clement is to
the effect that a distinction must be drawn between the
reason that was immanent in God and the Word which was
a Person—the Son.　Zahn thinks that Photius was wrong
in supposing that Clement denied the manifestation even
of the inferior Word, but seeks to show by passages taken
from the undoubted writings that he was right in affirming
that it was not the Word of the Father, but the Son-Word,
that became incarnate.　He points to the fact that Clement
makes a sharp distinction between the Son and Word who
was begotten or created before the rest of creation and the
alone Unbegotten God and Father, that he names this not
rarely a divine power, that he says that the Word who
appeared incarnate in Christ was not only the mediator of
the Old Testament Revelation but the source of all reason
and morals, the one true Teacher of all humanity.　But are
such characteristics irreconcilable with the conception that
it was the one Word that became incarnate?　"The Word
of the Father of the universe," says Clement, "is not the
'uttered word,' [3] but the wisdom and most manifest kindness of God, and His power, too, which is almighty and

---

[1] Photius, Cod. 109.　　　[2] Zahn puts a , after "incarnate."
[3] λόγος προφορικός, St. v. 1 b.

truly divine, and His almighty will." But surely Bethune-
Baker is right when he says, "Clement seems to me to
be certainly objecting to the term λόγος προφορικός as
applied to the Son on the ground that it depreciates His
dignity, and not, as Harnack and Zahn take it, himself
sanctioning a distinction between the higher λόγος ἐνδιάθετος
and the lower λόγοι προφορικόι."[1]   "There lies here a
polemic," says Dorner, "against the opinion that He is
simply the spoken, empty word, and not rather intelligence,
real, creative power."[2]

Another passage has to be examined in this connection. "An image of God is His Word, the genuine
Son of 'nous,' the divine Word, the archetypal light of
light; and an image of the Word is the true man, the
'nous' which is in man, who is therefore said to have
been made in the 'image and likeness' of God."[3] This
means, according to Zahn, that Clement teaches that the
Word who became incarnate was not the Son of God the
Father but the Son of the "nous" of the Father, and,
therefore, clearly to be distinguished from the Word
(reason) of God Himself; that the Son-Word was only the
Son of the higher Word. But it seems to me that Clement
uses "nous" not for the reason that was eternally immanent in God, but for God Himself. In the Stromateis
he quotes from Plato to the effect that he who contem-
plates the ideas will live as a god among men, and he adds
that "nous" is the place of ideas, and God is "nous."[4]
On the whole, therefore, it is much more natural to suppose
that Photius misinterpreted, not a part, but the whole of
the passage which he cited from the 'Hypotyposes.' "The
only safe canon of criticism is that which bids us inter-

---

[1] Bethune-Baker, 'History of Early Christian Doctrine,' p. 129.
[2] Vol. i. p. 289.   [3] Prot., x. ⁹⁵.
[4] Plato, Soph., 216 B; Str., iv. 25 ¹⁵⁵. Cf. Str., iv. 25 ¹⁶².

pret the less known in a sense in keeping with the more known." [1]

So far in his teaching as to the Word we move in a Christian atmosphere. But there are passages which take us out of the sphere of Christian thought. When we read that the Platonic idea is a thought of God, and that the barbarians call this the Word of God, we see the perilous side of his eclecticism.[2] When we read that the Son is the "circle of all the powers rolled into one and formed into a unity," [3] we are reminded of Neo-Platonic ways of thinking. Most important of all is the relation to Philo. In estimating the relation of the doctrine of the Word in Clement to that of Philo, two points have specially to be kept in view. On the one hand, as there is no doubt as to the dependence of Clement on Philo in some weighty matters of doctrine and criticism, other than his doctrine of the Word, the presumption is in favour of his dependence here. On the other hand, there are many points of affinity between the New Testament and Philo; and as Clement is saturated not only with the thoughts but with the words of the Scriptures, where Philo and the New Testament and Clement have common expressions, it is as probable that the New Testament was the primary source. "Image" (εἰκών), "impress" (χαρακτήρ), "high-priest" (ἀρχιερεύς), are found

---

[1] Bethune-Baker, p. 134. The passage from Photius is examined by Ziegler, ' Die Logoschristologie des Cl. Al.,' pp. 87-90. He puts the words ἀλλ' οὐχ οὗτός ἐστιν ὁ σὰρξ γενόμενος before λέγεται, and translates : " But it is not this" (that is, the "nous," who is in the hearts of men) " that is the Incarnate Word, nor the Word of the Father, but a certain power of God, as it were an emanation of His reason, became ' nous ' and pervaded the hearts of men." All, therefore, that Clement here meant to explain was the relation of the human reason to the primal reason of God—namely, to affirm that "a certain power of God, an emanation of His reason, became ' nous ' and pervaded the hearts of men."

[2] Str., v. 3[16].

[3] Ib., iv. 25[150]. Cf. Aal. 'Geschichte der Logosidee in der christlichen Litteratur,' pp. 393-429.

in all as designations of the Word; but from the context it would seem that it was the language of Scripture that floated before the mind of Clement.[1] There are numerous expressions common to both which are not found in the New Testament, such as τὸ ὄργανον τοῦ θεοῦ, ὁ πρωτόγονος θεοῦ υἱός ;[2] and there are kindred expressions, such as ὁ δεύτερος θεός, in Philo, and τὸ δεύτερον αἴτιον in Clement, ὁ πρεσβύτατος θεοῦ υἱός in Philo, and τὸ πρεσβύτερον ἐν γενέσει in Clement.[3] In such cases the dependence is manifest, as the expressions are not only not in Scripture but unscriptural. On the other hand, there are many characteristic designations of the Word in Philo which are not employed by Clement, and in some cases he has substituted a New Testament term for the Philonic word. Thus, neither "shadow" (σκία) nor "divider" (τομεύς) is found in Clement; and the absence of the latter is all the more noteworthy as he loves to support his views by sayings of Heraclitus, from whom Philo borrowed the expression. Though he speculates much, like many others, in part in dependence on Philo, on the mystic meaning of the number "seven," he does not, as the latter, relate it to the Word. When Philo employs ἑρμηνεύς for the interpretative function of the Word, Clement, in accordance with New Testament usage, prefers ἐξηγητής.[4] The key-word παιδαγωγός is not found in Philo, nor is Clement's favourite designation of the Word as Σωτήρ. The matter, therefore, is not so simple as it seems, and it is surely an exaggeration to say that the foundation is not scriptural but Philonic, as if Clement accepted only the epithets and teaching applied in the Scriptures to the Word, in so far as they were in harmony with kindred epithets and teaching in Philo. The opposite

---

[1] Str , v. 6 38 ; vii. 3 16 ; Prot. xii. 120. Cf. Col. i. 15 ; Heb. i 1, iv. 14.
[2] Prot., i 6 ; Str , vi. 7 38.   [3] Str., vii. 3 16 ; vii. i. 2.
[4] Ib., i 26 169. Cf. John i 18.

may with more reason be maintained.   To the mind of Clement there was no contradiction or irreconcilability between the purely philosophical and the purely Christian elements in his conception of the Word.   If so, the question is, What was the primary or assimilative principle? That Philonic conceptions had permeated Christian circles even in the first century, we see from the New Testament itself; but is there any evidence that thinkers of any school outside of Alexandria had become so imbued with the system of Philo, apart from its infiltration into Christian thought, that it occupied a prominent place in their teaching?   Or, if such teachers existed, is there any evidence that Clement had sat at their feet?   The fact that his eager spirit had no rest until he found Pantænus is against the supposition.   A common use of the allegorical method of exegesis proves nothing, for such was common and inevitable, while as yet the Old Testament was the only authoritative collection of sacred books, if they were to be interpreted in a Christian sense.   If, then, there be no evidence of the influence of this distinctive feature in the teaching of Philo in any teacher with whom it is probable that Clement had associated before his arrival in Alexandria, he would only learn to know the writings of Philo after his religious thought had been moulded on a definitely Christian basis, and he would read the works of Philo with Christian eyes rather than read Philonic conceptions into his Christian thought.   No doubt this is largely a matter of hypothesis, but it is a hypothesis which finds powerful confirmation in the fact that to Clement the Incarnation of the Word—an impossible conception with Philo —was a fundamental fact and truth.

"*That He came, and how.*"   The Word who was with God, the Word by whom all things were made, "He who is in Him who truly is," has appeared.   He, who as

Creator bestowed life upon us at first when He formed us, has appeared as a teacher, and taught us to live well, that as God he might afterwards bestow upon us eternal life.[1] Though despised in outward form, He was in reality adored. He truly is most manifest God. He was made equal to the Lord of the universe, because He was His son.[2] "If thou dost not believe the prophets, the Lord Himself will speak to thee," "who being in the form of God counted it not a prize to be on an equality with God, but emptied Himself," He, the compassionate God, eagerly longing to save man.[3] John, the herald of the Word, exhorted men to be ready for the advent of God the Christ.[4] The Son of God was conceived in the womb of the virgin.[5] The Lord Christ was the fruit of the virgin.[6] By this all generation has been sanctified.[7] The very Word has appeared as man. He alone is both—God and man.[8] A manifest mystery, God in man, and man God. The Mediator accomplishes the will of the Father. For He is the Word common to both, Son of God, but Saviour of men, His minister, our teacher.[9] He that ate from a homely bowl and washed the feet of the disciples was the unpresuming God and Lord of the universe.[10] He was God in the form of man.[11] So closely are the divine and the human interpenetrated that Clement assigns names and functions and attributes to the human side, that, strictly speaking, can only be applied to the divine side, and *vice versâ*. He applies the epithet "eternal" to Jesus.[12] Our Tutor is the holy God, Jesus, the Word who is the guide of all humanity, the philanthropic God Himself.[13] The Word poured forth His own blood for us.[14]   "Believe,

[1] Prot , i. 7.   [2] Ib., x 110   [3] Ib., i. 8.
[4] Ib., i. 10.   [5] Str , vi. 15 127.   [6] Pæd., i. 6 41.
[7] Str., iii. 17 102.   [8] Prot., i. 7.   [9] Pæd., ii 1 2.
[10] Ib., ii. 3 38.   [11] Ib., i. 2 4.   [12] Prot., xii. 120.
[13] Pæd., i. 7 55.   [14] Ib., i. 6 43.

O man, Him who is man and God. Believe, O man, in
Him who suffered and is adored. Believe, ye slaves, in
the living God who was dead. Believe, all ye of human
kind, the only God of all. Believe, and receive salvation
as a reward."[1] The Word alone is sinless.[2] The Saviour
surpassed all human nature.[3] He alone who for us assumed
humanity is perfect in all things at once.[4] The relation
of this perfection to His baptism had been a matter of
controversy with the Gnostics in Alexandria. As God,
He had nothing in addition to learn; yet, when "begotten
in baptism" He received the illumination that is given in
baptism. "If He were perfect, why was He, the Perfect
One, baptised? It was necessary, they say, to fulfil the
condition of His assumption of humanity. Most excellent.
Coincidently, then, with His baptism by John, He became
perfect? Manifestly. He did not, then, learn anything
from him? Certainly not But He is perfected by the
washing of baptism alone, and is sanctified by the descent
of the Spirit? Such is the case."[5] Clement, therefore,
seems to solve the problem by distinguishing between the
divine consciousness in Him to which nothing was unknown, and the human consciousness which received
enlightenment in the act of baptism.[6]

In consequence of his interest being limited mainly to
the teaching of the Lord, Clement takes little notice of
the events in the life other than those of His birth, death,
and resurrection. Incidents such as the crowning with
thorns[7] or the anointing in Bethany[8] are only introduced for the teaching which they are held to symbolise.
Though he professes to have little sympathy with such

[1] Prot., x. 106. Cf Pæd., ii 8 73.   [2] Str., iv. 12 85; Pæd., i. 2 4.
[3] Str., ii. 5 21.   [4] Ib., iv. 21 130.   [5] Pæd., i 6 25.
[6] Cf. Gore, 'Dissertations on the Incarnation,' p. 114.
[7] Pæd., ii. 8 73.   [8] Pæd., ii. 8 62.

investigations, he fixes the date of the birth of the Lord as having taken place on 18th November 2 B.C.[1] On account of the prophetic saying, adopted by Jesus, "He hath sent me to preach the acceptable year of the Lord," he concluded that the ministry of Jesus lasted only one year.[2]

On the ground of the rendering in the Septuagint,[3] he inferred that the Lord was unseemly in appearance. "He had no form nor beauty, but His form was without honour, defective as compared with other men." But this only brought out by way of contrast the spiritual beauty. "For who was better than the Lord? But it was not the beauty of the flesh visible to the eye that He exhibited, but the beauty of both soul and body, the beneficence of the soul, the immortality of the body."[4] This choice of a mean form of body was not without a purpose. Its aim was that no one in his admiration of the material beauty should lose sight of the spiritual teaching.[5] Was this body a real body or only an appearance? Among the charges that Photius brings against Clement is the averment that the Word did not really assume flesh, but only seemed to do so;[6] and in this charge he has been followed by others. Now, Clement himself refers to docetism as a heresy which, along with other heresies, must be rejected as out of harmony with the doctrine of the Church.[7] In quoting, in order to condemn, the opinions of Cassianus, he refers to him as the founder of the docetic heresy, and attributes his false teaching to the slandering of generation.[8] Could Clement,

---

[1] Str., i. 21 [145]. "One hundred and ninety-four years, one month, and thirteen days before the death of Commodus." See Herzog, R.E. [3], vol. xxi , p. 149.

[2] Str., i 21 [145]; Isa. lxi. [2]; Luke iv. 19.

[3] Isa. liii 2.   [4] Pæd , iii. 1 [3].

[5] Str , vi. 6 [151]. Cf. ib., iii. 17 [103]   ἀειδὴς δὲ ἐλήλυθεν καὶ ἄμορφος εἰς τὸ ἀειδὲς καὶ ἀσώματον τῆς θείας αἰτίας ἀποβλέπειν ἡμᾶς διδάσκων.

[6] Cod. 109.   [7] Str., vii. 17 [108].   [8] Ib., iii 13 [91]; iii. 17 [102].

then, have been guilty of teaching which was thus opposed
to the rule of faith, and repugnant to him on moral
grounds? *Prima facie*, it should be impossible; and it is
certain that he could not have been so consciously. But
in Clement we must always be prepared for apparent contradictions. Take the positive evidence. God, he says,
proclaimed the good tidings in a body.[1] He showed His
power in a body of flesh.[2] From His exceeding love to
men the Saviour did not despise the susceptibility of the
flesh of men, but invested Himself with it, and came for
the common salvation of men.[3] For our sakes He took
upon Him our flesh which is liable to suffering.[4] Having
assumed flesh which by nature is susceptible of suffering,
He trained it to the condition of passionlessness.[5] He
assumed flesh that He might speak with the mouth of a
man.[6] He is introduced in the Gospel as weary with
toil.[7] When the prophet says, " Remember us, for we are
dust," [8] he is praying to the Lord—" Sympathise with us,
for Thou hast known from Thine own experience of suffering
the weakness of the flesh." [9] The evidence in favour of the
real human nature of Christ might seem irresistible. But
there is another side. One passage on which undue stress
has been laid may be set aside. He speaks of the Word of
God taking upon Him the mask of a man, and fashioning
Himself in flesh, and acting the drama of human salvation:
for He was a true champion and fellow-champion with
the creature.[10] Does this mean that His earthly life was
only of the nature of a dramatic performance? The second
clause is against this contention. To begin with, the word
rendered "mask" may also be rendered "person." The
word "drama" does not involve unreality, for it is used

[1] Str., iv. 8 ⁶⁶.   [2] Ib., vi. 16 ¹⁴⁰.   [3] Ib., vii. 2 ⁹.   [4] Ib., vii 2 ⁶.
[5] Ib., vii. 2 ⁷.   [6] Ib., vii 11 ⁶¹.   [7] Pæd., i. 9 ⁸⁵ ; John iv. 6
[8] Ps. ciii. 14   [9] Pæd , i. 8 ⁶².   [10] Prot., x. ¹¹⁰.

elsewhere of the gnostic who plays irreproachably the drama of life.[1] It might as well be urged because he speaks of captivating the Father with the spell of prayers,[2] that he looked upon prayer as a magical incantation, in spite of the singularly spiritual view of prayer that he sets forth.[3] But there are other passages which present greater difficulty. "In the case of the Saviour," he says, "it were ludicrous to suppose that the body as a body de-manded the necessary aids in order to its continuance in life. For He ate not for the sake of the body which was held together by a holy energy, but in order that it might not enter into the minds of those who associated with Him to think otherwise about Him; as, of a truth, some afterwards supposed that He was manifested in appearance. But He was entirely passionless, inaccessible to any move-ment of emotion, whether of pleasure or pain."[4] "It is re-ported in the 'Traditions,'" he says elsewhere, "that John touching the external body of Christ sent his hand into the depths of it, and that the hardness of the flesh offered no resistance, but gave way to the hand of His disciple."[5] Unless this be interpreted of the resurrection-body of Christ, it is language which might well have been used by any ad-herent of docetism. As to the first passage. Little weight can be attached to the word "passionless" as a denial of true humanity, as to be passionless represents the ideal con-dition of the highest Christian type. On the face of it the passage seems to mean that Christ only ate and drank to prevent the disciples from giving way to docetic misunder-standings. Does not this indicate a humanity that was

---

[1] Str., vii. 11 [65].

[2] Q. D., 41.   λιτανείαις συνήθεσι μαγεύων τόν πατέρα.   [3] Cf. vii. 7 [39].

[4] Str., vi. 9 [71].   Cf. Str., iii. 6 [81], where he quotes without disapproval a saying of Valentinus of an undoubted docetic type.

[5] Adum. in 1 Joan, vol. iii. p. 210 (Stah.).

H

shadowy and unreal, a humanity that transcended earthly
conditions, a manifestation akin to the theophanies of the
Old Testament rather than a true incarnation?   It has
been suggested that the solution of the apparent conflict
in the statements of Clement is to be found, not in denying
the reality of the body of Christ, but by denying that He
had a human soul, the place of which in Him was taken by
the Word, and thus regarding Clement as a precursor of
Apollinarianism.[1] But in view of his representation of the
relation of soul and body, to deny the reality of the human
soul of Christ was surely a graver form of docetism—if
that be an appropriate word—than to deny the reality of
His body.   Moreover, Clement refers to the soul of Christ,
and assumes its identity with the soul of man.   " Our Tutor
was irreproachable and passionless in soul. . . . He is to us
a spotless image: to Him we must strive with all our
strength to assimilate our soul."[2]   Must not the archetype
be as the type?   " By the precious blood with which the
Lord bought us is meant the soul, pure through righteousness, which is offered to God."[3]   Further, it is a general
principle with Clement that there is the closest possible
relation between the person and mission of Christ and the
nature of man ; that what was to be saved by Him had to
be assumed by Him and sanctified in His own person ; and
to this end He must have assumed a human soul as well as a
body.[4] The wavering language is rather due to the fact that
Clement approached the question of the person of Christ
from the divine side, from that of the Word, and was think-

---

[1] Cf. Gieseler, 'Commentatio qua Clementis Alexandrini et Origenis doctrinæ
de corpore Christi exponuntur' (1837). The passage (Pæd., i. 5[20]) to which
Dahne appeals as favouring docetism, and Gieseler as proving the contrary, is
corrupt. Cf. Stah.

[2] Paed., i 2[4].   [3] Adum. in 1 Pet., Stah., vol. iii. p. 204.

[4] Cf. Schwane, 'Dogmengeschichte,' p. 240. Cf. Ec. Pr., 23. τὸ γὰρ ὅμοιον
τῷ ὁμοίῳ ἐξυπηρετεῖν κατάλληλον πρὸς τὴν ὁμοίαν σωτηρίαν.

ing not so much of the influence of the human on the divine as of the influence of the divine on the human; and, accordingly, he does not ask what limitations the human embodiment put on the divine, but what prerogatives the divine imparted to the human. His interest lay mainly in securing that there should be no imperfection in the work of Christ as a teacher of absolute truth concerning God; to that end the body of Christ was mainly important to Him as a fitting instrument for carrying out the will and the mission of the Word; and from this point of view a tendency in the direction of docetism was inevitable. It is true that passages can be quoted from later ecclesiastical writers closely akin to docetic passages in Clement,[1] but a statement of a docetic cast made at a time when docetism was dead occupies a different position from a statement made when docetism was a dangerous force. In his doctrine of the human nature of Christ, more plainly than anywhere else, Clement has been wounded by the weapons which he captured from his opponents.

"*And for what?*" What was the primary end of the Incarnation? In accordance with His pre-incarnate function and ministry, it was essentially a work of revelation and tuition. It was a continuation of, and an advance on, that ministry. From the Word came the gift of life; from the Word Incarnate came the gift of living well. Clement takes illustrations of His method of working indifferently from the sayings of the prophets whom He inspired and from His own sayings on earth. The only difference is that in the one case the Lord speaks by the mouth of others, in the other case by His own. The revelation which He brought was in part a revelation of God to man, in part a revelation through a man of his highest self and of the

---

[1] Basil, quoted by le Nourry, p. 175 (Migne, vol. ix. p. 1132).

method of realising it. "No man knoweth the Son but the
Father, and no one knoweth the Father save the Son, and
he to whom the Son shall have revealed Him."[1] If the
importance of a doctrine is to be measured by the frequency
with which it is repeated, this is vital in Clement's view of
the purpose of the Incarnation. Because the soul of man
was too feeble to apprehend things as they are, we needed
a divine teacher. Accordingly, the Saviour was sent down,
the ineffable and holy manifestation of the great Providence.[2] God was inaccessible to the senses. Hence the
Son is said to be the Father's face, because by the Incarnation He became accessible to the senses. He is the Word,
the revealer of the distinctive nature of the Father.[3] By
the Incarnation he was seen in more immediate relation to
the world.[4] The only-begotten Son of God has taught us
the divine mysteries.[5] He who was not of the world came
as one who was of this world to men. He sought to lead
men through knowledge to sovereign truth, from this world
to another.[6] He assumed flesh in order to show what was
possible to man in the way of obedience to the commandments.[7] From love He willingly assumed the lot of man,
that, having been brought to the measure of the weakness
of us whom He loved, He might in turn bring us to the
measure of His own power.[8] "The Word of God became
man, that, in truth, thou also mayst learn from man how
man may become God."[9] He seeks to transform man the
earth-born into a holy and heavenly man. He alone has
completely realised the divine purpose in the creation of
man. "Let us listen to the Word and take on the impress
of the truly saving life of our Saviour, henceforward cultivating the heavenly citizenship in accordance with which
we are being deified."[10] He is the creator of types of which

---

[1] Luke x. 22.   [2] Str., v. 1 [7].   [3] Ib., v. 6 [34].   [4] Ib., v. 6 [39].
[5] Ib., vii. 1 [4].   [6] Ib., vi. 15 [126].   [7] Ib., vii. 2 [8].   [8] Q. D., 37.
[9] Prot., i. 8.   [10] Pæd., i. 12 [98].

He Himself is the archetype.[1] Having described the Word as the New Song, Clement asks, " What, then, does this instrument, the Word of God, the Lord, the New Song will ? " " To open the eyes of the blind, to unstop the ears of the deaf, and to lead by the hand unto righteousness those that were lame in their feet or who had wandered, to manifest God to feeble men, to put an end to corruption, to conquer death, to reconcile disobedient sons to their Father. The instrument of God is a lover of men. The Lord pities, instructs, exhorts, admonishes, saves, guards, and abundantly promises the kingdom of heaven as a reward for our instruction ; and the only harvest that He reaps is that we are saved. For wickedness feeds on the destruction of men ; but truth, like the bee, injuring nothing that exists, delights only in the salvation of men." [2] He showed to men the height of salvation that they might repent and be saved, or disobey and be judged.[3]

"*And concerning His passion.*" If it were a mere matter of names and general phrases, there can be no doubt that Clement taught the doctrine of a vicarious atonement. He applies to Christ the epithets — " Mediator," " Truce-bringer," " reconciler," " great high-priest." He applies a saying of Plato about a "great and unprocurable sacrifice " being offered by the seeker after God to Christ, a truly unprocurable sacrifice, the Son of God consecrated for us.[4] In like manner he applied a saying of Euripides about " a sacrifice without fire " to Christ, a whole burnt-offering, without fire, for us.[5] He uses the word " ransom " with reference to the death of Christ, and likewise " propitiation," though only in a quotation in the latter case ; [6] and he explains it as meaning that Jesus heals both soul and body. Isaac was a type of the Lord, for he was a " victim " as the Lord was.

[1] Str., vii. 3[16].   [2] Prot., i. [6]   [3] Ib., xi. [116].
[4] Str., v. 10[66] ; Plato, Rep., ii. 378 A.   [5] Str., v. 11[70].
[6] Pæd., iii. 12[98] ; 1 John ii. 2.

But he was not offered in sacrifice as the Lord; only as the
Lord bore the wood of the cross, so he bore the wood of the
sacrifice.[1] We have been brought into kinship with Christ
through His blood by which we are ransomed.[2] Christ
willed to suffer that by His suffering we might live.[3] Our
life was hung upon the wood with a view to our faith.[4] He
drank the cup for the cleansing of those who plotted against
Him and of the unbelievers.[5] When He might have been
Lord, He willed to be a brother, and so good was He that
He died for us.[6] For the sake of each of us He laid down
His life—a life that was equal in worth to the universe.[7]
Still more plainly is it set forth in the appeal which he puts
into the mouth of the Saviour. " I begot thee again, when
miserably begotten by the world with a view to death. I
set thee free, I healed thee, I ransomed thee. I will pro-
cure for thee life unceasing, eternal, a life above this world.
I will show to thee the face of the good Father. . . . I will
lead thee into the rest and enjoyment of good things, unspeakable and untold. . . . I am thy nurse, giving myself as
bread, of which no man having tasted again has experience
of death: I give thee daily to drink immortality. I am
teacher of super-celestial instruction. For thee I fought
against death, and paid in full thy penalty of death, which
thou didst owe because of the former sins and thy faithless-
ness towards God."[8] "When about to be offered and giving
Himself as a ransom, He leaves a new covenant: My love
I give unto you."[9] No doubt, the most striking of these
passages are in the form of a rhetorical appeal, but the
appeal could have had no force unless based on admitted
truths. On the other hand, he puts an interpretation on
some passages of Scripture that seems to indicate an uncertain grasp of the sacrificial import of the work of Christ.

[1] Pæd., i. 5[23]   [2] Ib., i. 6[49].   [3] Str., iv. 7[43].
[4] Ib., v. 11[72].   [5] Ib., iv. 9[75].   [6] Pæd., i 9[83].
[7] Q. D., 37   [8] Ib, 23   [9] Ib, 37.

He interprets the saying, " The Lord delivered Him for our sins," as meaning that He was to be the amender and corrector of our sins.[1] By the "lamb of God" he does not think of the "lamb that had been slain," or "that taketh away the sins of the world," but regards it as equivalent to the "child of God," the Son of the Father.[2] By "the blood of Christ that cleanseth us" he understands the teaching of Christ, which is very powerful.[3] "He laid down His life for us" means for the Apostles.[4] Yet these passages cannot be allowed to outweigh the general force of others, as well as the definite statements to the effect that Christ died for our sins. In consequence of his view of sin as that which was irrational and the fruit of ignorance, he did not give the doctrine of the atonement any prominent place in his teaching, nor did he find it necessary to formulate any theory of the atonement, nor to speculate on the meaning of ransom. He is not thinking so much of sin from the divine standpoint as of its effect on the nature of man. The work of Christ as mediator is not clearly related to His death. Clement himself had passed through no spiritual crisis; enlightenment rather than the need of forgiveness, intellectual unrest rather than an accusing conscience, drove him to the Christian faith.

Sin is defined as anything that is contrary to right reason. Disobedience in relation to reason is the generator of sin. To sin against reason is to be likened to the beasts.[5] Sin is slavery. It is eternal death. It is the death of the soul—not the death which dissolves the union between soul and body, but that which dissolves the union between the soul and the truth.[6] Hence to be instructed and disciplined by the Lord is to be set free from death.[7] All sins are due

---

[1] Pæd., i. 8 67 ; Isa. liii. 6, LXX.   [2] Pæd., i. 5 24.
[3] Adum. in I Joan i. 7 ; Stah., vol iii. p. 211.
[4] Adum. in Jud , 16, vol. iii. p. 214.   [5] Pæd., i. 13 101 ; Ps. xlix. 20.
[6] Prot , xi 115 ; Str., iii. 9 64 ; ii. 7 34.   [7] Pæd., i. 7 61.

to choice and inclination.[1]   The only sins which are not
"imputed" are those which are not the result of choice.[2]
Though the actions of men are infinite in number, the causes
of all sin may be reduced to two—ignorance and weakness.[3]
One falls into a ditch, for example, either from ignorance of
its existence, or from inability to leap across it.[4]   No one
chooses evil as evil, but, beguiled by the pleasures attaching
to it, he supposes it to be good, and considers it a thing to
be desired.   But we are responsible for such misconceptions.
For to be set free from ignorance and to refuse assent to
deceptive phantasies rests with ourselves.[5]   This emphasising of individual sin seems to leave no place for inherited
sin, still less for inherited guilt.   The introduction of sin
into the world is in some sense associated with the fall of
Adam, and this in turn with the victory of Christ over
death ; but of the relation of that sin to us and our sins
there are no clear indications.   The first man sported in
Paradise in freedom, for he was a child of God ; but when
he fell under the power of pleasure—the serpent means
pleasure—he was carried away by his desires and fettered
to sins.   The Lord Himself in the fetters of flesh enslaved
the tyrant death.   He stooped down and man rose up.[6]
Adam was not perfect in the sense that he could not trans-
gress, but in the sense that he was adapted by nature to
receive virtue,[7] and that he lacked none of the distinctive
characteristics of "the idea and the form" of a man.[8]   By
his deliberate choice of evil he exchanged an immortal for a
mortal life, but not for ever.[9]   Man by nature has a tendency
towards giving assent to falsehood, though he possesses
helps for faith in the truth.[10]   But we only lie under the sin
of Adam in respect of likeness of sin.[11]   When Job said,

---

[1] Str., i. 17 [84].   [2] Ib , ii. 15 [66].   [3] Ib., vii. 16 [101].   [4] Ib., ii. 15 [62].
[5] Ib , i. 17 [84].   Cf. vii. 16 [101].   [6] Prot., xi. [111].   [7] Str., vi. 12 [96].
[8] Ib., iv. 23 [100].   [9] Ib., ii. 19 [98].   [10] Str , ii. 12 [88].
[11] Adum. in Jud., Stah., vol. iii. p. 208.   "Sic etiam peccato Adae subjacemus
secundum peccati similitudinem."   Clement, like Origen and Ambrosiaster, seems

"Naked came I out of my mother's womb, and naked shall
I return hither," he did not mean naked of possessions—
that were a small and common matter—but naked of
wickedness and sin.[1] If the entrance into life is to correspond to the return, the child must be conceived as naked of
sin. When David said, "In sin did my mother conceive
me," he referred to Eve the mother of the living; and in
any case, if he were conceived in sin, yet he himself was not
in sin, nor was he himself sin.[2] "By sin, death has passed
to all men,"—that is, by a natural necessity of the divine
economy death follows on birth, and the dissolution of
soul and body necessarily follows their union.[3] But this
necessary relationship involves no participation on our part
in the sin of Adam. "There is no entailed necessity
between his sin and ours."[4]

No name is more frequently given to Jesus than that of
the Saviour; no word is employed so frequently to denote
the goal and work of Christ as salvation. His soul glows
with the fire of love to Christ as Saviour; repeatedly in the
course of his discussions he breaks forth in prayer to Him;
and whenever he mentions His name, he loves to shower
upon it a series of descriptive epithets, as if striving to
express the fulness of his devotion. But we must not read
into the words "Saviour" or "salvation," as used by him,
the ordinary connotation of the words.[5] For his conception
of sin determines in large measure the conception of salvation. If sin be slavery, salvation is freedom; if sin be
moral disorder or disease, salvation is moral health; if sin
be ignorance, salvation is knowledge; if sin be death, salvation is life. A preliminary, but fundamental, element in

to have omitted the μή in Rom. v. 14. See Souter, 'A Study of Ambrosiaster,'
p. 198.
    [1] Str., iv. 25 [180].   [2] Ib., iii. 16 [100].
    [3] Rom. v. 12 ; Str., iii. 9 [64].   [4] Bigg, p. 81.
    [5] Cf. Ec. Pr., 16, where he speaks of the prophets and apostles as saviours
of men.

salvation is the forgiveness of sins. "The Lord ministers
all help, both as man and God; as God, forgiving our sins;
as man, training us not to sin."[1]   Forgiveness of sins precedes the training.   It is associated with Baptism, which
is a washing by which our sins are thoroughly cleansed, and
a grace by which the penalties of our sins are remitted.[2]
The Lord buys us with His precious blood, setting us free
from our former harsh masters—that is, the sins because of
which the "spiritual forces of wickedness" lorded it over
us.[3]   Of all good things salvation is the greatest[4]   To save
men is the eternal purpose of God.   For this reason the
good God sent the good Shepherd.   The Word unfolded
the truth and showed to men the height of salvation.[5]   The
salvation of men is His only work.[6]   As sin is disease, a
moral disease due to ignorance, the work of the Saviour is
pre-eminently that of a physician, and His medicine is
tuition or discipline.   Passions are diseases of the soul.[7]
The Word is the all-healing physician of human infirmities
and the holy charmer of the sick soul.[8]   "The Word has
been called the Saviour, as He has found out for man those
rational drugs which tend to quickness of perception and
salvation—watching for the favourable opportunity, reprov-
ing moral injury, laying bare the causes of passions, and
cutting out the roots of irrational desires, pointing out from
what we ought to abstain, bringing all the antidotes of
salvation to the sick; for this is the greatest and most
kingly work of God—the salvation of mankind."[9]   As a
good physician uses all methods—fomentation, cautery,
amputation—to heal the bodies of the sick, so the Saviour
has a voice of many tones and varied methods in the salvation of men.[10]   His aim is to create true health in the soul.[11]

---

[1] Pæd, i. 3[7].   [2] Ib., i. 6[26].   [3] Ec. Prop., 20.   [4] Prot., xii. [123]
[5] Ib, xi. [116].   [6] Ib., x. [87].   [7] Ib, xi. [115].   [8] Pæd., i. 2[6].
[9] Pæd., i. 12[100].   Cf. Q. D, 29; Pæd., i. 1[1].
[10] Prot., i. [8].   [11] Pæd., i. 11[96].

As all are sick in respect of passions and evil desires, all need a Saviour. "Sick, we truly stand in need of the Saviour; having gone astray, we need one to guide us; blind, we need one to lead us by His light; thirsty, we need the fountain of life, of which those who partake shall no longer thirst; dead, we need life; sheep, we need a shepherd; we who are children need a tutor; nay, all mankind stands in need of Jesus, so that we may not as intractable men and sinners fall at the end into condemnation, but may be separated from the chaff and stored up in the garner of the Father."[1] The Sun of righteousness has changed sunset into sunrise, He has crucified death so that life may be won.[2] Sometimes this salvation is represented as one with knowledge of God, and only to be attained by such knowledge. Sometimes it is represented as the guerdon of faith. It is so precious that if it were for sale, the whole wealth of Pactolus would not buy it, yet it can be bought with faith and love.[3] The fundamental conception of salvation in Clement is that of spiritual health.

The manner in which Clement exhibits the unity and catholicity of the Church, and its authority in relation to heretical schools and teaching, has already been noticed.[4] Here is only to be noted the relation of the Church to those within her fold. The Church is of divine origin, and is closely identified with salvation. "Only to believe and to be born again is perfection in life. For God is never weak. For as His volition is work, and this is called the world, so also His counsel is the salvation of men, and this has been called the Church."[5] "It is a holy temple,—not the place but the congregation; not built by mechanical art, nor adorned by the hand of angel, but formed by the will of God into a sanctuary."[6] The Church on earth is an image of the Church in heaven.[7]

[1] Pæd., i. 9 83.   [2] Prot., xi. 114.   [3] Ib., ix. 85, 86.   [4] See Lecture II., p. 60.
      [5] Pæd , i 6 27.   [6] Str., vii 5 29.   [7] Ib., iv. 8 66

The grades of bishops, presbyters, and deacons are an imitation of the angelic glory and of different degrees of felicity
among the perfected.[1] Of the whole Church Christ is the
crown, the head.[2] She is administered by the Word.[3] She
is the mother who nurses her children with holy milk.[4] Her
sacrifice is speech rising as incense from holy souls, while
every thought is unveiled to God along with the sacrifice.[5]
The Church is the "holy mountain" on which our Tutor
feeds His flock.[6] In this pasturing, what place is to be
assigned to the sacraments of Baptism and the Eucharist?

The many baptisms of Moses are embraced in the one
Baptism. Baptism is represented as the first stage in a
process that ends in immortality, and as that which gives
impulse to the process. "Being baptised, we are enlightened; being enlightened, we are made sons; being
made sons, we are perfected; being perfected, we are made
immortal. The work is variously called a gift of grace, and
enlightenment, and perfection, and washing. It is a washing by which we thoroughly cleanse our sins; grace by
which the penalty of our sins is remitted; enlightenment
by which the holy light of salvation is beheld—that is,
by which we have a keen vision of God; and perfection
which wants nothing."[7] It is the removing a film from
the eye of the spirit, so that it may have a clear
vision of God, the Holy Spirit flowing down to us from
above. The perfection, it is true, is only a potential perfection, for the goal is reserved for the resurrection of
believers; but the attainment is one with the promise.[8]
The Gnostic phrase "filtration" may be applied to Baptism.
As filtration, as described by them, is the separation from
what is worse, derived from the reminiscence of what is
better, and as he who remembers the better must repent of

---

[1] Str., vi. 13 [107].   [2] Pæd., ii. 8 [71]; i. 5 [18].   [3] Str., iv. 20 [172].
[4] Pæd., i. 6 [42]. Cf. iii. 12 [99].   [5] Str., vii 6 [32].
[6] Pæd., i. 9 [84].   [7] Ib., i. 6 [26].   [8] Ib., i. 6 [28], [29].

the worse, so we who have repented of our sins are
"filtered" by Baptism.[1] The Baptism of the Word is the
one all-healing medicine by which transgressions are taken
away. The character is not the same as before our washing.[2] It is a washing unto the forgiveness of sins, and by it
forgiveness for previous sins is obtained once for all.[3] We
are born again through water, which is a different kind of
sowing from that in the creation.[4] As we came naked of
sin from the womb, so from the womb—water—God hath
begotten us naked of sin[5] As a spiritual bath, it has a
natural relationship to spiritual nourishment.[6] The water
of baptism receives consecration.[7] The Saviour was baptised, though He had no need Himself to be so, that He
might sanctify the whole water for those who are being
regenerated.[8] Though Clement does not use the word
Baptism any more than the word Eucharist in his "Exhortation to the Greeks," he uses language which shows
that that ordinance and its purpose and result were before
his mind. "Take the water of the Word; wash yourselves,
ye who have been defiled; cleanse yourselves from custom
by the drops of truth."[9] Heretical baptism was the passing through "alien water"; it was not native and genuine
water.[10] Sins committed before baptism are remitted;
those wrought afterwards are cleansed by discipline. In one
passage he speaks as if there were a gnostic baptism in
contrast with common baptism. "Ye washed yourselves"
—not simply as the rest, but with knowledge ye cast off the
passions of the soul.[11] As illumination was not only an
essential constituent of baptism but synonymous with it,
this cannot mean that it was a different baptism, but is only an
illustration of his tendency to exalt knowledge which marks

[1] Pæd., i, 6 [32]   [2] Ib., i. 6 [30].   [3] Str., ii. 13 [58].   [4] Ib., iii. 12 [88].
[5] Ib., iv. 25 [160]. Cf. Pæd., ii. 12 [118].   [6] Pæd., i. 6 [50], [51].
[7] Ex. Theod., 82—probably from Theodotus, not Clement.
[8] Ec. Pr., 7.   [9] Prot., x. [99].
[10] Str , i. 19 [96] ; Prov. ix. 18, LXX.   [11] Str., vii. 14 [86] ; I Cor. vi 11

especially his later writings. Even when all allowance has been made for the rhetorical element in his phrases and imagery, it is plain that Clement associated the working of baptism with the forgiveness of sin, regarded it as the implanting of the germ of a new life, and ascribed to it a spiritual force as an essential stage in the progress towards salvation. It is equally plain that throughout he is thinking only of the baptism of those of riper years.[1]

The uncertain character of the teaching of Clement as to the Eucharist in itself and its place in the spiritual life is indicated by the contradictory conclusions that have been drawn from the same data. It has been argued that he taught the doctrine of the Real Presence in the Roman Catholic sense of the word;[2] it has been maintained that his teaching is closely akin to that of Zwingli,[3] or even might be expressed in the language of the apologist of Quakerism.[4] The obscurity arises in part from the fact that most of the allusions are quite incidental, in part from the cloudy rhetoric and symbolism that here in an unusual degree conceal rather than illustrate the thought.

Clement refers to its institution by Christ. "The Saviour," he says, "took the bread and first spoke and blessed. Then having broken the bread He set it forth, that we might eat it according to reason."[5] He blessed the wine, saying, "Take, drink, this is My blood." The blood of the vine, the Word who was poured forth unto the remission of sins, He figuratively calls a holy stream of gladness.[6] Clement designates it the Eucharist. He applies the passage about the "secret bread and stolen water" to the heretics who celebrate the Eucharist with water contrary to the rule of the

---

[1] See Bigg, p. 81.

[2] Dollinger; Probst. 'Liturgie der drei ersten christlichen Jahrhunderte,' p. 130 *et seq.* More recently, A. Struckmann, 'Die Gegenwart Christi nach den schrift-lichen Quellen der vornizanischen Zeit,' 1905, pp. 115 *et seq.*

[3] Hofling See Bigg, p. 106, who agrees with Hofling.

[4] Mayor, *op. cit.*, p. 383.   [5] Str., i. 10⁴⁶.   [6] Pæd., ii. 2²².

Church, and speaks of the whole ordinance under the name of the "offering."[1] By way of enforcing the mutual duties of scholar and teacher, he refers to some who in distributing the Eucharist permit each one of the people to take the portion himself.[2] In condemning extravagance in eating and drinking, he makes allusion to the abuse of the agape. To give this name to luxurious suppers was to insult the fair and saving work of the Lord—the consecrated love-feast. Nor was the name to be given to ordinary social gatherings,[3] still less to the immoral suppers of the followers of Carpocrates.[4] From the comment of Clement that those who indulged in delicate and costly feastings were mistaken in supposing that the promise of God was to be bought with such suppers, it would appear that in Alexandria the Eucharist was still associated with the agape. In support of the contention that Clement held the doctrine of the Real Presence, the following passages are adduced. "The Word is all things to the child, both father and mother and tutor and nurse. 'Eat My flesh,' He says, 'and drink My blood.' This appropriate nourishment the Lord provides, and holds out flesh and pours forth blood, and nothing is awanting to the growth of His children."[5] But elsewhere he says that the knowledge of the divine essence is the eating and drinking of the divine Word.[6] He bound, it is said, "the colt to the vine."[7] This means, says Clement, that He bound the simple and child-like people to the Word who is a vine. For the vine produces wine as the Word produces blood, and both produce drink to the saving health of men, the one, wine for the body, the other, blood for the spirit.[8] The bread and wine set forth by Melchisedek was consecrated food—a type of the Eucharist.[9] The good Samaritan is Christ who pours the wine, the blood of the wine of David,

---

[1] Str., i. 19 [96]; Prov. ix. 17.   [2] Str., i. 1 [5].   [3] Pæd , ii. 1 [4].
[4] Str., iii. 2 [10].   [5] Pæd., i. 6 [42].   [6] Str., v. 10 [66]. Cf. Pæd., i 6 [38].
[7] Gen. xlix. 11.   [8] Pæd., i 5 [15].   [9] Str., iv. 25 [161].

upon our wounded souls.[1] " The bread and the oil are consecrated by the power of the name of God, being in appearance the same as when they were received, but transformed
by the power into a spiritual power."[2] This might mean
that the bread had been altered in substance, or simply that
it had become the vehicle or medium of a spiritual power.
But it cannot be pressed into the argument, for in all
probability it belongs to Theodotus, not to Clement. In
one passage the literal and the symbolic seem intermingled.
" The blood of the Lord is twofold. The one is fleshly, by
which we have been redeemed from corruption ; the other is
spiritual, by which we have been anointed. To drink the
blood of Jesus is to share in the incorruption of the Lord.
The Spirit is the force of the Word, as the blood is of the
flesh. Analogously, therefore, the wine is mingled with
water and the Spirit with man. The mixture furnishes a
banquet for faith, the Spirit conducts to immortality. The
mixture of both—of that which is drunk and the Word—
is called Eucharist, a grace renowned and fair. Those who,
according to faith, participate in it are sanctified in body
and soul, the will of the Father mingling in mystical fashion
the divine mixture—the man—with the Spirit and the
Word."[3] So further he speaks of heavenly food,[4] of divine
and spiritual food,[5] of the eating of Christ, of the nourishment
—the Lord Jesus—sanctified human flesh.[6] On the strength
of these passages it has been argued that in the Eucharist
the body and blood of Christ are received, the Lord Himself
in His humanity and His Godhead, and that the effects of
this participation are union with Christ, holiness in body
and soul, the conquest of the passions and the immortality
of the body.[7] On the face of it, the contention has apparent

[1] Q. D., 29.   [2] Ex. Theod., 82.   [3] Pæd., ii. 2 [19], [20].
[4] Ib., ii 1 [4].   [5] Ib., ii. 1 [9].   [6] Ib., i. 6 [43].
[7] Struckmann, *op. cit.*, pp. 115-139. Cf. Batiffol, ' L'Eucharistie,'[5] pp. 248-261.

force; and he who comes to the reading of Clement with faith in this doctrine may without undue violence read it in, and into, these and kindred passages. But other passages show that the language of metaphor is an unsafe basis for dogmatic superstructure. For elsewhere he speaks of love as heavenly nourishment, a rational banquet,[1] of a righteous meal as a Eucharist,[2] of hope as the blood of faith.[3] "It is an admirable thing," he says, "to look up to the truth and cling to the nourishment which is from above and divine, and to be filled with the insatiable vision of Him who truly exists, tasting of the pleasure which is sure and abiding and pure."[4]   It has been argued that "if we read Clement as a whole, and reflect upon his strong antithesis of the letter, the flesh, to the spirit, and his language on the subject of priest and sacrifice," we shall conclude that he is nearer to Zwingli than to the doctrine of transubstantiation.[5]   But in an eclectic like Clement the argument from logical consistency cannot be pressed too far, and is only valid when there is an immediate relation between the principle and the conclusion. The language of Clement is based throughout on the sixth chapter of the Gospel of St John more than on the words at the institution of the ordinance : he nowhere quotes the words, "This is My body"; but the symbolic language presupposes a truth and a certain conception of that truth. It is the case that Clement was far from narrow in his conception of the nature and sphere of sacramental grace; but it is certain that his teaching went far beyond the mere symbolism usually associated with the name of Zwingli.[6]   He regarded the Eucharist as an ordinance instituted by Christ, whose method of administration

---

[1] Pæd., ii 1 [5].   [2] Ib., ii. 1 [10].   [3] Ib., i. 6 [88]
[4] Ib., ii. 1 [9].   [5] Cf. Bigg, p. 107.
[6] See, however, on the teaching of Zwingli, Lambert, 'The Sacraments of the New Testament,' p. 292, note 2.

I

was determined by the Church, and which, when received in faith, was a veritable means of "spiritual nourishment and growth in grace."

With regard to the period when the full fruition of salvation takes place, its final scope and extent, as generally with regard to all eschatological matters, the language of Clement is often obscure. This obscurity is due in part to the fact that not only the proposed section or treatise on the Resurrection[1] was not written or has been lost, but also the sections on the Soul,[2] the Devil,[3] the Angels,[4] have met with like destiny. The obscurity, further, is partly due to the fact that he deliberately in reverent silence omits discussion when it might naturally have been expected;[5] and that, here as elsewhere, there are individual statements not in harmony with his general principles or their logical development.

The soul, according to Clement, never sleeps, and the life of the blessed immediately after death is a self-conscious life. The promise as to seeing God face to face is fulfilled after our departure hence.[6] The blessedness of a holy life here is followed by increase of blessedness hereafter.[7] To be set free by death is but an exchange of life;[8] to the martyr the gate of death is the beginning of life.[9] Such an one goes with good courage to his friend the Lord, and is greeted by the Saviour as a "dear brother."[10] He is received with the joyous acclamations of angels, and led by the Saviour to the bosom of the Father, to the life eternal.[11] Of the millennium he says nothing; of the Parousia he says little. He alludes to it in an exposition of the nineteenth Psalm, in an annotation on the First

---

[1] Pæd., i. 6 47; ii. 10 104.   [2] Str., iii. 3 13; v. 13 88.   [3] Ib., iv. 11 86.

[4] Ib , vi. 2 38.   [5] Ib., vii. 3 13.   [6] Pæd., i. 6 37.

[7] Str., v. 14 122.   [8] Ib., iv. 11 80.   [9] Ib , iv. 7 44.

[10] Ib , iv. 4 14.   [11] Q. D , 42.

Epistle of St John, and in his address to the Newly-
Baptised;[1] but it has no prominence as a motive in the
spiritual life. His intention to write on the Resurrection,
whether carried out or not, may partly account for the
meagreness of the teaching in his extant writings.

Special difficulty arises in regard to Clement's views
concerning the extent and final scope of the salvation
wrought by Christ. One general principle is laid down—
that no one shall be finally condemned without having had
an opportunity of accepting or rejecting the message of
salvation, as otherwise the condemnation would be unjust.[2] "It would have been an act of no ordinary arrogance
that those who had departed before the advent of the
Lord without having had the good news proclaimed to
them, or having of themselves given ground of approval or
condemnation in respect of their belief or unbelief, should
participate either in salvation or punishment. For it
were not right that they should be condemned without
trial, and that only those after the advent should reap
the fruit of the divine righteousness."[3] As to save is the
work of the Lord, He preached to the spirits in ward.
If He preached both to Jews and Gentiles, all who
believe will be saved when they have made confession of
their sins, since the punishments of God are saving and
disciplinary. If He preached only to the Jews in Hades,
then the Apostles in harmony with their mission must
have preached to the Gentiles there. Apparently this
offer of salvation is limited to those in Hades who before
the advent had lived righteously; and it does not of itself
imply that even all such would accept the message or be
finally saved, but only that all may be saved; but it is
plain that the principle of equality of opportunity which

---

[1] Ec. Pr., 56. Adum. in 1 Joan. ii. 28; Stah., vol. iii. p. 213; ib., p. 223.
[2] Str., vi. 6 [51].   [3] Ib., vi. 6 [48].

underlies it is one capable of indefinite expansion in the direction of universal salvation.

With reference to the destiny of the unrighteous, three views have been ascribed to Clement — the hypothesis of annihilation, that of eternal punishment by fire, and that of universal salvation. In support of the first hypothesis two passages are adduced. The law, it is said, inflicts penalties for moderate transgressions, "but when it sees any one in such a condition as to seem incurable, and advancing to the lowest point of unrighteousness, then already in its care for others, in order that they may not be corrupted by him, as if cutting off a part of the whole body, so it puts to death such an one in the highest interests of health." [1] But from the context this can only mean that the man dies lest his influence should corrupt others; and of what takes place after death there is no indication. Again, " It is the highest and most perfect good when one is able to lead back any one from evil - doing to well-doing; and this is effected by the law. So that when any one is overcome by unrighteousness and greed, and falls into evil past all remedy, it would benefit him to be put to death." [2] This cannot mean that annihilation is better than eternal punishment for such an one, as there is no suggestion of such an alternative in the passage. But as he had already said that it was for the good of others that the incurable and unrighteous one should be put to death, so here he says that it is for the good of the man himself As in the previous case, he says nothing as to what takes place after death; but the implication is that "the flesh is destroyed that the spirit may be saved." [3] The hypothesis of annihilation may therefore be set aside.

[1] Str , i. 27 [171].   [2] Ib., i. 27 [173].
[3] I Cor. v. 5.   Cf. Adum. in i P.; Stah., iii. p. 206.

The hypothesis of eternal punishment occupies a different position.

That in a general way it will be well with the righteous after death, and not well with the unrighteous or unbeliev-ing, Clement often affirms. More definitely, in his "Exhortation to the Greeks" does he repeatedly insist on the alternative between acceptance and judgment, the choice of life or of death, of eternal life or the "fire which the Lord hath prepared for the devil and his angels."[1] He supports this view by the witness of Greek poets and thinkers as well as by the authority of Scripture. "If death were the end of all," as Plato said, "the wicked would have had a good bargain in dying."[2] Sophocles and Pindar alike emphasise the contrasted destiny.[3] Socrates says that good souls depart hence with good hope, and that the wicked live with an evil hope. Heraclitus says that there awaits for men after death what they look not for or dream of.[4] And this, so far as the wicked are concerned, he explains elsewhere as meaning fire.[5] These ideas, more-over, were extracted from the barbarian philosophy. The "fierce men of fiery aspect" in Plato are the angels who lay hold of and chasten the righteous. For, it is said, "He maketh His angels winds, and His ministers a flame of fire." What the barbarians call Gehenna, Plato calls Tartarus.[6] By over-scrupulousness in discriminating be-tween the claims of the worthy and the unworthy, we may neglect some who are dear to God—the punishment for which is "eternal fiery punishment."[7] Clement inter-prets the saying in Zechariah, "Is this not a brand plucked

---

[1] Prot , ix [84]; x. [95]; xii. [122]; viii. [89].   [2] Str., iv. 7 [44].
[3] Prot , x. [90]; Str., iv. 26 [167].   [4] Str., iv. 22 [141].   [5] Prot., ii. [22].
[6] Str., v 13 [89], [91]. Cf. Pæd., i. 7 [61].
[7] Q. D., 33. Cf. Q. D., 13, 39. Cf. Matt. xxv. 41

from the fire," as referring to Satan, and asks, " Why have they fled to the death-bringing brand with whom they will be burned, when it is in their power to live well and not according to custom ? For God bestows life, but evil custom after our departure from the world inflicts vain repentance together with punishment." [1]   To the like effect is a fragment preserved in an Armenian version.[2] So else-where he speaks of the "fire that cannot cease because of sin " [3] From these passages it would seem to follow that it is the teaching of Clement that eternal punishment by fire awaits the unrighteous, and that in the case of such repentance is profitless and vain.[4] The exact weight, how-ever, to be attached to these statements cannot be gauged without considering what he meant by " fire," as well as by examining other passages and principles with which these positions are in open or implicit antagonism.

"Fire" in the Scriptures is always interpreted by Clement figuratively, is represented not as outward and material but inward and spiritual, and its function as that of a force to cleanse and discipline, not to destroy.[5] There is a fire which convicts and heals superstition.[6] The cleansing of the blood of the sons and daughters of Israel "by the spirit of judgment and the spirit of burning" is likened to a spiritual bath which washes away the filth of the soul.[7]   Fire is conceived as a force, good and powerful,

---

[1] Prot., x. [90]; Zech. iii. 2. Cf. Prot., i.[8].   [2] Stah., iii. p. 229, fr. 69.

[3] Pæd , iii. 11 [83]. From the context, however, it may be that the thought is rather akin to that of 2 Peter ii 14.

[4] The passages in Potter, p. 1020, often quoted as decisive of the question, are not genuine See Stah., vol. iii. p. lxxi. The passage in Q. D., c. 39, denying the possibility of forgiveness for sins committed after baptism, is plainly corrupt, and in all probability, with Dindorf, Mayor, and Barnard, we should insert a negative, and read, "even this man is *not* altogether condemned by God."

[5] Ec. Pr , 26 ; Str., v. 14 [100]. Cf Ex. Theod., 81.

[6] Prot , iv. [58].   [7] Pæd., iii 9 [43] ; Isa. iv. 4.

destructive of what is worse, preservative of what is better.[1]
" We say that fire sanctifies not flesh but sinful souls,
and by fire we mean not that which is all-devouring and
common, but the discerning fire which penetrates the soul
that walks through the fire." [2]   As with the symbol so with
the thing signified.   Cocytus, Acheron, and the like, referred
to by Plato, are places of punishment, but punishment with
a view to discipline.[3]   " The gnostic pities those who are
chastened after death, and by punishments are involuntarily
made to make confession of their sins." [4]   " Those who
have reached a higher degree of insensibility are forced to
repent by the necessary chastisements, by the goodness of
the great Judge." [5]   In some instances it is difficult to determine whether Clement is speaking of punishments here or
hereafter, but the above are quite explicit; and in any case
the aim of punishment is represented by him as the same
in both.   In view of the apparent conflict of opinions, the
determining factor must be assigned to general principles.

That, in the judgment of Clement, repentance after
death was possible, there can be no doubt.   The measure
of that possibility is limited rather by the free-will of man
than by the nature of God.   Even for the devil repentance
was possible, because of his possession of freedom.[6]   Such
possession, it is plain, made equally possible the condition
of final impenitence.[7]   The justice of God, as we have
seen, is inseparably related to His goodness.   " As children
are corrected by their teacher or their father, so are we
corrected by Providence.   God does not take vengeance,
for vengeance is a retaliation for evil, but He corrects with
a view to the good, both public and private, of those who

---

[1] Ec. Pr., 26.   [2] Str., vii. 6 ³⁴.   [3] Ib , v. 13 ⁹¹
[4] Ib., vii. 12 ⁷⁸.   [5] Ib., vii. 2 ¹²   [6] Ib., i. 17 ⁸³ ; but cf. vol. iii. p. 214
[7] Cf. Adum. in Jud., vol. iii. p. 207

are corrected." [1]   Christ handed over those who judged him
unjustly to God that they might receive punishment and
be disciplined.[2]   The possibility of repentance elsewhere
than here is distinctly affirmed, and that on the ground
that there is no place where the beneficent activity of God
is inoperative.[3]   Moreover, the Lord is the power of God,
and His power can never lose its strength.[4]   The principle
of equality of opportunity, as alone consistent with divine
righteousness, tends in the same direction, especially when
accompanied, as it is in Clement, with the hypothesis that
disembodied spirits possess clearer vision of the things of
God.[5]   If that be so, and no further opportunity were to be
given to those who had heard here the call of Jesus, not
to have heard the call of the Gospel in this life at all would
have been a preferential position, which Clement in his
missionary zeal could not have admitted for a moment.
Further, the possibility of repentance after death is alone
consistent with the conception of punishment as discipline.
For, if divine punishment be disciplinary, and only disciplinary, it must continue as long as, and only so long as,
the educative process has been ineffective.   But is it possible that Clement ascribed to God a method of discipline
that finally failed in its aim, or ascribed to the great
Physician a virtual acknowledgment of His impotence?

Is this discipline, in the life to be, limited to the unrighteous?   Or does it extend to those who die in a state of
spiritual imperfection?   Or is it universal?   No such discipline can attach to the martyr, because after death he goes
straight to the highest bliss.   From the circumstance that
the gnostic pities those who undergo punishment, the presumption is that he himself is exempt from such discipline.

---

[1] Str., vii. 16 [102].

[2] Adum. in 1 Pet., vol. iii. p 205.

[3] Str , iv. 6 [37].

[4] Ib., vi. 6 [47].   [5] Ib., vi. 6 [46].

But for those who are neither gnostics nor martyrs there would seem to be discipline, especially for sins committed after baptism. This is associated with the idea of gradations of status in heaven. The " mansions " vary according to the lives of men, according to the desert of believers.[1] The three elect mansions are indicated by the thirty, the sixty, and the hundred-fold, in the Gospel. The perfect inheritance belongs to the perfect man.[2] " The man of faith (the simple believer) is distressed yet further, either because he has not yet attained, or not fully attained, what he sees that others have shared. And, moreover, he is ashamed because of the transgressions which he had committed, which in truth are the greatest punishments to the man of faith. And though the punishments cease, as a matter of fact, at the completion of the full penalty and the purification of each, those who have been deemed worthy of the ' other fold ' have the greatest abiding sorrow, the sorrow of not being along with those who have been glorified because of righteousness." [3]   The punishment, then, from one point of view, is the consciousness of failure to reach an ideal; from another, it is the exaction of a penalty. Whether such souls always remain in a relatively lower sphere is not distinctly stated ; but for them, as for others, the law is continuous progress.

The pre-eminence given to the doctrine of the Word is the most distinctive feature in the theology of Clement. He found in it the key to a right conception of God, of nature, of history, and of man. As against every form of polytheism, the unity of God is postulated not less by philosophical thought than by the religious spirit. But the unity which might be admitted by the speculative reason, the conception of a solitary being in inaccessible isolation,

[1] Str., ıv. 6 ³⁶.   [2] Ib., vi 14 ¹¹⁴.   [3] Ib., vı. 14 ¹⁰⁹

could not satisfy the hunger of the heart which cries out for a Father in heaven. Nor could the conception of the Fatherhood of God find complete realisation in the thought of His relation to the world or man, or even the highest order of created spirits; for neither the world, nor man, nor angels, had existed from the beginning: there was a time when they were not. But did God only become a Father when the creation sprang into being at His word? Was the Fatherhood of God only an accident, or, irrespective of creation, was it an inalienable characteristic of His? To the Alexandrian thinker the last seemed the true thought. Fatherhood implied sonship; the Son must, therefore, have been eternally begotten, and thus stood in an altogether different relation to the Father from the universe or man which were formed by Him, not begotten of Him. As a revelation of the Father, the Incarnation of the Son was not regarded by Clement as an isolated act, but only as the highest and final act in a series of manifestations of the Word. The universe owed its existence to the Word, and thus bears upon it the impress of rationality. It is the result and the embodiment of a divine thought, and is, therefore, not dead, but informed with life; and it is our duty to search and discover the divine thoughts that are there operative. But there is another sphere for the working of the Word of God. Thought is that in man which is most akin to the essence of God; and the Word wrought in the minds of men. The progressive education of humanity by the Word, altogether apart from its applications, was surely a magnificent conception. In a way of which they themselves were unconscious, the thinkers of Greece had been illuminated by the Word; and, if the light had been obscured by the medium through which it shone or came only in fitful gleams, it was none the less light from Him;

and the partial truth created the longing for the future manifestation. In a more direct way and prior to this, the Word had intervened in the history of mankind. To the people of the Jews, alone among the nations of antiquity, He had given a direct revelation of Himself; and the record of that revelation had been preserved for the guidance of men. But something more than this was needed. The possibility of communication between God and man was an evidence of God's relation to man and of man's kinship with Him. But a theophany was only a transitory manifestation, and left the relation between God and man as external as before; the word in man was still alienated from the Word who was with God; the theophany must be consummated by an Incarnation; and so, the "Word became flesh, and tabernacled among us." When men began to search into the divine content of these words, new problems were created. Two things the Church sought to maintain and reconcile—the absolute deity of Christ and His complete humanity: it sought to show that He was not a dual personality, half human, half divine, but one divinely-human personality, in which the divine and human aspects were alike to be acknowledged, neither aspect being exaggerated nor minimised. The humanity of Christ had been assailed in Alexandria; and, as has been noted, Clement was not altogether uninfluenced by the speculations in his environment. But he held so firmly by the humanity of Christ that he regarded the Incarnation as the basis and archetype of that which was in a measure possible for all His followers. In the fact and in the doctrine of the Incarnation he saw the bridging of the gulf, hitherto impassable, between man and God. He saw in it the consecration of nature and its redemption from the charge of being the cause of evil and antagonistic to God, as well as from the Epicurean charge that it was outside the abiding love and care of the Almighty. He saw in it the consecration of the history of humanity as an ever-operative sphere for the activity of the Word. He saw in it the consecration of every son of man by presenting to him the possibility of becoming a son of God. Clement might have said with Browning [1]—

> " I say, the acknowledgment of God in Christ
> Accepted by thy reason solves for thee
> All questions in the earth and out of it."

---

[1] Cf Chase, Lectures on Ecclesiastical History (Norwich Cathedral), 1896, p. 296.

LECTURE V.

THE ETHICS OF CLEMENT.

WITH regard to the sources of the moral ideas in the teaching of Clement, as well as of the psychology that underlies them, there has been much discussion and controversy. According to Merk, he is an adherent of the Stoics;[1] according to Reinkens, of Aristotle;[2] Ritter regards him as fundamentally a Platonist;[3] Dahne as a Neo-Platonist.[4] The truth is, if we accept his own statement, that he refused to be considered a narrow partisan of any school; that we find in his writings terms and definitions drawn indifferently from Plato or Aristotle; that in his conception of virtue, and even of its detailed applications, he has learned much from the Stoics. This need excite no surprise. Stoicism in its highest reach had much in common with Christianity, and even before his conversion it must have been attractive to an earnest spirit such as his; and it is probable, as we have noted, that Pantænus, in whose teaching he found intellectual rest, was an adherent of that system. But in delineating the Christian ideal he professed to exhibit the gnostic according to the rule of

---

[1] Clemens Alexandrinus in seiner Abhangigkeit von der griechischen Philosophie. 1879.

[2] De Clemente Presbytero Alexandrino, 1851, pp. 300-309.

[3] Geschichte der christlichen Philosophie, p. 447 *et seq.*

[4] De Γνώσει, 1831, pp. 1-18, 69-112.

the Church;[1] his ultimate authority is Scripture; and he
would have accepted no maxim from any quarter as
authoritative of which he did not regard Scripture as the
source, or which could not in his opinion be reasonably
deduced from it. "The Platonic and Stoic features are
mingled with an inner confidence in the power of the
spirit of Christianity."[2]

Of man, his nature and destiny generally, Clement presents a high conception. Man is a plant of heavenly origin.[3]
It is his natural prerogative, as man, to have fellowship with
God.[4] By nature he is a lofty and majestic being, seeking
after the good, as befits the creation of Him who alone is
good.[5] All men are the work of one God, invested with
one likeness upon one nature.[6] As the image of God is
His Word, so the true man, the mind in the man, is the
image of the Word.[7] To be "after the image and likeness"
does not apply to the body but to the mind and the
reasoning faculty on which the Lord puts the seal of
likeness.[8] Man is superior to the animals in this, that by
the inbreathing of God he shares in a purer essence than
they, and that in him alone an idea of God has been
instilled at his creation.[9] As to the origin of the soul, the
doctrine of traducianism is definitely set aside.[10] Like the
centaur, man is compounded of a rational and an irrational
element—soul and body. The soul is superior to the body.
But the soul is not good by nature, nor the body evil by
nature. These two are diverse, but not opposite.[11] Christ
healed the soul as well as the body. If the flesh had been
the enemy of the soul, He would not have restored it to

[1] Str., vii. 7 ⁴¹.   τὸν τῷ ὄντι κατὰ τὸν ἐκκλησιαστικὸν κανόνα γνωστικόν.
[2] Gass, 'Geschichte der christlichen Ethik,' vol. i. p. 78.
[3] Prot., ii ²⁸.   [4] Ib., x.¹⁰⁰.   [5] Pæd., iii. 7 ³⁷.   [6] Str., vii. 14 ⁸⁵.
[7] Prot., x.⁸⁶.   [8] Str., ii. 19 ¹⁰².   [9] Ib., v. 13 ⁸⁸; vii. 2 ⁵. Cf. v. 14 ⁹⁴.
[10] Ib., vi. 16 ¹³⁵.   [11] Ib., iv. 3 ⁹; iv. 26 ¹⁶⁴.

health and fortified it in its hostility to the soul.[1] The soul
never sleeps.[2] It is immortal and indestructible. Being
formed of finer material, it suffered no injury in the flood
from water, which is of grosser material.[3] Without the
spirit the body is nothing but dust and ashes.[4] The soul is
the final cause of the body.[5] The body is the instrument,
the seat, and the possession of the soul.[6] The whole body,
and not the upper part merely, was formed by God.[7] Man
by his constitution has been formed erect for the vision of
heaven, and the mechanism of the senses tends to knowledge. All the parts are well ordered with a view to good,
not pleasure. The body is the dwelling-place of the soul,
and shares in the sanctification wrought by the Holy
Spirit.[8] The harmony of the body contributes to the
goodly disposition of the mind.[9] Yet, because of the
passions inevitably associated with the body, it is a fetter to
the soul.[10] Natural death is the dissolution of the chains
that bind the soul to the body, and this severance is the
life-long "study" of the philosopher.[11] The little piece of
flesh tends to obscure the vision of the soul.[12] Clement
quotes with approval the saying of Plato,[13] that the soul of
the philosopher dishonours the body and seeks to be alone
by itself,[14] and without disapproval the saying that the
body is the grave of the soul.[15] A fleshly element involves
a dead element.[16] The hypothesis of transmigration of the
soul and of purification by transmigration is to be rejected.
The soul has not been sent into the world as into a prison-
house.[17] It is plain that we have here two different, if not
contradictory, conceptions of the relation of the body to the

[1] Str., iii. 17 [104].   [2] Pæd , ii. 9 [82].   [3] Str., v. 14 [81] ; vi. 6 [52].
[4] Ib., iii. 6 [46].   [5] Ib., iii. 17 [100].   [6] Ib., vi. 18 [183].   [7] Ib., iii. 4 [34].
[8] Ib., iv. 26 [163].   [9] Ib., iv. 4 [18].   [10] Ib., vii. 7 [40].   [11] Ib., iv. 3 [19].
[12] Ib., vi. 6 [46].   [13] Phædo, 65 C.   [14] Str., iii. 3 [18].
[15] Ib., iii. 3 [16] ; Plato, Krat., 400 B.C   [16] Ib., iii. 4 [25].   [17] Ib., iii. 3 [13].

soul, — a conception which admits the possibility of the transfiguration of the body and all its activities, and a conception which involves the crushing of the body as the seat of the passions and an obstacle to the development of the highest life. According as the one conception or other predominates, the ethical ideal varies, the ascetic element gains or loses in prominence. The former conception is chiefly emphasised in his refutation of the heretics who vilified the body and creation generally; the latter conception comes out incidentally, but may none the less indicate a dominating principle in his ethical ideals.[1]

Clement puts great emphasis on human freedom. In a fragment of the lost treatise on Providence he defines willing as the natural, voluntary movement of the self-determined mind, or the mind moved of its own choice with reference to anything. Freedom of will is the mind moved according to nature, or it is an intellectual, independent movement of the soul.[2] Like the words or phrase which are employed by him to denote the conception,[3] this definition emphasises the self-determination of the will and its ground in the natural or divine constitution of man. The will takes precedence of all: the rational powers are ministers of the will.[4] That is in our power of which and its opposites we are equally masters; as, for example, we can philosophise or not philosophise, we can believe or disbelieve.[5] This is a gift of God, who has bestowed upon us free and sovereign power to live as we will, and has left the soul unfettered in respect of rejection or refusal.[6]

---

[1] For a full discussion of the nature of the soul, and of the psychology generally, see the treatise of Ziegler, 'Die Psychologie des T Fl. Clemens Alexandrinus,' 1894, especially pp. 1-16, 53-66.

[2] Stah., vol. iii. p 220.

[3] τὸ ἐφ' ἡμῖν, τὸ αὐτεξούσιον, προαιρετικὴ δύναμις, τὸ αὐθαίρετον τῆς ἀνθρωπίνης ψυχῆς, αἵρεσις καὶ φυγὴ αὐτοκρατορική, &c.

[4] Str., ii. 17[77]   [5] Ib., iv. 24[153].   [6] Ib., ii. 4[12]; iii, 5[41]; vii. 3[15].

The choice or rejection of the truth is a voluntary action.[1] Clement seeks to prove and illustrate this by the statements of Scripture, on general moral grounds, and as being in accordance with the relation of God to man. The very giving of the commandments was a recognition of freedom, for it implied that man had it in his power what to choose and what to shun [2] The prophet Hosea rebuked the people inasmuch by the possession of the understanding, which is the eye of the soul, they showed that they had sinned voluntarily.[3] The Apostle gives the name of "men" to those who in the enjoyment of freedom of will believed and were saved by voluntary choice.[4] The reply of the Saviour to the rich young man, "if thou willest," indicated the free-will of the soul; the man was free to choose as God was free to give.[5] In opposition to the natural determinism of Basilides, Clement showed that moral freedom was essential to responsibility. If faith were only an advantage of nature, as Basilides maintained, there could be no room for praise or censure in the case of belief or unbelief, for man would be the creature of a natural, if divine, necessity. If men were moved like lifeless puppets by natural forces, the distinction between voluntary and involuntary is super-fluous; and the same is true of the impulse which leads to choice.[6] From this conception of freedom as absolute, important conclusions in the matter of salvation are drawn. God wishes us to be saved of ourselves.[7] Because man is not a lifeless instrument, he must hasten to salvation willingly and of set purpose.[8] Readiness of mind is our contribution to salvation.[9] Faith as well as obedience depend on freedom.[10] Choice and life are yoked together.[11]

[1] Str., i 18 [89], [90].   [2] Ib., vii. 7 [42]   [3] Pæd., i. 9 [77].
[4] Ib., i. 6 [33].   [5] Q. D., c. 10.   [6] Str., ii 3
[7] Ib., vi 12 [96]; Ec. Pr., 22.   [8] Str, vii 7 [42]   [9] Ec. Pr., 22
[10] Str., ii. 3 [11]; ii. 6 [26]; ii. 20 [113]. Cf iv. 23 [150].   [11] Prot., xi. [117]

K

He who sins of his own will makes choice of punishment.[1] That which is involuntary is not judged.[2] God only requires of us the things that are in our power.[3] By instruction we are taught to will to choose what is best.[4] God Himself has respect to this freedom, and exercises no compulsion in the matter of salvation. No one will be saved against his will, for force is hateful to God.[5] Man must co-operate with God.[6] Those who are foreordained were foreordained because God knew before the foundation of the world that they would be righteous.[7] Even, as has already been noted, the argument from the miraculous must not be such as to compel the assent of the spirit of man; for such compulsion were out of harmony with the nature of God and man.[8] But though God will not compel man, there is a sense in which man may exercise compulsion upon God. The kingdom of God is not for the slack or the sleepers; the "violent take it by force," and snatch life from God; for in such conflicts He rejoices to be defeated.[9]

The prominence thus given by Clement to the self-determination of man seems to leave little scope for the action of divine grace in the specifically Christian sense of the word. True, the God-given wisdom, which is a power of the Father, stimulates the will.[10] In a general way, too, no progress in virtue or knowledge is possible apart from the assistance of God. Because we wander in the darkness of the world, we need a guide who does not stumble nor go astray.[11] By confidence in the Lord we can war against the principalities of darkness.[12] The thoughts of

---

[1] Pæd , 1. 8 69.   [2] Str., ii. 14 60. Cf. ii. 15 62.   [3] Ib., ii. 6 26; vii. 7 48.
[4] Ib , 1. 6 38. Cf. ii. 16 78.   [5] Q. D., c. 10.
[6] Str , vi 17 157.   [7] Ib., vii. 17 107.
[8] Stah., vol. iii p 217. Cf. p. 55.   [9] Q. D., c. 21.
[10] Str , v 13 83.   [11] Pæd., i. 3 9   [12] Str., iv. 7 47.

virtuous men derive their origin from the inspiration of God, from the contact of the divine will with the souls of men.[1] Apart from the Saviour the film of ignorance cannot be removed that man might thus gain true knowledge of himself or of God.[2] The unknown God can only be apprehended by divine grace.[3] But all that refers to the grace of revelation rather than to grace in the usage of the New Testament. When he quotes "by grace are ye saved," he adds, "not, however, without good works."[4] More specifically, the divine grace and the drawing of the Father are required for the pursuit of the good without afterthought, though this must be associated with a holy willingness to learn.[5] The highest and only true form of continence is unattainable without the grace of God.[6] In particular, the effect of the illumination of grace of illumination in Baptism is emphasised.[7] Faith is a grace.[8] By faith on the part of man and divine grace the bonds of ignorance are loosened.[9] The attainment of the perfect good does not depend wholly on ourselves.[10] In spite of such sporadic expressions and the occasional use of the word, the function which grace plays in the teaching of Clement is relatively unimportant.

Virtue is defined by Clement as the harmonious disposition of the soul in harmony with reason in every relation of life.[11] It is described indifferently as a habit or a disposition. Thus self-control is designated as a disposition,[12] purity as a habit, simplicity as a habit, contentment as a habit, goodness as a habit.[13] Virtue is a habit because it depends not on others but on ourselves, and is the property of the

---

[1] Str., vi. 17 [157].   [2] Ib , i. 28 [178].   [3] Ib , v 12 [82]; v. 13 [83].
[4] Ib , v. 1 [7].   [5] Ib.   [6] Ib., iii. 7 [57].
[7] Pæd., i. 6 [30].   [8] Str., i. 7 [38].   [9] Pæd , i. 6 [29].
[10] Str , v. 1 [7].   [11] Pæd., i. 13 [101]. Cf. ib., i. 12 [99].
[12] Str , ii. 18 [80].   [13] Pæd., iii. 11 [85]; Str., vii. 7 [38].

man who has power to exercise it.[1] We are not born
with the possession of virtue, nor does it arise in us
afterwards as by natural development, for in that case it
would not have been voluntary or praiseworthy; nor, like
the faculty of speech, does it arise and become perfected by
family intercourse.[2] It is natural only in the sense that we
are by nature adapted for its acquisition.[3] There are, no
doubt, differences in natural aptitude; but the advantage
which one derives from nature may be lost by neglect, and
one less gifted by nature may strengthen his gift by discipline; for perfection in virtue is not the prerogative of
those who have by nature the higher aptitude in the direction of virtue.[4] Righteousness is an attribute independent
of race or nationality; one righteous man as such differs
not from another righteous man.[5] Virtue is one in power;
all the virtues are mutually related.[6] So he that has one
virtue gnostically has all the virtues.[7] Because virtue is a
habit or disposition, it reaches its ideal when habit becomes
nature.[8] Alike in definition and in detail, Clement has
much in common with the Stoics;[9] much inevitably
followed from the emphasis which he placed on moral
freedom.

The question as to "man's chief end" is dealt with at
some length by Clement.[10] He details the opinions of the
representatives of various schools of philosophy, for the
most part without criticism or comment, though he promises
to give a refutation of some of them in due time.[11] But both

---

[1] Str., iv 19 [124]   [2] Ib., vii. 3 [19].
[3] Ib., vi. 11 [95]. Cf. ib., i. 6 [34], οὐ γὰρ φύσει, μαθήσει δὲ οἱ καλοὶ κἀγαθοὶ
γίνονται
[4] Ib , i 6 [34]; vi 12 [69].   [5] Ib., vi. 6 [47].
[6] Ib., i. 20 [97]; viii. 9 [30].   [7] Ib., ii. 18 [80].
[8] Ib., vii. 7 [46]; iv. 22 [128]   [9] See the parallels quoted by Stahlin
[10] Str , ii. 21, 22 [127.136]   [11] Ib., ii 21 [134].

by direct approval and by specific appropriation of the words, he accepts the Platonic conception of the end as assimilation to God.[1] This assimilation may also be described as "assimilation to right reason," but in this connection associated with our restoration through the Son to perfect adoption.[2] The end, he says, is precisely described by the Apostle in the words, "But now being made free from sin, and become servants to God, ye have your fruit unto holiness, and the *end* eternal life."[3] It is the ideal set forth in the exhortation to "be perfect as the Father in heaven."[4] This likeness is closely related to, if not dependent on, and one with, the knowledge of Him. The greatest thing assuredly is the knowledge of God.[5] To know God is to share in immortality.[6] The most perfect good is gnosis, for it is chosen for its own sake.[7] The one end of good and of life is to become a lover of God.[8] But this likeness has its limitations. We are called upon by the Scripture to strive to know God as far as possible.[9] It is impossible and impracticable for any one to become perfect as God is perfect, for that were to imply that the virtue of man and God is the same. All that is demanded is that, living according to the obedience of the Gospel, we should be irreproachably perfect.[10] Moreover, by assimilation to God is meant assimilation to God the Saviour, and that only as far as possible for human nature[11] For to this, too, there is a limit. "It is sufficient if we be as the Master, not in respect of essence, for it is impossible that that which is by adoption should be equal in point of subsistence to that which is by nature."[12] Such being the end, the question arises, Was this end a universal

---

[1] Str , ii 22 [136].
[2] Ib , ii. 22 [134].
[3] Ib.; Rom. vi 22, τὸ δὲ τέλος.
[4] Str., vii 14 [88]. [5] Ib., vii. 7 [47]. [6] Ib., iv. 6 [27].
[7] Ib., vi. 12 [96]. [8] Ib., v. 14 [96]. [9] Ib , ii. 10 [47]
[10] Ib , vii. 14 [88]. [11] Ib., ii. 9 [45]; vi. 12 [104]. [12] Ib , ii. 17 [77].

end, or one to be pursued by, and restricted to, a limited
spiritual aristocracy? Was it open to, and incumbent on,
the man of faith—the simple believer—or the prerogative
and ideal only of the man of gnosis?

The relation of faith to gnosis—with the twofold ideal of
Christian life based thereon—is one of the most distinctive
features in the ethical teaching of Clement. The fluctuating
character of his conception of faith or its application may be
illustrated by the varying interpretations which he puts on
the same passage of Scripture. He quotes four times the
saying in Isaiah, "Unless ye believe, ye shall not understand,"[1] and on each occasion he puts a different interpretation on the word "believe." In one case he takes it in
the sense of belief in contrast with unbelief, and asks, confirming his view by a saying of Heraclitus, How could a
soul admit the transcendent contemplation of the things of
God, while belief in regard to the instruction created an
inner conflict?[2] In another passage he interprets it as
meaning that a belief in Christ, who was prophesied through
the law, was essential to the understanding of the Old
Covenant which He Himself interpreted at His coming.[3]
Elsewhere he characterises faith as a reasonable standard
of judgment which gives a firm basis for the recognition of
the divine words and begets full persuasion.[4] In another
passage he finds in it a confirmation of the definition—
likewise confirmed by a saying of Heraclitus—that faith
is a preconception of the mind, and adds that as preconception is essential to understanding, no one can understand
without faith.[5]

Faith is opposed on the one hand to unbelief, which is
the mere negative supposition of opposition to belief, and
on the other to hardness of belief, which is a habit that

---

[1] Isa. vii. 9.   [2] Str., ii. 2 §.   [3] Ib., iv. 21 §34.
          [4] Ib., i. 1 §.   [5] Ib., ii. 4 §17.

is slow to admit faith.[1] Unbelief dies when faith is shed over us.[2] To believe the truth brings life, as to disbelieve it brings death.[3] The change from unbelief to belief is a divine change.[4]

Faith is not a vain and barbarous thing, as the Greeks calumniate it, but it is a voluntary preconception, the assent of piety, "the assurance of things hoped for, the proof of things not seen." It has also been defined as the assent of the intellect to an unseen object, as certainly the demonstration of a thing unknown is a manifest assent. It is the beginning of action, for it is the foundation of the intelligent choice which is based on the demonstration given by faith, and choice is the beginning of action.[5] It is the rational assent of the self-determining soul.[6] It is thus an activity of the reason as well as of the religious spirit. From the former point of view it is essential to the learning of anything; for if faith be a preconception of the intellect, one will never learn without faith, since one cannot learn without preconception.[7] As an assent, it is the basis of opinion and judgment and of all that makes possible our intercourse with our fellow-men.[8] It is in every relation of life universally necessary.[9] The past and the future fall within its scope.[10] It is no barren assent, for it is the doer of good things and the foundation of doing justice.[11] So more distinctly is it with faith on its religious side as the assent of piety. It is a certain inward good, and without seeking after God it both confirms His existence and glorifies Him as existent.[12] It is no mere human acquirement, but something divine.[13] It is a power of God, being the force of the truth.[14] It is a force unto salvation and a power unto eternal

[1] Str , ii. 6²⁸.   [2] Ec. Pr., 12.   [3] Str., iv 3⁸.   [4] Ib., ii. 6³¹.
[5] Ib , ii. 2⁸·⁹.   [6] Ib., v. 1³   [7] Ib., ii. 4¹⁷.   [8] Ib , ii. 12⁸⁵.
[9] Ib., ii. 5⁵².   [10] Ib., ii. 12⁵⁴.   [11] Ib., v. 13⁸⁶.   [12] Ib., vii. 10⁵⁵.
[13] Ib., ii. 6⁸⁰.   [14] Str., ii. 11⁴⁸.

life.[1] The teaching of philosophy is a gift, but faith is a grace.[2] The Holy Spirit is breathed into those who have believed.[3] By bare faith, without demonstration, the power of God is able to save.[4] He who believes the Scriptures as the voice of God has a demonstration that cannot be gainsaid.[5] Faith is the irrefragable criterion.[6] It is essential to salvation,[7] but works must follow if salvation is to be secured.[8] It justified even those who were before the law, and made them partakers of the divine promise.[9] Yet to those who were righteous according to law, faith was wanting; wherefore the Lord said, "Thy faith hath saved thee." [10] Faith is twofold, the faith of science and the faith of opinion.[11] When the Apostle speaks of the "righteousness of God as revealed from faith to faith," [12] he seems to proclaim a twofold faith, or rather one faith which admits of growth and perfecting; for the common faith lies beneath as a foundation. The special faith, which is built upon it, is perfected along with the believer, and brought to completion along with that which results from instruction and fulfilling the commandments of the Lord. Such was the faith of the apostles which could remove mountains [13] Perfection of faith is to be distinguished from the common faith.[14] Faith is akin to trust, but trust is more than faith. For when one knows that the Son of God is Teacher, he trusts that His teaching is true. And as instruction, according to Empedocles, will make the mind grow, so he that trusts in the Lord will make faith grow.[15] Faith, then, in the conception of Clement, is at once an intellectual act and a spiritual act or attitude, a divine force, yet voluntary, no mere theological or even religious principle, but one of

---

[1] Str , ii 12 [88].   [2] Ib., i. 7 [38].   [3] Ib., v. 13 [83].   [4] Ib., v. 1 [9].

[5] Ib., ii. 2 [9].   [6] Ib., ii. 4 [12].   [7] Ib., i. 7 [38].   [8] Ib , vi. 14 [108].

[9] Ib., ii. 4 [12].   [10] Ib., vi 6 [44].   [11] Ib , ii. 11 [48].   [12] Rom. i. 17.

[13] Str , v. 1 [2]   [14] Ib., iv. 16 [100].   [15] Ib., v. 13 [85].   Cf. ib., ii. 6 [28].

universal sweep and significance, one in its origin but varied in its development, sometimes related to teaching rather than to a person, unless so far as a person is behind the words and commands assent and gives authority to that which is believed,—the faith of the Epistle to the Hebrews rather than the justifying faith of St Paul.

As the conception of faith is fluctuating, so also is the conception of knowledge. Of knowledge in general— apart from any Christian or religious application—Clement says that the word is used in a twofold sense. The first, the knowledge commonly so called, is that which appears universally in all men, in which not only the rational powers but also the irrational powers participate, whose nature it is to apprehend through the senses. To such he refuses the name of knowledge. Knowledge, properly so called, derives its impress from judgment and reason, and thus only the rational powers form cognitions, which are applied to things intellectual by the bare activity of the soul.[1] From this point of view, knowledge is the peculiar property of the rational soul. It is the beginning and author of all rational action. For action is based on impulse, and impulse is based on knowledge.[2] In a narrower sense knowledge is used of the esoteric tradition given by the Lord to the Apostles, and transmitted by them to the few in an unwritten form.[3] This is supported by Scripture, in particular by the authority of St Paul. He says, " We know that we all have knowledge," that is, common knowledge in common things, and the knowledge that there is one God. For he was writing to believers. " But *the* knowledge is not in all " — that is, the knowledge which was transmitted among the few.[4] Prophecy was full of this knowledge.

---

[1] Str , vi. 1 [3].   [2] Ib., vi. 8 [68], [69].   [3] Ib., vi 7 [54], [61].
[4] Ib., iv. 15 [97]; 1 Cor. viii. 1, 7.   Cf. Stäh., vol. iii. p. 227, fr. 60.

Related to this, but not to be identified with it, is a third
form of knowledge—that of gnosis in Clement's sense of
the word. It may be defined as "a kind of perfection of
man as man, being completed by the science of divine
things, in respect of character and life and speech,
harmonious and consistent with itself and the divine
word." All knowledge is wisdom; but all wisdom is not
knowledge.[1] Knowledge is wisdom,—that is, it is a sure
and firm science and apprehension of the things that are,
and will be, and have been.[2] This wisdom is to be contrasted with the wisdom which furnishes experience of the
things relating to life. It is eternal, while the other is
useful in time; it is one and the same, while the other
assumes many and diverse forms; it is without any
movement of passion, while the other is accompanied
with passionate desire.[3] The pre-eminence of knowledge
is indicated by the prophet when he says, "Goodness
and instruction and knowledge teach me," thus presenting in progressive order the guiding principle of perfection.[4]
Its goal is contemplation, the immediate vision of God.[5]
But it is not a barren contemplation. For the vision of
God purity is necessary, and by knowledge the purification of the ruling principle of the soul is effected.[6] A tree
is known by its fruit, not by its blossom, so knowledge
is not characterised by word and blossoms but by fruit
and way of life. For it is not a mere word but a certain
divine science, and the light which, springing up in the
soul, makes all things luminous in their origin, and prepares man to know himself and teaches him how to attain
to God.[7] Knowledge is perfected by word and deed.[8]
Works follow knowledge as the shadow the body.[9]   It

[1] Str., vii. 10 [68].   [2] Ib., vi. 7 [61].   [3] Ib., vi. 7 [54].
[4] Ib , vii 7 [36]; Ps. 119 [66], LXX.   [5] Str., ii. 10 [47].
[6] Ib., iv. 6 [39].   [7] Ib., iii. 5 [44].   [8] Ib , iv. 17 [109].
[9] Ib , vii. 13 [82].   Cf. Ec. Pr., 28.

teaches us to discern the things that contribute to the permanence of virtue. As the greatest of all things is the knowledge of God, in this way virtue is so preserved that its loss is impossible.[1] These are the more general characteristics of knowledge, its source, its goal, its fruit: to know more fully what it is, we must look at it more narrowly as contrasted with, and as related to, faith, and as embodied in the gnostic.

Two false views of the relation of faith to knowledge must be set aside. The Valentinians, says Clement, assign faith to us the simple and knowledge to themselves. They hold that knowledge springs up in those who are saved by nature in accordance with the superiority of a germ of excellence, and that it is as widely separated from faith as the spiritual from the psychical. But, rejoins Clement, if that were so, if faith were not a voluntary assent but an advantage of nature, moral responsibility would be plainly destroyed.[2] Another error, dealing not with the origin or nature of faith but with its object, has also to be rejected. Clement refers to some who held that faith was concerned with the Son but knowledge with the Father. He replies that Fatherhood implied Sonship, and that the two cannot in this way be separated. To believe in the Son we must know the Father, and to know the Father we must believe in the Son; for it is through the Son that the Father comes from faith to knowledge. The knowledge of the Son and Father is the comprehension of the Truth by the Truth.[3]

The general principle is that faith and knowledge are indissolubly related. "Neither is knowledge without faith, nor faith without knowledge."[4] By a certain divine sequence and reciprocity faith is an attribute of know-

---

[1] Str., vii. 7 ⁴⁷.   [2] Ib., ii. 3 ¹⁰, ¹¹.
[3] Ib., v. 1 ¹.   [4] Ib.

ledge and knowledge is an attribute of faith.[1] Between
them there is a natural relationship and adaptation. " As
to the man who has hands it is natural to grasp, and to
him who has healthy eyes to see the light, so to him
who has received faith it is the natural prerogative to participate in knowledge." [2] Faith is as essential to the gnostic
as respiration is to life. As without the four elements it
is not possible to live, so without faith it is not possible
to follow after knowledge.[3] In one sense, faith is more
authoritative than science and its criterion; [4] in another
sense, to know is more than to believe.[5] In one sense,
faith is independent of knowledge, and has to do with a
sphere where science cannot act. For faith deals with
first principles, and first principles, being incapable of
demonstration, can only be apprehended by faith, which
leads up from that which cannot be demonstrated to that
which is universal and simple.[6] In another sense, knowledge rests upon faith, enriching and extending its scope,
and on the ground of things which are already believed,
creates faith in things which are not yet believed, the faith
so created being, as it were, the essence of demonstration.[7]
Faith is the foundation of knowledge,[8] and by knowledge
is faith made perfect.[9] " Knowledge is a kind of perfection of man as man. To have no doubt in reference to
God, but to have faith in Him, is the foundation of knowledge; and Christ is both the foundation and the superstructure, through Whom also are the beginnings and
the ends." [10] In contradistinction to gnostic perfection, the
Apostle sometimes calls the common faith the foundation,
sometimes " milk " as opposed to gnostic food.[11] " Faith,

---

[1] Str., ii 4[16]. Cf. vi 8[68]; vi. 9[74].   [2] Ib , vi. 17[152]   [3] Ib , ii. 6[31].
[4] Ib., ii. 4[15].   [5] Ib., vi. 14[109].   [6] Ib., ii 4[13], [14].
[7] Ib., vii 16[96].   [8] Ib , v. 1[5], vii. 3[20]; ii. 11[51].   [9] Ib., vi. 18[164].
[10] Ib , vii. 10[55].   [11] Ib., v. 4[26].

then, so to speak, is a summary knowledge of the essentials, but knowledge is a demonstration sure and firm of the things received through the faith, being built on the faith by means of the teaching of the Lord, carrying us on to that which is irrefragable and scientifically apprehended."[1] In such passages faith seems to be used for the contents rather than for the act of faith. Faith, then, is perfect in the sense that a foundation is perfect; it is imperfect in the sense that a foundation is imperfect without a superstructure. The superstructure is knowledge, which, however, is not to be conceived as standing in any merely external relation to faith, but as to something with which it is in vital union, as a natural development of it, and a scientific demonstration of its sphere and object.[2]

This is the ruling conception of the relation of faith to knowledge, though at times, in antagonism to the heretical depreciation of faith, he represents faith as perfect and complete in itself.[3] It is to be noted, moreover, that in depicting the ideal Christian under the designation of the gnostic, he emphasises the points in which knowledge is superior to faith, ignoring the common aspects, much more the points of equality.

The relation of the leading virtues to one another is not uniformly set forth. " The consideration that he is ignorant is the first lesson given to the man who is walking according to the Word. An ignorant man has sought, and having sought he finds, the Teacher; and having found he believed; and having believed he hopes; and having loved he is thenceforward assimilated to Him who has been loved, eager to be that which he first loved."[4] Thus the order is,

---

[1] Str., vii. 10 [57].

[2] How strongly Clement felt the necessity of faith being supplemented by knowledge is seen by the addition of the words "ac speculatione" to "fide" in his Adum. in 1 P 1. 5 (Stäh., vol. iii. p. 203).

[3] Cf. Pæd., i. 6 [29]. [4] Str., v. 3 [17].

ignorance, faith, hope, love. And love is perfected by knowledge.[1] So elsewhere he says that knowledge has for its foundation the holy triad—faith, hope, and love.[2] In a later book of the Stromateis he reverses this relation of love and knowledge. "To him that hath shall be added, to faith knowledge, and to knowledge love, and to love the inheritance."[3] The first saving change is from heathenism to faith, a second from faith to knowledge, and this finding its end in love, makes that which knows the friend of that which is known.[4] The perfection of a man of faith is love.[5] Thus in every case faith precedes knowledge and love; but sometimes knowledge is represented as the crown of love, sometimes love as the crown of knowledge. The last is the dominant thought. Knowledge can be taught; it stands between faith and love, which are not taught.[6]

The man of faith and the man of knowledge differ widely in their attitude towards divine truth generally, and, in particular, in their apprehension of the Scriptures. The man of faith only tastes the Scriptures; the gnostic is their true interpreter. The man of faith is as the layman to the skilled craftsman in the matters of daily life.[7] Without letters it is possible to be a man of faith, but not to comprehend the things spoken of in the faith.[8] The gnostic is the scholar of the Spirit. To him the law is not merely a stepping-stone, but he comprehends it as delivered by the Lord.[9] This knowledge is intrusted as a deposit to those who show themselves worthy of the teaching.[10] The difference in content and scope is indicated by the Apostle in the Epistle to the Colossians.[11] The mysteries which were

---

[1] Str., ii. 9 45.   [2] Ib., iv. 7 54.   [3] Ib., vii. 10 55.
[4] Ib., vii. 10 57.   [5] Ad. in 1 Joan. 4 18, vol. iii p. 214.
[6] Str., vii. 4 56.   [7] Ib., vii. 16 95.   [8] Ib., i. 6 35.
[9] Ib., iv. 21 130.   [10] Ib., vii. 10 55.   [11] Col. i. 9,11; i. 25,27.

hidden until the time of the apostles, and were delivered by
them as they received them from the Lord, and " now manifested to the saints," are one thing; and a different thing
is "the riches of the glory of the mystery in the Gentiles,"
—that is, the faith and the hope in Christ, elsewhere called
the foundation.[1] This insight of the gnostic is conditioned
by righteousness ; for as one increases in righteousness, the
nearer to him is the Spirit who is the source of illumination.[2] Such an one apprehends what seems to be incomprehensible to others; for he has believed that nothing is
incomprehensible to the Son of God, and therefore, nothing
that is untaught,—for He who suffered from love to us would
have kept back nothing with a view to our instruction in
knowledge.[3] The Word designed the truth to be a living
force, and not to be a pretext for intellectual indolence.[4]
The difference between the man of faith and the gnostic
in regard to the truth of Scripture is thus the difference
between the pupil, who has learned and is satisfied with
the rudiments, and the advanced scholar; between him who
merely grazes the surface and him who searches into the
deep things of God; between him who is startled as by
a sudden light breaking in upon him in the twilight and
him whose eye has been trained for the sure vision and
apprehension of the truth;[5] between him who has but
entered on the path that leads to life and him who has
been initiated into the mysteries of the esoteric tradition.
The difference is one not of nature but of training ; it is
not a difference of kind but of degree or status in the
spiritual life; there is no impassable barrier between the
stages ; any man may " seek and find," and from being
a man of faith may become a man of knowledge.

   While on the purely intellectual side the distinction

[1] Str., v. 10 [60, 61].   [2] Ib., iv. 17 [107].   [3] Ib., vi. 8 [70].
          [4] Ib., i. 10 [51].   [5] Cf. Ec. Pr., 35, 32.

between the man of faith and the gnostic is not absolute but one of natural gradation, yet when we pass into the sphere of ethical ideals the transition is not so easily bridged. No doubt, here too they have much in common. All the principles and their applications in questions of practical morals, which are enforced in the Pædagogus, are incumbent on both. The gnostic not less than the man of faith must carry out his life in conformity with the precepts of the Word, must direct all his affairs in accordance with reason, must be on his guard not only against every form of vice but every form of extravagance, must fulfil in every detail the principle of doing nothing contrary to nature, dare not, like the heretical gnostic, claim on the ground of special illumination to be indifferent to or superior to the conditions of ordinary morality,—must, in a word, be faithful to all the prescriptions necessary for securing moral health. On the other hand, when it is a question of ethical motives and ideals, there seems a clear antagonism of principles.

The gnostic recognises sin in itself. He condemns not any particular sin but all sin absolutely. His is not the repentance common to all believers, which is the result of past transgressions, but that of him who, knowing the nature of sin, aims at the goal of entire abstinence from sin, the ideal result of which is not-sinning.[1] His repentance has no relation to fear; it is the shame of the soul in itself arising from conscience.[2]

But this does not imply a merely negative goal for the gnostic, but the contrary. While the virtue of the man of faith, his absolute perfection, is purely negative, lying in the mere abstinence from evil, that of the gnostic is positive,

---

[1] Str., vi. 12 [97].

[2] Ib., iv. 6 [37]   Cf Ec. Pr., 15.   "He that hath believed has obtained forgiveness of sins from the Lord, but he that is in the condition of knowledge, as one who sins no longer, obtains from himself the forgiveness of the rest."

having as its goal the unchangeable habit of well-doing after the will of God.[1] The man of faith is limited in the range of his moral activities; he may successfully accomplish one or two things, but not all things nor with the highest science.[2] The righteousness of the man of faith is not true righteousness, for it lacks the notes of progress and perfection that mark the righteousness of the gnostic.[3] Only the action of the gnostic can claim to be moral in the strict sense of the word. "Every action of the gnostic is right action, but that of the simple believer might be called intermediate, as not yet perfected in accordance with reason; but every act of the heathen, on the other hand, is sinful. For not simply to do well, but to perform actions with a certain goal in view and to act in accordance with reason, is exhibited in the Scriptures as morally fitting."[4] This is in harmony with the action of God Himself. He created all things by the Word (Reason), and the man who becomes a gnostic performs good actions by the reasoning faculty.[5]

The higher ethical stage is marked in a very specific manner by the purity of motive, which gives to every action a distinctive character. While the man of faith is influenced by fear of punishment or hope of recompense, the gnostic is spontaneously good, acts only under the influence of love, and for the sake of the good itself, and not for the sake of its results.[6] His self-control is not like that of the dog which refrains because it fears the uplifted hand.[7] The motive of his abstinence is not fear, but love.[8] As little does it rest on love of honour or riches or bodily health.[9] His courage is not the irrational courage of the child, the wild

---

[1] Str., vi. 7 60. Cf. Ec. Pr., 12.   [2] Str., vii. 14 84.
[3] Ib., vi 12 102.   [4] Ib., vi. 14 111.   [5] Ib., vi 16 136.
[6] Ib., iv. 22 135, 143, 144; vi. 12 96.   [7] Ib., iv. 22 146.
[8] Ec. Pr., 19. Cf. Adum. in 1 Joan. 2 3, vol. iii. p. 212.   [9] Ib., vii. 11 66.

beast, or the juggler, but the courage which is in accordance
with reason, and is inspired by the love which is the fruit
of knowledge.[1] All thought even of recompense after death
must be eliminated from the service of the gnostic.[2] He
practises piety, drawn by the love of Him who is the Beloved. "So that, not even supposing that he were to receive
permission from God to do what is forbidden without being
punished for it, nor even if he were to receive a promise that
he would receive as reward the good things of the blessed
on these terms, nor if he were persuaded that what he
did would escape the knowledge of God—which is impossible—would he ever wish to act contrary to right reason,
having once for all made choice of that which is truly good
and to be chosen for its own sake, and on this ground
beloved."[3] Nay, even the pursuit of knowledge itself must
be freed not merely from base alloy or any consideration of
practical need, but even from the desire of salvation. "For
I would dare to affirm that he who pursues knowledge for
the sake of the divine science itself will not choose knowledge from a wish to be saved. If, therefore, one were,
ex hypothesi, to offer to the gnostic which of the two he
would wish to choose, knowledge of God or eternal salvation, and if these two, which are absolutely identical,
were separable, he would without any hesitation whatsoever choose the knowledge of God, having formed
the judgment that the distinctive quality of faith, which
through love has mounted to knowledge, is to be chosen
for its own sake."[4] Truly the utterance of a "bold and
joyous thinker."[5]

Of all the characteristic features in the portrait of the
wise man of the Stoics which Clement has transferred to
his representation of the Christian ideal, the most distinc-

---

[1] Str., vii. 10 [50]. [2] Ib., iv. 22 [114]; vii. 12 [69]. [3] Ib., iv. 22 [148], [149].
[4] Ib., iv. 22 [136]. [5] Harnack, 'History of Dogma,' vol. ii. p. 328.

tive, even if the most alien to the spirit of Christianity, is that of "apathy"—passionlessness. It would be easy to point out differences between the Stoic wise man and the gnostic in respect of the conceptions of freedom, wealth, beauty, kingship; but that has little bearing on the question of Clement's indebtedness in the matter of apathy. He not only has borrowed the word and the conception, but the theory of relation of other virtues to this fundamental virtue. By apathy or the passionless state he distinctly states that he does not mean mastery over the passions, but their extirpation.[1] Self-control is necessary, as man is by nature subject to passion.[2] It is the mark of the man who restrains the impulses that are contrary to right reason, or who restrains himself that he has no impulse contrary to right reason.[3] But even this absolute self-restraint is but a stage in the direction of that complete emancipation from passion which apathy implies.[4] The gnostic is subject to the passions, such as hunger, thirst, and the like, that exist for the continuance of the body,[5] but otherwise every element of passion must be cut out from the soul.[6] He who has not willed to root out the passions of the soul kills himself.[7] As God is passionless, it were unseemly that the friend of God should be engrossed with the restraint of passion.[8] As his Teacher is passionless, so by fellowship with the Beloved must the scholar become.[9] This condition was attained by the righteous men of old, who, while yet in the body, enjoyed passionlessness and imperturbability.[10] When the Lord says in the Psalm, "Ye are gods, . . . and sons of the Highest, all of you," he refers to the gnostics who have mastered the passions, who reject as far as possible everything that is

[1] Str., vi. 9 [74].　　[2] Ib., ii. 18 [81].　　[3] Ib., ii. 18 [89].
[4] Ib., vi. 13 [105]; iv. 22 [137], [189].　　[5] Ib , vi. 9 [71].　　[6] Ec. Pr., 31.
[7] Str., vii., 12 [72].　　[8] Ib., vi. 9 [76].　　Ib., vi. 9 [72]　　[10] Ib., iv. 7 [55].

human.[1]   Though the word "apathy" is not applied to
the apostles, it is implied that they possessed it after the
resurrection of Christ, as they are represented as not being
subject even to such movements of feeling as seem good,
but as abiding always in one unchangeable habit of discipline.[2]   And this unity of the moral life is one with the
condition of apathy, and is to be contrasted with the
varying condition that arises from the passionate attach-
ment to things material.[3]   Apart from these allusions,
nowhere is the virtue of apathy supported by any reference
to the teaching of the Scriptures.   In the chapter[4] in
which the apathy of the gnostic is exhibited in most detail,
there are allusions to the "tent," and to "putting to death
the desires," which suggest passages in the Epistles of St
Paul,[5] but there is no direct appeal to any passage of Scripture.   It has only scriptural basis so far as his distinction
of the carnal spirit from the ruling faculty may be held to
be based on the teaching of St Paul as to the enmity
between the flesh and the spirit with which he formally
connects it.[6]   This complete conquest of the passions
logically involved sinlessness; but though, indeed, he says
that the gnostic is bound to be sinless,[7] he expressly dis-
claims elsewhere the possibility of sinless perfection on the
part of any man.[8]   This illustrates the danger, in the case
of a writer like Clement, of putting a dogmatic construction
on an incidental phrase or phrases.   Clement's conception
of apathy, however, though it represents the same attitude
to the sensuous nature of man, differs from the Stoic
conception in respect of the love which was no less an
essential attribute of the gnostic, and in respect of the goal

[1] Str., ii. 20 [125].   [2] Ib., vi. 9 [71].   [3] Ib., iv. 23 [152], 22 [139].
[4] Ib., vi. 9   [5] 2 Cor. v 1; Col. iii 5.
[6] Str., vi. 16 [131.130]; Gal. v. 17.   [7] Str., iv. 9 [75]. Cf. vii. 3 [14]; Col. iii 5.
                [8] Str., iv. 21 [190], ii. 12 [70]; Pæd., iii. 12 [95].

of assimilation to God with the immediate vision of Him as its necessary concomitant. Of one object to this union of love with the passionless state Clement takes notice. "If close union with that which is good is accompanied by longing, how can he abide passionless who has a longing for that which is good?" Clement rejoins that love is free from longing or desire, because it is already in possession. "Such objectors do not know the divinity of love. For love is not a longing on the part of him who loves, but a loving union which restores the gnostic to the 'unity of the faith,' as he is independent of time and place. But he who by the agency of love is already among the things in which he shall be, has anticipated hope through knowledge, and does not long for anything, as he has as far as possible the very thing for which he longed."[1] The relation of apathy to knowledge and likeness to God is frequently noted. "Pure, therefore, in respect of bodily desires and of holy thoughts he wishes them to be who arrive at the full knowledge of God, in order that the ruling principle of the soul may have nothing spurious to stand in the way of its power. When he who shares in gnostic fashion in this holy quality devotes himself to contemplation, holding pure converse with God, he comes more immediately into the condition of passionless identity, so as no longer to have science and possess knowledge, but to be science and knowledge."[2] "When a man has transcended passion and desire, and loves the creation for the sake of the God and Creator of all, he will live gnostically. He has acquired the effortless habit of self-control, in accordance with the assimilation to the Saviour. He has formed into a unity knowledge, faith, love; he is one henceforward in judgment and truly spiritual; he is absolutely incapable of admitting the

---

[1] Str., vi. 9 [73].   [2] Ib., iv. 6 [40]

thoughts that arise from passion and desire, being perfected 'after the image' of the Lord by the Artificer Himself, a perfect man, worthy to be called 'brother' by the
Lord, being at once friend and son."[1]

The vision of God is the supreme felicity of the gnostic.
In some passages it is hard to say whether Clement is referring to the present earnest or the future realisation; but
the complete realisation is yet to be. He seeks to explain
in ordinary language what St Paul meant by "seeing God
face to face," what Jesus meant by the vision which He
promised to "the pure in heart," and when He spoke of the
"many mansions in His Father's house." It is indifferently
described as the soul's rest in God and as God's rest in the
soul. "Knowledge," it is said, "easily transplants a man
to that which is akin to the soul and divine and holy, and
by a light of its own carries him through the mystic stages
of progress until it restores him to the crowning place of
rest, having brought him who is pure in heart to behold
God face to face with science and apprehension."[2] "The
gnostic souls come to places even better than those that
preceded, no longer greeting the divine vision in mirrors or
by means of mirrors, feasting with loving souls on the
vision that is never sated. This is the 'apprehensive presentation' of the pure in heart."[3] It is characteristic of
Clement that just as he employs the Stoic term "apathy"
to express the goal of the gnostic on the ethical side, so
he uses the "apprehensive presentation" of the Stoics to
express the highest end of the gnostic on the intellectual
and spiritual side. By this term is meant, according to
Professor Edward Caird, "a presentation or idea which
grasps or enables the mind to grasp the object as it really
is."[4] This well expresses the thought of Clement. His

[1] Str , iii. 10 [69].   [2] Ib., vii. 9 [57].   [3] Ib., vii. 3 [12]. Cf. vii. 3 [10].
[4] 'Evolution of Religion in the Greek Philosophers,' vol. ii. p. 132.

conception of eternal life is "an end that knows no end,"[1] a goal that never reaches completion, a continuous advance, a vision of God ever growing in fulness and clearness, a fellowship with God ever growing in nearness and intensity. Can any conception be more ennobling and inspiring? At every stage in that life the soul's thirst after God will be satisfied; but, as God is infinite, and man though endowed with immortality is finite, eternal life must mean eternal progress, new revelations of God awakening ever-renewed activities, new insight into the unfathomable depths of the love of God in Christ, new glimpses of the beauty of Absolute Holiness.

To what extent is this ideal of the Christian life attainable here and now, or is it only to be attained in the future? Some of the features in the portrait of the gnostic are not his prerogative or exclusive goal. That his every thought may be a prayer, his every deed a sacrifice, his soul a temple, that the unseen and the future may be as real as, nay more real than, the things that lie at his feet, that by fixing his thought on spiritual things he may become detached from material things, is the aspiration of every Christian spirit.[2] But there are other elements in the delineation of which this cannot be said. The science of the gnostic becomes indefectible, being as much an essential attribute of him as weight in a stone.[3] By his knowledge he has all things potentially, though not numerically.[4] By knowledge itself he becomes a partaker of the divine will.[5] He has already become, as it were, out of the flesh and above the world.[6] Such an one has already attained the condition of being equal to the angels.[7] He is destined

[1] Str., ii. 22 [134]; vii. 10 [56].   [2] Cf. ib., vi. 12 [102]; vii. 12 [78]; iv. 23 [149].
[3] Ib., vii. 7 [46]; iv. 22 [139]   [4] Ib., vii. 7 [47].   [5] Ib., vii. 12 [78].
[6] Ib., vii. 14 [86].   [7] Ib., vi. 13 [105], vii. 12 [78]. Cf. Ec Pr., 37.

to be a god, and even now is being likened unto God.[1]
He is divine and holy, God-bearing and God-borne.[2] He
is a god moving about in the flesh.[3] Perfection takes
place when any one hangs on the Lord by means of faith
and love and knowledge, and ascends with Him to the
place where the God and Guardian of our faith and love
is.[4] He cleaves the heavens through his science, and
passing through the spiritual essences and every prin-
cipality and power, he lays hold of the highest thrones,
hastening to that alone which alone he knows.[5]

On the face of it, it would seem that this angelic being,
this God in human form, utterly unfettered by the flesh,
this knowledge incarnate, can, in the intensity of his gaze
and concentration on the unapproachable heights, have
little interest in men or in human affairs. But the duty
of teaching and moulding others is an essential mark of
the gnostic faculty.[6] "These three things our philosopher
holds fast: first, contemplation; in the second place, the
fulfilment of the Commandments; thirdly, the making of
good men. These in their union perfect the gnostic. If
any of these be wanting, the contents of the knowledge
are defective."[7] He who is likened to the Saviour is given
to saving.[8] In imitation of the divine purpose, he does
good to all who are willing to the best of his power.[9]
In respect of the beneficence of his teaching, he may be
called a living image of the Lord.[10] Thanksgiving and
prayer for the conversion of his neighbours are the work of
the gnostic.[11] In such service of humanity is true devoutness. The best harvest of the piety of the gnostic is that
of the men who have believed through his instrumentality

---

[1] Str , vii. 1 [3].   [2] Ib., vii. 13 [82].   [3] Ib., vii. 16 [101].
[4] Ib., vii 9 [56].   [5] Ib., vii. 13 [82]. Cf vi. 13 [105]   [6] Ib., vii. 1 [4].
[7] Ib , ii. 10 [46].   [8] Ib., vi. 9 [77].   [9] Ib., vii. 3 [16]
[10] Ib., vi. 9 [82].   [11] Ib., vii. 7 [41].

and have been brought into the way of salvation.[1] In such an atmosphere mysticism in the narrower sense of the word cannot live. "The mystic ideal," it has been said, "is not a life of ethical energy among mankind; it is the eye turned wholly inwards, the life spent in contemplation and devout communion."[2] To this type of mystic Clement did not belong. There is a mystic element in his ideal, as in every attempt to express in words the intercourse of the spirit of man with God, and he uses language which any mystic could appropriate; but nothing could be further from his mode of thought than any form of selfish ecstasy or the loss of self-consciousness in communion with God. If he "stands on earth on tiptoe,"[3] to use his own metaphor, he never loses contact with earth and with the needs of men. If, like Moses, he ascends the mountain to hold unbroken fellowship with God, he comes down transfigured indeed with the radiance of that fellowship, but with the Commandments in his hand. In the presence of this love for others mysticism loses its self-centred note, and apathy, save in the limited sense of self-conquest with a view to the higher service of others, becomes impossible. The moral ideal of Clement was an endeavour to harmonise elements that were discordant and antagonistic: formally, the victory lay with Stoicism; in reality, with Christianity.

To questions of social ethics Clement attached great importance. Of these the most urgent in Alexandria were the question of marriage and the relation of the Gospel to men of wealth.

Clement's conception of marriage was determined in part by his view of the relation of man to woman

---

[1] Str., vii. 1 ³.　　[2] Prof. Pringle-Pattison, "Mysticism" (Ency. Brit.)
[3] Pæd., i. 5 ³⁶.

generally, in part by his Hellenic birth and training, in part by the necessity of refuting the teaching of heretics, but by all these elements as modified and permeated by the teaching of Scripture, especially of Christ and the Apostles.

Man and woman have one God and one Tutor. They have a common life, a common grace, a common salvation, a common virtue and way of life.[1] Woman has the same nature as man, and should possess the same virtue. Virtue is not a matter of sex. Woman is to cultivate temperance and righteousness as well as man. Woman differs from man in the distinctive constitution of the body and the functions relating thereto; but in respect of the soul they are the same.[2] Women, therefore, are to philosophise in like manner as men, but men, unless they have become effeminate, should carry off the highest honours.[3] The Church is full of women who, like philosophers, have all their life made a "study" of death.[4] As it is a noble thing for a man to die for virtue and for freedom, so it is for a woman. For this is not an attribute peculiar to the nature of the male, but to the nature of the good.[5] Marriage is an equal yoke.[6] The difference of sex may show that marriage is natural; but the attitude of the Christian towards marriage must be influenced by consideration of the fact that the distinction of sex is earthly and temporal, and not spiritual and eternal.[7]

In accordance with the Greek way of thinking, Clement teaches that the primary end of marriage is the procreation of children as a duty that we owe to the State.

---

[1] Pæd , i 4[10].
[2] Ib., iv. 8[62].   Cf. Plato, Rep., 455 C.
[5] Ib., iv. 8[67].
[3] Str., iv. 8[59], [60].
[4] Str., iv. 8[58].
[6] Pæd., i. 4[10].
[7] Pæd., i. 4[10]; Str., iii. 12[87]; vi. 12[100].

We must by all means marry for our Fatherland, for the succession of children, and for the perfection of the world, as far as it lies with us. He quotes with approval the action of legislators like the Spartans and the view of philosophers with respect to the unmarried.[1] From a like point of view he commends marriage because of the intense sympathy of a wife in sickness and old age. The duty of marriage, however, is to be fulfilled in accordance with a fitting time and person and age, and with discrimination. The man and the woman should be in every respect alike, and the woman be fond of the man who loves her, not by force or necessity.[2]

In Alexandria there were two types of heretics who from different points of view had promulgated tenets equally subversive of Christian morals. There were those who in the name of liberty and knowledge taught the moral indifference of actions, and claimed that the more they abused the lower nature the more they honoured the higher, and that the ordinary laws of morality were not binding on those who reached the dignity of being "sons of the highest God" and "lords of the Sabbath," as they described themselves.[3] Of such Clement says that they acted not like kings but whipped curs.[4] A much more dangerous class were those who, partly from dogmatic motives, partly in the name of a professedly loftier moral ideal, maintained an unconditional asceticism and said that marriage was a sin, no better than fornication, that it derived its origin from the devil, and that we should not introduce into the world other unhappy beings and furnish food for death.[5] Those who say so, rejoins Clement, under the guise of self-control are ignorant and godless.[6] To say that marriage is sin is to say that

[1] Str., ii. 23 [139,149].   [2] Ib , ii. 23 [137].   [3] Ib., iii 4 [30].   [4] Ib.
[5] Ib , iii. 12 [84]; iii 6 [49], iii. 6 [45].   [6] Ib., iii. 6 [43], [60]

God, who instituted marriage, commanded what is sin.
Fornication and marriage are as far apart from one
another as the devil is from God.[1] Generation is holy.
By means of it the world subsists and the whole
economy of creation and salvation.[2]   To calumniate
generation is to calumniate the Lord and the virgin
who brought Him forth.[3]   In vainglorious fashion such
false teachers claim that they imitate the Lord, who
never married. They forget that He had His own bride,
the Church; that He was not a common man and needed
no helpmeet according to the flesh; that He had no need
to beget children to succeed Him, seeing that He was
and remained for ever the only Son of God.[4]   Those
who declare that marriage was permitted by the Law
but not by the New Covenant are in direct contradiction to the authoritative teaching of Paul, who approves of the marriage of bishop, presbyter, and deacon.[5]
If marriage were an obstacle to salvation, neither the
just men before the advent who married, nor those after
the advent who do so, will be saved, though they be
apostles.[6]   Monogamy is the true and only ideal of
marriage. The reasons for the temporary permission of
polygamy have passed away. A second marriage is permitted by Clement on grounds similar to those con-
ceded by St Paul; but he does not regard it as fulfilling
the ideal of the perfect way of life according to the
Gospel.[7] The conjugal relationship is to be divorced as
far as possible from all sensuous desire. It is to be
fulfilled in the spirit of one who is co-operating with
God.[8] It is to be carried out by those and after the
standard of those who are children not of desire but of

---

[1] Str., iii 12 [84].   [2] Ib., iii. 17 [103].   [3] Ib., iii. 17 [102].
[4] Ib., iii 6 [49].   [5] Ib., iii. 12 [90]; iii. 18 [108].   [6] Ib., iii. 12 [80].
          [7] Ib., iii. 12 [82]; iii. 2 [4].   [8] Pæd., ii. 10 [83].

will.[1] We are to bear witness to the Lord in all our life by piety in the soul, by purity in the body.[2] The wife is to be in all things a helpmeet to her husband. In all domestic trials she is to remember that God is her helper in her great task, her true comrade and Saviour both for the present and the future. She is to make Him her leader in every action, regard temperance and righteousness as her work, and make the love of God her goal.[3] Like the pattern wife in the Book of Proverbs, she should clothe both herself and her husband with finery of her own workmanship, by which all are made glad—the children for their mother, the husband for his wife, she for them, and all for God.[4] The happy marriage is not to be judged by wealth or beauty, but by virtue.[5] The married life was not to be put on a lower level than the life of celibacy. No doubt, generally speaking, it was a good thing "for the sake of the kingdom of heaven to cut oneself off" from all desire;[6] but on the other hand all desires were pure and holy in the sphere of the Lord.[7] "We pronounce chastity blessed in the case of those to whom God has given the gift, and we admire the stately dignity that belongs to a single marriage."[8] Each condition of life has its own distinctive ministries for the Lord.[9] The gnostic does not prefer children or marriage or parents to the love of God and righteousness in life; but he may marry.[10] In this he has the apostles for patterns. True, he eats and drinks and marries—not as if such things were the primary end of life, but regarding them as necessaries. The single life is not the best sphere for exhibiting true manhood. Such an one lacks the cares

---

[1] Str., iii. 7 ⁸³.   Cf. Pæd., ii. 10 ⁹⁰.   [2] Str., ii. 23 ¹⁴⁵.

[3] Ib., iv. 20 ¹²⁶, ¹²⁷.   [4] Pæd., iii. 11 ⁶⁷.   [5] Str., iv. 20 ¹²⁶.

[6] Ib., iii. 7 ⁵⁹.   [7] Ib., iii. 17 ¹⁰³.   [8] Ib., iii. 1 ⁴.

[9] Ib., iii. 12 ⁷⁹.   [10] Ib., vi. 12 ¹⁰⁰; vii. 12 ⁸⁰.

and temptations which family life brings. He has not
to master them, and at the same time to retain a firm
hold of the love of God. So far as progress towards his
own individual salvation is concerned, the celibate may
have the advantage; but in respect of the conduct of life
he is inferior to the married man, as the latter preserves
a faint image of the true Providence.[1] In accordance
with his interpretation of the teaching of Jesus, Clement
regards the marriage tie as indissoluble save by death.[2]
It is plain that the teaching of Clement agrees in all
essential points with the teaching of St Paul, but it is
modified and necessarily expanded by antagonism to the
heretical tendencies of his age.

The perennial question of the relations of wealth and
poverty occupies considerable space in the teaching of
Clement. His consideration of the general question was
called forth by the extravagance and luxury in Alexandria;
a special problem was forced upon him by the presence of
some men of wealth in the Church.

Like all moralists, Clement points out that material wealth
is not the highest form of riches. The truly rich man is he
who possesses what is worth most.[3] Righteousness is true
riches, and the Word is more precious than all treasure,
being the gift of God.[4] True wealth is to abound in virtuous
actions.[5] Like the wise man of the Stoics, the Christian
alone is rich. He who has the Almighty God, the Word, is
in need of nothing.[6] The good man can never be in want
so long as he keeps his confession secure towards God. He
can ask and receive from the Father of the universe what
he needs.[7] In respect of things necessary no one is ever
poor, and no man is ever disregarded by God.[8] He who
has attained to the condition of being in need of nothing

---

[1] Str., vii. 12 [70].   [2] Ib., ii. 23 [145].   [3] Pæd., ii. 6 [33].   [4] Ib., iii. 6 [36].
[5] Str., vi. 12 [99].   [6] Pæd., iii. 7 [39].   [7] Ib., iii. 7 [40].   [8] Ib , ii. 1 [14].

has no envy of riches.[1] He is pre-eminently rich who desires nothing because by reason of his knowledge of the good he possesses every good thing in superabundance.[2] The best wealth is poverty of desire,[3] and true poverty is not narrowness of means but increase of desire. Material wealth when not under proper control is an acropolis of wickedness.[4] It may be compared to a serpent which, unless grasped firmly and kept at a distance, will twist round the hand and bite, and which must be taken captive by the charm of the Word, if he who owns it is to be untouched by passion.[5] The moral danger may be avoided by the consideration that while all things have been made for the most part for the use of man, it is not good to use all things nor to use them always,[6] that such use must be sanctioned by reason[7] and must not exceed the limit of what is necessary,[8] and that they must be possessed and used without passionate and overmastering desire.[9] In carrying out these principles we must keep before us our own spiritual goal and our duty to others. Because we are journeying towards truth, we must be as unencumbered as possible.[10] Worldly possessions are not "our own," because we do not abide in them for ever, but are handed down in succession to others.[11] Properly used, wealth may be no barrier to, but a means of, spiritual progress. He that would ascend to the heavens " by violence " must carry the fair staff of beneficence. This is in accordance with the declaration of Scripture that " his own riches is the ransom of a man's soul "[12]—that is, if he be rich, he will be saved by distributing it.[13] It was

---

[1] Pæd., iii. 7 [40]. Cf. Stah., vol. iii. p. 223, fr. 46. [2] Str., vii. 3 [18].
[3] Pæd., ii. 3 [39]. [4] Ib., ii. 3 [38]. [5] Ib., iii. 6 [35].
[6] Ib., ii. 1 [14]. [7] Str., vii. 11 [62]. [8] Ib., vi. 12 [100].
[9] Ib., iv. 6 [31]; iv. 13 [94]. Cf. Ec. Pr., 47. [10] Pæd., ii. 7 [58].
[11] Str., iv. 13 [94]. [12] Prov. xiii. 8. [13] Pæd , iii. 7 [19].

in the power of God to make no one poor, but to do this would have extinguished beneficence to others and sympathy.[1] Self-sufficiency apportions something from itself to our neighbours.[2] This imparting to others must not be done in a vulgar or braggart fashion,[3] nor must it be indiscriminate but in accordance with justice and desert; for so to distribute is a form of the highest justice.[4] In his enforcement of the duty of liberality, and in denunciation of the extravagant fads of the rich, Clement uses language which suggests a Christian socialism. He refers to what he calls the astounding apology of women absolutely agape for jewels—"What God hath provided why may we not use? It is in my possession, why may I not enjoy it? For whom have these things been made, if not for us?" To use such language, says Clement, is to betray absolute ignorance of the will of God. Things which are necessary, such as water and air, He has supplied openly to all; things which are not necessary, like gold and pearls, He has concealed in the earth and water. To say and act so is to be out of harmony with the Scripture which calls upon us to "seek first the kingdom of God and His righteousness." Moreover, though it is true that "all things are in our power," it is also true that "all things are not expedient." Such selfish use is opposed to the divine constitution of human society. God Himself introduced the principle of "communion" into the race of men, when He first imparted of what was His own, and provided His own Word common to all men, having made all things for all. All things, therefore, are common, and it is not for the rich to claim a larger share. The saying, "What I have, and what I have in superfluity, why should I not daintily enjoy," is alike unworthy of man in himself and as a social being.

---

[1] Stah., vol. iii. p. 224, fr. 47.   [2] Pæd., ii. 1[7].
[3] Ib., iii. 6[34].   [4] Str., vii. 12[69].

Much more is it in accordance with love to say, "I have, why should I not impart to those who are in need?" For that is the true luxury, the expenditure which is "treasured up." God has given to us the liberty of use, but only so far as necessary, and He has willed that the use should be common. It is monstrous that one should be in luxury, while many are in penury.[1]

These principles touching the duties attaching to wealth in general are applied by Clement to the more pressing question of the attitude of the Gospel to men of wealth in the Church. As treated by him, it was not primarily an ethical or economical question, but one with a practical bearing, to be settled on exegetical and dogmatic grounds. He devoted to it a special homily under the title, "Who is the rich Man that is being saved,"[2] an exposition of a passage in the Gospel of St Mark.[3] The following is an outline of the leading points:—

Those who basely flatter the rich are at once guilty of impiety and treacherous to the true wellbeing of the rich themselves, by inflaming their malady instead of seeking to heal it and helping them to the attainment of salvation.[4] The saying of the Saviour about the rich man and the eye of the needle has caused some only to cling the more closely to this life as if they had no hope of true life, while others have failed to use their wealth with a view to its attainment.[5] Accordingly, he who loves the truth has a twofold duty to the rich, first to expound the Word so as to drive away their groundless despair, and then to show how the man may secure the hope and the prize of the victor in the conflict.[6] The sayings of the Saviour are not to be understood in a carnal sense, but we must seek to penetrate into their inmost meaning[7] It was natural for Him who was

[1] Pæd , ii. 12 [119], [120].   [2] Τίς ὁ σωζόμενος πλούσιος   [3] Mark x. 17-31.
[4] c., I.   [5] Ib., 2.   [6] Ib , 3.   [7] Ib., 5.

M

the Life to be questioned about life. The crowning lesson was to know God; for only in full knowledge of Him was life.[1] Hence the young man was exhorted to know God, and then to understand, as one trained under the law, the newness and the necessity of the grace and mission of the Saviour, who alone could give the life which he lacked, though he had fulfilled all the requirements of the law.[2] "Sell that thou hast," said the Saviour. That does not mean that he was to cast away his property, but to banish from his soul the excessive desire for it, the morbid excitement concerning it, all the things that choke the seed of true life. To renounce wealth save for life is no great thing. Otherwise the poorest would alone possess eternal life. Many men of old before the coming of the Saviour gave up their possessions, but only increased their arrogance and vanity thereby. Though released from the load of wealth, the desire for it remained. Moreover, he that is in want of the necessaries of life has no leisure for higher things.[3] Much better to be free from such anxiety, and so be able to help others and fulfil the teaching of the Lord. Who is to care for the hungry and the homeless if every one is destitute? The Lord did not command Zaccheus and Matthew to give up their wealth, but only enforced its just use. If He were to command us to give up our wealth, and at the same time to assist the needy, were not that most irrational?[4] Wealth is like a tool which may be used skilfully or the reverse, may be a servant of righteousness or unrighteousness. Its nature is to serve, not to rule. In itself it is neither good nor bad. The blame for misuse rests with the mind of man. What is required is not the suppression of our possessions but of the passions which prevent the better use of them.[5] Better to get rid of the

[1] c., 6, 7.   [2] Ib., 8-10.   [3] Ib., 11, 12.   [4] Ib., 13.   [5] Ib., 14.

passions within the soul, by the removal of which wealth may be of good service, than to get rid of the wealth which is outside of the soul and leave the passions the more violent because of the lack of means to satisfy them. External things are not injurious in themselves. Wealth of passions is death-bringing; their destruction is salvation. He who uses God's gifts for the salvation of men, who does not carry about his possessions in his soul and circumscribe his life within them, is pronounced blessed by the Lord. He is not the rich man who is incapable of gaining life.[1] But the man who bears his wealth in his soul, who carries about not a heart but a mine or land, can have no desire nor anxiety about the kingdom of heaven. "Where the mind of a man is, there is his treasure also." As treasure may be good or bad, so there is a wealth of good things and a wealth of bad things. So spiritual poverty is blessed; but wretched are the poor who have no share in God and still less in human possessions.[2] Salvation does not depend on external things, but on the excellence of the soul, nor has it any relation to beauty or strength of body. A man though destitute may be drunken with lusts; a rich man may be poor in sensual indulgence.[3] To sell what we have is not to exchange one kind of wealth for another, but to introduce into the soul a different kind of wealth, which makes man as God and ministers eternal life, treasure in the heavens.[4] The wealthy man who had been trained under the law did not understand how the same man could be both poor and rich, and went away downcast, himself making what was difficult a thing impossible. For he might have withdrawn from material wealth to that which was intellectual, and learned to use indifferent things as one who had set out for eternal life. The alarm of the disciples could not be due to the

[1] c., 15, 16.   [2] Ib., 17.   [3] Ib., 18.   [4] Ib., 19.

scanty possessions which they had abandoned, but sprang rather from the consciousness that they had not entirely laid aside their passions. For it is to passionless and pure souls that salvation belongs.[1] "That which is impossible among men is possible with God." The man toiling in his own strength effects nothing, but with the power of God he succeeds. Not that God saves men against their will. For the kingdom of God is for the men of violence who snatch life from Him by force.[2] To leave kindred for the sake of Christ means that if such stand in the way of our higher life, the fleshly relationship must be broken up because of the spiritual enmity.[3] Consider the matter as a lawsuit. Listen first to the father who begat thee, telling thee not to obey the law of Christ.   Listen then to the Saviour who re-generated thee, who gives Himself as bread.   Then give thy vote for thine own salvation[4] Canst thou gain the mastery over wealth ?   Christ does not drive thee away from it.   Art thou worsted by it ?   Fling it away, flee from it.   So is it with the possessions of " lands and wealth and houses and brethren, *with persecutions*."   If wealth bring thee persecution from without or the more maddening form of persecution of lusts within the soul, leave it, get rid of the persecution, choose before all the Saviour, the Prince of endless life. Salvation is in no way fenced off from the rich, if they are willing to submit to the yoke of the commandments of God. What wrong does a man who by thrift before his conversion has gathered a competency ?   Or, if God, who allots for-tune to all, has placed him in a rich home, is he not still less to be blamed ?   If because of his involuntary birth in wealth he has been banished from life, he has been wronged by God.   If wealth be the purveyor and ally of death, why should it ever have sprung up from the earth at all ?[5]   The

---

[1] c., 20.   [2] Ib., 21.   [3] Ib., 22.   [4] Ib., 23   [5] Ib., 24-26.

well-to-do must not be negligent of their own salvation as if they had been condemned beforehand, nor cast their wealth into the sea, but learn how to use it and obtain life. To this end the Teacher says that the greatest of the commandments is "to love the Lord thy God." With good reason : for He is our Father, and He loved us first. The second, but not the less, is, "to love thy neighbour as thyself." What neighbour means, He shows in the Samaritan. The Samaritan is no other than Christ Himself. We are to love Him equally with God ; and He loves Christ Jesus who does His will. What one does for a disciple the Lord accepts as for Himself.[1] We are urged to "make friends by means of the mammon of unrighteousness."[2] A possession which a man regards as absolutely his own is by nature unrighteous ; but from this unrighteousness we may effect a righteous and saving deed. We are not to wait to be importuned, but to seek out those who are to be benefited and are worthy disciples of the Saviour. The reward is an eternal tabernacle.[3] Surely a divine marketing ! With such reward in view, supplicate the poor to receive ; be fearful lest they treat thee as unworthy of honour. Not that such rewards are the gift of the benefited, but are given by the Lord because of His friendship for them. You may err as to "the friends of God." Better to benefit the unworthy for the sake of the worthy than by being on your guard against the less good neglect some who are loved by God. To all who are enrolled among the disciples of God open your heart, paying no heed to the body, or outward estate, or appearance. Choose with thy wealth pious old men, orphans beloved of God, widows armed with meekness, men adorned with love, as guards for thy body and soul.[4] They are for you effective soldiers, trustworthy

[1] c., 27-30.   [2] Luke xvi. 9.   [3] c., 31.   [4] Ib., 32-34.

guards. They minister to you, as needed, encouragement, sympathy, teaching, warning, counsel, without hypocrisy or flattery.[1] He who laid down His life for us demands that we owe our lives to our brethren. Thus the rich man may use his possessions so as to avoid the reproach of wealth and the hindrance which it offers in the way of life.[2] The man who is a swaggerer, powerful and rich, should set over himself some man of God as trainer and pilot. Let him reverence at least one man, fear at least one man, listen at least to the bold speech of one man. Such a man will keep sleepless vigil for the rich man, interceding for him with God.[3]

Whatever may be thought of this setting up of a *quasi* spiritual director or external conscience, whatever reserve we must maintain with regard to the validity of the quaint exegesis on which his conclusions are partly based, the moderation of his views on wealth, its nature, its responsibility, and use, commands our admiration. His bias towards asceticism was restrained by the soundness of his judgment. His love of allegorical exegesis did not weaken his moral perceptions. He glorifies neither wealth as such nor poverty as such, but recognises that poverty no less than riches has spiritual difficulties of its own.

In the Cambridge series of 'Texts and Studies,' published in 1897, Barnard published a fragment of what he suggested might be a part of the lost treatise that bore the title, 'Exhortation to Patience — to the Newly - Baptised.'[4] The suggestion is accepted by Stahlin,[5] and there can be little doubt as to its genuineness. As it stands, it is almost entirely taken up with practical counsels in complete harmony with the teaching of Clement; as it is only a frag-

---

[1] c., 35.   [2] Ib., 37-39.
[3] Ib., 41-42. At the close of the Homily Clement tells the well-known story of John the Apostle and the young robber.
[4] Eus., H. E., vi. 13.   [5] Vol. iii. pp. lx. and 221.

ment, we do not know whether any specifically dogmatic instruction preceded. It shows how simple and direct Clement could be when the occasion demanded. Alike because of its interest, as a specimen of an address to catechumens in the end of the second century, of its brevity, and of its direct bearing on the subject of this chapter, I quote it in full.

"Cultivate restfulness in words and deeds, and likewise in tongue and gait. Avoid headstrong vehemence. For so will the mind continue steadfast, and, untroubled by vehemence, will not become enfeebled, nor shallow in perception, nor dull in vision. Nor will it be overcome by gluttony; but it will be overcome if anger boils, and it will be overcome by the other passions, being exposed as a ready prey to them. For the mind must gain mastery over the passions, sitting aloft as on a quiet throne, with vision fixed on God. Be not swift to wrath in respect of the passions, nor sluggish in words, nor over-hesitating in thy movements, to the end that thy restfulness may be adorned with a fair symmetry, and thy bearing appear a divine and sacred thing. But be on guard against the tokens of arrogance, the haughty mien, the head carried high, and the stride of the feet delicate and high-stepping. Let thy words to those thou meetest be gentle, and thy greetings sweet, and let there be reverence towards women, with the eye turned to the ground. And speak all things with circumspectness, and return a useful answer, adapting thy voice to the use of the hearers until it shall be heard, not eluding the hearing of those present by reason of too great lowness, nor deafening them by too great loudness. And take care that thou never speakest anything which thou hast not considered and thought on beforehand. Nor cast down thy words rashly and interrupt the words of another; for it is necessary to hear and converse in turn, apportioning a time

for speech and silence. But learn gladly and teach un-
grudgingly, neither concealing wisdom from others from
envy, nor turning aside from instruction from a sense of
shame. Give way to thy elders as to thy fathers; honour
the servants of God; lead the way in wisdom and virtue.
Do not wrangle with thy friends, nor scoff nor laugh at
them. Falsehood and fraud and insolence strenuously
avoid. Endure with fair words the haughty and the in-
solent, as beseems a meek and magnanimous man. And
let all thy affairs be dependent on God, both words and
deeds; and refer all things to Christ, and often turn thy
soul to God, and lean thy thought on the power of Christ,
as though in some haven, through the divine light of the
Saviour, it were resting from all talk and action. And by
day often give a share of thine own thought to men, but
to God as often as possible, both by night and day; for let
not much sleep deprive thee of thy prayers and praises
to God. For prolonged sleep is like to death. Become
always a partner with Christ, who caused the divine ray to
shine down from heaven; let Christ be to thee a continuous
and unceasing joy. Relax not the tone of the soul by
feasting and indulgence in wine, but regard as sufficient
what is useful for the body. And be not the first to hasten
to meals before the time of supper arrives; but let the
supper be bread, and let there be set forth the seeds of the
earth and the fruits of the trees. And go to thy food with
steady step, and not showing a furious gluttony. And be
not an eater of flesh nor a lover of wine, unless when some
sickness calls for this remedy. But in place of pleasure in
such things, choose thy joys in divine words and hymns
which are supplied by the wisdom of God, and let heavenly
thought' always lead thee heavenwards. Give up anxious
cares about the body, encouraged by hopes that rest in God,
because He will provide for thee things necessary, sufficient

food for life, and covering for the body, and protection against the winter cold. For to thy King belongs the whole earth and all the things that spring up out of it. As the bodies of His own servants are His members, He tends them with surpassing care, as His holy places and sanctuaries. Wherefore be not afraid of violent ailments, nor shrink from the onset of age, which must be expected as the years pass. For also the sickness will cease when with whole-hearted resolution we keep His commandments. Knowing these things, make thy soul strong against disease, be of good courage like a man in the racecourse, equipped in the best way for enduring toils with unflagging strength. Crush not thy soul altogether with sorrow if a sickness come upon thee and weigh thee down, or any other distress befall thee; but nobly oppose thy thought to the hardships, offering thanksgivings to God even in the midst of distresses; for He has wiser thoughts than men, and such as it is not possible nor easy for men to find. Have pity on those who suffer wrong, and ask assistance from God in the case of men; for He will grant grace to his friend who asks it, and will provide assistance to those who have suffered wrong. For He wills to make His own power known to men, that having come to full knowledge they may return to God and enjoy eternal blessedness, when the Son of God shall appear restoring good things to His own."

The defects in Clement's representation of the Christian ideal lie on the surface. The merits in view of the circumstances of the time are not less conspicuous. The fundamental defect lay in the very conception of a twofold ideal, irrespective of the principles on which the line of demarcation was based. Many of the features are but half-truths or the exaggeration of one side of truth. The truth in the outline is, that men are unequal in spiritual apprehension. The exaggeration is, that the inequality is as absolute as he seems sometimes to assume, even if this furnished a critical dividing-line. In rescuing the word "gnosis" from the degradation which had fallen upon it, he has not escaped the exclusiveness that was all but inseparable from its use. He has not quite got rid of the distinction of different classes of men derived from the Gnosticism which he is combating; though, by enforcing individual liberty as the true ground of distinction, he has got rid of the most pernicious element in it, that which attributed this classification to nature, and therefore conceived it as arbitrary. Notwithstanding the rigour of some of his precepts and the prominence given to the passionless state in relation to all outward and transitory things, and the ascetic spirit which breathes in some allusions to the body, the attitude of Clement to the world is on the whole genial and sympathetic. So far as it was unsympathetic, it was determined in large measure by antagonism to the extravagance and luxury around him, and in part by his acceptance as authoritative of some sayings of Jesus and St Paul without any endeavour to weaken the absoluteness of their claims. To him the unconditional alternatives of Jesus were no paradoxical way of enforcing a precept, but a law to be fulfilled in the letter and the spirit. The avoidance of all conformity with the world and its ideals was to him a categorical imperative of universal validity. If he treats the body at times as the enemy of the spirit, if he protests against the devotion to games in Alexandria as opposed to a grave view of life and its responsibilities, if he puts the emphasis rather on the saying, "all things are not expedient," rather than on "all things are lawful," is he on these grounds disloyal to the teaching of St Paul? If on one occasion he speaks of the world as a "wilderness," and represents the gnostic as using this world only as a temporary stopping-place, is he alone in this, or is there any religious literature of any age in which

kindred thoughts do not find expression ? If, in consideration of the vice and luxury around him, he thinks rather of
the suppression than the transfiguration of natural desire,
shall we forget that a rigid asceticism, if not the most
effective weapon in the long-run, is the best immediate
weapon with which to combat moral corruption ? That in
his ethical fervour he condemned some things in themselves
innocent and unimportant, and showed at times a lack of
moral perspective, is in no way surprising. Much more
surprising is the general sanity of his outlook on life,
especially on the social side. He sanctioned, nay, welcomed
all forms of culture in which no irreligious or non-ethical
element was involved. He had little sympathy with Greek
art; for, historically, its growth had been coincident with
error and was its glorification, and it had been for the most
part the ally of the paganism which it was his life-work to
undermine and overthrow. But while condemning its misuse, he praises the art itself.[1] He loved the joyousness and
beauty of outward nature. He objected to no music save
that which weakened the moral fibre. As in his attitude to
the world generally, so in his conception of the duty of the
Christian in the face of persecution, and in all questions of
social ethics, he is marked by great soberness. Like his
own gnostic, he sought to harmonise the intellectual, ethical,
and mystical elements in the Christian faith, and to assign
to each its true place, to weld into a unity elements which
God hath joined together — faith, knowledge, love — but
which man has often put asunder ; and to exhibit Christian
life not as a congeries of inconsistent and unrelated sections,
but as a unity in relation to self, to society, and to God.

[1] Prot., iv. 57.

LECTURE VI.

IF the foundation of a true Christian theology be a right conception of God, and that of a true Christology a right conception of the person of Christ, our attitude towards Scripture must determine in large measure the foundation of both doctrines. The fundamental question is, Whether we are to regard Scripture as primarily the record of man's interest in God or of God's interest in man, the record of the efforts of man's spirit "to feel after Him and find Him," or of the Spirit of God entering into fellowship with man to satisfy the longing which He Himself has implanted? If the former conception be adopted as primary, the Scriptures are only of interest in the history of religion, and as exhibiting the genius of the Jewish race in this lofty province of human inquiry; and all question of authority must be eliminated, and the assertion of their inherent fitness for man's nature and needs be not merely their highest but their only prerogative and claim to our allegiance. If the latter conception be adopted, we have a revelation of and from God, truth manifested through human spirits and of necessity limited by the material forms in which it has been embodied, but none the less His truth, and as such rightfully claiming to furnish an authoritative rule for faith and life. Clement lays down without any reservation the unconditional authority of Scripture and of the whole of what

he held to be Scripture. It is true that he uses the words
" prophet," " inspiration," and " Scripture " in a wider as
well as in a more restricted sense. He designates the Sibyl
as a prophetess,[1] and quotes sayings of hers as illustrating
and confirming the teaching of a pure theism as opposed to
idolatry. He speaks of prophets of the Egyptians as well
as of the Greeks in an incidental fashion without quoting
any prophecy from them.[2] But for the latter usage may he
not claim the authority of St Paul, in connection with whose
designation he himself applies the word ?[3] He ascribes
inspiration to Plato as well as to an Epicurean.[4] But he
draws a clear line of demarcation between such prophecy
or inspiration and that exhibited in the Scriptures. For
while, in accordance with his theory of theft as well as
with his view of universal inspiration, he is ever seeking
in the philosophy and poetry of the Greeks for analogies
to the truths of Scripture, and quotes sayings which,
because of the truth expressed or because of its harmony
with the Scriptures, he regards as divinely inspired, he does
not consider such writings as authoritative as a whole, and
limits their inspiration to the particular citation which
he makes. It is otherwise with the Scriptures. These
derive their validity from the authority of the Almighty.[5]
The prophets of the Almighty God were the instruments
of the divine voice.[6] Not one tittle of the Scriptures
shall pass away, because they are the utterances of

---

[1] Prot., ii. 27 ; ib., viii. 77.   [2] Str., i. 14 62 ; i. 15 71 ; i. 14 59.

[3] Ib , i. 14 59. Cf. Tit. i. 12.

[4] Ib., v. 14 138 ; i 8 42. In Str., iv. 1 3 he says of his own work that it shall be
written ἣν θεὸς γε ἐθέλῃ καὶ ὅπως ἂν ἐμπνέῃ. But to transform this natural
expression of a reverent spirit into a claim for inspiration in the scriptural sense,
or to regard it as proving a loose conception of inspiration, is surely meticulous
criticism. It is true, also, that he uses the word " γραφή " for a written composition, including his own (Str., i. 1 4 ; iv. 1 4. Cf. i. 1 7) ; but that he uses it
constantly in the technical sense there can be no doubt.

[5] Str., iv. 1 2.   [6] Ib , vi. 18 168. Cf. ib., i. 21 135.

the mouth of the Lord—the Holy Spirit.[1]   If the Platonic saying be true that he who declares what takes
place in his own family is to be believed, shall we not
believe what God spake by His Son in the Old and the
New Testaments?[2]   For the determination of any controversy between him and the adherents of heresy, the
bringing forward of a passage from Scripture is final.[3]
God spake at one time by "the pillar and the bush";
thereafter, as flesh of man is more precious than such,
by the mouth of the prophets. Now the Lord Himself
has spoken, putting man's unbelief to shame.[4]   So far as
the Old Testament is concerned, that authority belongs not
only to the Hebrew but to the Greek translation.   The
translators were so guided by the Spirit of God that they
agreed in a miraculous manner in thought and expression,
and the Greek translation was such that the Hebrew
prophecy became a prophecy in the Greek tongue.[5]   In
the most literal sense of the word the Scriptures were given
by inspiration of God, and to this is due their authority.
For the same reason they form a unity with entire harmony
of contents.   This unity, as Clement conceived it, was the
unity of a common authorship, with one end in view, the
salvation of men.   All is the work of God; all therefore
must be worthy of Him from whom it came, and perfectly
harmonious in all its parts.   A human medium was required, but that in no way affected either its authority
or unity.   The impossibility of conflict between the different parts is with Clement an axiomatic presupposition;
and he often seeks to set aside apparent contradictions,
as well as to find points of analogy and contact.   One

---

[1] Prot , ix [82].   [2] Str., v. 13 [84.5].   [3] Ib., iv. 26 [170].   [4] Prot., i. [8].
[5] Str., i. 22 [148]. That Clement was ignorant of Hebrew seems probable from
his mistakes in regard to Hebrew names.   For what may be said to the contrary,
see 'Jewish Quarterly Review' for 1893.

God was truly proclaimed by the Law and the Prophets and the blessed Gospel.[1] The Son will keep the things which the Father commanded. It is the same One who is lawgiver and evangelist, and He is never at conflict with Himself.[2] The Covenants—the Old and the New—are two in respect of time and name, but one in respect of power, having been provided by the One God through the Son. The Apostle declares the one salvation which has been perfected from Prophecy to Gospel through one and the same Lord.[3] Of this unity Clement gives a somewhat quaint illustration, which may be interpreted either as showing his ever-present consciousness of this unity, or as an indication of his desire to enforce it. When the Almighty God of the universe first gave the Law by the Word, there appeared to Moses a godlike vision in the form of light in a thorny plant. When the Word had brought to a close His legislative work and His sojourning on earth, He was again mystically crowned with thorns. By this He summed up at the close what had been the first stage of His ancient descent, and showed that the whole had been the work of one Power.[4] Thus Prophecy and Gospel agree, and the Apostle agrees with the Gospel.[5] The Apostle is confirmed by the prophetic word.[6] The Law given through Moses and that given through the Apostles were both used by the Word for the instruction of humanity.[7] Paul is recent in point of time, as he was in his prime immediately after the Ascension of the Lord; but his writing depends on the Old Covenant, deriving breath and expression from it. For faith in Christ and the knowledge of the Gospel are the

[1] Str., iv. 1 [2]; iv. 13 [91]; ii. 23 [147].
[2] Ib., iii 12 [88]. Cf. ii. 23 [147]; iii. 10 [70]; iii. 11 [76].
[3] Ib., ii. 6 [29] (Rom. i. 17).   [4] Pæd., ii. 8 [75].   [5] Str., vii. 16 [95]; 3 [14]
[6] Str., v. 14 [35].   [7] Pæd., iii 12 [94].

interpretation of the Law and its fulfilment.[1]　All the Epistles prove the logical relation of the Law to the Gospel.[2]　There cannot be even an appearance of conflict between a metaphorical saying of St Paul and a metaphor in the Law; and the former must be so interpreted as to be in perfect harmony with the latter.[3]　In the time of Clement the objections to this unity mainly took the form of an attack on the religious conceptions and the practical ethics of the Old Testament.　The attack on the former came from the Gnostics, who denied the unity of the Testaments, and held, on the contrary, that the conceptions of these as to God were so irreconcilable that they could only be explained by the hypothesis of their having derived their origin from different Gods,—the New Testament from One whose essential attribute was goodness, the Old Testament from One whose essential attribute was justice.　Clement, as we have seen, denies that these attributes were antagonistic, and in defence of the Law, as of divine authority, appeals to its beneficent results.　The greatest and most perfect good for man is the transformation from evil-doing to well-doing, and that is effected by the Law.[4]　The fact that it involves penalties is no argument against its perfect goodness.　Nor is the appeal to fear any ground for denying the divine origin of the Law.　The nature of fear as a moral motive is determined by the persons or objects which are feared.　On this ground, as well as by its results, the fear of the Law is justified.　It is a fear of God, and it is determined by His nature.　As He is passionless, so there is no element of passion in this fear; it is the falling away from God that is feared.[5]　The objects of this fear are not things such as poverty, disease, and the like, but things truly evil, vice in all its forms, and death, not the

---

[1] Str , iv 21 [134].　　　[2] Ib , iii, 12 [86].　　　[3] Pæd , i. 6 [35].

[4] Str., i. 27 [173].　　　　　[5] Ib., ii 8 [39,40].

death which dissolves the union between soul and body,
but that which dissolves the union between the soul and
truth.[1] The fear, whose fruit is abstinence from evil,
cannot but be good.[2] That cannot be an irrational affection which is the result of a commandment given by the
Logos.[3] If the Law were given to be "a tutor unto
Christ," can it be anything but good?[4] Some heretics appealed to the saying of St Paul, "By the Law is the knowledge of sin," arguing that that was a condemnation of the
Law. But this only showed their misunderstanding of the
Apostle, who did not say that sin derived its existence from
the Law, but only that the Law manifested it.[5] In proof
of the humanitarian character of the Law, in close dependence on Philo, he adduces many details. He points to the
laws against usury, to the payment of daily wages, to the
provision for the poor, which was based on the principle
that the love of men to the Creator must manifest itself
in love to our fellow-men, to the law enforcing humanity
toward beasts, which by the inculcation of kindness
toward creatures which were not of the same genus
emphasised a fortiori the duty of kindness towards those
of the same genus; and to the generous features in the
regulations affecting those of a different nationality.[6] On
all grounds, therefore, the Law and the Gospel are to be
regarded as the energy of the one Lord, and the same
God is demonstrated to be good from the beginning to
the end.[7]

As the Scriptures form the short road to salvation,[8] we
might have expected that Clement would have taught that
the road was easily traversed and accessible to all; but,
on the contrary, in harmony with the spirit of his time, at

---

[1] Str , ii. 7²⁴.   [2] Ib , ii. 8³⁹.   Cf. Ec. Pr., 20.   [3] Str., ii. 7³².
[4] Ib., ii 7⁴⁵.   [5] Ib , ii. 7³¹.   [6] Ib., ii. 16⁷⁸,⁹⁵.
            [7] Ib , i 27¹⁷⁴.   [8] Prot., viii. 77.

least in Alexandria, he maintains that the most distinctive
characteristic of Scripture was its symbolic and parabolic
character. This symbolic feature was in harmony with the
deepest wisdom in all religions and all philosophies. It
was a characteristic of the Egyptians, who did not intrust
their mysteries indiscriminately.[1] It was a characteristic
of the Greeks, who made extensive employment of the art
of concealment.[2] It was a characteristic of the Pythagoreans.[3] Not only did representatives of the most
intellectual class adopt this method, but such of the
barbarians who had devoted themselves in any measure
to philosophy had prosecuted the symbolic method.[4] In
brief, all who had theologised (thought on the deep
things of God) had veiled the first principles of things,
and transmitted the truth in enigmas, and symbols, and
allegories, and metaphors.[5] That being so, it was not
unnatural that the barbarian philosophy should prophesy
in occult fashion and by means of symbols.[6] And this
may be proved from the language of Scripture itself.
That the holy word was hidden is shown by David.
" He made darkness His hiding-place, His pavilion round
about Him darkness of waters, thick clouds of the skies.
At the brightness before Him, thick clouds passed, hail-
stones and coals of fire." That is, words are sent down
from God which to the gnostic are transparent and re-
splendent as hail, but dark to the multitude, like extinguished coals which, unless lighted up and kindled anew,
will not produce fire or light.[7] In like manner, the Spirit
says by Isaiah, " I will give to thee treasures, dark, secret."[8]
The Lord and His disciples used parables in accordance
with the express statements of Scripture itself.[9] Nay, the

---

[1] Str., v 4[20] ; v. 7[41].   [2] Ib., v. 8[45].   [3] Ib., v. 8[40]

[4] Ib., v. 8[44].   [5] Ib., v. 4[22].   [6] Ib., v. 8[51].

[7] Ib., vi. 15[116].   [8] Ib., v. 4[22].   [9] Ib., vi. 15[127]; v. 4[26].

Saviour Himself put the seal on these things when He said, "To you it is given to know the mysteries of the kingdom of heaven"; and by the Parable of the Leaven He showed the like conception of concealment.[1] To the like effect said the noble Apostle, "We speak the wisdom of God hidden in a mystery."[2] On what grounds is this symbolic feature of the Scriptures to be explained or defended? The method of symbolic interpretation contributes to a right theology, and to the display of intelligence and the practice of brevity and the exhibition of wisdom.[3] These are mainly intellectual gains. But there are other and higher grounds. One main reason is that we may cultivate the spirit of investigation and always keep vigil with a view to the discovery of the saving word.[4] The Scriptures desire the true theology to be the property of those who often approach them and have made proof of them in respect of faith. Like fruits shining faintly through water, or like figures which are invested with new features when seen through a veil, the truth gains in grandeur when it is veiled.[5] Clement seems to regard it as a defect if a passage of Scripture could only be interpreted in one way, and approves of truth in symbol because of the great diversities of possible interpretation. The Scriptures are not to be conceived as characterised by a bald uniformity.[6] Because truth does not appertain to all, it is veiled in many modes; the light only arises on those who are initiated unto knowledge, who seek the truth for the sake of love.[7] To seek out the logical coherence of the divine teaching calls for the keenest exercise of the faculty of reasoning.[8]

---

[1] Str., v. 12 80.   [2] Ib., v. 4 25 (1 Cor. ii. 7).   [3] Ib., v. 8 46.
[4] Ib., vi. 15 126.   [5] Ib., v. 9 85.
[6] Ib., i. 28 179: οὐ γὰρ δὴ μία Μύκονος ἡ πᾶσα πρὸς νόησιν γραφή.
[7] Ib., vi 15 129.   [8] Ib., i. 28 179.

In conjunction with this symbolic conception of Scripture, Clement held the theory of verbal inspiration. In
controverting the views of Tatian, he emphasises the fact
that in Genesis the reading is not simply θεός, but that by
the addition of the article ὁ the Almighty is indicated.[1]
So, too, of a passage in the New Testament, "The Law
was given through (διά) Moses, not by (ὑπό) Moses, but by
the Word, and through Moses, His servant." Wherefore
also, it became temporary. But eternal "grace and
truth were through Jesus Christ." Mark the expressions
of Scripture. Of the Law it is only said, "it was given";
but truth, being the grace of the Father, is the eternal
work of the Word, and it is no longer said "to be given,"
but "to have come into being" through Jesus Christ,
without Whom nothing came into being.[2] The exact
grammatical sense would, therefore, seem to be the
foundation on which the symbolic structure is to be
reared. The interpretation of Scripture, however, was
subject to certain general principles which to some extent defined the lines on which allegorical exegesis had
to proceed. Restrictions were based on the nature of
God from whom the Scriptures came, on the contents
of the Scriptures as a whole, on the tradition that was
the property of the Church, and the ecclesiastical norm
of teaching. Scripture being of divine origin, it must be
interpreted in a manner perfectly fitting and appropriate
to the Lord and the Almighty God.[3] It is obvious that
this principle if primarily a principle of restriction, as it
appears from the context, was capable of being developed
into a principle of expansion of the allegorical method,
and even of justifying its use. For, in the absence of
any idea of historical development, it logically led to the
elimination or the explaining away of much in the earlier
books of the Old Testament. Scripture being a whole

---

[1] Pæd , iii 12 81.   [2] Ib., i. 7 60.   [3] Str., vii. 16 96.

and a unit, the analogy of Scriptural usage had to be
maintained in order to preserve unbroken harmony in all
its parts.[1]   The tradition derived from Christ Himself
was a further restrictive factor.   He who gave the Law
was also the exegete of the Law, He who interpreted
the bosom of the Father.[2]   The Saviour taught the apostles,
and from them has been transmitted to us the unwritten
interpretation of the written Scriptures.[3]   The teaching
of the Church limited the range of the operation of
the allegorical method by compelling the exegete to keep
in view the theological doctrines to which its application should conform.   This was emphasised by Clement
specially in his refutation of heretical opinions.   He accuses the heretics of interpreting Scripture in accordance
with their cosmical conceptions, of doing violence to the
plain meaning of Scripture by severing passages from the
context, by attributing to God what was quoted by the
prophet as the murmuring of the people,[4] and by giving
an allegorical exposition of what was literal and a literal
exposition of what was allegorical.[5]   He passes much
acute criticism on their method of procedure; but in the
advocacy of his own position he has recourse to much
perverse interpretation of a similar kind; and in his belief
in the symbolic theory he propounds explanations that
are purely fantastic, as, in spite of the limitations which
I have noted, they could not fail to be.   In his eagerness,
for example, to prove that the highest wisdom was not
given to all, he explains Colossians i. 28, which was
directed against such limitation, in a manner contrary to
its natural meaning.   By "admonishing every man, and
teaching every man in all wisdom," the divine Apostle
did not mean "every man absolutely"—for in that case
no one would have been unbelieving—nor did he mean

---

[1] Str., vii. 16 96.   [2] Ib , i 26 169.   [3] Ib., vi. 7 61 ; iv. 21 130.
          [4] Ib., iii. 4 38.   [5] Ib., iii. 11 76 ; iii. 12 86.

every believer perfect in Christ, but "all the man," "the whole man," as if purified in body and soul.[1] But exegesis like this is exceptional; and in his discussion of heretical tenets, for example, he adheres for the most part to the literal sense. In illustration of his thesis of the difference between the external meaning of Scripture and the inner meaning which is the prerogative of "men," he adduces a legend to the effect that on the death of Moses one Moses only was seen by Caleb, while two were visible to Joshua. In like manner some look only to the body of the Scriptures, the expressions and names, corresponding to the body of Moses; while others look to the thoughts and what is signified by the names, seeking earnestly for the Moses who is with the angels. In the case of the latter, too, insight is gradual; we cannot all at once look the splendours of the truth in the face.[2] So far as the Old Testament is concerned, most of his illustrations of the allegorical method of getting at the hidden meaning are taken from Philo and Barnabas, and may be justified in some cases by the usage of the writers of the New Testament themselves.[3] The same may be said of the allusions to Isaac as a type of Christ, and the exposition of some incidents which may be treated as parabolical. But when everything is allegorised, the historical becomes a secondary matter, facts are treated as parables, poetry is made to masquerade as science and philosophy. The most grotesque illustrations of his method are those in which he has followed closely the interpretation of Philo or some other of his predecessors. Setting these aside, I give some illustrations which are not so borrowed.

The meaning of the Law is to be taken in three ways—as exhibiting a sign, as ratifying a precept for a right way of

---

[1] Str., v. 10[61].   [2] Ib., vi. 15[132].
[3] Cf. Gal. iv. 24; Heb. vii. 1-3.

living, and as predicting like a prophecy. To make such distinctions is the prerogative of men. In Str. vi. 16, he gives what he calls a specimen of gnostic exposition of the decalogue. As the tables were written by the finger of God, that is the power of God and His work, they are found to exhibit the physical creation, to contain symbols of heaven and earth. In accordance with this is the physical decalogue of heaven and earth.[1] The Two Tables may be a prophecy of the two covenants. They were therefore renewed in mystic fashion, when ignorance together with sin abounded. The commandments are written in twofold wise for the twofold spirits—the ruling spirit and that which is subject.[2] So actions are twofold—those of thought and those of activity.[3] As there are ten commandments, so there is a "ten" in man.[4] The first commandment teaches that there is only one Almighty God, who conveyed the people through the wilderness to their fatherland that they might apprehend His power, as far as they were able, through the divine workings, and that they should be done with the idolatry of things created, and fix their entire hope in the true God.[5] The second word indicated that we should not take and give a name to the majestic power of God—(for that is His name, for this alone they were able to learn, as even yet the multitude),—nor transfer His title to things created and vain, which have been made by human craftsmen, in which "He that is" is not ranked. For in uncreated identity "He that is" is by Himself alone.[6] The third word[7] declares that the world has been made by God,

---

[1] Str, vi 16[133]   [2] Ib., vi. 16[134].   [3] Ib., vi. 16[137].
[4] Ib, vi 16[134]. τά τε αἰσθητήρια πέντε καὶ τὸ φωνητικὸν καὶ τὸ σπερματικὸν καὶ τοῦτο δὴ ὄγδοον τὸ κατὰ τὴν πλάσιν πνευματικόν, ἔνατον δὲ τὸ ἡγεμονικὸν τῆς ψυχῆς καὶ δέκατον τὸ διὰ τῆς πίστεως προσγινόμενον ἁγίου πνεύματος χαρακτηρισ-τικὸν ἰδίωμα.   [5] Ib., vi. 16[137].
[6] Ib. Here follows a mystic interpretation of the number six and the number seven. Ib , vi. 138 et seq.
[7] I give the numbers as stated by Clement.

and that He has given the seventh day as rest to us because
of the distress in life. For God is unwearied, and passionless, and free from want. But we who bear flesh need rest.[1]
The fifth word is that with reference to the honour of father
and mother. This clearly calls God Father and Lord.
Wherefore also to those who know Him is given the name
of sons and gods. The Creator of the universe is then Lord
and Father ; and the mother is not, as some hold, the
essence out of which we have come into being, nor as others
have taught, the Church, but the divine knowledge and
wisdom, as Solomon says, who calls wisdom the mother
of the just. And it is chosen for its own sake. The knowledge of all that is good and venerable comes from God
through the Son.[2] Next follows the word about adultery.
It is adultery when one leaves the ecclesiastical and true
knowledge concerning God, and goes over to the false
opinion which is not becoming, whether by defying anything among things created, or by forming an "idol" of
non-existent things, with a view to stepping beyond knowledge, or rather stepping out of it. For false opinion is
foreign to the gnostic, as true opinion is kindred and wedded
to him.[3] The word about murder follows. Murder is a
violent removal. He who wishes to remove the true word
about God and His eternity in order to give sanction to
falsehood by saying that the universe is not ordered by a
providence, or that the world is uncreated, doing violence
to that which is in harmony with true teaching, is most
destructive.[4] Then follows the word about theft. Those
who assign any influence to the stars in the matter of
growth and life deprive the Father of the universe of His
unwearied might.[5] The tenth is the word concerning all
lusts. As, then, he who desires what is not becoming is
called to account, so in the same way he is not permitted

---

[1] Str., vi. 16 [137].   [2] Ib., vi. 16 [146].   [3] Ib.   [4] Ib., vi. 16 [147].
[5] Ib., vi 16 [148].   He gives no exegesis of the ninth commandment.

to desire false things, nor to suppose that of things created, such as are animate have power of themselves, but such as are inanimate cannot at all save or injure.

The being "after the image and likeness" does not apply to the body, for it is not lawful for the mortal to be likened to the immortal, but to likeness in understanding and reasoning. On this the Lord appropriately puts the seal of likeness, both in respect of doing good and of ruling.[1] The eunuch is the man who is barren of truth.[2] In Isaiah the saying, "Hear, O heaven, and give ear, O earth,"[3] is to be interpreted thus. "Heaven" is the soul of the gnostic who has taken on himself the vision of heaven and the things of God; "earth" represents the man who has made choice of ignorance and hardness of heart. The "hear" refers to the understanding; the "give ear" is the ascription of carnal things to those devoted to things of sense [4] "Day utters speech to day"—that which has been written without disguise; "night unto night proclaims knowledge"—that which has been hidden mystically.[5]

His interpretation of the Gospels may be illustrated from the Sermon on the Mount, from Parables and separate sayings, from miracles and incidents which are recorded.

"Blessed are the poor," whether in spirit or in substance—that is, of course, for the sake of righteousness. Perhaps it is not the poor simply, but those who have willed to become poor for the sake of righteousness that He pronounces blessed,—those who have despised earthly honour with a view to the acquisition of the good.[6] "Blessed are they that mourn, for they shall be comforted." They who have repented of the evils of their former life shall come to the calling, for that is to be comforted.[7] "Blessed are

---

[1] Str , ii. 19[102] [2] Isa. lvi. 3-5 ; Str., iii 15[99]. [3] Isa. i. 2.
[4] Str., iv 26[169]. [5] Ib , v. 10[64]. [6] Ib , iv. 6[26].
[7] Ib., iv. 6[37] : εἰς τὴν κλῆσιν παρεσόνται· τοῦτο γάρ ἐστι τὸ παρακληθῆναι.

the meek, for they shall inherit the earth." The meek are
those who have laid to rest the implacable conflict of anger
and lust in the soul. The meek referred to are those who
are meek from deliberate choice, not from necessity.[1]
" Blessed are they that hunger and thirst after righteousness, for they shall be filled." They are called blessed by
Him who approves of the genuine longing which not even
famine can cut off.[2] " Blessed are the merciful, for they
shall obtain mercy." Mercy is not sorrow for the calamities
of others, but something good. By the merciful are meant
not only those who do what is merciful, but those who wish
to show mercy though they may not be able, those with whom
the actualising is present in respect of choice.[3] " Blessed
are the pure in heart, for they shall see God." Pure in
respect of bodily lusts and holy in their reasonings He
wishes them to be who come to the knowledge of God,
when the ruling faculty shall have nothing spurious in the
way of its own power.[4] " Blessed are the peacemakers."
They are such as have tamed and subdued the law which
was against the thought of the mind, as well as the threats
of anger, and the baits of lust and the rest of the passions
which fight against the reason. These having passed their
life attended by the science both of good works and true
reason, shall be restored to that adoption of sons which is
dearest. The perfect peacemaking may be that which in
every circumstance maintains unchanged a peaceful state ;
calling the dispensation of Providence holy and good, and
regarding the opposing elements in the world as the
most beautiful harmony of creation. They, too, are peacemakers, who teach those who are warring here against the
stratagems of sin to pass over to the faith and to peace.[5]
" Blessed are they that are persecuted for righteousness'
sake." He teaches us clearly in every circumstance to seek

[1] Str , iv. 6 36.   [2] Ib., iv. 6 26.   [3] Ib., iv. 6 38.   [4] Ib., iv. 6 39.
[5] Ib., iv. 6 40.

out the martyr who, if he be poor for the sake of righteousness, bears witness that the righteousness which he loved is
a good thing.[1]

The " night " in which the lamps of the wise virgins were
lit was the great darkness of ignorance. Wise souls, pure as
virgins, understand themselves to be in the ignorance that
marks the world. They kindle the light, rouse the mind,
light up the darkness, and drive out ignorance, seek the
truth, and await the manifestation of the Teacher.[2] The
faith which the apostles asked for is " as a grain of mustard,"
which bites the soul to its profit and grows to a great height
in it, so that transcendent reasonings rest upon it.[3] Or, the
mustard-tree is the Church of Christ which filled the world,
so that the birds of heaven—that is, divine angels and transcendent souls—lodged in its branches.[4] In the Parable of
the Rich Man and Lazarus, the poor man is represented by
the grass, πόα. For we who are bedewed by the grace of
God are the grass, and though cut down we shall spring up
again. The rich man is represented by the hay, χόρτος,
which is to-day in the field and to-morrow is cast into the
oven, being made partaker of the fire.[5] The " neighbour "
in the Parable of the Good Samaritan is the Saviour Himself. When we had been all but put to death by "the world-
rulers of the darkness " with many wounds—fears, lusts,
deceits, pleasures—He took pity upon us. For such wounds
the only physician is Jesus, who cuts out the passions by
their roots, and not, like the Law, their effects merely. It is
He who pours wine on our wounded souls. It is He who
has brought the oil, the mercy from the heart of the Father.[6]
It is He who has exhibited the indissoluble bonds [7] of health
and salvation—love, faith, hope. It is He that appointed
angels and principalities and powers to minister to us for a

---

[1] Str., iv 6 25.   [2] Ib., v. 3 17.   [3] Ib., v. 1 2.
[4] Stah., vol. iii. p. 226, fr. 54.   [5] Pæd , ii. 10 104, 105.   Cf. Luke xii. 28.
[6] Playing on the words ἔλαιον and ἔλεος.   [7] Cf. κατέδησεν, Luke x 34.

great reward,[1] because they too shall be set free from "the vanity" of the world at the revelation of the glory of the sons of God.[2]

The fish which Peter caught at the command of the Lord indicates food with which one is easily satisfied, God-given, and temperate. From those who rise from the water of baptism to the bait of righteousness we should take away dissoluteness and love of money, like the coin from the fish, in order to separate the vainglory, and by giving the stater to the tax-gatherer and rendering to Cæsar "the things that are Cæsar's," to preserve to God "the things that are God's."[3]

The "adversary" with whom Jesus calls us to agree is not the body, as some suppose, but the devil and those who are likened unto him.[4] "The foxes have holes"—that is, men of evil disposition and earth-born, engrossed with money which is mined and dug. "The birds"—flying fowls—"of the heaven have nests"—that is, those who are separated by heaven from the other birds, those really pure, that are able to fly to the knowledge of the heavenly word.[5] The "mother" whom we are called upon to forsake is figuratively interpreted fatherland and sustenance; "fathers" are the law of the State.[6] Who are the "two or three who are gathered together in the name of the Lord, in the midst of whom He is"?[7] Does He not mean the husband, the wife, and the child, seeing that "by God the woman is joined to the man"? Otherwise, the three may

---

[1] Cf. ἀποδώσω, Luke x. 35.

[2] Q. D., c. 29. Origen (Hom. in Luc., 35) gives as from "quidam de presbyteris," a kindred explanation, but entering into every detail for analogies. He regards it as explained "rationabiliter pulchreque." A like mystic interpretation is found in most of the Fathers.

[3] Pæd., ii. 1[14]. Cf. Matt. xxii. 21.   [4] Str., iv. 14[95]. Cf. Matt v. 25.

[5] Str., iv. 6[31]. Cf. Matt. viii. 20.   [6] Str., iv. 4[15]. Cf. Mark x. 29.

[7] Matt. xviii. 20.

be anger, desire, and reasoning, or flesh and soul and spirit. Perhaps it may mean the one Church, the one man, the one race. The Law and the Prophets, together with the Gospel, are gathered together in the name of Christ into the one gnosis.[1]

The silence of Zacharias was a type of the mystic silence of the prophetic enigmas which was broken by Christ, the light of truth, the Word.[2] With reference to the anointing of the feet of the Lord, Clement identifies the incident recorded in St Matthew with that recorded in St Luke, or mixes them up together. The anointing may be a symbol of the Lord's teaching and of His passion. The feet are the Apostles, which received the fragrance of the unction of the Holy Ghost. Of them also the Holy Spirit prophesied through the Psalmist, " Let us adore at the place where the feet stood"[3]—that is, where the Apostles arrived, through whom being preached He came to the ends of the earth. The tears are repentance, and the loosened hair proclaims the loosening of the old vainglory for the sake of the new faith. Moreover, mystically understood, the anointing is a symbol of the Passion. The oil ($\tau\grave{o}$ $\check{e}\lambda a\iota o\nu$) is the Lord Himself, from whom is the mercy ($\tau\grave{o}$ $\check{e}\lambda\epsilon o\varsigma$) which is towards us. But the ointment ($\tau\grave{o}$ $\mu\acute{v}\rho o\nu$), which is adulterated oil, is the traitor Judas. As the dead are anointed, it may be said that the feet of the Lord were anointed by Judas. We, sinners, who have repented and believed in Him, are the tears. The loosened hair is mourning Jerusalem. Thus the anointed feet were a prophecy of the treachery of Judas when the Lord was on His way to His Passion.[4] The washing of the feet of the disciples by the Saviour intimated their journeying for the benefit of the nations, making this fair and pure by His own power. The ointment in them smelled sweetly,

[1] Str., iii. 10 68, 69.   [2] Prot., i. 1 10.
[3] Ps. cxxxi. 7, LXX.   [4] Pæd., ii. 8 61,63

and the work of fragrance reaching to all has been proclaimed.[1] The crowning of the Lord with thorns prophet-
ically pointed at us. For we were once fruitless, but are
bound as wreaths round about Him through the Church, of
which He is the Head.   But it is also a type of the faith,—
of life, because of the substance of the wood ; of joy, because
of the appellation of " crown "; of danger, because of the
thorn ; for it is not possible to draw nigh to the Word without shedding of blood. It is a symbol, too, of the right
action of the Master. He bore on His head, even on the
sovereign principle of the body, all our misdeeds by which
we were pierced. He by His own Passion saved us from
offences and sins and suchlike thorns.[2]

A like method of exegesis is applied to the Epistles of St
Paul   To get rid of what he regards as the incongruity
between the promise in Exodus and the statement of St
Paul in the First Epistle to the Corinthians, " I have fed
you with milk, not with meat,"[3] he enters into physiological details as to the nature of milk, with the view of
showing that the milk is not to be regarded as something
different from the meat, but the same in essence. Blood is
a kind of liquid flesh, and milk is the sweeter and finer part
of blood. The essence of the human body is blood, and
milk is a product of the blood. If food by digestion is
changed into blood, and blood is changed into milk, then
the blood is a preparation for the milk.[4] Elsewhere he
interprets the same saying in a natural sense. Dealing
with the passage—" The wild olive is ingrafted into the
fatness of the olive,"[5] he touches on various methods of
ingrafting. He finds in one method an analogy of the
way in which the unlearned converts from the Gentiles
are instructed, who receive the word in surface fashion.

[1] Pæd., ii. 8 62.   [2] Ib., i. 8 73, 74.   [3] 1 Cor. iii. 2. Cf. Ex. iii. 8, 17.
          [4] Pæd., i. 6 34,02.   [5] Rom. xi. 17.

Another method represents the way in which the truth is acknowledged by those who have studied philosophy, and also by the Jews. A third method is symbolic of the way in which the uncultivated and heretics are brought by violence to the truth. A fourth method is a symbol of gnostic teaching.[1]

These illustrations may suffice to show to what extent Clement was dominated in his exegesis by the hypothesis of the symbolic character of Scripture and his method of applying it. Fantastic alike in its conception and in its results as the allegorical exegesis was, it may be claimed for it that in the hands of Clement it had behind it certain great truths or principles. Like the Rabbinical exegesis of the Old Testament, it was based on implicit belief in the divine origin of Scripture. " Turn it over and over again," we read in the 'Sayings of the Jewish Fathers,' " for the all is therein, and thy all is therein." [2] This being assumed, it followed that analogies between it and the nature of man, as well as the outer universe, were to be expected. This explains, at least in part, the psychological, mathematical, and physical analogies which were read into the simplest words of Scripture. This exegesis had behind it a true conception that the truths of Scripture, like those of nature itself, do not lie on the surface for the careless looker or reader to gather, but demand reverence and patient inquiry for their interpretation. The saying that the Scriptures are pregnant to the gnostic but dismissed by the heretics as barren[3]—to which strong exception has been taken as a " bad feature "—is but Clement's way of saying that spiritual insight is essential to fruitful apprehension. The allegorical theory had behind it, though expressed in a grotesque form and almost unconsciously, the idea of the unity and continuity of revelation.

[1] Str , vi 15[119].   [2] 'Sayings of the Jewish Fathers,' v. 32.
[3] Str., vii. 16[94].

"The thought was akin to reverence, but it was also akin to that superstition which is most fatal to reverence." [1]   And the history of exegesis shows that the latter tendency always tended to become dominant, that the Scriptures were apt to be degraded to the rank of a book of riddles, the interpretation of which was little better than a form of literary frivolity of no higher dignity or worth than the manufacture of anagrams.   The fascination of such a hypothesis is still powerful, even in critical circles, though the *motif* be purely literary or historical or dogmatic.   But though the principle is different, the application leads to similar results. If we take the Old Testament, for example, the physiological exegesis of some portions of the book of Ecclesiastes and the pathological exegesis of the Song of Solomon produce results compared with which the Alexandrian exegesis is comparatively sober.   And the rigorous application of the same hypothesis to the Fourth Gospel in the hands of the school of Réville and Loisy, in their search for historical facts veiled in its symbolism, is productive of results not less fantastic.   Does the fact that such interpretations are put forward in the august name of modern critical science, and not in that of an antiquated exegesis, alter their essential character ?

We pass on to inquire — to what books did Clement ascribe the qualities which have been indicated ?   What books did he recognise as authoritative in questions of faith or controversy?   What, in other words, was the Canon of Scripture in the Church of Alexandria, if he be regarded as a representative man?

With regard to the Canon of the Old Testament there is no controversy.   His Canon is that of the Septuagint, and included books that have been recognised by the Church of Rome as canonical, but are designated and regarded

[1] Maurice, *op. cit.*, p. 238.

by the Protestant Churches as apocryphal. In particular,
he has been greatly influenced by the ' Wisdom of Solomon '
and the book of ' Ecclesiasticus,' especially in the ethical
sections of his writings; and in this respect differs markedly
from Philo, who never mentions them. Yet, though there
is no conflict of opinion as to his view of the canon of the
Old Testament, his attitude to that canon may throw im:
portant light on the controverted question, that of the
canon of the New Testament.

The forms of citation or allusion may be thus classified.
(1) We have words or phrases which imply authority or
inspiration, as ἡ γραφή, ἡ θεία γραφή,[1] αἱ γραφαί,[2] αἱ θεῖαι
γραφαί,[3] αἱ κυριακαί γραφαί,[4] αἱ θεοπνεύσται γραφαί,[5] γέγραπται, τὸ πνεῦμα, τὸ ἅγιον πνεῦμα, τὸ πνεῦμα διά, φησί,
εἴρηται, and kindred words.   (2) We have reference to the
names of the writers with or without honorific epithets,
as ὁ Μωυσῆς, παρὰ τῷ Μωυσεῖ, ὁ πάνσοφος Μωυσῆς, ὁ
θεσπέσιος Μωυσῆς—ὁ Δαβίδ, κατὰ τὸν Δαβίδ, ὁ μακάριος
Δαβίδ, ὁ προφήτης, ὁ ψαλμῳδός, κατὰ τὸν μακάριον ψαλμῳδόν,
—ὁ Σολομῶν, κατὰ τὸν Σολομῶντα,—ὁ Ἡσαίας, παρὰ Ἡσαίᾳ,
ὁ προφήτης—ὁ Ἱερεμίας, ὁ προφήτης.   (3) We have a few
references to the books, as, οἱ ψαλμοί, ὁ ψαλμός, ἐν τοῖς
ψαλμοῖς γέγραπται, γέγραπται ἐν τῷ Δαβίδ,—αἱ παροίμιαι,
ἡ τοῦ Ἰησοῦ σοφία, ἐν τῇ σοφίᾳ εἰρημένον, ἐν τῷ Ἱερεμίᾳ
γέγραπται, ἐν τῷ Ἰεζεκιὴλ γέγραπται.   (4) In a very large
number of instances we have passages introduced without
any indication of their source—though sometimes a comment implies scriptural authority,—but simply incorporated
into his text.   (5) In a large number of cases, also, we have
only indication by a word or phrase that some particular
passage was before the mind of the writer—an evidence

[1] Str , 1 3 [24].   [2] Ec. Pr., 1, &c.
[3] Pæd , iii. 2 [9], &c.   [4] Str., vii. 1 [1].
[5] vii. 16 [101].   For illustrations of the other forms, see details that follow.

O

more weighty in some respects than direct citation would
be of his knowledge of Scripture and of the way into which
it had become inwoven into the texture of his thought, as
well as, it may be, of the measure of knowledge which he
expected from his readers.

The book of Genesis is mentioned by name.[1] It is
nowhere quoted in the Protrepticus as ἡ γραφή, but it is
so quoted in the Pædagogus, and more than once in the
Stromateis.[2] It is also quoted with γέγραπται absolutely.[3]
It is nowhere quoted with the formula τὸ πνεῦμα διά or
kindred formulas. Some passages are introduced by the
formula ὁ παιδαγωγὸς διὰ Μωυσέως,[4] numerous passages by
φησί[5]—either in the sense that God says or that Scripture says; occasionally we have εἴρηκεν, or ἐκείνη ἡ θεικὴ
φωνή.[6] Sometimes it is quoted under the designation ἡ
προφητεία,[7] more frequently with ὁ Μωυσῆς λέγει, or διδάσκει,
or the like,[8] sometimes with a honorific epithet, as ὁ
πάνσοφος.[9] Sometimes passages are introduced into the
text without any indication that they are quotations;[10]
sometimes by a supplementary comment or allegorical
exegesis it is indicated that Scripture is implied. Very
many passages are only alluded to in connection with some
incident or suggested by the phraseology.

The book of Exodus is not mentioned by name. It is
quoted as ἡ γραφή, both in the sense of Scripture and in
the sense of a passage of Scripture, in the Pædagogus,
and repeatedly in the Stromateis.[11] It is nowhere quoted
with the words τὸ πνεῦμα. It is quoted in the Pædagogus
and the Stromateis under the phrase ὁ παιδαγωγὸς διά, ὁ

---

[1] Ec. Pr., 1.
[2] Pæd., ii. 11[51].
[3] Ib., ii. 10[94].
[4] Str., vi. 16[146].
[5] Ib., iv. 25[161].

[2] Pæd., i. 5[22]; Str., iv 20[126].
[4] Pæd., 1 9[81].
[6] Ib., 1. 12[98].
[8] Ib, i 21[142]; ii. 5[20], &c.
[10] Pæd., iii. 10[50], &c.

[11] Pæd, i. 6[34]; Str., 1. 4[25], &c

λόγος διά, φησί, and the like.[1]   It is quoted as the work of
Moses, and as ὁ νόμος.[2]   There are passages incorporated
and suggestions of others.

The book of Leviticus is mentioned by name.[3]   It is
quoted in the Stromateis, and by implication in the Pædagogus, as ἡ γραφή.[4]   It is quoted with the formula ὁ λόγος
διὰ Μωυσέως.[5]   The word φησί is not associated with any
quotation, but the kindred word λέγει is found.[6]   Sayings
are quoted as the work of Moses, and under the designation ὁ νόμος.[7]   There are allusions to particular sayings
or incidents or regulations.

The book of Numbers is mentioned by name,[8] but it is
seldom quoted, and never under the designation of ἡ γραφή
nor with the formula τὸ πνεῦμα διά.   It is quoted with
φησί,[9] and with the formula, ὁ παιδαγωγὸς διὰ Μωυσέως.[10]

The book of Deuteronomy is not mentioned by name.
It is quoted as ἡ γραφή in the Pædagogus.[11]   It is quoted
under the designation τὸ πνεῦμα τὸ ἅγιον,[12] or with a phrase
of like import, ὁ λόγος διά.[13]   It is quoted as the work of
ὁ προφήτης,[14] and as the work of Moses ὁ πάνσοφος, ὁ
θεσπέσιος.[15]   It is quoted with φησί, λέγει, and ὁ νόμος.[16]
Passages are incorporated with and without comment.   As
in the previous books, there are allusions and suggestions.

The book of Joshua is mentioned by name.[17]   A knowledge
of it is further indicated by a reference to the dividing of
the waters.[18]

The book of Judges is mentioned by name, and many
historical and chronological details are taken from it.[19]

[1] Pæd , i. 11 ⁹⁶, &c.   [2] Str., v. 1 ⁷; iii 11 ⁷¹.   [3] Ib., i. 21 ¹²⁰.
[4] Pæd., ii. 10 ⁹¹ ; Str., ii. 10 ⁴⁶, ⁴⁷.   [5] Pæd., ii. 10 ⁹¹.
[6] Str., v. 6 ⁴⁰.   [7] Ib , ii. 15 ⁶⁷; ii. 23 ¹⁴⁷.   [8] Ib., iii. 4 ³².
[9] Ib., ii. 19 ⁹⁷.   [10] Pæd., i 2 ⁸.   [11] Ib., i. 7 ⁵⁶.
[12] Ib.   [13] Ib , iii 3 ²⁰.   [14] Prot , x. ¹⁰⁹.
[15] Ib , viii. ⁸⁰.   [16] Ib., x. ⁹⁵ ; Pæd., i. 8 ⁶⁹ ; Str., vii. 3 ¹⁴.
[17] Str., i 21 ¹⁰⁹.   [18] Ec. Pr., 6.   [19] Str., i. 21 ¹⁰⁹.

Knowledge of it is only further indicated by an allusion to Samson and his hair.[1]

There is no citation from, nor allusion to, nor suggestion of, the book of Ruth.

The First Book of Samuel is mentioned by name, and some historical facts are taken from it.[2] It is quoted with φησί, and also with ὁ λόγος διὰ τοῦ προφήτου Σαμουήλ.[3] There is, further, a reference to an incident in the career of Samuel.[4]

There is a reference to David which may be taken either from the Second Book of Samuel or the First Book of Chronicles.[5] The scantiness of allusion to this book is the more noteworthy because he attributes to Plato a knowledge of the incident referred to.

His knowledge of the First Book of Kings is attested by the historical data which are adduced.[6] There are, further, allusions to Elijah.[7]

The same may be said of his knowledge of the Second Book of Kings.[8] There is a reference to Elijah which may be due to his knowledge of this book.[9]

Save for the possible allusion already noted, there is no reference to the First Book of Chronicles.

The Second Book of Chronicles or the First Book of Kings is cited in a fragment of a lost treatise.[10]

From the books of Ezra and Nehemiah historical statements are taken.[11]

A passage is quoted from the Fourth Book of Esdras as a saying of Ἔσδρας ὁ προφήτης.[12]

[1] Pæd., iii. 11 [68]; Str., vi. 17 [153]; Ec Pr , 39.
[2] Str , i. 21 [109], i 21 [111], [112]; vi. 12 [101].
[3] Pæd , iii. 4 [27]; iii. 2 [12]; Str., vi. 3 [29].
[4] Adum. in i Joan , Stah., vol. iii. p. 211.
[5] Pæd., ii. 1 [18]. Cf. ib., ii. 8 [61], and 2 Sam. xii. 30.
[6] Str., i 21 [113].[116].   [7] Pæd , iii. 7 [38]; Prot., x. [92]; Str., iii. 6 [92].
[8] Str , i. 21 [116].[129].   [9] Pæd , ii. 10 [112]; Str., iii. 6 [53].
[10] Stah., vol. iii. p. 218.   [11] Str., i. 21 [124].
[12] Str., iii. 16 [100]. Cf. i. 22 [149].

The book of Psalms is quoted with greater variety of phrase than any other book of the Old Testament. It is quoted as ἡ γραφή or with γέγραπται in the Protrepticus, the Pædagogus, and the Stromateis.[1] It is quoted in the Pædagogus and in the Stromateis—much more frequently in the former—under the designation of τὸ πνεῦμα simply, or τὸ πνεῦμα διά.[2] We have not only τὸ πνεῦμα εἴρηκεν but even τὸ πνεῦμα ψάλλει, τὸ ἅγιον πνεῦμα ἔψαλλεν.[3] We have the full formula ὁ Δαβίδ, τουτέστι τὸ πνεῦμα τὸ δι' αὐτοῦ.[4] We have διὰ τοῦ ψαλμῳδοῦ τὸ πνεῦμα,[5] ὁ παιδαγωγὸς διὰ Δαβίδ,[6] ὁ λόγος διὰ Δαβίδ.[7] We have quotations with the designation ὁ προφήτης, ἡ προφητεία, ὁ προφητικὸς λόγος, ἐκεῖνο τὸ προφητικόν.[8] We have φησί and kindred words.[9] We have ὁ Δαβίδ many times, ὁ μακάριος Δαβίδ, κατὰ τον μακάριον Δαβίδ,[10] ὁ ψαλμῳδός, κατὰ τον μακάριον ψαλμῳδόν,[11] γέγραπται ἐν Δαβίδ, ὁ ψαλμός, οἱ ψαλμοί.[12]

We have, further, passages incorporated without any indication of their source; in some cases, however, with a comment which implies that they were Scripture or authoritative.[13]

The book of Proverbs is quoted by name in the Stromateis.[14] It is quoted as ἡ γραφή repeatedly in the Pædagogus and the Stromateis.[15] It is nowhere quoted with the designation τὸ πνεῦμα. It is, however, quoted with other phrases which imply inspiration or authority, such as ὁ παιδαγωγός, ὁ θεῖος παιδαγωγός,[16] ὁ λόγος, ὁ λόγος διὰ Σολομῶντος, ὁ ἅγιος λόγος,[17] θείως λέλεκται, ἐνθέως εἴρηται,[18]

---

[1] Prot , ix 85; x. 105; Pæd, i. 9[78]; Str , iv. 25[155].
[2] Pæd , ii. 8[62]   [3] Str., ii. 20[125]; Pæd., ii. 4[41], i. 8[73].
[4] Pæd., i. 9[87].   [5] Ib , ii. 8[62].   [6] Ib., i. 9[90].
[7] Ib., ii 10[110]   [8] Str , vii. 7[36]; i. 27[172]; Pæd., i 6[51]; Str , vi. 8[64]
[9] Prot., x. 103, &c.   [10] Str., vi. 16[145], &c.   [11] Ib., vi 3[30], &c.
[12] Ib., vii 13[83]; vii 7[41].   [13] Prot , iv. 63, &c.   [14] Str., ii. 2[4].
[15] Pæd , ii. 1[4]; ii. 2[29]; Str., ii. 7[33], &c.   [16] Pæd., iii 10[49], iii. 2[9]
[17] Ib , iii. 11[67], &c.   [18] Str., ii 7[35], i. 5[29].

οἱ χρησμοί οἱ θεῖοι, τὸ λόγιον ἐκεῖνό.[1] It is very frequently quoted as the work of Solomon, sometimes as ὁ προφήτης,[2] sometimes as the words of ἡ σοφία, where σοφία is represented as speaking, as well as when it is not so represented.[3] It is also quoted with φησί.[4] As in other books, passages are incorporated without any indication that they are quotations, save in one or two cases where a comment implies it.[5]

The book of Ecclesiastes is quoted by name, and also with γέγραπται.[6] Ecclesiastes i. 2 is represented as having inspired part of the teaching of Epicurus[7] Otherwise there is no indication of its use or influence.

The book of Job is not quoted nor referred to in the Protrepticus or the Pædagogus, but it is quoted several times as ἡ γραφή in the Stromateis.[8] It is quoted twice or thrice with sayings of Job himself, in one case with comment.[9] One passage is quoted with the indefinite ὥσπερ εἶπέ τις.[10] A passage of Job is erroneously described as written in the Kings.[11] There are references to Job himself based on incidents in the book.[12]

The Wisdom of Solomon is mentioned by name.[13] There is a possible allusion to it as ἡ γραφή in the Pædagogus[14] and an undoubted reference in the Stromateis.[15] Scripture is implied in a comment upon it.[16] It is nowhere quoted with the designation τὸ πνεῦμα. It is quoted with φησί, and also with εἴρηται.[17] It is quoted with the phrase ἡ σοφία λέγει, ἡ θεία σοφία,[18] but more frequently with the name of its author.[19]

---

[1] Str , ii. 7 [34].   [2] Ib , ii. 2 [7], &c ; iii. 17 [107], &c.
[3] Ib , i. 19 [96] , ii 18 [83]. Cf. ἡ πανάρετος σοφία ; Str., ii 22 [136].
[4] Pæd., iii. 4 [30], &c   [5] Str., ii. 18 [79].   [6] Ib , i. 13 [88].
[7] Ib., v. 14 [90]   [8] Ib , iv. 2 [6]; vi. 8 [65].   [9] Ib., iii. 16 [100] ; iv 26 [109].
[10] Ib., iv. 12 [83].   [11] Ib , iv. 26 [179].   [12] Ib., iv. 5 [19]; iv. 17 [108].
[13] Ib , v 14 [89].   [14] Pæd., ii, 10 [99]   [15] Str., v. 14 [108] ; vi 11 [92].
[16] Ec. Pr , 41.   [17] Pæd., ii. 1 [7]; Str , vi. 14 [113].
[18] Pæd , ii. 1 [7], Str., iv. 16 [103]   [19] Str., vi. 11 [93], &c.

The book of Ecclesiasticus is twice quoted by name as ἡ τοῦ Ἰησοῦ σοφία[1] It is very frequently quoted as ἡ γραφή in the Pædagogus.[2] It is quoted with γέγραπται.[3] It is never quoted under the designation τὸ πνεῦμα. It is quoted as the utterance of ὁ παιδαγωγός.[4] It is quoted very frequently in the Pædagogus with φησί.[5] It is still more frequently quoted as the sayings of ἡ σοφία.[6] In some cases it is correctly described as the "Wisdom of Jesus";[7] but in others its authorship, or rather some quotations from it, are erroneously assigned to Solomon.[8]

A reference to Esther and her mission shows his knowledge of the book of Esther.[9]

There is a possible reference to the book of Judith.[10] The narrative of Judith is referred to.[11]

The book of Tobit is twice quoted without name as ἡ γραφή.[12]

The book of Hosea is nowhere quoted as ἡ γραφή. It is quoted with the form ὁ λόγος διά, and ὁ παιδαγωγὸς διά,[13] with φησί,[14] and with the name of the writer, and with ὁ προφήτης.[15] In the Protrepticus, and also in the Stromateis, a passage in Amos is erroneously referred to as a saying of Hosea, though forms implying inspiration and authority are employed in both cases.[16]

The book of Amos is quoted as ἡ γραφή,[17] and also with the forms τὸ ἅγιον πνεῦμα διά, ὁ λόγος διά.[18]

---

[1] Str., i. 4 ⁷⁷, i. 10 ⁴⁷.
[2] Pæd., i 8 ⁶²; ii. 2 ³⁴.
[3] Str , i. 13 ⁵⁸, Stah., vol. iii. p. 225.
[4] Pæd., ii. 10 ⁹⁹, ¹⁰¹, ¹⁰⁹.
[5] Ib., ii. 2 ⁶¹, &c
[6] Ib., i. 8 ⁶⁹
[7] Str., i 4 ²⁷, i. 10 ⁴⁷.
[8] Ib., ii. 5 ²⁴; vii. 16 ¹⁰⁵.
[9] Pæd., iii. 2 ¹². Cf. Str., i. 21 ¹²³.
[10] Str., ii. 7 ⁵⁵.
[11] Ib., iv. 19 ¹¹⁸.
[12] Ib., ii. 23 ¹³⁹; vi. 12 ¹⁰⁹. Cf. i. 21 ¹²³.
[13] Pæd , i. 7 ⁵³.
[14] Ib., ii. 12 ¹²⁶.
[15] Ec. Pr , 4; Str , vi. 15 ¹¹⁵.
[16] Prot., viii. ⁷⁹; Str., v. 14 ¹²⁶.
[17] Str., vi 15 ¹¹⁵. Cf. v. 14 ¹³ᵇ.
[18] Pæd., ii. 2 ³⁰; i. 8 ⁶⁹.

The book of Micah is quoted with Μιχείας ὁ προφήτης and as one of the Twelve Prophets.[1]

The book of Joel is quoted with διὰ Ἰωήλ—one of the Twelve Prophets—εἴρηται.[2]

The book of Obadiah is not named nor quoted.

The book of Jonah is quoted by name and he is called a prophet.[3] There is a reference to his prayer.[4]

The book of Nahum is quoted once, without any reference, but with an implication that it is a saying of the Tutor.[5]

The book of Habakkuk is quoted with ὁ προφήτης.[6]

The book of Zephaniah is quoted with διὰ τοῦ Σοφονίου τὸ πνεῦμα,[7] and with ὁ προφήτης.[8]

The book of Haggai is quoted with φησί, and with γέγραπται.[9]

The book of Zechariah is quoted with ὁ προφήτης Ζαχαρίας,[10] and once without reference but with a comment.[11]

The book of Malachi is quoted with Μαλαχίας ὁ προφήτης and with ὁ Μαλαχίας φησί.[12] A phrase is incorporated without reference.[13] In the historical narrative Malachi is designated as the " Angel in the Twelve." [14]

The book of Isaiah is quoted as ἡ γραφή in all the three leading works of Clement.[15] The same is true of the application of τὸ πνεῦμα, τὸ ἅγιον πνεῦμα διά.[16] We have, further, ὁ παιδαγωγὸς διά, ὁ θεός διά, ὁ κύριος διά [17] It is also quoted with φησί, ἡ προφητεία, τὸ ἐκεῖνον προφητικόν, ὁ προφήτης, and with the name of the writer or his book.[18]

---

[1] Str., iv. 26 [169]; iii. 6 [101].   [2] Ib , v 13 [68].

[3] Ib , v. 14 [135].   [4] Q. D , c. 41 ; Jonah ii.

[5] Pæd., i. 9 [81].   [6] Str., ii. 2 [8].   [7] Pæd., ii. 12 [126].

[8] Str , iii. 12 [86].   But the reference is uncertain.

[9] Pæd , ii. 3 [39]; Str , iii 6 [56]   [10] Prot , x. [90].

[11] Pæd., i. 5 [18]   [12] Str., v. 14 [136]; iii. 4 [39].   [13] Prot., xi. [114].

[14] Str , i. 21 [122].   [15] Prot , i. [9]; Pæd., i. 5 [24]; Str., vi. 6 [49].

[16] Prot , viii. [79], Pæd., ii. 1 [8], Str , v. 14 [119].

[17] Pæd., i. 9 [76]; Prot., viii. [93], Str , iii. 15 [98]   [18] Pæd., i 5 [21]; i. 8 [67], &c.

Many passages are incorporated, and there are numerous references or allusions. The book of Jeremiah is quoted very rarely in the Pædagogus and the Stromateis as ἡ γραφή,[1] and in the Protrepticus not at all. It is quoted in all of them with τὸ πνεῦμα, and once with the elaborate formula, ὁ Ἰερεμίας ὁ προφήτης ὁ πάνσοφος, μᾶλλον δὲ ἐν Ἰερεμίᾳ τὸ ἅγιον πνεῦμα.[2] We have also ὁ παιδαγωγὸς διά.[3] It is quoted with ὁ προφήτης, ἡ προφητεία,[4] and very frequently with the mere name, φησίν Ἰερεμίας,[5] and once with γέγραπται under the name of the book.[6] There are some allusions to words or phrases.

The book of Baruch is quoted as ἡ θεία γραφή,[7] and with the formula (implied from the context) ὁ παιδαγωγὸς διὰ Ἰερεμίου.[8]

A saying from the Lamentations of Jeremiah is quoted in like manner.[9]

The book of Ezekiel is nowhere quoted as ἡ γραφή, though once with the form ὥς ἐν τῷ Ἰεζεκιὴλ γέγραπται [10] It is quoted once with the form τὸ πνεῦμα διά.[11] We have, further, ὁ κύριος διὰ Ἰεζεκιήλ, ὁ παιδαγωγος διὰ Ἰεζεκιήλ.[12] There are passages quoted without reference and some suggestions.

The book of Daniel is nowhere quoted as ἡ γραφή, nor with the phrase τὸ πνεῦμα διά, nor with φησί. It is quoted with the name of the writer and with ὁ προφήτης.[13]

Of the apocryphal additions to the book of Daniel, we have a reference to Susanna as a heroine,[14] to the Song of the Three Holy Children,[15] and to an incident in Bel and the Dragon.[16]

---

[1] Pæd., i. 9⁷ᵇ; Str., v. 5²⁷.
[2] Pæd , ii. 10⁸⁷; Str., iv 26¹⁶³, Prot., viii ⁷⁸.
[3] Pæd., i 9⁸¹.   [4] Prot , viii. ⁷⁸.   [5] Ib , viii. ⁸⁰.
[6] Str , i· 11⁵⁰.   [7] Pæd., ii. 3³⁶   [8] Ib., i 10⁸¹.
[9] Ib , i 9⁸⁰.   [10] Str., iv. 25¹⁵⁸.   [11] Ib , ii. 23¹⁴⁷.
[12] Ib., ii. 15⁶⁹ , Pæd., i. 9⁷⁶, ⁸⁴.   [13] Str., i. 21¹²⁵, ¹⁴⁶.
[14] Ib., iv. 19¹¹⁹.   [15] Ec. Pr , 1; Str., i 21¹²³   [16] Str , i 21¹²².

There is a reference to the books of the Maccabees.[1]

It would thus appear that of the books in the Hebrew canon Clement shows no knowledge of Ruth, the Song of Solomon, and Obadiah, and that all the apocryphal books are quoted or referred to except the Epistle of Jeremiah and the Third and Fourth Books of the Maccabees.

From this survey of Clement's use of the Old Testament in its bearing on our conclusions as to his use and appreciation of the books of the New Testament, the most important points to be adduced are these. No conclusion adverse to his knowledge of, or appreciation of, any particular book can be drawn from the absence of reference to any such book. Otherwise we should have to draw the inference that the books of Ruth, the Song of Solomon, and Obadiah were not in his copy of the Septuagint. The same applies to the writer's more or less infrequent reference to particular books as bearing on the measure of authority which he attached to them. In both cases the omission or infrequency is due to the personality of the writer, and to the degree in which he found certain writings more in harmony with his spiritual individuality and better adapted for exhortation and argument. The absence of the words ἡ γραφή or γέγραπται, where other indications of authority are present, throws no doubt on the authority of a book; or in that case we should have to eliminate the books of Numbers, all the historical books from Joshua to the Second Book of Chronicles, Daniel, and all the Minor Prophets except Amos and Haggai. No conclusion adverse to the inspiration of a writer can be drawn from the absence of τὸ πνεῦμα διά. For in that case we should have to eliminate from Clement's list of inspired books Genesis, Exodus, Leviticus, Numbers, Job, Proverbs, Ecclesiasticus, the Wisdom of Solomon, Ezekiel, Daniel, and all the Minor Prophets

---

[1] Str., i. 21 [123]. The genuineness of this passage is disputed.

except Amos and Zephaniah. No conclusion adverse to
the authority and inspiration of certain books can be drawn
from the omission of both ἡ γραφή and τὸ πνεῦμα, as in that
case we should have to omit from his list of authoritative
and inspired books Numbers, Daniel, and all the Minor
Prophets except Amos, Haggai, and Zephaniah. No conclusion as to the relative authority which he assigned to
any book of the same class or group can be drawn from
the number of phrases or epithets implying authority or
inspiration which he employs in reference to such, or the
relative frequency of such phrases or epithets. Otherwise
we should have to conclude that in his eyes Jeremiah was
unequal in authority or value to Isaiah, and Ezekiel
inferior to both. And, further, our conclusions as to the
usage of Clement in regard to the authority or inspiration
of particular books would be modified if one or other of
the great works of Clement had perished. No doubt, it
may be urged that there was no need for him to pay
attention to such matters in view of the fact that no one
disputed the authority of the books in question. But in
view of the incidental character of the phraseology and
the absence of design in the case of his references to both
Testaments, the same argument can be applied to his
usage in the case of the New Testament writings. Accordingly, in deciding as to the canonical status of any book
in the New Testament in the eyes of Clement, we cannot
be controlled solely by the application of a particular word
or phrase, but must also have regard to the general attitude
of the writer to such book or books and to the principles
which underlie his application of the same.

Apart from his formulas of citation, his method of
quotation throws light on the same question. His ascription of a passage in Job to the Second Book of Kings is a
slip of memory which is only interesting in view of his
otherwise almost complete ignorance of the latter book.

The ascription of a passage in Amos to Hosea in writings separated by such an interval as the Protrepticus and the Fifth Book of the Stromateis is an illustration of a familiar experience—the stereotyping of an error, not recognised as an error, in the mind of a writer. Apart from such errors, in view of his belief in the literal inspiration of the Old Testament, he deals with it with great freedom.[1] There can be little doubt that in many cases he quoted it from memory, and that in some cases, when he did not wish to quote the whole of a passage, he quoted only what was relevant to his purpose. As for his detachment of passages from the context, and without any regard to the context, or the transposition of clauses where the separate clauses are correctly quoted, is it a paradox to say that that shows his reverence for the authority of the words of Scripture ? All were transcribed from one authority. And as passages from different books could be quoted and put together and treated as parts of a whole, so clauses might be abbreviated or reversed without any sense of impropriety. In a mass of solid gold it does not matter where you break off a piece, or how the pieces so broken off are welded or mixed together. In any case, if we find such freedom of treatment in regard to the Old Testament, we need not be surprised to find like freedom in regard to the treatment of the New Testament, without looking on it as an adverse testimony to the authority of the latter.

Before forming any conclusions as to whether Clement had an official canon of New Testament writings, which he regarded as of equal authority with the books of the Old Testament, or whether we can speak in his case of a canon at all, it may be well to look at the evidence for the

---

[1] For example, in Str., i. 19 [96] he attributes the saying in Prov. ix 17 to ἡ σοφία instead of to γυνὴ ἄφρων. In Pæd., i 11 [96] he quotes Ex. xxxii. 6, χορτασθέντες γοῦν ἀνέστησαν παίζειν, and comments on the word χορτασθέντες, though it is not in the text of Exodus. Cf. Prov xv. 17 with Pæd ii. 1 [16].

separate books, applying to them the same tests that we have applied to the books of the Old Testament.

According to Eusebius,[1] Clement recorded in the 'Outlines' the following tradition of the earliest presbyters with reference to the order in which the Gospels were written. The Gospels containing the genealogies were written first. The Gospel of Mark was held to be a reproduction of the sayings of Peter, though Peter neither forbade nor encouraged its production "Last of all, John, perceiving that the outward facts had been made plain in the Gospels, at the instance of his friends, and under the inspiration of the Spirit, composes a spiritual Gospel." The implication that there were only four Gospels traditionally recognised by the Church is confirmed by an explicit statement in the extant writings.[2]

That Clement regarded the Four Canonical Gospels as a unit and as forming a whole in spite of difference in expressions which in no way affected the harmony of the thought, there can be no doubt. This he designates as τὸ εὐαγγέλιον. After the phrase ἐν τῷ εὐαγγελίῳ or τὸ εὐαγγέλιον, we have quotations, for the most part introduced as sayings of the Lord, indifferently from the Gospels of St Matthew,[3] St Mark,[4] St Luke,[5] and St John.[6] It should be noted, however, that the passage assigned to St Mark, as it is quoted only in part, might have been taken from the parallel passage in St Matthew, so that the conclusion as to St Mark in this connection is uncertain.

The Gospel of St Matthew is mentioned by name in the Stromateis.[7] It is quoted as ἡ γραφή in the Protrep-

[1] H. E., vi. 14, Stäh., vol. iii. p. 197.   [2] Str., iii 13⁹³.
[3] Pæd, i. 5¹³; i 9⁷⁶; i 9⁷⁹; i. 9⁸⁰; i. 9⁸⁵; Str., iv. 4¹³; vii. 12⁷²; Ec. Pr, 57   [4] Str., iv 4¹⁵.
[5] Pæd., ii. 12¹²⁵; Str., i. 21¹³⁸ (ἐν τοῖς εὐαγγελίοις); iii. 6⁵⁶, Ec. Pr., 50.
[6] Pæd, i. 5¹²; i. 9⁸⁵; Adum. in 1 Joan., Stäh., vol iii. p. 210
[7] Str., i. 21¹⁴⁷.

ticus,[1] the Pædagogus,[2] and the Stromateis.[3]   It is quoted
with γέγραπται in the Pædagogus[4] and the Stromateis.[5]
Passages are quoted as sayings of ὁ κύριος,[6] ὁ παιδαγωγός.[7]
The form φησί is found in the Pædagogus.[8]   In one case
we have the form τὸ προφητικὸν πνεῦμα.[9]   In a fragment
of the Commentary on St Jude there is a reference to a
saying in "other Gospels" than the Gospel of St Mark,
which occurs in the Gospel of St Matthew.[10]   A passage
which may either refer to St Matthew or St Luke is
introduced with the phrase ἡ προφητικὴ φωνὴ συνῳδὸς
ἀληθείας.[11]

There are few certain references to the Gospel of St
Mark.   A definite allusion to it by name is found in the
"Quis Dives,"[12] and in the fragment of the Commentary on
St Jude.[13]   The allusions to the Lord's Prayer[14] and to the
Parable of the Fourfold Seed[15] are too indefinite to enable
us to determine the source of the reference.   The same is
true of other sayings which may be taken from, or have as
their background any one of, the Canonical Gospels.

The Gospel of St Luke is specifically mentioned by
name in the Stromateis and in the Pædagogus.[16]   It is
quoted as ἡ γραφή in the Pædagogus[17] and the Stromateis.[18]
It is implicitly referred to as such in the Pædagogus,[19]
and either it or St Matthew is referred to as ἡ γραφή in
various passages.[20]   It is quoted as the saying of the

---

[1] Prot., ix. 82.   [2] Pæd., i. 5[14], i. 5[17]; ii. 12[118]; ii. 12[120], iii 11[70].

[3] Str , ii. 5[22]; v. 14[91]; vi 18[164].   [4] Pæd., ii. 6[50].

[5] Str., iv. 14[95].   [6] Prot., ix. 87; Pæd., i. 5[12]; Str., vii. 15[89].

[7] Pæd., ii. 6[51]; iii. 12[93].

[8] Pæd , ii. 6[49]; iii. 4[30]; iii. 5[33]; iii. 6[36].   [9] Ib., i. 5[11]

[10] Stäh , vol. iii. p. 209..   [11] Prot , i. 4.

[12] Q. D , 5   [13] Stäh., vol. iii. p. 209.

[14] Pæd., i 8[71]; Stah., vol iii. p. 205.

[15] Str , iv. 6[31].   So Clement designates the Parable of the Sower.

[16] Str., i 21[145]; Pæd , ii. 1[15].   [17] Pæd., ii. 12[120].   But cf. note 4.

[18] Str., ii. 5[22].   But cf. note 5.   [19] Pæd., ii 1[6], compared with ii. 1[4].

[20] Ib , ii. 12[120], iii. 11[70].   Cf. note 4.

Word,[1] the Lord,[2] the Saviour.[3] It is quoted with φησί
in the Pædagogus.[4] A passage is quoted in the Protrepticus as one of the λόγιοι νόμοι καὶ ἅγιοι λόγοι[5] There
are allusions to the Parable of the Two Brothers,[6] to the
Parable of Lazarus,[7] to Zaccheus,[8] and to a saying of
the Baptist[9] which is regarded as authoritative.
  The Gospel of St John is referred to by name in the
Pædagogus.[10] Sayings of John or John the Apostle taken
from the Gospel are quoted in the Protrepticus,[11] the
Stromateis,[12] and a fragment of the Περὶ τοῦ πάσχα.[13]
It is quoted as ἡ γραφή in the Protrepticus and the
Stromateis.[14] The same passage is quoted as Scripture,
and as a heretical watchword with the words ναί φασι
γεγράφθαι.[15] It is quoted with sayings of the Lord,[16] the
Word,[17] the Tutor.[18] It is quoted with φησί,[19] and once
with a ὅτι εἶπεν.[20]
  In all the writings of Clement there are numerous passages
from the Gospels, and many suggestions by word or phrase of
passages therein incorporated into his own text, occasionally
with a comment, but much more frequently without.
  The important points that arise from this survey are
these. The word " Gospel "—with the possible exception
of St Mark—is applied indifferently to all. All the Gospels
are mentioned by name. The Gospel of St Matthew is
most frequently referred to as ἡ γραφή: the Gospel of
St John comes next in order. It is very infrequently
applied to St Luke, and to St Mark not at all. This

---

[1] Pæd., i 8⁷².   [2] Ib., ii. 1⁴; Q. D., 39.   [3] Ec. Pr., 26.
[4] Pæd , i. 4¹⁰; ii. 9⁷⁹; iii. 12⁹¹.   [5] Prot., x. 108.
[6] Str., iv. 6³⁰. So Clement designates the Parable of the Prodigal Son.
[7] Str, iv. 6³⁰.   [8] Ib., iv 6³⁵   [9] Pæd , iii. 12⁹¹   [10] Ib., i. 6³³.
[11] Prot , iv 59   [12] Str., v 12⁸¹.   [13] Stah., vol iii. pp. 216, 217.
[14] Prot , ix. 82 ; Str , i 21¹⁴⁵.   [15] Str., i 20¹⁰⁰; i. 17⁸¹.
[16] Pæd , i. 3⁸; i. 5¹³, i. 6²⁸, ³⁶; i. 8⁶⁶; Adum in I Pet., Stah , vol. iii.
p. 204; fr. 39, p. 220
[17] Pæd , i 6⁴⁶.   [18] Ib., i. 7⁵³.
[19] Ib., i. 6²⁹. Cf i. 7⁵³; Prot., ii. 10 (φησί που.)   [20] Pæd., i. 8⁶².

fact is a striking illustration of the danger of drawing conclusions from too narrow a basis. For not only is the Gospel of St Mark referred to as a separate Gospel, but, so far from occupying an inferior position in his eyes, it is the text of that Gospel which he employs as the basis of his tractate, "Quis Dives." The favourite Old Testament phrase τὸ πνεῦμα is found, and in an altered form, with reference to a saying in St Matthew only. The word φησί is applied very rarely to St Matthew, not frequently to St Luke, and not at all to St Mark or St John. The sayings are ascribed to the Lord Himself most frequently in St John, less frequently in St Matthew and St Luke. It is difficult to account for this varying usage; but to whatever cause it may be due, it is not due to any distinction in the mind of the writer as to the relative authority and sacredness of the different Gospels, all of which are recognised as forming a unity, in perfect harmony with each other, and alike authoritative.

"The Acts of the Apostles," says Leipoldt,[1] "is not regarded by Clement as canonical. His successor Origen first takes this step." This statement is open to question. The authorship of the Acts of the Apostles is specifically assigned to St Luke.[2] It is quoted with the designation of "The Acts" simply,[3] and "The Acts of the Apostles."[4] It is quoted with reference to the education of Moses.[5] It is quoted as giving authentic sayings of St Peter and incidents in his life.[6] It is quoted in like manner as giving authentic sayings of St Paul, and incidents in his career.[7] In defence of his own exegesis of 2 Cor. xii. 5, he quotes the evidence

[1] Enstehung d. ntl. Kan., p. 220.

[2] Str., v. 12[92].   [3] Ib., i. 23[183], [184]; vi. 8[63].

[4] Pæd., ii. 1[16], Str., i. 11[80]; i. 19[91], iv. 15[97]; v. 11[71]; vi. 18[105].

[5] Str., i. 23[153].   [6] Pæd., ii. 1[16]; Str., vi 8[63]; i. 23[151].

[7] Str., i. 11[80]; i. 19[91]; v. 11[75]; v. 12[92]; vi. 15[124].

of Acts as to the missionary activity of St Paul.[1] It is
quoted with γέγραπται.[2] Reference is twice made to the
"Catholic Epistle of all the Apostles," once with mention
of the Book of Acts by name, once without such mention.[3]
The statement in Acts vi. 12, with reference to the Twelve
and their action in regard to the distribution of the common
funds, is quoted without reference to Acts, as though the
source of the allusion were well known.[4] An important
clause of Acts i. 7 is incorporated without reference, but
from the context the implication is that it is a saying
of Christ.[5] "We have learned," He says, "that God is
a knower of hearts." The word παρειλήφαμεν cannot
be pressed as indicating an authoritative source of teaching. But the word καρδιογνώστης is found nowhere else
in the Scriptures save in the Book of Acts, where it is
found twice.[6] In the literature prior to the date of
Clement it is found in the "Pastor" of Hermas, but
there it is given as an attribute of the Lord, not of
God,[7] and the most natural conclusion, in view of his
otherwise attested knowledge of the Book of Acts, is that
it is a reminiscence of that book. The use of Acts as
a historical book must be compared with his use of the
Historical Books of the Old Testament; and, compared
with the scanty reference to them from Joshua to the
Second Book of Chronicles inclusive, the knowledge and
use of Acts are all the more noteworthy. In view of the
fact that so many spurious Acts were current at this period,
the use of the form, "The Acts" simply, implies that it
occupied a unique and distinctive place, as the one historical record of the apostolic age that could claim universal
recognition. A writing whose author is declared to be the

[1] Str , vi. 18 165   [2] Pæd., ii. 1 16.   [3] Str., iv. 15 97 ; Pæd., ii. 7 56.
[4] Pæd., ii 7 56   [5] Str., iii. 6 49.
[6] Ib., vi. 12 101 ; Acts i. 24 ; xv. 8.   [7] Hermas, Mand , iv 3.

P

writer of the Third Gospel, whose sayings can be incorporated without specific reference to their sources, which
can be quoted as authoritative in support of his own attitude to Greek philosophy as well as in questions of practical ethics[1]—to say nothing of the term γέγραπται—was
certainly to the consciousness of Clement a document of
the first rank and invested with canonical authority.

"Unless all appearances be deceptive," it is averred, "it
was strictly speaking only the Four Gospels that Clement
considered and treated as completely on a level with the
Old Testament. The formula, ' The Law and the Prophets
and the Gospel,' is frequently used, and everything else,
even the Apostolic writings, is judged by this group. He
does not consider even the Pauline Epistles to be a court
of appeal of equal value with the Gospels, though he
occasionally quotes them as Scripture."[2]   Now, if the question could be decided by the extent of his knowledge and
use of the Pauline Epistles, there could be no doubt of the
answer. But it is always possible to hold that they were
not used because recognised as authoritative, but became
authoritative because they were so used,—though the ground
for their use has in this case to be explained; and not the
use but the method of use must be the determining factor.

Clement declares the harmony of the Law, the Prophets,
and the Apostles with the Gospel.[3] He takes for granted
that a conflict between Paul and the language of the
Old Testament is impossible, and adopts altogether fantastic exegesis to get rid of the apparent conflict. He
speaks of the Law given through Moses and that given
through the Apostles as alike of service to the Word in
the education of mankind; and all the illustrations that

[1] Str., i. 19⁹¹; Pæd., ii 1¹⁶.
[2] Harnack, ' History of Dogma,' vol. ii. p 58.
[3] Str., vi. 11⁶⁸; vii. 3¹⁴.

follow are taken from the Epistles of St Paul.[1] He says
that the Greeks must be taught by the Law and the
Prophets and then by the blessed Apostles.[2] He puts the
injunction of the Apostle on a line with the Gospel and
affirms their agreement.

The Pauline Epistles are marked by the symbolic note[3]
which was the highest characteristic of religious writings,
and could be allegorised so as to bring out their hidden
meaning. For the unbelieving to reject the message of so
great an apostle could only issue in condemnation.[4] By
heretics and orthodox alike his words were adduced as a
final court of appeal.[5] The only question of controversy
betwixt Clement and the heretics was not the question of
their authority but of their interpretation. The Pauline
Epistles are αἱ θεῖαι γραφαί.

In the Pædagogus he gives some passages from what he
designates by these words—and the numerous quotations
which follow are taken from the Epistles to the Ephesians,
Galatians, 1st Thessalonians, Colossians, First Epistle to
Timothy, and Romans.[6] The First Epistle to Timothy
and the Epistle to Titus belong to the " Sacred Books."[7]
Setting aside some doubtful cases where it is uncertain
whether a passage from the Old or the New Testament
was before his mind, we find that the technical term ἡ γραφή
or γέγραπται is applied to Romans, the Epistles to the
Corinthians, Ephesians, Colossians, 1st Thessalonians, 1st
Timothy. A saying in 2nd Corinthians is the cry of " The

---

[1] Pæd., iii. 12[94].   [2] Str., vii. 16[95].   [3] Ib., vi. 15[119]. Cf. vi. 18[164].
[4] Pæd., ix. [84] ; Str., vii. 16[104].   [5] Str., iii. 8[61] ; iii. 1[2] ; ii. 7[34].
[6] Pæd , iii. 12[94,96]. It has been urged against the weight to be attached to
this that Clement mixes up with these passages quotations from profane writers.
It is true that he interpolates a saying from Pindar, but giving it as a quotation
from Pindar, and some lines from Menander, without stating his authority But
that only proves that he could not resist an apposite poetical quotation.
[7] Pæd., iii. 12[97]. ἐγγεγράφαται ταῖς βίβλοις ταῖς ἁγίαις.

Truth." We have also the phrase that most clearly indicates inspiration, τὸ ἐν τῷ ἀποστόλῳ ἅγιον πνεῦμα.[1] In the sense of Scripture we have φησί applied several times to passages in the Epistles; and we have once κελεύει in a similar usage. One saying is quoted as a command of the Tutor, another as an exhortation of the Word.

All the honorific epithets that are applied to Moses, David, Solomon, and others whose writings are quoted by the name or designation of the writer, are applied with much greater profuseness to St Paul. He is repeatedly characterised as ὁ θεῖος ἀπόστολος,[2] ὁ θεσπέσιος,[3] ὁ μακάριος,[4] ὁ γενναῖος,[5] less frequently ὁ ἅγιος, ὁ καλός. He is the apostle of the Lord.[6] He is further an unerring witness.[7] A saying of his is characterised as expressed in an inspired and prophetic manner, as most mystically and holily uttered.[8] The great majority of the quotations are simply given as sayings of the Apostle without any epithet. In all the writings of Clement there are numerous passages from the Pauline Epistles incorporated into his text, for the most part without any indication that they are quotations, sometimes with a comment which implies that they are quotations. In many cases it is clearly shown by a word or a phrase that he is saturated not only with the teaching but with the vocabulary of St Paul.

From all the points indicated, from the relationship in which they are described as standing to the Old Testament and the Gospel, from the general notes that mark their character and authority, from the specific phrases and words that indicate a written authority, from the epithets that are bestowed upon him and his teaching, and from the extent of Clement's knowledge of them, in the light of the method of his use, there would seem to be little doubt that

---

[1] Pæd., i. 6 [49].   [2] ±9 times.   [3] ±5 times.   [4] ±6 times.
[5] ±8 times.   [6] Prot., ix. [87].   [7] Str., v. 1 [2].   [8] Ib., iv. [149].

the Pauline Epistles were to Clement canonical Scriptures in the fullest sense of the word. Let us look at the details.

The Epistle to the Romans is repeatedly quoted by name.[1] Quotations from it belong to the Divine Scriptures.[2] It is quoted with ἡ γραφή in the sense of a passage of Scripture, and also with γέγραπται.[3] It is quoted as a saying of "the Apostle"[4] and of "Paul,"[5] sometimes with, sometimes without, honorific epithets. Numerous passages are incorporated without reference.[6] Sometimes a word or phrase suggests that the phraseology or thought of Paul was in his mind.[7]

The First Epistle to the Corinthians is quoted by name,[8] and also in the more general phrase "to the Corinthians,"[9] and by the indefinite phrase "in a certain Epistle."[10] It is quoted as ἡ γραφή in the technical sense of a passage of Scripture.[11] A saying is quoted as that of τὸ ἐν τῷ ἀποστόλῳ ἅγιον πνεῦμα.[12] It is also quoted with φησί.[13] The form ὁ ἀπόστολος[14] is associated with quotations, and also the form ὁ Παῦλος,[15] sometimes with, sometimes without, honorific epithets. Numerous passages are incorporated without reference.[16] There are suggestions of many others.

The Second Epistle to the Corinthians is mentioned by name.[17] It is quoted as ἡ γραφή,[18] and as the utterance of the Truth,[19] and as the exhortation of the Word.[20] We have also the forms ὁ ἀπόστολος,[21] ὁ Παῦλος, with or without

---

[1] Pæd., i. 5[19]; Str., ii. 6[29], iii. 4[39]; iii. 11[73]; iv. 3[9]; v. 4[26].
[2] Ib , iii. 12[97].   [3] Str., iii 8[61]; iii. 12[85].   [4] ±42 times.
[5] ±8 times.   [6] Pæd., i. 8[69]; ii. 1[10]; Prot., x. 59.
[7] Prot , x. 98.   [8] Pæd , i. 6[33]; Str., ii. 22[136]; v. 12[80]; vii 14[84].
[9] Pæd., i. 7[61]; Str., i. 14[59], &c.   [10] Str., iii. 6[53]. ἔν τίνι ἐπιστολῇ.
[11] Cf. Str , vii 14[84].   [12] Pæd., i. 6[49].
[13] Ib , ii. 1[6]; ii. 1[10]; ii 1[13].   [14] ±42 times.   [15] ±9 times.
[16] Pæd., ii. 1[10]; iii. 11[79].   [17] Str., iv. 16[100].
[18] Ib , vi. 8[66].   [19] Prot., xi. 116.   [20] Pæd., iii. 2[11].   [21] ±10 times.

honorific epithets.   Passages are incorporated without
reference.   There are suggestions of many others by a
word.[1]

The Epistle to the Galatians is referred to by name.[2]
Passages taken from it belong to the "Divine Scripture."[3]   We have the phrase ὁ ἀπόστολος[4] and also
ὁ Παῦλος.[5]   A few passages are incorporated without reference; and there are suggestions of others.

The Epistle to the Ephesians is quoted by name.[6]   It is
plain from the exegesis of Origen that the words ἐν Ἐφέσῳ
were not in his MSS.   Whether they were in those used by
Clement or not, the Alexandrian tradition as represented by
him is in favour of the Ephesian destination of the letter;
and it must have been in the superscription.   The Epistle
belongs to the "Divine Scriptures."[7]   It is quoted with
ἡ γραφή.[8]   We have the forms ὁ ἀπόστολος[9] with honorific
epithets and ὁ Παῦλος.   Some passages are incorporated
without reference, sometimes with a comment.   There are
suggestions by words or phrases of others.[10]

The Epistle to the Philippians is referred to by name.[11]
It is nowhere designated as ἡ γραφή.   It is quoted
with the indefinite "ἐν τίνι ἐπιστολῇ."[12]   We have the
forms ὁ ἀπόστολος,[13] ὁ Παῦλος.   One or two passages are
quoted without reference;[14] and there are suggestions of
others.[15]

The Epistle to the Colossians is quoted by name.[16]   It
belongs to the "Divine Scriptures."[17]   ἡ γραφή is used in

---

[1] Pæd., iii. 11[79]; iii. 12[94], Prot., x. [94], καπηλεύω.   Cf. 2 Cor. ii. 17.
[2] Pæd., i 9[83], Str., iii. 15[99].   [3] Pæd., iii. 12[97].   [4] ±5 times.
[5] ±4 times   [6] Pæd., i 5[18]; Str, iv. 8[64].
[7] Pæd., iii. 12[97].   [8] Str, v. 5[27].   [9] ±16 times.
[10] Prot., ii. [27]; Pæd., i. 6[29]; Prot., x. [90].
[11] Str., iv. 13[92].   Cf. Prot., i. [8].   [12] Str. iii. 6[53].   [13] ±5 times.
[14] Prot , i [8].   [15] Pæd., iii. 12[99].   Cf Phil iii. 20
[16] Str., i. 1[15]; iv. 8[63], &c.   [17] Pæd., iii. 12[97].

the sense of a passage of Scripture.[1] We have the forms
ὁ ἀπόστολος,[2] ὁ Παῦλος.

The First Epistle to the Thessalonians is not quoted by
name. It belongs to the " Divine Scriptures."[3] It is quoted
as ἡ γραφή.[4] We have ὁ ἀπόστολος.[5] One passage is quoted
without reference; and there is a suggestion of another.[6]

The Second Epistle to the Thessalonians is not quoted
by name, nor are any passages from it quoted as ἡ γραφή.
One passage is quoted without reference.[7] There is a
possible suggestion of another.[8]

The First Epistle to Timothy is quoted as addressed to
Timothy.[9] There is a reference to the Second Epistle by
mistake for the First.[10] It is quoted as ἡ γραφή[11] and also
with γέγραπται.[12] Passages from it are quoted as belonging
to the " Divine Scriptures."[13] Precepts in it are taken from
the " Sacred Books."[14] Passages are quoted under the form
ὁ ἀπόστολος, ὁ Παῦλος, with or without a honorific epithet.[15]
One passage is incorporated without reference. There are
suggestions of others.[16]

The Second Epistle to Timothy is mentioned by name,
and as addressed to Timothy.[17] Passages are quoted with
ὁ ἀπόστολος, with and without honorific epithet.[18] No
passages are quoted with the name of ὁ Παῦλος simply.
No passages are quoted without reference. Clement states
that the heretics rejected the authenticity of the Epistles to
Timothy on dogmatic grounds.[19]

---

[1] Str , iv. 8 66.   [2] ±6 times.   [3] Pæd., iii. 12 97.
[4] Ib., ii. 9 80.   [5] ±4 times.   [6] Str., vii. 10 57.
[7] Ib., v. 3 17.   [8] Prot., x. 94.   [9] Pæd., ii. 2 19 ; Str., i. 1 4 ; ii. 2 33.
[10] Str., iii. 6 53.   [11] Ib., iv. 3 9.   [12] Ib., iv. 16 100.
[13] Pæd., iii. 12 97.   [14] Ib.
[15] Str., i 10 49 ; iii 6 61.   [16] Prot., ix. 86.
[17] Str., iii. 6 53 ; iv. 7 49.   [18] Ib., i. 10 49 ; v. i 5.
[19] Cf. ii. 11 52. ὑπὸ ταύτης ἐλεγχόμενοι τῆς φωνῆς (i.e., 1 Tim. vi. 20) οἱ ἀπὸ τῶν αἱρέσεων τὰς πρὸς Τιμόθεον ἀθετοῦσιν ἐπιστολάς.

The Epistle to Titus is quoted by name.[1] Precepts contained in it are assigned to the " Sacred Books." [2] A passage is quoted as ἡ ἀποστολικὴ γραφή.[3] Another passage is
quoted as from the divinely-inspired apostle of the Lord.[4]

The Epistle to Philemon is nowhere quoted or referred
to. That this does not necessarily imply ignorance of its
existence or doubt of its authority is plain from his apparent
ignorance of certain books of the Old Testament. The
omission was probably due to its brevity and its personal
note. The contents were of no special interest to him, as
the question of slavery was to all appearance not urgent in
the Church in Alexandria.

The Epistle to the Hebrews is quoted by name, and as
the work of Paul.[5] A passage is quoted as from the divine
apostle.[6] We have also ὁ ἀπόστολος simply.[7] A passage is
quoted without reference, and there are suggestions of
others.[8] In a passage from the "Hypotyposes," preserved
by Eusebius, the position of Clement with regard to the
authorship of Hebrews is given as follows : "The Epistle to
the Hebrews was the work of Paul, and was written to the
Hebrews in the Hebrew language, but Luke translated it
carefully and published it for the Greeks. Hence the similarity in the complexion of style between Acts and Hebrews.
The words, Paul the Apostle, were probably not prefixed,
because in sending it to the Hebrews, who were prejudiced
and suspicious of him, he did not wish to repel them at the
outset by putting his name." [9] The interest of this hypothesis is that Clement has observed the difference in style
between Hebrews and the Pauline Epistles and its likeness
to St Luke.[10]

---

[1] Str., i. 14[69]; iv. 20[128].   [2] Pæd., iii 12[97].   [3] Prot., i. [4].   [4] Ib., i. [7].
[5] Str., v. 10[62]; vi. 8[69].   [6] Ib., ii. 2[8].   [7] ±7 times.
[8] Prot., ix. [83].   [9] Eus., H. E., vi. 14.
[10] Cf. Adum. in 1 Pet v. 13; Stah., vol. iii. p. 206.

From this record it appears that, with the exception of Philemon, all the Epistles of St Paul were used by Clement; that, with the exception of 1st and 2nd Thessalonians, all the Epistles are mentioned by name; that, with the exception of the Epistles to the Philippians, 2nd Timothy, and Hebrews, all the Epistles are quoted as Scripture, or in phrases which imply scriptural authority; that, apart from cases where a honorific epithet is attached to the name of Paul or to him as the apostle, the form ὁ ἀπόστολος, most naturally interpreted as the Apostle *par excellence*, occurs more than 120 times, most frequently in 1st Corinthians, Romans, and Ephesians, least frequently in Philippians and the Pastoral Epistles, and not at all in 2nd Thessalonians; that, with the exception of 1st Thessalonians and Titus, we have passages incorporated without reference or suggestions of passages. As has been shown in the survey of references to the Old Testament Scriptures, the absence of the word ἡ γραφή cannot be pressed as showing that Philippians, 2nd Timothy, and Hebrews occupied in his mind a lower level than the other Epistles; and the detailed examination leads to the same conclusion as that drawn from the more general principles previously considered, that the Epistles of St Paul were normative in all questions of doctrine and ethics for the Church of Alexandria in the time of Clement.

According to the statement of Eusebius, Clement commented on all the catholic Epistles. To what extent is this confirmed by the evidence of the extant writings?

There is no clear evidence of Clement's knowledge of the Epistle of St James. The passage, "faith is perfected through gnosis," [1] can hardly be regarded as an allusion to "faith was perfected by works." The explanation of the word "God of all grace"—because He is good and

---

[1] Str., vii. 10⁵⁵. διὰ ταύτης (i.e., γνώσεως) γὰρ τελειοῦται ἡ πίστις.

the Giver of all good things—is slender evidence of his knowledge of St James ii. 22.[1] The references to Abraham as the "friend of God" from the context are most naturally referred to the Old Testament.[2] The passage in St James iv. 6 is twice given; but in one case it is taken from Clement of Rome,[3] and in the other case it is impossible to say whether it is taken from the Epistle of St James, or from the parallel passage in the First Epistle of St Peter, or from the Book of Proverbs.[4] As it is quoted as ἡ γραφή, which no other passage of 1st Peter is, it is most probably to be assigned to Proverbs. The saying quoted in the Stromateis might be taken either from St Matthew or from St James.[5] It is nearer in form to the latter than the former; but, as in the first instance noted, it is quoted as a saying of the Lord, and in the latter case it is incorporated without reference, the probability is that he was thinking of the passage in St Matthew. By Justin and others the passage in St Matthew is quoted in the form employed by Clement. The strongest case for his knowledge of St James is the reference in the Stromateis, where, it is true, the command to love one's neighbour is associated, not, as in James, with a "royal law," but with "royal persons."[6] This difference in the case of Clement, whose memory was often tenacious of single words, does not disprove that that passage was in his mind. But of itself the passage is hardly sufficient to prove the thesis, as it is not clearly confirmed by other testimony. At the most, the evidence in regard to St James does not go beyond a "non liquet."

The First Epistle of St Peter is quoted by name.[7] No

---

[1] Adum. in 1 Pet.; Stah., vol. iii. p. 206.
[2] Pæd., iii. 2[12]; iii. 8[42]; Str., ii 5[20]   [3] Str., iv 17[106].
[4] Ib., iii. 6[49]; 1 Pet v. 5.; Rom. iii. 34.
[5] Str., v. 14[99]; vii 11[67]. Cf. vii. 8[54]. Cf. Matt. v. 37 with James v. 12.
[6] Str., vi. 18[164]. Cf., however, 1 Pet. 2[9].   [7] Str., iii. 18[110]; iv. 20[129].

passage is quoted with ἡ γραφή. A passage is quoted with
φησί, or as a saying of the Tutor.[1] One passage is quoted with
the words τὸ εἰρημένον ἁγίως.[2] Peter is designated ὁ μακάριος[3]
and ὁ θαυμάσιος.[4] Numerous passages are quoted simply
as the sayings of Peter.[5] Several passages are quoted
without reference,[6] and there are numerous suggestions.[7]

The Second Epistle of St Peter is nowhere mentioned nor
quoted. The fact that he only seems to have known one
epistle because he uses the phrase ἐν τῇ ἐπιστολῇ[8] does not
prove that he knew only one; for he uses a like phrase of
1st John,[9] though he knew of more than one, and also of
1st Corinthians.[10] Potter gives two references to 2nd Peter.
The first proves nothing; the second is a mistake for 1st
Peter. In Strom. i. 1[2] some have found a possible reference
to 2nd Peter ii. 22; but on a phrase so proverbial nothing
can be built. There is a possible suggestion of 2nd Peter
i. 10 in Strom. vii. 11[66] and Quis Dives, c. 36; but the possibility is barely established. As in the case of St James, the
statement of Eusebius may be held to demonstrate Clement's
knowledge of 2nd Peter; but in his extant works there is no
evidence of such knowledge. As the emphasising of knowledge in the Epistle was in harmony with his way of thinking, the absence of reference here is the more noteworthy.
In one case, moreover, where he accuses the heretics of
twisting the Scriptures with a view to their own pleasures,
a reference so apposite to the context as that of 2nd Peter
iii. 16 might naturally have been expected.[11]

Part of his commentary on the Epistle of St Jude survives in a Latin version. Elsewhere the Epistle is definitely

[1] Pæd., iii. 11[66].   [2] Ib., iii 11[53].
[3] Stah., vol. iii. p. 219.   [4] Str., iii. 11[75].
[5] Pæd., i. 6[44]; iii. 11[74]; Str., iv. 7[46]; Ex. Theod, 12   [6] Prot., iv. 59.
[7] E.g., Str., i. 28[178]; iii. 4[31]; vii. 7[35].   [8] Ib., iii. 18[110].
[9] Ib, iii. 4[32].   [10] Ib., v. 12[80].   [11] Ib., iii. 4[39].

assigned to St Jude.[1]   A passage is quoted with " Jude
says," [2] and another with the words διδασκαλικώτατα
ἐκτίθεται.[3]   A passage is quoted without reference.[4]

The First Epistle of St John is specifically mentioned.[5]
A passage is quoted as having been spoken by John θείως
γε καὶ ἐπιπνόως,[6] another passage with φησί.[7]   Several
sayings are quoted as sayings of John.[8]   One passage is
quoted without reference.[9]   Part of the commentary survives in a Latin version.

Clement knew of at least two Epistles of St John, as
he refers to the " larger epistle." [10]   Part of a commentary
on the Second Epistle survives in a Latin Version.
Clement regards ἐκλεκτή as a proper name, and says that
the letter was addressed to a certain Babylonian.[11]

There is no trace of the Third Epistle in the extant
writings of Clement.

The Book of Revelation is assigned to St John.[12]   It is
quoted as " The Apocalypse." [13]   If this does not prove that
the Apocalypse of St John occupied a higher platform than
the other Apocalypses then current, it shows that at least
it was more widely known.   A reference to the Word as
Alpha and Omega is found twice, and there is a kindred
reference to the Lord.[14]   With the indefinite phrase, " we
have heard," there is a reference to the precious stones on
the walls and gates of the Jerusalem that is above.[15]   A
comment implies that it is " Scripture."   There is a refer-

---

[1] Str , iii. 2[11].   [2] Pæd., iii. 8[44].   [3] Ib., iii. 8[48].   [4] Str., vi. 8[65].
[5] Ib., ii 15[66]; iii. 4[32].   [6] Q. D., 37.   [7] Str , iii. 5[42].
[8] Pæd., iii. 11[82]; iii. 12[98]; Str., iii. 5[44]; iii. 6[45]; iv. 16[100].
[9] Str , v. 1[13].   [10] Ib , ii. 15[66].
[11] " Scripta vero est ad quandam Babyloniam Electam " (Stah. vol. iii
p. 215) (2 John 1.)
[12] Str., vi. 13[106].   [13] Pæd., ii. 10[108].
[14] Ib , i 6[36]; Str , iv. 25[137].
[15] Pæd , ii. 12[119]. τὸ συμβολικὸν τῶν γραφῶν.

ence to the contents of Rev. v. 6.[1]   There are suggestions of other passages.[2]

If the positions here supported be adopted, it would appear that in the extant works of Clement we have clear evidence of his knowledge and recognition of all the books that now form the canon of the New Testament, with the exception of Philemon, 2nd Peter, and 3rd John, and that in the case of James the evidence is inconclusive.

From the evidence it would appear that Clement was acquainted with at least two groups of authoritative books other than the writings of the Old Testament—the one designated τὸ εὐαγγέλιον, the other ὁ ἀπόστολος.   Though the Gospels could not have been formed into one roll,[3] they are virtually regarded as forming one book.   As in the New Testament we find the "Law" given as a denomination for the whole of the Old Testament,[4] so it has been suggested that Clement uses the word "Gospel" for the whole writings which he recognised as belonging to the New Testament.   But the arguments are inconclusive; and it is all but certain that he used the word to express the four canonical Gospels only.

A second group seems to be quoted under the name of "The Apostle."   In an overwhelming number of cases the word simply means St Paul.   But in some cases—though we nowhere find the phrase "in the Apostle" as a parallel phrase to that "in the Gospel"—it seems to refer to writings.   As it is nowhere applied to any quotation from the Epistles of the other Apostles, it is probably to be interpreted as meaning the Epistles of St Paul only.   In the plural form the phrase does not seem to be applied to writings but to individuals, whose writings for that reason

---

[1] Str , v. 6[25].   [2] E g., Pæd., iii. 3[25].
[3] Kenyon, 'Handbook to the Textual Criticism of the N. T.,' p. 31.
[4] 1 Cor. xiv. 21.

are recognised as authoritative. In this way the term might include both the Catholic Epistles and the Pauline Epistles.

The manner in which "Gospel" and "Apostle" are referred to implies their authoritative character. But it does not follow that they were regarded as parts of an exclusive whole, of a canon in the latter sense of the word. Clement uses the word "canon" in various ways. He speaks of the "canon of the truth," of the "canon of the faith," of the "canon of the Church," of the "ecclesiastical canon."[1] This last is defined as "the harmony and agreement of the Law and the Prophets with the Covenant delivered at the coming of the Lord."[2] It is therefore a canon of interpretation, not of the contents of that to which the canon applied, though it implies a certain relationship between the things interpreted. The question of a canon, considered as an authoritative collection of writings, turns rather on the interpretation to be put on the word $\delta\iota\alpha\theta\dot\eta\kappa\eta$. The word is used by him in the New Testament sense of "covenant," without any reference to a written testament, sometimes in a sense that fluctuates between these conceptions. But in some cases the natural interpretation suggests a written document. He speaks of the importance of philosophy in enabling us to distinguish synonymous expressions in the Testaments.[3] After quoting a saying of the Lord in the Gospel of St Matthew, he asks, quoting a passage from the Book of Proverbs, "Does He not legislate to the same effect in the Old Testament?"[4] Elsewhere he contrasts the saying of the Law with a saying of the Lord Himself in the New

[1] Str., vii. 16 [94]; iv. 15 [98]; vii. 16 [105]; vii. 7 [41].

[2] Ib., vi. 15 [125].   [3] Ib., i. 9 [44].

[4] Ib., iii 6 [54].   οὐχὶ δὲ τὰ αὐτὰ καὶ ἐν τῇ παλαιᾷ διαθήκῃ νομοθετεῖ; Prov. xix 17; Matt. xxv. 40.

Testament.[1] The one was a written authority; is it not most natural to regard the other, the contrasted, source, as also written? So he speaks of the Epistles of St Paul as depending on the Old Testament.[2] But though there is this conception of a written Testament, and though the conception of a New Testament was logically prior to any collection of writings, and may have been at work unconsciously, it is plain from Clement's treatment of other works that the conception was not consciously realised nor logically developed.

The extensive use of writings not regarded as canonical is one of the most pronounced features in the works of Clement. Of some a mere mention must suffice. The Book of Enoch is quoted as the work of Enoch, and an allusion to the same passage is found elsewhere.[3] In view of the precedent in the Epistle of St Jude, this is in no way surprising.[4] The Apocalypse of Elias is quoted without reference as Scripture.[5] There is a probable reference to "The Acts of Paul,"[6] and to "The Acts of John."[7] The limited use of such as compared with the "Acts of the Apostles" would seem to indicate that he had no direct knowledge of them, or that he regarded them as relatively unimportant. One passage seems to be taken from "The Apocalypse of Zephaniah."[8] There are two references by name to "The Traditions of Matthias," and another passage with the name of Matthew only.[9] Some have identified this work with the "Gospel according to Matthew," to which Origen makes allusion,[10] but so far as can be gathered from

---

[1] Str , iii. 10 [71]. Cf. v. 13 [85]; vii. 16 [100].
[2] Ib., iv. 21 [134].
[3] Ec. Pr., 53; Str , i. 17 [8].
[4] Jude v. 14.
[5] Prot , x. [94].
[6] Str., vi. 5 [43].
[7] Stah., vol. iii. p. 210.
[8] Str., v. 11 [77].
[9] Ib., ii. 9 [45]; vii. 13 [82]; iii. 4 [26].
[10] Hom. in Luc. 1.

Clement's use of it, it contained not sayings of Jesus but of Matthew the Apostle.[1]

The most important questions arise in connection with his use of the Apocryphal Gospels, the Didache, the First Epistle of Clement of Rome, the Epistle of Barnabas, the Pastor of Hermas, the Apocalypse of Peter, and the Preaching of Peter.

Two Apocryphal Gospels, the Gospel according to the Egyptians and the Gospel according to the Hebrews, are mentioned by name. In speaking of the first-mentioned he says: " In the first place, we have not the saying in the Four Gospels handed down to us but in the Gospel according to the Egyptians." [2] Apparently, therefore, Clement does not recognise the authority of any Gospel other than the canonical four; and we might have expected that that would have ended the discussion, and that his use of it was only to be regarded as an "archaism." [3] But the matter is not quite so simple as it seems. For on the first occasion on which he refers to the passage, he explains the answer of the Lord in allegorical fashion; and on the second occasion he accuses the heretics who had adduced the passage of not noting the context, and explains the addition which they had omitted allegorically. No doubt this might be interpreted as meaning that he was willing to discuss the matter from their standpoint, or on the assumption of their premises. But it is much more probable that it was to him a genuine saying of the Lord. He distinguishes in effect between the validity to be ascribed to the particular saying itself and the ecclesiastical authority of the book in which the saying is recorded. Another saying of the Lord may be taken from this Gospel.[4]

The " Gospel according to the Hebrews " is mentioned

by name, and a saying is quoted with the formula, " It is written in the Gospel according to the Hebrews." [1] There it is classed as parallel to a thought in the ' Theætetus ' of Plato, and in the ' Traditions of Matthias.' The same saying is adduced without reference,[2] the context, however, suggesting that he regarded it as authoritative. Clement seems to have regarded the saying as a genuine saying of the Lord, though he does not expressly say so, and does not even clearly indicate that it is such; but, as in the case of the " Gospel according to the Egyptians," this does not imply that he recognised the canonical authority of the whole book. Individual sayings are quoted with ἡ γραφή and λέγει ὁ σωτήρ,[3] which may have come either from oral tradition or some non-canonical Gospel; but so far as they are not explained on the principle just suggested, they may be due to a slip of memory, or may be regarded as the survival of the influence of an earlier period, when he had not yet definitely formulated a distinction between what was canonical and what was not. There is no saying quoted with the phrase " In the Gospel " that can be definitely assigned to any non-canonical Gospel.

Though relative frequency of quotation does not furnish an absolute criterion of relative value, it has a certain force. While the Gospel of St Matthew is quoted or referred to from three to four hundred times, and there are references to some passage in every chapter of the Gospel of St Luke, and to all but the ninth chapter in the Gospel of St John, there is only one quotation, twice repeated from the " Gospel according to the Hebrews," and two or three, dealing with the same incident, from the " Gospel according to the Egyptians." If Clement or his antagonists had put any non - canonical Gospel in the same

---

[1] Str., ii 9⁴⁵. See Appendix G.   [2] Str , v. 14⁹⁶.
        [3] See Appendix G.

category as the canonical Gospels, it is inconceivable that
the references to them should have been so few. It is a
proof that the non - canonical Gospels stood in a purely
external relation to his inner development, and had contributed little or nothing to it. In any case, it shows that
in the non-canonical Gospels there was little that was
not found in the canonical Gospels, and that that little
was not of much value.

The " Didache " was familiar to Clement. This is proved
by the form in which he quotes the Decalogue.[1] It is
often said that the " Didache " is quoted by Clement as
ἡ γραφή. From the previous sentence to that in which
the term is used it is more probable that the reference
is to John x. 8.[2] The " Didache " is, however, quoted in
the next sentence with φησί.[3]

If we apply to the Epistles of Clement of Rome and
Barnabas the same criteria which we have applied to the
Pauline Epistles, we find the results to be as follows. The
Epistle of Clement to the Corinthians is quoted by name,
and as the work of Clement.[4] It is nowhere quoted as
ἡ γραφή. It is quoted with γέγραπται with the Epistle to
the Corinthians by name,[5] and in one case as the " Epistle
of the Romans to the Corinthians." [6] It is quoted with
φησί,[7] though in one case the subject may be Clement of
Rome himself.[8] In the series of quotations from the
Epistle of Clement in Strom. iv.,[9] he is designated as
the apostle Clement. He is not named with any such
honorific epithets as are attached to the name of Paul.
It is doubtful whether Clement could have regarded as
Scripture in the fullest sense, or as on a level with the

---

[1] Pæd., iii. 12 [89]; Str., iii. 4 [36]. οὐ παιδοφθορήσεις·
[2] Str., i. 20 [100].   [3] Ib. ; Did., iii. 5.   [4] Str., i. 7 [38]; iv. 17 [108], vi. 8 [65].
[5] Ib., iv. 17 [110].   [6] Ib., v. 12 [80].   [7] Ib., iv. 17 [108].
[8] Ib., iv. 18 [111].   [9] Ib., iv. 17.

Pauline Epistles, a letter in which he conceived of the writer as the spokesman of a church; but it is certainly a writing which he treats with great respect, and it was probably regarded by him as authoritative.

The question as to the Epistle of Barnabas is more complicated. One passage is quoted with φησί.[1] Barnabas is designated as the Apostle[2] or apostolic,[3] as "one of the Seventy and a fellow-worker with Paul,"[4] as "one who proclaimed the Gospel along with the Apostle,"[5] as "one of the Seventy who received gnosis from the Apostles."[6] Sometimes Clement quotes or appropriates the fanciful interpretations of the Old Testament which are characteristic of Barnabas.[7] The evidence in favour of its canonicity in his eyes seems so far cogent. But there is evidence of a contrary kind. When quoting the exposition of the First Psalm by Barnabas, he quotes other expositions with no indication that that of Barnabas stood on a different platform from the others, and, apparently, with a preference for another than that of Barnabas.[8] From this attitude of his two opposite conclusions may be drawn. We may say with Leipoldt that to the consciousness of Clement there was no clear distinction between Scripture and valuable historical sources, and that his attitude to a "work which he certainly regarded as canonical" shows that his "corpus ecclesiasticum" was not a fixed quantity.[9] Or, we may hold that a work whose authority is not unquestionably accepted by him cannot have had in his eyes canonical authority. He never dreams, for example, of differing from St Paul, or St Peter, or St John, but is satisfied with expounding them. If that be so, the designation "the

[1] Pæd., iii. 12 [90].   [2] Str., ii. 6 [31]; ii. 7 [35].   [3] Ib, ii. 20 [116]
[4] Ib.   [5] Ib., v. 10 [63]   [6] Stah, vol iii. p 199.
[7] Pæd., iii. 11 [75]; Str., v 8 [52]; vi. 11 [84].
[8] Str, ii. 15 [68].   [9] *Op. cit.*, p 234.

apostle " cannot of itself in that case involve authority; and the phrases that are attached to his name only indicate that he was entitled to such deference as might be awarded to a fellow-worker of Paul. The citation with φησί might, then, be regarded as a slip of memory. This gains a measure of support in the fact that on the only other occasion of its use the same passage is attached to a passage in the book of Isaiah.[1] Further doubt as to the position of Barnabas is suggested by the circumstance that in the Pædagogus he seems to be giving a direct contradiction to a statement of his. At any rate, he emphatically contradicts a hypothesis which from his knowledge of the immediate context in the Epistle of Barnabas he could not fail to know was held by Barnabas.[2] This seems decisive. The work of Barnabas, accordingly, was to him that of one who was to be honoured as a fellow-worker of Paul, and with whom as an exponent of the Old Testament he had himself some intellectual sympathy, rather than an authoritative Scripture.

No doubt attaches to his recognition of the canonical authority of the 'Pastor' of Hermas. It is regarded as what it claims to be, the record of a revelation granted to Hermas in a vision.[3] It is quoted under the name of 'The Shepherd.'[4] A saying of Hermas is commented on as if it were a passage of Scripture.[5] It is quoted in support of his dogmatic thesis that the apostles preached the Gospel to the heathen in Hades.[6] It is quoted on the relation of the Christian virtues to one another,[7] and

---

[1] Str., ii. 18 79.

[2] Pæd , ii. 10 88 : οὔκουν οὐδὲ τὴν ὕαιναν μεταβάλλειν τὴν φύσιν πιστευτέον ποτέ. Barn., x   τοῦτο γὰρ τὸ ζῶον παρ' ἐνιαυτὸν ἀλλάσσει τὴν φύσιν.

[3] Str., i. 29 181 ; ii 1 3.   [4] Ib., ii. 12 85 ; iv. 9 74.

[5] Ec. Pr., 45   [6] Str., vi. 6 48.   [7] Ib., ii. 12 55.

also alongside of a saying of St Paul and a saying of the Lord.[1] It is quoted in support of his contention as to the difference between the letter and the inner meaning,[2] and as to the utterance of some truths by the false prophets.[3]

Clement regards as authoritative and authentic all the literature that circulated in the name of Peter. Of these the most important are 'The Apocalypse of Peter' and 'The Preaching of Peter.' According to Eusebius, Clement commented on the 'Apocalypse of Peter' in his 'Hypotyposes';[4] and the passages in the 'Selections from the Prophets' support this statement.[5] The fact that the teaching of 'The Apocalypse of Peter,' in the fragmentary form in which we now have it, is so entirely out of harmony with Clement's own teaching on punishment for sin, may mean that the document has undergone many interpolations. If not, that he should have accepted a document as authoritative which was so foreign to his own way of thinking, proves how dominant in his mind was the conception of apostolic authority as a guarantee of inspiration. It must have required all his allegorical subtlety to explain away its details.

'The Preaching of Peter' is quoted by name, and as the work of Peter.[6] It is quoted in support of his view that the souls in Hades must have had an opportunity of hearing the Gospel.[7] It is quoted with great regard for the letter of the passage in support of his contention that the Greeks had an imperfect knowledge and worship of the true God,[8] that Greeks, Jews, and Christians all knew God, though in a

---

[1] Str., iv. 9 [74].   [2] Ib., vi. 15 [131].
[3] Ib., i. 17 [85].   [4] H. E., vi. 14.
[5] Ec. Pr., 41, 48, 49. From a comparison of Fragments 41 and 48 it is plain that he regarded it as Scripture and commented on it as such.
[6] Str., i. 29 [182]; ii. 15 [68]; Ec. Pr., 58.
[7] Str., vi 6 [48].   [8] Ib., vi. 5 [39, 40].

different way,[1] and that God gave philosophy to the Greeks.[2] A saying from it is quoted and put alongside one assigned to the Apostle Paul.[3]   It is also quoted in support of his view as to parabolic teaching and the interpretation of the Old Testament.[4]   Though it is not quoted with any of the ordinary forms that imply inspiration or authority, there can be no doubt from his method of use that he regarded it as a canonical Scripture, simply because, as in the case of the Apocalypse, he regarded it as the work of the Apostle Peter.

The conception of a canon logically involved that of a closed canon and a clear recognition of the principles on which it should be formed; but the use of apocryphal books by Clement shows that in Alexandria the conception was yet in flux, that the question of an authoritative record had not yet been definitely settled, nor the principles of its formation formulated. All the books of the New Testament, with the exceptions already noted, were known to Clement and used by him as authoritative; but alongside of these, some as equal in rank, some as lower in rank, were placed other productions believed to belong to the apostolic or sub-apostolic age.   Clement witnesses to the importance that was attached in the formation of the canon to apostolic authorship or apostolic sanction, and to the part played by the Catholic Church, as claiming to be the custodier of apostolic tradition, in determining what was, or was not, cognate to itself and its teaching.   In estimating his position as a representative man, we have to keep in mind his strong individualism, his belief in the universality of inspiration, his genial outlook on Greek literature, and the influ-

---

[1] Str., vi. 5⁴¹.   [2] Ib., vi 5⁴².
[3] Ib , vi. 5⁴³.   The saying is from 'The Acts of Paul.'
[4] Str , vi. 15¹²⁷, ¹²⁸.

ence which these exercised.   But as a counterpoise to this
have to be placed his official position and his extensive
journeyings in pursuit of Christian truth, which entitle
him to be regarded as a representative not of Alexandria
merely, but of the Church in widely scattered districts of
the Roman Empire.

APPENDIX A.

In Greek song and story we read how Amphion built the walls
of Thebes by his skill in music, how Orpheus tamed the wild
beasts, how the grasshopper took the place of the broken string
on the lyre of Eunomus. But my Eunomus sings not in Phrygian
or in Lydian measure, but He sings the new song—"a song to
lull all pain and error, and bring forgetfulness of every sorrow."
Orpheus and Amphion corrupted the life of man under the mask
of music, my Singer has destroyed the bitter slavery of the
demons, and by the might of His song such as were but "stones"
and "beasts" become men.[1] This song has brought the whole
universe into harmony. The Word of God—the New Song—is
the philanthropic instrument of God Our salvation is His only
harvest from us. Though designated by me the New Song, "He
was before the morning-star"; He "was in the beginning." The
source of our being and our wellbeing, the Word, by whom all
things were created, has appeared as our teacher to bestow on us
eternal life. His pity is an eternal pity Like those who bind
captives to the dead, the wicked serpent binds living men to dead
idols. He who now exhorts men to salvation is He who once
spoke to men through the thorn and the cloud, and by the pillar of
fire terrified men. Then He spoke by the mouth of the prophets;
now, the Lord Himself, the compassionate God, speaks clearly to
men. The Word of God became man that thou mightst learn from
man how man may become God. Be very earnest in regard to
Christ. He is the door to a true conception of God : only through
Him is God truly discerned by the initiated [2] Do not concern

[1] i. 1.4.   [2] ; 8.10.

yourselves with oracles and other insane forms of divination, artifices of unbelieving men. The mysteries are a seed of wickedness and corruption. What you are not ashamed to worship I shall not refrain from describing What of Aphrodite, her origin and rites? Are not the mysteries of Demeter an insult and a jest? What of Zeus and his intercourse with Persephone? What of the inhuman mysteries of Dionysus and the savagery of the Titans? The mysteries of the Cabiri are but murders and funerals.[1] Their mysteries are mysteries of atheists. Are they not atheists who do not recognise the truly existent God, and call those gods who are nothing but a name? Strange that men like Euhemerus, who saw clearly the errors of men in regard to God, should have been called atheists. The extreme points of atheism are ignorance and superstition. By it the primal fellowship between God and man was darkened, and man, the child of God, has been turned aside from the heavenly way of life Some have deified the stars and worshipped the sun. Some have made gods of the fruits of the earth. Some have deified retribution and calamities. Some have made idols of the passions. Some deify incidents that befall men. Some manufacture gods and speak of their birth. Some attribute the beneficence of God Himself to "saviours," as Heracles and Asclepius.[2] The things recorded of your gods really happened to dissolute men. Their fatherland, their crafts, their way of life, their graves, prove that they were but men. Listen to the loves of your gods—the monstrous legends of their dissoluteness, their wounds and their battles, their laughter and tears. The games, Isthmian, Olympian, and the like, were primarily gatherings at tombs. The mysteries seem to have been held in honour of the dead Your gods ate and drank, sometimes unwittingly of the flesh of men like Zeus. The myths about Zeus are antiquated ; he is dead and buried in Crete.[3] Your Zeus, your Apollo, have different names and characteristics. Better than such worship the Egyptian worship of creatures without reason ; they at least are not unnatural in their lusts. You scoff at the Egyptians , but do not some of you worship the stork, the weasel, and the ant ? The impure demons are no "guardians of articulate-speaking men." Do they guard you from committing sin, as, of course, they have had no experience of it ?

[1] ii. [11], [12]   [2] ii. 23-26.   [3] ii. [27],[37].

Like gluttons they are enticed by the smoke, "the drink-offering and burnt-offering which is their due."[1]   Those gods of yours are inhuman and enjoy human sacrifices.   A place does not transform a murder into a sacrifice   To sacrifice a man to Artemis is as much a murder as if done in passion or from lust of gold.   You turn aside from a serpent, why not from man-hating demons?   Can truth or profit be got from the wicked?   Your temples are but tombs.   Yourselves dead, you have put your trust in the dead; "your heads are shrouded in night."[2]

Statues are the work of men.   As art flourished, error grew. The statue of Zeus at Olympias was fashioned by Pheidias.   Other statues are the work of other sculptors, as the Egyptian Serapis— the so-called "made without hands."   Well says the philosopher Heraclitus, "and they pray to their images as if one were to talk with houses."   Statues are less worthy of honour than the meanest living creatures; these possess life and growth, though their senses be undeveloped.   Your image is but dead matter, we have an intellectual image of the only true God.   Men plunder idols; birds defile them.   Fire and earthquake have no fear of images.[3]   Kings of old, even private persons, claimed for themselves divine honours. How can phantoms and demons be gods?   Why forsake heaven and honour earth?   Matter needs art to fashion it; God is in need of nothing.   I dare not intrust the hopes of my soul to soulless things.   You have been deceived by art—though apes are not deceived by pictures in wax or clay.   You have peopled the woods, fields, rivers, and seas with a mob of satyrs, nymphs, nereids, and nereiads.   You have made a stage of heaven.   We carry about in the living statue—man—the image of God, an image which is our guest.   We are "not from beneath."[4]   You have pictures of wantonness everywhere.   We are forbidden to practise an art that deceives.   The sculptor has a better claim to divine honours than the statue which he moulded.   Take heed lest you become as void of perception as statues.   What folly to worship the work of God, sun, moon, and stars, and not God Himself.   The universe sprang into being by a mere act of His will.   Do not deify the cosmos, but seek for its Creator.   In the Divine wisdom is a holy asylum.[5]

[1] ii. 38.41.   [2] iii. 42.45.   [3] iv. 46.53.   [4] iv. 54.59.   [5] iv. 60.63.

Turn to philosophers. They have a dream of the truth. Think of the divergent views of Thales, Anaximenes, and Parmenides, &c., with regard to the first principles. The Stoics utterly disgrace philosophy by representing Divinity as permeating all matter. Epicurus, utterly impious, thinks that God cares for nothing.[1]

You fashion gods out of winds or air or fire or earth. I yearn for the Lord of the fire, the Creator of the cosmos, for God Himself, not for His works. In his conception of God Plato grazed the surface of the truth. He speaks truth as in a riddle. For true laws and opinions concerning God he is indebted to the Hebrews. By the inspiration of God not Plato alone, but many philosophers like Antisthenes and Cleanthes, have declared that God is the only true God.[2]

The witness of poetry is as that of philosophy. Take Aratus or Hesiod or Euripides. They have glimmerings of the truth, but only glimmerings; for to speak of God apart from the word of truth is to walk without feet.[3]

Turn to the Prophetic Scriptures. They are a short road to salvation. Mark how Jeremiah, Isaiah, the whole prophetic choir, set forth God. Listen to the divine Moses, the blessed psalmist, the holy apostle of the Lord.[4] Thousands of Scriptures might be adduced. As a gentle Father, not as a master, God admonishes His children. You must become little children. The church of the first-born is formed of many good children. Be not slaves too proud to become sons. Do not prefer bondage to freedom, death to salvation. Scripture sets before us the threatening, the exhortation, the reward. The Lord exhorts all men to a full knowledge of the truth. If eternal salvation were for sale, the whole wealth of Pactolus would not suffice to purchase it; but with love and faith you can buy it. God alone can teach man and make him like to God.[5] The apostle calls the sacred books God-inspired. No exhortation has such force as that of the Lord Himself, whose sole work is the salvation of men. He says, "The kingdom of heaven is at hand"; and the apostle interprets that divine voice. Faith will introduce you, experience will teach you, the Scriptures will train you. The Word shines for all men. "Let us who are many hasten to be gathered together into the one love. Let us follow after oneness, seeking out the good Monad," that we may come to rest in the one truth, saying, "Abba, Father."[1]

"It is not reasonable," you say, "to subvert the customs handed down to us from our fathers." Why not, then, use the milk of infancy? Why not slobber as we did when children? Abhorrent to piety is this insane custom   But for it you would never have rejected God's greatest boon to the race of men.   Superstition destroys, piety saves.[2]   Look to those who serve the idols—their filthy hair, their ragged raiment, their nails like wild beasts' claws   They seem to be mourning for their gods, not to be worshipping them.   Why not look up to the Lord of the universe?   Monstrous that you, who are His absolute property, should become the slaves of another master.   Let us pass from ignorance to knowledge, from unrighteousness to righteousness, from godlessness to God.   Our loving Father never ceases to admonish or save.   Why not prefer life to death?[3]   By your obsession with ancestral customs you keep off the truth   Let us fight in the stadium of truth, with the Holy Word as umpire, and the Lord of the universe as presiding in the contest.   The prize is immortality.   Heed not the loafers in the market-place and their harangues.   Heed not the image-makers who have had the audacity to make gods of men.   No artist, great or mean, ever formed a living image.   Only the Creator of the universe has formed a living image—man.   Statues are but earthly images of the visible and earth-born man.[4]   As a man, seek out the Creator.   As a son, acknowledge thy Father.   By nature man is formed for intercourse with God.   Piety is his peculiar prerogative—a sufficient viaticum for eternity.   Till the fields, if you will, but, as you till, know God.   Sail, if fond of seamanship, but invoke the heavenly pilot.   If knowledge has come to you when soldiering, listen to the general who commands what is right.[5]   Awake out of your drunken stupor.   Why love the darkness?   Neither halo, nor iris, nor sun, nor moon, nor punishment, nor destiny, nor sleep, nor death, is a god.   Only one God truly exists.   "The earth is the Lord's."   Why ignore the owner?[6]   Are stones and birds sacred, but not men?   Wretched men to suppose that God speaks through the croaking of a raven or the chattering of a jackdaw, but not

[1] ix 67, 68.

[2] x. 89, 90,

[3] x 91,95,

[4] x. b. s

[5] x. 99, 100,

[6] x 102, 103.

through the articulate speech of men. To be deprived of spiritual vision and to be deaf to divine instruction is of all things the most pitiable. Yet nothing can hinder a man who is determined to know God. Receive, then, the gentle word, and spit out deleterious poison. "Believe, O man, Him who is man and God. Believe Him who suffered and is adored Believe the living God, whom to find is to possess life." [1] More blessed are the wild beasts than men in their errors. Fishes are not superstitious, birds are not idolaters. Gain knowledge of God, if even at the end of life. Let heaven be thy fatherland, and God thy lawgiver. Better the bitter drug of truth than the sweet of custom. Cast aside the playthings of childhood. [2] The Son—the Word—took the mask of a man and acted the drama of human salvation. The universe has been flooded with His benefits. [3]

Regard His beneficence. Man, the child of God, fell under the power of the serpent—that is, pleasure. The Lord overcame the serpent, and he who lost paradise receives heaven as his due. [4] With the coming of the Word from above, recourse to the men of Athens or Ionia is superfluous. The true wisdom, only dimly guessed at by the highest philosophers, we have apprehended. The Word gives clear vision to the darkened mind. Let us admit the light, that we may admit God. Let us remove the ignorance which like a mist obstructs the vision, and contemplate the God who truly exists. The Sun of righteousness has changed sunset into sunrise. By heavenly teaching He has made man as God.

Let us give to God the guerdon of a thankful heart and obedience. Those who put their trust in jugglers receive amulets that claim "saving" power, why not rather take for an amulet the Heavenly One Himself—the "Saving" Word? Let the light shine in the heart. [5] God sent the Good Shepherd to save the flock of men. He proclaims good news to the obedient, judgment to the disobedient. He blows the trumpet of the Gospel, and gathers the soldiers of peace. With His armoury we are prepared for battle with the evil one. Better to become at once the servant of the best of beings, and by holy service to imitate Him. I exhort you to be saved. Christ truly bestows life upon you. He banishes death, and makes man the temple and dwelling-place of

[1] x. 104-106.   [2] x. 107-109.   [3] x. 110.   [4] xi. 111, 112.   [5] xi. 113-115.

God. Offer thyself to Him, that thou mayst be not the work only, but also the grace of God.[1]

Custom is as dangerous as the Charybdis or the mythic sirens. But if bound to the cross, thou art saved from destruction : the Word of God will be thy pilot, the Holy Spirit will bring thee to anchorage in heaven, where thou shalt have the vision of God and be instructed in the holy mysteries. Come, O frenzied one, to the true Cithæron, where no Maenades hold revel, but the daughters of God celebrate the sacred rites of the Word. Come, O blind Teiresias, and be led to the truth. Thou didst not see Thebes, but thou shalt see the heavens [2] " Hear," says Jesus, " ye men endowed with reason, barbarians and Greeks alike. To you alone of mortals I grant immortality. I confer on you the word, the knowledge of God, my perfect self. I seek that ye may be like unto me." [3] Let us run to Him, let us love Christ, the good charioteer of men. Let us acquire the greatest of all things—God and life. Let us long for the Word of Truth Himself. Let us not value least the things which are worth most. Not unreasonably the philosophers call ignorance a form of madness. Can we doubt whether it is better to be sane than insane ? All things are God's. If man be beloved by God, all things are His. The pious alone is rich, and wise, and of noble birth. He is the "image" of God as well as the "like-ness." He is like unto God. Choose judgment or grace. Surely life is not to be compared to destruction [4]

[1] xi. 116, 117.   [2] xii 118, 119.   [3] xii. 120.   [4] xii 121, 123.

APPENDIX B.

ANALYSIS OF THE PÆDAGOGUS.

BOOK I. Corresponding to the actions, habits, and passions of men, the Word discharges a threefold function. As Tutor, His aim is preliminary, not scientific, to train the soul to a virtuous, not a scientific, life. He diets our sick souls. By a series of stages leading to salvation, the Word first exhorts, then trains, and finally teaches.[1] Our Tutor is like God, His Father, sinless, free from passion. We need first to be delivered from passions, and then from proclivity to sin. Not to sin is the prerogative of God. To be free from deliberate transgression is the mark of the wise man. To avoid involuntary offences belongs to the well-instructed. Our Tutor heals body and soul. Man is His child, His greatest work.[2] The Lord ministers all good to men. Man, who was made by God, is loved by Him, and ought to return His love and live according to His will. This applies to women as well as to men. For men and women have a common grace and a common salvation, a common love and training.[3]

Pædagogy is the training of children. As is proved by the Lord in the Gospel, we are the children of the Tutor. The same is shown by the designations, "lambs," "sucking-calves," "doves," "chickens," and "young colts." We are "little children," not because we are at the age of unreasoning or devoid of learning, but because we are simple and guileless, as those who know the only God as their Father. As infants we are easily wrought to goodness, and, being a new people, are not perverse like the ancient race. Because the children are the simple ones we glory in the name. All young and feeble things meet with kindness. So God

[1] i. 1 1.3.   [2] i. 2 1.6.   [3] i. 3.4 7.11.

the Father of the universe treats with tenderness the children
whom He has begotten and adopted. The Spirit calls the Lord
Himself a child—the great God and the perfect child.[1] We are
not, then, called children, because our education is childish or
imperfect in character.   When regenerated we at once attain
perfection; illuminated, we know God.   We are already "light
in the Lord," though there is a difference between the earnest
and the attainment of the promise.   Yet faith is perfect and
complete in itself. It is the one universal salvation of men, and
equality of fellowship with the righteous and loving God is the
same to all.   In the same Word there are not gnostics and
psychical men.   The Master calls us "babes."   We are to be
as new-born babes of God.   Those under the Law are children;
those under faith are men and sons.   Compared with the Law,
childhood in Christ is full growth.[2]   When the apostle said, "I
have fed you with milk," he did not mean that which was childish
and imperfect.   For the milk is to be regarded not as something
different from the meat, but the same in essence.   Blood is a kind
of liquid flesh, and milk is the sweeter and finer part of blood.
The essence of the human body is blood.   Milk is a product of the
blood.   The affinity of milk for water, its mixture with honey and
sweet wine, the butter made from milk, may all symbolise spiritual
truths.[3]

Our Tutor, Jesus, calls Himself the good shepherd.   As such
He leads the children to salvation.   He has said—"I am your
Teacher."   Divine instruction is a right directing of truth with a
view to the vision of God, and is a possession for ever; whereas
human instruction fails to mould moral character.   Once He said,
"Thou shalt fear"; to us He says, "Thou shalt love."   Moses
predicted His name and office.   By Prophecy He is invested with
a rod.[4]

"But can He be good who uses the rod?"   To say so is to
forget that in love for us the Lord became man.   From experience
of suffering He knows the weakness of the flesh.   God hates nothing, nor does His Word.   He loves, and man most of all.   "If
so, how does He punish?"   Punishment cures the passions;
reproof acts as a surgeon.   Censure is a mark of goodwill, not

[1] i. 5 $^{12.34}$.   [2] i. 6 $^{25.84}$.   [3] i. 6 $^{38.52}$.   [4] i. 7 $^{53.61}$.

of hatred. He adjusts His reproof to the distinctive habits of each. He cuts off the impulse to sin by declaring its consequences. He punishes, but without feeling of revenge. God is good and just. His Son, the saving Word, may wound in a saving fashion the soul that has grown apathetic, and may do so by manifest methods. The affection of anger, if such a word may be used, is inspired by love to man. The Incarnation is a proof.[1] The Tutor of humanity has devoted Himself to the saving of the "babes." The prophetic testimony shows the varied manner of His loving training. He employs all forms of admonition, reproof, and censure His rhetorical use of fear is a spring of salvation. He leads to self-control those who were being carried away to dissoluteness. When He threatens more harshly, it is to draw us back from rushing to death. The goodness that always shows kindness is disregarded; that which reminds us by the loving fear of righteousness is held in reverence. There is a fear which is associated with reverence, and a fear which is associated with hatred, such as slaves feel towards a harsh master. There is an absolute difference between voluntary and forced piety. The physician is not the cause of the fever, he only demonstrates its existence. So God only shows the sins which are in the man who is sick of soul. The same love that caused God to make His sun to shine caused Him to send down His own Son.[2] As by fault-finding He seeks to induce repentance and dissuade us from sinning, so He employs persuasion and praise. He appeals to the past, the present, and the future. By all forms of cure He calls mankind to salvation. He invites us to the possession of blessings. He calls men of understanding to the love of knowledge. He brings the light of truth to the erring. Praise as well as blame is an essential medicine. Some men need to be beaten out like iron; others grow by praise. Such is His method of instruction. By the Law and the Prophets He trained men who were hard to bridle. The Law was "a tutor to bring us to Christ." Our Tutor is Jesus, the Word of God, to Him God has intrusted us. He is worthy of trust, because He is adorned with three of the fairest graces—knowledge, benevolence, and boldness of utterance.[3]

The Tutor delineates for us the ideal of the true life and trains men in Christ. He formed man out of the dust, and transforms

[1] i. 8 62.74.　　　　[2] i. 9 75.88.　　　　[3] i. 10-11 89.97.

him into a holy and heavenly being. From the tutorship of Christ a noble temper springs, and in those who have been taught the scope of its energy the whole life is conspicuous for gravity.[1] As everything contrary to right reason is sin, he who transgresses is not rational. Christian action is an energy of the rational soul which is perfected through the body, the soul's consort and fellow-combatant, in accordance with a right judgment and desire of the truth.[2]

Book II. What should the Christian be in his whole life? How is he to deal with his body? We must purify the eye of the soul and sanctify the flesh itself. We are to eat that we may live. Food is to be simple and artless, correspondent to truth, befitting simple and artless children, sufficient for life—not for luxury. Such food conduces to health and strength; variety of foods is a source of disease. Men sweep the world as with a drag-net in pursuit of dainties. It has driven them to invent many forms of dessert. We who seek the heavenly food must master the belly. Let the supper be plain and economical, suitable for sleepless vigil. The natural use of food is indifferent. But it is not in accordance with reason for those who share in divine food to take part in the tables of demons We must be lords over meats, not their slaves. We should partake of few and necessary things.[3] We are to take part in social gatherings in a harmless and unsated way, to eat with thanksgiving, to win our fellow-guests by self-control. But to eat flesh or drink wine is not to sin Only we are to partake temperately, not greedily, and not violate decorum in eating. The Lord fed the disciples with loaves and baked fishes—a pattern of simple food. It is lawful to partake of all things; but "all things are not expedient." It is not good to use all things, nor always. In the sphere of a temperate simplicity there is ample variety. Boiled flesh is to be preferred to roasted. Dried fruits and honey may be partaken of. The apostle Matthew and John the Baptist ate the simplest fare, though Peter was taught that the use of food was a thing indifferent. The Tutor by Moses enforced frugality on the Jews by prohibiting the use of many things[4] As for food, so with drink. The natural drink for the thirsty man is water.

[1] i. 12 98-100.   [2] i. 13 101-103.   [3] ii. 1 1-9.   [4] ii 1 10.18.

Such the Lord supplied to the Hebrews. Boys and girls with fire
in their blood should not have access to wine. To be heavy with
wine is not compatible with interest in the things of God. The
advanced in years may partake more freely, they can withstand the
stormy surge of passions But they must not drink to the point of
shaking their reason. It is well to mix the wine with much water.
Both are works of God. Reason should be a partner in the feast.
The picture of the drunkard is at once ridiculous and pitiful. The
divine wisdom despises such a life, if life it be. Christ made water
into wine at the marriage, but He does not permit drunkenness
Wines are imported for jaded appetites. Why should not the wine
of the country satiate desire? In drinking regard must be had
to seemliness The Lord partook of wine, but with decorum. At
all times we must conduct ourselves in a decorous way, as in the
presence of the Lord.[1]

Gold and silver vessels only deceive the vision. They provoke
envy when they go beyond what is necessary. So with furniture in
ebony and ivory. Such vulgar display is banished by the absolute
authority of the Lord. "Sell what thou hast, and give to the poor."
The Lord took His food in a homely bowl. He did not carry about
a silver foot-bath from heaven. He made use, not senseless mag-
nificence, His aim. In like manner all the possessions of the
worshippers of the one God should show forth the symbols of
the one beautiful life. Cheaper things are better than costly. For
self-sufficiency only a few things are required.[2]

At social gatherings musical instruments provocative of lust or
gluttony must be abandoned. The pipe and the flute are more
appropriate to beasts than men. The harp or the lyre may be
used without blame. We are to banish the liquid harmonies which
by base artifices minister to ribaldry, and leave chromatic harmonies
to bacchanalian songs.[3] Buffoons are to be banished from the
Christian polity. We must not make a mock of speech, the most
precious of all human possessions. It is lawful to be playful, but
not to play the buffoon We are to laugh, as in all things, in
a temperate fashion. One should not be grim, but grave. We
must not smile at what is disgraceful or painful We are not to
be always laughing, neither before our elders, nor before everybody,

[1] ii. 19.34.　　　　[2] ii. 3 35.39.　　　　[3] ii. 4 40.44.

nor about everything.[1] From filthy speaking we must absolutely refrain. The divine Tutor invests us with temperate words for ear-guards. By forbidding the utterance of what is unseemly, the Tutor protects us in advance against licentiousness. Let jeering be far removed from us. It is opposed to the friendly feeling which is the end of a banquet. Young men and women are to be absent from such festive gatherings. Unmarried women are not to be present at a banquet of men. Men are not to indulge in any movements or actions suggestive of levity or greed. At a rare time elderly people may quiz children. If one has to sneeze or hiccup, let it be done as quietly as possible. In a word, that which is distinctive of the Christian is composure, tranquillity, stillness, repose.[2]

For Christians the use of crowns and ointments is not necessary. Perfumes and dyes should not stealthily slip into the city of truth. Let women savour of Christ, the truly royal ointment. Some sweet scents are salutary, and may be employed to stimulate sinking strength. We are to choose what is useful. Silly men who dye their hair only make it the grayer. Men of temperance are not to wear a crown of flowers at home. This is neither to enjoy the beauty nor the fragrance of flowers. For us, who have heard that the Word was crowned with a wreath of thorns, to bind our head with flowers would be a mockery of His passion.[3]

As for sleep. Costly rugs of all sorts are to be banished. To sleep on down, moreover, is hurtful to the digestion. Ivory which comes from a lifeless body is not lawful on beds. Yet it indicates vanity to make a point of sleeping "under a bull-hide," unless in an emergency. Let the bed be unadorned, with no elaborate carvings. Sleep is for recreation, not for enervation. We must sleep wake-fully. We who have the wakeful Word indwelling in us should not sleep the whole night. Still less must we sleep by day. The soul needs no sleep, for it is "ever in motion."[4] *

We are not to seek after costly clothing. The Lord enjoined, "Consider the lilies." If He takes away anxious care for food and clothing, what will He say of false hair, of the use of rouge and the like, and the base arts which deceive? Those devoted

---

[1] ii. 5 $^{43-48}$.   [2] ii. 6-7 $^{49-60}$.   [3] ii. 8 $^{61-76}$.   [4] ii. 9 $^{77-88}$.

* Chapter 10 $^{83-102}$ is taken up with the question of marriage. The main points are noted in Lecture V.

to the shadow of the beautiful, not to the beautiful itself, are to
be banished from the truth. Clothes are only required for protection against cold or heat. Hence men and women should be
clothed alike. As a concession, women may be allowed softer
clothes, but not thin, nor of elaborate workmanship, nor decked
with bright colours. Dyeing of clothes is to be rejected. Those
who are white and genuine within should use white and simple
raiment. Life should not be a parade. The Lord derided those
who "lived in gorgeous apparel." Trailing garments indicate a
bragging spirit. Beauty of body in women should not be a trap
for men. They must not make themselves the cynosure of all eyes
by using a purple veil. Why prefer what is rare and costly to what
is accessible and cheap? Why seek with eagerness things that seem
instead of realities?[1] In the matter of shoes women show great
stupidity. Sandals with flowers of gold are really base. The
mincing walk of many stamps the wantonness of their thoughts.
Women may wear white shoes, except on a journey, and then they
must use greased shoes with nails. As a rule, women should wear
shoes; but a man may go barefoot. Jesus wore nothing elaborate
in the way of shoes [2]

To be astounded at green stones and things which are but the
scum of the sea is childish. Women are very anxious about a little
oyster, when it is in their power to adorn themselves with the sacred jewel, Jesus, who is called by Scripture a pearl. The stones in
the Jerusalem that is above are to be interpreted symbolically.
Women put forth the defence, "why may we not use what God
has provided?"[3] Better surely to gain decorous friends than
lifeless ornaments! Women should be beautiful within. The
distinctive excellence of each plant or animal is that which marks
its beauty. Only the beautiful is good. To apply things unsuit-
able to the body as if they were suitable, begets a habit of deceit.
Golden necklaces and anklets are but fetters. Women who are
tutored by Christ should adorn themselves not with gold but with
the Word. If they are beautiful, nature suffices. Let not falsehood
contend with truth. For women who serve Christ, it is fitting to
embrace simplicity. The chains wrought in gold by God are

---

[1] ii. 10 [109-115]   [2] ii. 10 [116, 117].
[3] For Clement's answer and discussion of the right use of wealth, see Lecture V.

modesty and temperance. To pierce the ears is contrary to nature. The best ornament for the ear is true instruction.[1]

Book III. To know oneself is to know God. To know God is to be made like unto Him, by well-doing, and by needing the fewest things possible. The man who has the Word for indweller does not embellish himself. He is the true beauty; for he is also God; he becomes God, for so God wills it. There is another beauty of men—love. "Love does not seek what is not her own." The truth calls that its own which is native to it, but the love of ornament seeks that which is foreign to the true self. "The Lord had no form or comeliness"; yet He exhibited the true beauty.[2] The soul is to be adorned with goodness. Women who beautify the outward appearance and leave waste that which is within are unconsciously adorning themselves after the fashion of the temples of the Egyptians—all gorgeous with the gleam of gold and silver without, in the inner shrine a cat or a crocodile. They destroy their own beauty by washes and dyes. They dishonour the Creator as if the beauty which He gave them was of no worth. Even heathen poets condemn them, how much more shall they be cast away by the Truth? Love of dainties and love of wine can be satiated, but love of finery is insatiable. Horses and birds rejoice in ornament which is their own by nature. Is it not monstrous that women should need a beauty, foreign, bought, and unreal? They have even invented mirrors for this manufactured shape of theirs. Esther, it is true, ransomed the people from massacre by her beauty. But, on the other hand, think of the Trojan war and the desolation which it produced, or of the transgression of the angels and their due reward.[3]

Even men pursue the disease of luxury. To dye the hair is to oppose God who alone "can make the hair white or black." To shave for the sake of beauty of appearance is womanly. The beard is the mark of the man and the symbol of his superior nature. Man should adorn his mind. The Lord wishes us to be naked of vulgarity, separated from sin, intent only on salvation.[4]

Women deserve censure for their great wealth of slaves. They have slaves to carry them everywhere, and associate with worthless

[1] ii. 12 118.129.   [2] iii. 1 1.3.   [3] iii. 2 4.14.   [4] iii. 3 16.25.

creatuies. They nurture parrots, but neglect the orphan and even old men with a reputation for temperance. Like sated fowls they scratch the dung of life.[1] Their baths, too, minister to self-indulgence, vulgarity, and immodesty. Men should be to women a noble pattern of truth. At home, in the stieets, in solitude, and everywhere, they should exhibit reverence. If we are always conscious of the presence of God, we shall keep from stumbling.[2]

Wealth is to be partaken of rationally and imparted in a spirit of love. Masters only differ from slaves in that they have been brought up in a more sickly fashion and are feebler The Christians alone are rich. If God denies nothing, all things belong to the pious man The good man cannot be in straits so long as he keeps fast his confession towards God. Our Tutor gives to us the true riches.[3] Examples often turn the balance towards salvation. So the Tutor in His love by example dissuades from evil, and builds up others on a firm foundation with a view to endurance. Those who have not the power to receive sonship may be preserved from wantonness by fear.[4]

To touch again on baths. They are not to be used on the ground of pleasure. Nor must we bathe on all occasions, nor with the aid of an attendant, nor often in the day. Let due proportion be the standard.[5]

Gymnastic exercises within limits are good both for body and soul. Women are to exercise themselves in spinning, weaving, and cooking. Such exercise tends to sound health. Men may join in various games, or take a walk, or do some economic bye-work, such as using a hoe. In this is nothing ignoble. We are not to enter into athletic contests from a vain spirit of rivalry, but wrestle with composed strength and in the interests of health as befits men free in status. In everything and everywhere we are to be trained to a way of life harmonious and temperate. To be one's own servant, to watch by a sick-bed, to be of service to the impotent, to provide for one in want, is an exercise of righteousness Fishing is permitted, though the better catch is to be "a fisher of men."[6]

Clothing should be simple and white, like the truth, it should be one, not varied. To men of light white is appropriate. Cloth-

[1] iii. 4 26.30.   [2] iii. 5 31.33.   [3] iii. 6-7 34.40.

[4] iii. 8 41.45.   [5] iii. 9 46.48.   [6] iii. 10 49.52.

ing is an index to character. Let the raiment be in harmony with age, person, position, nature, calling. A gold finger-ring may be allowed, not for ornament but for use as a seal. Let the seals be a dove, or a fish, or a lyre, or an anchor—not some idol, nor a sword, nor a goblet.[1] As for the hair. Let the head be closely cropped, but let the chin be covered with hair. Women may dress their locks and bind up the hair simply with a plain pin ; but there must be no meretricious braidings. False hair must be absolutely rejected. It is a most impious thing to put dead tresses on the skull. For on whom will the presbyter lay his hand ? The hair of another, and therefore the head of another. This is to deceive men, disgrace the Lord, and dishonour the head. Nor is the hair to be dyed. Old age is worthy of trust, and should not be veiled. Women are not to besmear their faces with the juggling tricks of knavish art. Natural beauty is best attained by moderation , this produces health ; and beauty is the free flower of health [2] As for walking, we are to adopt a leisurely but not a loitering step A noble man must have no unmanly disfigurement either in movements or habits. Men are not to waste their time in barbers' shops or taverns. Gambling with dice is to be prohibited. Nor will the Tutor bring us to the spectacles, the race-course, or the theatres. Such gatherings are the source of moral disorder. The cities in which sport is seriously pursued lack wisdom. For unpitying contests for glory are not sports, nor is the name to be given to the zealous pursuit of frivolities, and to the irrational ambitions and the senseless waste of money connected with them. " But," you say, "we do not all philosophise." Do you not then follow after life ? How dost thou love God and thy neighbour, if thou dost not philosophise ? To carry on worldly affairs in an orderly way according to the mind of God is not forbidden Let the buyer or seller have only one price for his goods , if he does not obtain his price, he at least obtains the truth [3] Men and women—the latter entirely veiled—are to go to church in seemly fashion, delighting in silence, pure in body, pure in heart, fit to pray to God The whole life of the Christian should be such as they fashion themselves in the church. But some seem to change their manner with the place, and leave within the church what they have heard.

---

[1] iii II ⁵³⁻⁶⁰.   [2] iii. II ⁶¹⁻⁷³.   [3] iii II ⁷⁴⁻⁷⁸

Let the kiss in church be the kiss of true love and holy. By the well-instructed the sight of women will be avoided. The chaste must not only be self-controlled, but beyond the range of censure. We must not only be trusty but appear worthy of trust.[1] Our dividing line in all things must be the cross. Let us nail ourselves to the truth. If some counsels seem harsh, they are designed to bring about the salvation which is the fruit of correction. So the Tutor sets forth bare injunctions, adapting them to the period of guidance, but entrusting the interpretation of them to the Teacher.[2] "Hear, O child, who art being rightly trained," says the Tutor, "the principal heads of salvation." Clement then quotes the all-embracing precept in the Gospel, Christ's summary of the commandments, and the decalogue. He gives practical counsels based on the Scripture on prayer, fasting, forbearance, love, civil government in various aspects, faith, servants, liberality, and the like. After numerous quotations from the teaching of the apostles, he concludes with a prayer to the Tutor.[3]

[1] III. 11 79, 83.   [2] III. 12 84-96.   [3] III. 12 97-101.

APPENDIX C.

BOOK I. Should books be written, and if so, by whom? Shall we
approve the writing of books by men like Epicurus, and forbid men
who proclaim the truth to leave works that will benefit the generations after them? Words are the offspring of the soul. The
Saviour condemned the servant who returned the deposit without
increase. The writer as well as the reader must prove himself in
the light of conscience. There is an unwritten husbandry of the
Word and a written husbandry. We are to labour "for the meat
that endureth unto everlasting life." Souls have their own proper
nourishment. On him who labours in writing God will bestow
reward according to his need. But "men" should not even aim
at reward. To do so is to be in the grip of worldly custom.[1] As
for these memorials of mine they are designed to be a veritable
image of the living words of my teachers, though they are feeble
in comparison with the words of those gracious spirits If I pass
by some things I do so in no grudging spirit, but in the interests
of my hearers. I shall not scruple to use what is best in philosophy and Hellenic culture, to seek out the truth in them, like
the nut in the husk. For in a real sense philosophy is a work of
the Divine Providence.[2] Its use may be defended on the ground
that, even if it were of no use, it would be useful to prove that it
was so, that admiration and persuasion are begotten by learning,
that truth is wooed and won by a comparison of different opinions.
The seeds of knowledge are artfully hidden in the Stromateis, that
like the prey of the huntsmen the truth be caught with toil and

[1] i. 1 $^{1.10}$ [2] i. 1 $^{11.18}$.

search. "Why arrange your notes so?" Because there is a danger in betraying the secret word of the Christian philosophy to those who speak against everything without just reason Such scoffers, of whom there are many, jest at the barbaric element in the truth, manufacture objections, and spend their life about the distinction of names, the nature of sentences and their synthesis, more talkative than turtle-doves. Of such the Divine Scripture says, "I will destroy the wisdom of the wise."[1]

The word "wise" is varied in application. Homer calls a craftsman "wise." Hesiod speaks of a harper "skilled in all manner of wisdom" The saying of the Lord to Moses[2] shows that in Scripture every secular art or science is called by the common name of wisdom. There is wisdom in excellence in mechanical arts as well as in the higher departments of work and thought. Rightly, then, the Apostle called the wisdom of God "manifold," which had manifested its own power for the wellbeing of men by art, by science, by faith, by prophecy.[3]

While before the advent of Christ philosophy was necessary to the Greeks for righteousness, now it serves by way of a preliminary discipline. We are warned by the Scripture "not to be much with a strange woman,"[4] that is, we are to make use of secular culture, but not to linger over it, nor abide permanently with it.[5] Such preliminary training contributes readiness for the vision of duty, and re-illumines the soul. Moral perfection is not the fruit of nature but of instruction. To refute sophistry we must study the art of reasoning.[6]

Greek culture and philosophy came down from God, as showers fall on different soils. The Husbandman was One, the results varied according to place, time, and variety of seed All arts differ, but all are useful to life. So by philosophy I mean no special school. Some have fallen into well-doing by accident. But faith is essential. The Scriptures were translated into Greek to take away the pretext of ignorance. The paths to righteousness are many, and lead to the authoritative way of truth.[7] Neither in

---

[1] 1 2-3[19.24]; Isa xxix. 14; 1 Cor. i. 19.   [2] Exod xxxi. 1-5
[3] 1 4[25.27]; Eph. iii. 10.   [4] Prov. v. 20.
[5] 1 5[28.32]. Here, in close dependence on Philo, follows scriptural proof of the relation between secular culture and the true philosophy.
[6] 1, 6[33.36].   [7] 1. 7[37, 38].

sophistry, nor in rhetoric, nor in the logic of the schools, is truth at
all to be found. The Apostle calls the art of logic a disease. We
must not seek to please the multitude. The truth-loving Plato,
like one divinely inspired, says, "I obey only the word that seems
to me the best."[1]

To disdain philosophy and insist on bare faith alone is opposed
to the teaching of the Lord in the Parable of the Vine. In all arts
he is truly learned who has learned useful things; so he who takes
examples from Greek and barbarian alike is a much-experienced
tracker-out of truth and a man "of many devices." The prophets
and apostles were ignorant of philosophical arts; but methodical
teaching is required for the interpretation of what they said. There
is a saving word as well as a saving work. To save those eager to
be saved is the best thing, and not the composition of ornamental
little phrases. One hearer suffices the gnostic.[2] The philosophy
discredited by the Apostle is the Epicurean or any other system
which pays high honour to the elements. Deny Providence, and
the economy of the Saviour seems a myth. Christianity extends
Providence to particular events. Those who worship the elements
or posit atoms as first principles may be philosophers in name, but
are really atheists.[3] We must sanctify ear as well as tongue if we
are to share in the truth. We are not "to cast pearls before swine."
What we hear we are to "proclaim on the house-tops"—that is, to
expound them in a transcendental and pre-eminent way, and not
impart the truth to all absolutely. Truth is one. The sects both
of the barbarian and Hellenic philosophy have each a part. He
who puts together the separate pieces of truth will behold the Word
—the perfect truth.[4]

The form of philosophy among the "seven wise men" of the
Greeks was Hebraic and enigmatic. Plato says that the form of
brevity was zealously pursued by the Greeks of old.[5] The most of
the wise men and philosophers were barbarians by race. Plato
admits that he derived the best elements in his system from the
barbarians. Zoroaster was a Persian. Numa was a Roman. Wit-

[1] i. 8 $^{39.42}$.   ὁ φιλαλήθης Πλάτων οἷον θεοφορούμενος.   [2] i. 9-10 $^{43.49}$.
[3] i. 11 $^{50.54}$.   [4] i. 12 $^{57, 58}$.
[5] i. 14 $^{59.65}$.   Clement discussed some of the sayings of the wise men. Then he
gives a summary of the succession of philosophers among the Greeks with the view
of showing the higher antiquity of the Hebrew philosophy.

ness, too, the Egyptian prophets, the Druids, the Indian gymnoso-
phists, the disciples of Buddha, regarded by them as divine. By
far the oldest of these is the Jewish race. Philo has proved it. As
with philosophy, so with almost all arts. The Egyptians introduced
astrology and invented geometry. Augury was of barbarian origin.
Cadmus was a Phœnician In navigation, mining, dyeing, music,
rhetoric, grammar, the barbarians anticipated the Greeks The
first woman who was a philosopher was Theano of Crotona.[1]

In spite of its limitations philosophy paves the way for the truth
that is most kingly. But, is it not written, "all who were before the
advent of Christ were thieves and robbers?" "And is it not the
case that he who does not prevent an evil is a cause of it?" This
is an entirely wrong conception of causality.[2] As for the "all that
came," this does not mean all men, but all the false prophets, all
that were not authoritatively sent by the Word. And though they
were prophets of the liar, they told some true things. For Providence overruled their daring for good.[3] The really wise among
the Greeks are not discredited by Scripture, but such as were wise
in their own conceit. God has shown their wisdom to be foolish
and not true as they supposed. In the Book of Acts Paul shows
that God was worshipped by the Greeks in a roundabout way, but
that apprehension in the way of knowledge was necessary by the
Son. We do not receive all philosophy absolutely but that of
which Socrates speaks. "Many, as they say in the mysteries, are
bearers of the thyrsus, but the mystics are few." So Plato limits
philosophers to "the lovers of the vision of the truth." Philosophy
aids in the apprehension of the truth; but the alone authoritative
truth is that in which we are taught by the Son of God. This
teaching is self-sufficient and in need of nothing.[4]

The most ancient of all forms of wisdom is incontrovertibly the
philosophy of the Hebrews. Moses was older than most of the
Greek deities.[5]

---

[1] i. 15-16 [66, 80].   [2] See Lecture III.   [3] i. 17 [80, 87].   [4] i. 18-20 [88, 100].
[5] i. 21 [101, 147]. Clement gives the times of the prophets who succeeded Moses,
beginning with the Judges, followed by the Kings He holds that Homer and
Hesiod were later in date than Elijah; explains the seventy weeks of Daniel;
makes curious digressions, as, for example, on the number of dialects in the
world, the language used by irrational creatures. He discusses the date of the
birth of Christ. He brings down his chronology to the death of Commodus.

The Scriptures both of the Law and the Prophets were translated into Greek in the time of Ptolemy — whether the son of Lagos or Ptolemy Philadelphus   Seventy men of the highest repute with a knowledge of the Greek tongue carried out the task in such a manner that the translation, though separately done, agreed both in meaning and expression   Thus the Hebrew prophecy became a prophecy in Greek.   The Scriptures tell of the race, deeds, and life of Moses, the theologian, prophet, and interpreter of sacred laws.[1] He is a prophet, legislator, tactician, general, statesman, and philosopher.   Generalship is a section of kingly government.   The highest form of the kingly office is that which is according to God and His Holy Son.   There are three elements in generalship — caution, daring, and their union   All these things, and how to use them, the Greeks learned from Moses.   Plato lays down principles which seem to be interpretations of the Law.   Moses was a living law guided by the good Word.   He administered a good polity, seeking to train good and noble men.   The Lord is the true lawgiver.   He not only gave the Law, He is the exegete of the divine commands.   Strange that the Greeks say that the gods taught Minos and Lycurgus, while they do not believe that God gave the Law to Moses, and thus disown the archetypes of what is told by their own writers.[2]

The Law inflicts penalties, but it is none the less good.   Punishment is a surgery or cautery to the soul.   The Providence that administers the world must be both sovereign and good   From a "son of disobedience" you may become a "legal slave," then a "faithful servant," and then a "son."   Salvation is the goal of the terror begotten by the Law.[3]

The philosophy of Moses is divided into four parts — the historical, the legislative, the sacrificial, and the theological, that is, the initiation into the immediate vision of God   The true dialectic professes the knowledge not of mortal affairs but of divine, but this is accompanied by a proper use of human affairs in word

---

[1] I. 22 [148,150].   Chap 23 [151,167] contains an account of the birth and life of Moses down to the departure of the people from the land of Egypt.   It is taken from Philo, to whose work he once makes allusion, and includes some legendary matter from other sources

[2] I. 24-26 [158,170].   [3] I 27 [171,175].

and deed. The true dialectic leads to the true wisdom which
knows things that exist as they exist   This needs the Saviour
who removes the film of ignorance from the soul, shows us how
we are to know ourselves, and reveals the Father of the universe
to whomsoever He wills.   The apostle says that it was " by
revelation " that he knew the mystery.[1] The Egyptian priest in
Plato beautifully said that " the Greeks are always children," and
that " there is not an old man among the Greeks, nor any science
hoary with age."   By this he means the barbarian truth of very
ancient date.[2]

Book II. As to our plan of work note the following points. We
shall show that the Greeks are thieves, that they have plagiarised and
adulterated their most weighty opinions in matters of faith, wisdom,
the fear of God, and, in particular, the secret part of the barbarian
philosophy, the symbolic and enigmatical, which is most essential
to a knowledge of the truth. We shall then defend our opinions
from the attacks of the Greeks and give a friendly refutation of
the more noble of the philosophers—not to avenge ourselves on
detractors, but to convert them and take away their vanity.[3]

"In all thy ways acknowledge wisdom."[4] This shows that our
actions should be in harmony with reason, and that we should
select what is useful out of every discipline   Our philosophy is
perfect and true.   It leads up to the Governor of the universe, a
being difficult to track out, ever withdrawing from him who pursues, but who, though far off in respect of essence, is very near
in respect of His power.   To search into the deep things of God
demands faith.   He who believes the Divine Scriptures receives
a demonstration that cannot be gainsaid.[5] Faith is not a gift of
nature, as Basilides avers   For if so, there is no merit either in
faith or unfaith. Faith must be voluntary.   To us faith is an
irrefragable criterion. We have believed the Word, for the Word
is truth.   First principles are indemonstrable.   Only by faith is
it possible to know the First Principle of the universe. We need
a new eye, a new ear, and a new heart.   Faith and knowledge are
indissolubly related.   " Unless ye believe, ye will not understand."[6]

---

[1] i 28[176-179].   [2] i. 29[180-182]; Timæus, p. 22 B.   [3] ii. 1[1-3].
[4] Prov. iii. 6.   [5] ii. 2[4-9].   [6] ii. 3-4[10-19].

That all things belong to the wise man has come down to the Greeks from Moses. As Abraham was called "the friend of God," so by way of imitation Minos was called "the friend of Zeus." Moses was a wise man, king, lawgiver. But our Saviour surpasses all human nature. He is a king, rich, alone the High Priest, the king of truth, a lawgiver, of noble lineage, for God is His Father.[1] Plato proves the universal necessity of faith. Faithfulness embraces summarily the other virtues[2] "Faith cometh by hearing, and hearing by the Word of God."[3] The word of God, then, is demonstration. Teaching is trustworthy when faith co-operates. There must be receptivity on the part of the learner. Penitence is a work of faith. Hope, too, is constituted by faith. Hope is the expectation of good, and expectation involves faith. "God is faithful," that is, He is worthy to be believed when making an assertion. We believe in Him whom we have trusted, in God whom alone we know. Whether based on fear or love, faith is something divine. It is the foundation of truth.[4]

To attack fear is to run down the Law, and, therefore, God who gave the Law. "But fear is an irrational affection." How so, when the commandment was given through the Word (Reason)? The fear of the Law is a cautious fear; it is a turning aside from that which is truly hurtful, disease of soul. Can the Law be anything but good, which is our Tutor to Christ?[5] The Marcionites call the Law not evil, but just But the opposite of evil is not just, but good Fear is a good thing, for it takes away evil True fear does not fear God, but the falling away from God. "In the fear of the Lord is the hope of strength."[6] Such fear leads to repentance and hope. Faith rests on repentance and hope, and fear upon faith, and endurance and practice, along with instruction, find their goal in love, which is perfected by knowledge. An ignorant man, so long as he is ignorant, cannot philosophise, as he has not grasped the idea of wisdom.[7] By saying, "I am your God," the Scripture admonishes us to seek God, and as far as possible to strive to know Him. Righteous action is inseparable

---

[1] ii 5[20,22].   [2] ii. 5[23, 24]   [3] Rom x. 17.   [4] ii. 6[23,32].
[5] ii. 7[33,35] Here follows a criticism of the views of Basilides and Valentinus on fear, ii. 8[36,38].
[6] ii. 8[39, 40]; Prov xiv. 26.   [7] ii 9[41,45]

S

from such knowledge.[1] As there is a faith of knowledge and a
faith of opinion, so there is a demonstration of knowledge and a
demonstration of opinion. The demonstration of opinion is
human, the demonstration of knowledge implants faith through
comparison and opening up the Scriptures. He who is wise in
his own conceit does not touch the truth, but is wavering and
unstable, whereas by faith and true knowledge the soul remains
the same and unchanged.[2]

In regard to time there is memory in relation to what is past,
hope to what is future. We believe that the past has taken
place, that the future will take place. Fear is the beginning of
love, which by an addition becomes love, then faith. When I
fear the Father, I love when I fear. In all our intercourse with
men we require faith. As the Shepherd says, "All the virtues
are the daughters of faith."[3]

In order that the foundation of faith may be laid, the soul must
be cleansed by repentance. For those who sin in the faith a second
repentance is granted, but he who continuously repents is closely
related to him who sinned wilfully at first. Frequent prayer for
pardon for frequent transgressions is but an appearance of repentance. All passions are irrational appetites. That which is involuntary is not judged. This may arise from ignorance or
necessity. The Lord shows sins to be in our power by pre-
scribing forms of healing corresponding to the disorders. Pardon
does not consist in remission, but in healing.[4]

To interpret the will of the passionless God as akin to our
emotions is to interpret the Scriptures carnally. The ascription
of joy or pity to Him is a concession to our weakness. Our
only relationship to God is that we are the work of His will
Yet in His pity He cares for us. So our relationship to the Lord
is not that of essence, but in this that we have been made immortal, and have been called sons. In the gnostic, will, judgment,
and discipline are one.[5]

The Greeks derived from Moses the elements of their ideas
of the virtues, manliness, wisdom, self-control, and the like,
above all, piety. All these virtues are related. We are to be

[1] ii. 10 46, 47.   [2] ii. 11 48.52.   [3] ii 12 53.55.
        [4] ii. 13-15 56.71.   [5] ii. 16-17 72.77.

assimilated to the Lord. As God needs nothing, the good man being on the borderland between an immortal and a mortal nature, has few needs In all its precepts the Law encourages manliness and humanity.[1]

The Gnostic is he who is after "the image and the likeness," imitating God as far as possible, self-controlled, enduring, living righteously, king over his passions, given to impart of what he has. For God's gifts are for the common advantage of men. There is to be a moral change in mouth, heart, hands. Plato said that the goal is likeness to God as far as possible. So the Law says, "Walk after the Lord your God." So to follow creates likeness. The beneficent man who does good by which he himself receives good is the image of God.[2] The divine likeness is also gained by fortitude which reaps as its fruit apathy through endurance. Such endurance the gnostic, so far as he is a gnostic, possesses. Bearing about the cross of the Saviour, he follows the Lord, walking in His footsteps, "as if he were a God," having become a "Holy of Holies." To loose the soul from pleasure is "the study of death"[3] We must, therefore, "put on the panoply of God." Man who is endowed with reason ought not to give way to impulse like the animals.[4] A champion of heresy, calling himself a gnostic, used to say that he fought with pleasure through pleasure. So the Nicolaitanes say that we ought to wither up the attacks of the flesh by abusing it. This were to live like beasts. The affection of pleasure is not an absolute necessity, but only attends by way of consequence certain natural needs. It is not an activity, nor a disposition, nor a part of us, but has been introduced into life for the purpose of service. Peace and freedom are only won by untiring conflict with our passions. Our standard, no doubt, may seem severe to those without tone and feeble, as to the unjust that which befalls them may seem very stringent justice. We must shun things provocative of lust and luxury.[5]

In saying that there was a happiness equal to that of a God in not being hungry or thirsty or cold, Epicurus laid down a precept for dung-eating swine rather than for rational creatures. To live in

---

[1] ii 18 78-96.   [2] ii. 19 97-102.   [3] Phædo, 81 A.
[4] Here follows a criticism of the views of Basilides and Valentinus on the passions as appendages, ii. 20 103-117.   [5] ii 20 118-126.

accordance with virtue, to live in harmony with reason, to live in contemplation of the truth and order of the universe, to live according to knowledge, such are philosophical definitions of the chief end. Plato describes the most perfect good as likeness to God, and to be like to God is to be holy, just, and wise.[1]   Our aim is to attain the end that knows no end, to live according to the commandments without reproach and in a scientific spirit, through knowledge of the divine will.   " Be ye followers of me, as I also of Christ," says the Apostle.[2]   Assimilation to God, then, is the aim of faith, and the end is the restitution of the promise that rests on faith.[3]

The question of marriage falls under pleasure and desire. Marriage is a union for the production of lawful children.   Should one marry?   And when and in what condition should he marry? Some philosophers rejected marriage ; some looked on it as a thing indifferent , some as a good   Marriage is to be a school for the highest forms of self-restraint.   In regard to marriage the Gospel is not in conflict with the Law, for both come from the one Lord.[4]

Book III. Continence is not concerned merely with sexual desires, but with all things which the soul lusts for in an evil way.   As a divine grace it not only teaches self-control, it creates it.[5]   To say with the followers of Carpocrates that women should be common is entirely subversive of the Law and the Gospel.   No wonder that the agapæ of such are scenes of unbridled lust   It is a misunderstanding of the teaching of Plato to say that he taught the community of women.[6]   The Marcionites say that nature is evil, because derived from an inferior God—the just Creator.   Hence they abstain from marriage.   But though in their hatred of the Creator they will not marry, they use His food and breathe His air. No doubt the Greek poets and thinkers said many things about the hardships that attend existence, and even said that it was better not to come into existence than to be.[7]

---

[1] Theat., 176 B.   [2] 1 Cor. xi. 1.   [3] ii. 21-22 [127.136].
[4] ii. 23 [137.147]. See Lecture V. for the main points in Clement's views of marriage
[5] iii. 1 [1.4]   [6] iii. 2 [5.11].   [7] iii. 3 [12.24].

The self-control of Marcion, if it can be so called, is due to the Creator Himself. All that Nicolaus meant by "abusing the flesh" was that we must master pleasures, and that we cannot serve two masters, pleasure and God. The views of some are a disgrace not merely to philosophy but to humanity. "Ye have not so learned Christ" The followers of Prodicus boast of being "royal sons," but they act not like kings but whipped curs. They are opposed alike to human and divine law. Are they better than men of the world who are like the worst of such? They oppose one precept of the Creator Why not be consistent and oppose all? He said, "Make no graven image." Why not worship images? They pick out expressions from some prophetic section, patch them together, and interpret literally what was said allegorically. By transposing accents and stops they wrest the Scriptures to their own luxuries [1]

We may divide the heresies into two types—those which teach the moral indifference of actions, and those which proclaim self-control from impiety and a spirit of contentiousness. As to the former If any way of life can be chosen, the life of self-control can be chosen. If all things be lawful, self-control is lawful. If the most shameful way of life be indifferent, then we must obey desires in every respect, or we must avoid some desires, and then indifference ceases. But how can the man who is mastered by bodily pleasures be likened unto God or possess the knowledge of God? Those who follow the divine Scriptures must not live indifferently It is not possible to have knowledge and not be ashamed to pay court to the body. As well call bile sweet, as call slavery to pleasure liberty.[2]

As for the second class. Of them we say, "They went out from us, but they were not of us." The reply of the Lord to Salome [3] only meant that genesis in every case is followed by corruption. If they reject marriage because "they have accepted the resurrection," let them give up eating and drinking also. In saying that they imitate the Lord, they forget that they are entirely different from Him,[4] and that He said, "What God had joined together, let not man put asunder." Unless it spring from love to God, there is no virtue in chastity Paul condemns those who rejected marriage. Peter and Philip had children.[1] Christian self-control aims at mastery over the very desire of lusting. This demands the grace of God. True continence is better than that taught by philosophers. In regard to marriage or food or the like, we should choose only what is necessary. Self-control is not limited to sexual passion; there is self-control in despising money, or pleasure, or property, or the games, in controlling the tongue, in lording it over evil reasonings. We embrace self-restraint from love to God, sanctifying the temple of God.[2]

By supporters of the doctrine of indifference some passages of Scripture are violently wrested, in particular, the saying, "Sin shall not have dominion over you."[3] But the apostle himself divinely annuls the sophistical art of pleasure. As for the saying of the Lord to Salome, "I came to destroy the works of the female," that means desire and her works. The Lord only abolished love of money, love of strife, madness in lust, dainty living and the like. Why do they not quote the context which teaches that either self-control or marriage is in our power?[4]

The saying, "Where two or three are gathered together in my name, there am I in the midst of them,"[5] may be interpreted in various ways. In any case, in the number of those with whom the Lord is, those who do not marry from hatred or who from lust abuse the flesh are not found. The counsel of the prophet to "come out from among them and be separate"[6] does not mean to separate ourselves from the married but from the Gentiles and from impure and impious heresies. And the same God spoke through the Law and the Prophets and the Gospel[7] Paul teaches that both chastity and marriage have each their distinctive ministries for the Lord. Nowhere do the Letters of the Apostle annul marriage, but preserving the sequence of the Law with the Gospel, regard both the married woman and the virgin as holy in the Lord ——the one as a wife, the other as a virgin.[8] The saying adduced by Cassianus is not in the Four Gospels handed down by the Church, but in the Gospel according to the Egyptians, and, in any case, should be interpreted allegorically.[9] The saying about the beguiling

---

[1] iii. 6 45.56.   [2] iii. 7 57.60.   [3] Rom. vi 14   [4] iii. 8-9 61.66
[5] Matt. xviii. 20   [6] Isa. lii 11 ; 2 Cor. vi. 16.   [7] iii. 10-11 67.78.
[8] iii 12 79.90.   [9] iii. 13 91.93.

of Eve[1] does not mean that generation was due to deceit, but only that they sought pleasure greedily. The saying, " It is good for a man not to touch a woman," [2] means that we are not to be carried away by irrational impulses. When Paul speaks of being temperate in all things,[3] that does not mean abstinence from all things, but that he used in a temperate way what he judged should be used. If generation be evil, they must draw the blasphemous conclusion that the Lord, who shared in it, was evil. Thus they slander the will of God and the mystery of creation. Apart from the body the economy of salvation could not have been fulfilled; for He who was its Head passed His life in the flesh. And did He not cure the body as well as the soul from disorders?[4]

A life of chastity may therefore be chosen, but those who are joined in marriage are not to be despised. Both are to give thanks to God in their distinctive spheres. The plain teaching of Paul is that marriage is lawful not only according to the Law but according to the New Covenant. Such as, under the name of knowledge "falsely so-called," have given way to pleasure contrary to the rule of God, have entered on the path which leads to the outer darkness.[5]

Book IV. As to order of treatment. First, we shall discuss martyrdom, who the perfect man is, and relative points such as the universal duty to philosophise. Then we shall treat of faith, inquiry, the debt of Greeks to the barbarian philosophy. Then will follow an exposition of the Scriptures in opposition to Greeks and Jews, with supplementary matter. The physiological views of the Greeks will next be considered After a brief sketch of theology we shall treat of prophecy, the Scriptures and their divine authority in relation to heretics Then we shall treat of the true gnostic physiology. But it shall be written as God wills, and as He may inspire.[6] The Stromateis are designedly discursive, and require winnowing in order to pick out the wheat.[7]

The mass of men have a disposition like the storms of winter, unsettled and unreasoning. To disbelieve the truth brings death,

[1] 2 Cor. xi. 3.   [2] 1 Cor vii 1.   [3] 1 Cor. ix. 25   [4] iii 14-17 $^{9i-10i}$.
      [5] iii. 18 $^{105-110}$.   [6] iv. 1 $^{1-3}$.   [7] iv 2 $^{i-7}$.

as to believe brings life. He who was "made a little lower than
the angels" is the perfect man and the gnostic. Man is compacted
of soul and body. The body tills the ground, the soul reaches
forth to God Death is the fellowship of the soul, being sinful,
with the body, life is the separation from sin All his life the
gnostic makes it his study to sever in this sense the soul from
the body, and thus creates an eagerness to endure the natural
death which dissolves the chains that bind the soul to the body.[1]
Hence the gnostic will not from fear of death fall away from
the teaching of the Lord. He confirms the truth of the Gospel
by his deed. By his precious blood he puts unbelievers to shame.
Martyrdom is perfection, because it exhibits the perfect work of
love. The soul that has lived in purity along with the knowledge
of God is a witness both by life and word, pouring forth faith like
blood all his life and even up to his departure. Some heretics say
that the knowledge of the only true God is true martyrdom, and
that the man who makes confession by death is a self-murderer.
We assent to the former statement; and we also censure those who
have rushed on death from hatred of the Creator, giving themselves
up to a vain death. To live well, we must live. He who in the
body has studied the art of living well is being sent forward to immortality.[2] We must exercise care for the body for the sake of the
soul. By beneficence like that of the Lord, gnostic love shows
itself. Those who act for the sake of the gift promised are called
"hired servants" in the Parable of the Two Brothers. The Lord
teaches that from love to God we must gnostically despise death.
We are not to hate our persecutors, but regard every trial as an
opportunity for witnessing[3] He who denies the Lord denies himself; he denies life. Those who persecute the martyr do not know
that to such death is the gateway of life The gnostic will never
put the chief end in fortune, but in being a kingly friend of God;
and though he be subjected to dishonour, and exile, and confisca-
tion, and death, he will never be torn away from his freedom and
overmastering love to God Armed with weapons not carnal, he
says "O Lord, grant a critical opportunity and take a demonstration; let the terror approach; I despise dangers from love to

[1] iv 3[8.12].   [2] iv 4[13.19].   [3] iv. 5-6[20.41].

Thee." [1] Even barbarians have defied tyrants and faced most
cruel tortures.   The whole church is full of women as well as
of men who have made "a study of death" — the death that
quickens unto Christ.   Young or old, slave or Greek, can philosophise. Both servant and wife will practise the Christian philosophy.
The free man, though menaced with death, will never abandon
piety ; nor will the wife, nor son, nor servant, where husband or
father or master is hostile, fail to cling nobly to virtue.   There
can, surely, be no doubt that it is better to be a member of the
brotherhood of God than to choose the darkness of demons.   In
fighting for virtue we are to think of nothing save the possibility
of its being well done.[2]
    Consider the sayings of the Lord as to martyrdom.   With the
great part of the exegesis of Heracleon we agree.   He has over-
looked this point, that even if some have not by action and life
"confessed Christ before men," their confession at the tribunal
and endurance of torture even unto death show that they have
believed with the heart.   Even the martyrdom of those who make
confession at the end of life is a purging away of sins with glory.
The Lord drank the cup, and in imitation of Him the Apostles, as
being truly gnostics and perfect, suffered for the churches which
they founded.   So the gnostics who walk in their footsteps ought to
drink the cup, if circumstances demand it.   The gnostic who bears
witness not from hope or fear, but from love, is the truly blessed
martyr, surrendering himself wholly for God, giving up as a deposit
the "man" who is demanded [3]   When He says, "When they persecute you in one city, flee ye into another," He does not exhort us
to flee as if persecution were an evil thing, nor like men in fear of
death to turn and flee ; but He wishes us not to be a cause of evil
in the persecutor, nor to share in his evil.   To expose ourselves to
capture from rashness is to be a fellow-worker in the crime of the
persecutor.   We are not to keep hold of anything that belongs to
this life ; we are not to embitter by counter-claims those who take
us to law, and by our action stir them up to blaspheme the Name.[4]
"If God cares for you, why are you persecuted and slain?"   This
takes place in harmony with the prediction of God, the free-will of

[1] iv 7 [42-55].   [2] iv. 8 [56,69].   [3] iv. 9 [70-75].   [4] iv. 10 [76, 77].

the judge, and, in any case, is no real wrong to us.[1] In like conflict with human freedom is the theory of Basilides that the soul is punished here for sins committed previously in another life. If martyrdom be retribution by way of punishment, then the faith and the teaching for which martyrdom takes place are co-operators in punishment. What place, then, is there for love to God, or praise, or censure, or right citizenship? The Lord did not suffer by the will of the Father, nor are those who are persecuted, persecuted by the purpose of God. He does not prevent such things. His Providence is to be regarded as a disciplinary act, in the case of others for their own individual sins, in the case of the Lord and His apostles for ours. For the sake of our sanctification the Lord was not prohibited from suffering.[2]

We are to love the sinner, not as such, but in so far as he is a man and the handiwork of God. We are to love our enemies. Like Paul, we must bear all things lest we should cause hindrance to the Gospel of Christ. We must exhibit a pure example to our disciples.[3] The perfect righteousness both in word and deed is plainly outlined in the Epistle to the Romans. The divine apostle sets forth the gnostic rule thus. He speaks of one salvation in Christ for the righteous of the Old Covenant and for us.[4] "If I give my body and do not love," says the Apostle Paul, "I am become as sounding brass and a clanging cymbal." That is, if I bear witness not from an elect disposition through love, but from fear. If from a reward expected I clang my lips in witness to the Lord, I am a common man, sounding the name of the Lord, not knowing Him. The same work differs according as it is done by fear, or perfected through love, and whether it is wrought through faith or gnostically. Naturally the rewards are different. The gnostic who looks on beauty thinks of beauty of soul, admiring the body as a statue through the beauty of which he transports himself in thought to the artist and to that which is truly beautiful.[5] In this perfection man and woman can equally share. Scripture and history prove it. The temperate wife will, in the first place, seek to induce her husband to share with her in the things that contribute to happiness; and, if that be im-

---

[1] iv. 11 [78-80].   [2] iv. 12 [81-88].   [3] iv. 13-15 [89-98].
[4] iv. 16 [99-104]   [5] iv. 17-18 [105-116].

possible, will herself press on to virtue, obeying her husband in
all things save such as have a bearing on virtue and salvation.
Without instruction, study, and discipline, advance in virtue is
not possible. The wife must remember that God is her helper,
and her true comrade and Saviour, and make Him leader and
general in every action, and the love of Him as her goal.[1]

One may be perfected in one virtue and one in another. But
perfect in all things at once no man is, while he is still a man,
save Him alone who for us put on man   According to the mere
letter of the Law, perfection might be obtained by abstinence from
evil actions. But in the Gospel the gnostic advances not merely by
using the Law as a stepping-stone, but by comprehending it as the
Lord, who gave the command, delivered it to the apostles. Not till
life is ended will he have a claim to the title "perfect." The
divine apostle sets forth the differences of the perfect. Prophets,
martyrs, teachers, were prominent in their distinctive virtues, but
they shared alike in common virtues. "Each has his own gift
from God." But the apostles were complete in all. The writings
of Paul derive their breath and expression from the Old Covenant.[2]

The gnostic is a man of understanding and insight. His work
is not abstinence from evil—whether from fear or hope of reward—
he chooses well-doing for the sake of love. He does not aim at
the knowledge of God for any special need, nor does he even make
choice of knowledge from a wish to be saved. He does good
because he judges it right to do good. He has consecrated his
body into a holy temple. He is no longer self-controlled, but has
attained the state of passionlessness, waiting to be "clothed upon"
with the divine form. Such knowledge loves the ignorant and
instructs them to honour the whole creation of the Almighty.
"Purity is to think holy thoughts." A true and steadfast repentance is sufficient purification to a man. Though we are not to be
righteous for the sake of reward, there is a place for hope. But he
who obeys the call neither from fear nor from the hope of pleasure,
goes on to knowledge. Drawn by the love of him who is the Lover,
he cultivates piety.[3] To turn away from things of sense does not
of necessity produce close union with intellectual (spiritual) objects,
but the reverse is true. It is possible for the gnostic now to

[1] iv. 19-20 [117-129].   [2] iv. 21 [130-134].   [3] iv. 22 [135-146].

become God. When deified into the passionless state, man becomes a unit undefiled. "As, then, those at sea when they are attached to the anchor by a tight cable, when they pull at the anchor, draw not the anchor to themselves but themselves to the anchor, so those who in accordance with the gnostic life are drawing God to themselves are unconsciously bringing themselves to God. For he that gives service to God gives service to himself." [1]

To philosophise or not, to believe or not, is in our power. Sins before faith are forgiven by the Lord—not merely involuntary or ignorant sins, as Basilides would have it, as if it were a man and not God who provided so great a gift. Punishment does not undo the sin, but has as its aim that the sinner may sin no more, and that no one may commit like sin. [2]

As God cannot be demonstrated, He cannot be an object of science. But the Son is Wisdom and Science and Truth, and whatsoever things are cognate thereto. He is capable of demonstration and explication. He is the circle of all the powers rolled into one and formed into a unity. Hence to believe in Him is to be monadic, and not to believe is to be divided. We are introduced into the mysteries by the Saviour Himself. God is the first principle of physics, ethics, and logic. Hence the Son alone is the teacher of men. [3]

To run down the creation and vilify the body is unreasonable. The body is the dwelling-place of the soul; the soul of the gnostic deals with it in a grave and austere fashion. He uses the body as one going on a long journey uses the inns on the road. Euripides says, "I shall go into the wide ether to hold converse with Zeus." But I shall pray the Spirit to furnish me with wings to my Jerusalem [4]

Book V. To limit the sphere of faith to the Son and knowledge to the Father is opposed to the close relation between faith and knowledge as well as the inseparable union between the Father and the Son. The inquiry which goes along with faith, which builds the august knowledge of the truth on the basis of faith, is the best. Set aside inquiry into the obvious, the obscure which will always be so, and questions on which opinions equally valid may be adduced,

---

[1] iv 23 [147-152].   [2] iv. 24 [153, 154].   [3] iv 25 [155-162].   [4] iv. 26 [163-172].

and faith is established. It is God who speaks in Scripture, and
it were godless to disbelieve Him. Admit a Providence and the
economy of the Saviour must be admitted. Our feebleness made
the coming of the Saviour a necessity. To inquire concerning
God has a saving influence. We must become intimately united
to God, through divine love, that we may listen to the truth without
guile.[1] Turn to hope   The man who hopes sees things to be with
the mind only. What is just or true is in like manner invisible
to the senses. So the Truth—the Word of God—is apprehended
by the mind. The Word of God became flesh that He might be
seen. He who seeks to walk according to the Word believes, then
hopes, then loves [2]

All the highest truth is expressed in symbol. The mysteries
were not exhibited to every one indiscriminately, but only to the
perfected and the instructed. The Egyptians had three divisions
of the symbolic—that by literal imitation, that by figures of speech,
and that by allegorical enigmas   This veiling of the first principles
of things is universal   It was so with the oracles of the Greeks, the
maxims of the wise men, and the Greek poets. It is so with all our
Scripture. Sayings of the Apostle prove it.[3]

There is a secret relationship between the Pythagorean symbols
and the barbarian philosophy   To all his sayings there are Scripture parallels   For example, the saying, "Do not step over the
balance," is an epitome of the sayings of Moses concerning righteousness. The sphinxes before the Egyptian temples may mean
that the discourse about God is enigmatical and obscure, perhaps
that we ought to love and fear the Divine Being, to love Him as
gracious to the pious, to fear Him as just to the unholy, the twofold characteristic being indicated by the union of the wild beast
and the man.[4]

The oracles of Scripture are delivered in the form of enigmas.
The furniture of the tabernacle, the altar of incense, the veil into
the Holy of Holies, the four letters that mark the name of God,
the golden lamp, the table of shewbread, the ark, the Cherubim,
the bells and stones on the robe of the High Priest, all symbolise

---

[1] v. 1[113].   [2] v. 2-3[14,19].   [3] v. 4[20,26].
[4] v. 5[27,31]. In v. 7[42] he explains the sphinx as a symbol of the union of
strength and intelligence   In v. 8[45] he suggests other explanations.

truths. The golden lamp may be a symbol of Christ, as casting light "in diverse portions and diverse manners" on those who believe in Him. The 360 bells on the robe of the High Priest represent the space of a year, "the acceptable year of the Lord," proclaiming and sounding the mighty manifestation of the Saviour. The mitre indicates the most sovereign power of the Lord.[1]

The Egyptians likewise concealed mysteries in enigmas. The hawk, the crocodile, the dog, the ibis, were symbolical of various characteristics in men and God and natural phenomena.[2] The Scythians and the Greeks did the same. Take, for example, the Ephesian Letters and their interpretation. Take the interpretation of the words containing the letters of alphabet as given to children.[3] Even whole books like that of Heraclitus have been uttered in enigmatic form. Such being the case, it was fitting that prophecy should be uttered in secret and symbolic fashion.[4] This form is adopted by the Scriptures for the sake of memory and brevity, and to give a stimulus to the truth. Such veiling is in the interests of the genuine inquirer, as well as of the truth which is only partly revealed and diversely interpreted. For writing out the views of Pythagoras clearly, Hipparchus was expelled from the school. The scholars of Epicurus declare that some of his writings are esoteric. So the founders of the mysteries buried their own doctrines in myths. It was not expedient that the ignorant should fall in with them.[5] The divine apostle shows that the gnosis did not belong to all. Some things were handed down unwritten in tradition to the Hebrews. The "babe" is entrusted with the rudiments. "Day utters speech to day"—that which has been written without disguise; "night to night proclaims knowledge " — that which has been hidden mystically. Paul says, "I have fed you with milk, not with meat." The milk is catechetical instruction — the first food of the soul; meat is the contemplation, the immediate vision of God.[6]

A separation from the body and its passions is a sacrifice acceptable to God. Philosophy has naturally been called the study of death. The true philosophy is pursued by him who leaves out the

---

[1] v. 6 [39,40]. The first part is taken from Philo.   [2] v. 7 [41, 42].
[3] Clement gives various interpretations of βέδυ, ζάψ, χθών, πλῆκτρον, σφίγξ, and other forms, v. 8 [49]. See note in Kaye, p. 181.
[4] v. 8 [42,55].   [5] v. 9 [56,59].   [6] v. 10 [60,66].

senses in his thinking. Hence the silence enjoined by Pythagoras. The Greeks deify the gnostic life though they have not an intelligent knowledge of it. In the Greek mysteries purifications come first. This is followed by the minor mysteries with their groundwork of instruction, and these by the great mysteries which are taken up with the contemplation of nature and realities. To the first stage corresponds our baptism with confession; in the last stage analysis takes the place of contemplation. In this way we rise to the concept of the Monad, and come to know not what the Almighty is, but what He is not. God cannot be circumscribed. "What house will ye build me, saith the Lord?"[1] Plato says that it is a difficult task to discover the Father and Maker of the universe. Kindred thoughts are expressed in various passages of the Scripture. The reason is that, as the absolutely First Principle, He cannot be demonstrated, nor expressed in ordinary predicates. Only by divine grace can we form any conception of Him.[2] All knowledge of Him, whether due to the direct action of God Himself, or to the exercise of free-will on the part of man, is due to grace. If it is impossible, according to Plato, to disbelieve the children of the gods, though they speak without probable and certain proofs, is not that a proof that the prophets, sons of God, are true witnesses about divine things? It was through His Son that God proclaimed the Scriptures. He who knows that the Son of God is Teacher has confidence that His teaching is true; and such confidence makes faith grow. And this faith is the effective cause of good things and the foundation of right conduct.[3]

The Father and Maker of the universe is known innately, even without teaching. The belief in the sovereignty of God is universal. But even the Greeks with their search after knowledge only came to know God by way of circumlocution, which was true as far as it went. For they do not know what He is, nor how He is Lord and Father and Maker, unless they have been taught by the truth. When the shipmaster said to Jonah,[4] "Call on thy God that He may save us," the expression, "thy God," suggests one

---

[1] v. 11 [67.77]   [2] v. 12 [78.82].
[3] v. 13 [83.88]. Chapter xiv. [89.113] is entirely devoted to illustrations of "theft" from the barbarian philosophy by the Greeks. He has exhibited many interesting parallels and analogies. Cf. pp. 46-49.   [4] Jonah i. 6.

who knew by way of knowledge; the expression, "that God may save us," indicates the common consciousness of the Gentiles, who had applied their mind to the thought of Almighty but had not yet believed. The beneficence of God is eternal. Each one shares in it according as he wills.[1]

Book VI. In the Pædagogus we have set forth the way of life that prepares the soul for the reception of gnostic science. In the delineation of the gnostic we shall show to the Greeks that they are impious in persecuting the man who loves God. The Stromateis are like a variegated meadow, and such of set purpose. For if toil should precede food, much more should it precede gnosis. Our spiritual garden is the Saviour Himself. When transplanted into Him we become fruitful. He is the true gnosis.[2]

That the symbolic form was archaic and all but universal has been proved. The theft of Hellenic thought from the Scriptures has been demonstrated. As further proof we call to witness the Greeks themselves, for they steal from one another, and will, therefore, hardly refrain from what is ours. All the adherents of the various schools in philosophy admit their debt to Socrates for their authoritative tenets.[3] They have not only filched doctrines from the barbarians, but they have transformed the marvels in our records into marvels of Hellenic mythology.[4] Moreover, they took doctrines from the Egyptians, who follow a philosophy of their own, as is shown by their ritual.[5]

Peter says in his "Preaching,"—"Worship God not as the Greeks, but worship Him in a new way through Christ." He shows that the one God was known by the Greeks in a Gentile way, by the Jews in a Judaic way, and in a new and spiritual way by us The same is shown by the Apostle Paul.[6] To those who were righteous according to Law faith was wanting. But to the righteous according to philosophy not only faith was lacking, but

[1] v. 14 134.141.　　　　　　　　　　　　　　　[2] vi. 1 1.3.
[3] vi. 2 4.77.　Clement proceeds to quote parallel passages from Homer, Musæus, Archilochus, the tragedians, philosophers, historians, and rhetoricians.　He seeks further to show that they have been guilty of possessing stolen goods *en masse*.
[4] vi 3. 28.34.　　　　　[5] vi. 4 35.38.　　　　　[6] vi. 5 39.43.

they had to abandon idolatry. The Lord preached the Gospel
to those in Hades. He puts forth His might, because to save is
His work. If He preached to the Jews only, the apostles, there
as well as here, must have preached the Gospel to the heathen.
Both Gentile and Jew belong to the holy people. "The ox and
the bear," says the Scripture, "shall meet together." The ox is
the Jew, the Gentile is indicated by the bear. If in the flood all
sinful flesh perished, we must believe that the will of God, which
is disciplinary and operative, saves those who turn to Him. Water,
which is of gross material, could not injure the soul, which is of
finer material.[1]

Wisdom is the steadfast knowledge of things divine and
human. This the Lord taught us both through His advent and
through the prophets. With us those are called philosophers who
love wisdom,—that is, the knowledge of the Son of God,—but
among the Greeks, those who take up discussions on virtue. Some
dogmas the Greeks have borrowed, some they have misunderstood. Self-love is the cause of all their errors. In this way
they miss the truth. Knowledge and science are derived from
the instruction of a teacher. You name Pythagoras and others
as teachers. Who taught them? Who taught the first generation
of men? The First-begotten, the Wisdom of God, is the teacher
who from the very beginning of the world has trained and perfected man. As the whole family goes back to the Creator, so
the teaching which justifies goes back to the Lord. Some choked
the seeds of truth, like the Pharisees. But those who believed
in the coming of the Lord gained knowledge of the Law; just
as philosophers, when taught by the Lord, learn the true philosophy. Christ taught the apostles at the time of the advent;
through this knowledge, as delivered and revealed, cometh wisdom.
The gnosis has come down through succession to a few, having
been delivered unwritten by the apostles.[2]

Paul does not seem to censure philosophy, though he does not
deem it worthy of the man who has attained to the gnostic height
to run back to it. So to the Colossians he calls philosophy elementary teaching.[3] The gnostic must be fond of learning. He
must be prepared to meet argument with argument. All things

[1] vi. 6 ⁴¹⁻⁸³.   [2] vi. 7 ⁵⁴⁻⁶⁰.   [3] vi. 8 ⁶¹⁻⁶⁵.

T

profitable for life come from God; but there are tares in Greek philosophy. It, moreover, is elementary; while truly perfect science is conversant with intellectual and transcendent objects, and with objects still more spiritual. The true gnostic — such as James, Peter, John, Paul, and the rest of the apostles—knows all things. He comprehends what seems to others incomprehensible; for nothing is incomprehensible to the Son of God, nor untaught. He who in love suffered for us kept back nothing. Thus faith becomes certain demonstration.[1] No doubt the gnostic is subject to hunger, thirst, and the like, without which the body could not continue. This did not apply to the Saviour. The apostles were not subject to emotions apparently good—courage, joy, tranquillity. The gnostic does not need courage nor cheerfulness, is not angry, does not envy, and loves the Creator in the creatures. He becomes passionless like his teacher. He who feasts on the insatiable gladness of contemplation cannot be delighted with petty things. Why should he run back to the good things of the world who has gained the "light inaccessible"? To him the future is no matter of conjecture, through love it is already present. His gnosis, when perfected, becomes infallible through love. He has apprehended the First Cause. He has learned from the Truth the most exact truth. He models the administration of his own affairs from the archetypes above, as those who sail direct their ship by the stars. He requires few necessaries for life, and these not as primary, but because they are essential to his sojourn in life; for to him gnosis is the principal thing.[2] Accordingly, he devotes himself to subjects that serve as a training for gnosis. From music, arithmetic, geometry, astronomy, he takes what they may contribute to the truth. From astronomy, like Abraham, he ascends to the Creator from the creation. So he will utilise dialectics, which has a place in the interpretation of Scripture. To him all branches of study are only a means to an end, the transmission of the truth to others, and a defence against hindrances to the truth. What is craftily used by heretics he uses rightly.[3] The study of arithmetic is illustrated by Abraham. As an example of music take David, at once singing and prophesying. Astronomy helps to provide the soul with a keen vision of truth. Philosophy co-operates in the

[1] vi. 8 $^{66.70}$.   [2] vi. 9 $^{71.79}$.   [3] vi. 10 $^{80.93}$.

discussions about truth. We have been born by nature for virtue, not so as to have it from birth, but in the sense that we are adapted for acquiring it.[1] The same is true of Adam. He was not perfect as created, but adapted to receive virtue. Aptitude is an impulse in the direction of virtue, but it is not virtue. Much more is gnosis the fruit of toil. The gnostic is pure in deeds and thought and also in word. He does not condemn any particular sin, but all sin absolutely. He circumscribes his desires both in respect of possession and use. He deems it of more importance to live well than to live. He prefers the love of God and righteousness to children or marriage or parents. After the children are begotten he regards his wife as a sister. To those who have repented of their sins but not steadfastly believed, God grants their requests when they pray for them; but to those who live sinlessly He grants their thoughts. The gnostic prays in thought every hour. Having prayed for forgiveness of sin, he will then pray that he may no longer sin, then for the power to do well and to understand the economy of the Lord, that having become pure in heart he may be initiated into the beatific vision. Possessed of true righteousness he is glorified even here, as Moses was, with something of an intellectual effulgence like the glory of the sun. He grows in likeness to God the Saviour, so far as it is possible for human nature.[2] He who has cultivated apathy and grown to the beneficence of gnostic perfection is here equal to the angels. He hastens to the holy abode like the apostles. For those who have lived perfectly and gnostically may be enrolled among the presbyters. Both Greek and Jew meet in the unity of the faith, and the election out of both is one. Of the elect some are more elect.[3] Such will rest in the "holy mount," the church on high, in which are gathered the philosophers of God, the true Israelites, the pure in heart, who devote themselves to the pure vision of the contemplation that is never sated. To be deemed worthy of the highest honour after being saved is more than being saved. Simply to be saved belongs to things intermediate, but to be saved rightly and fittingly is right action. Those who do not accomplish good things do not know what is profitable for them. Being ignorant of what is truly good, they cannot pray so as to receive good

[1] vi. 11 84,95.   [2] vi. 12 96,104.   [3] vi. 13 105,108.

things from God; nor if they received it would they profit by it, in their ignorance of the proper use of divine things.[1]

The gnostic receives the impression of the more immediate image, the mind of the Master. He teaches "on the house-tops" those who can be taught; he teaches, as he acts, the pattern of the Christian citizenship. It belongs to Him to know when to speak, and how, and to whom. "The wild olive is engrafted into the fatness of the olive." By engrafting worthless shoots are made noble, and the barren fruitful. There are four modes of grafting, and each symbolises a separate class of disciples. Solomon teaches that the love of knowledge makes a man immortal; it should, therefore, be sought so as to be found. With discovery inquiry ends. The discovery concerning God is the teaching given through the Son. We aim at learning from God Himself, with whom the truth is. From the divine oracles we claim to have been taught the truth by the Son of God. "The Saviour spoke all things in parables." They must, therefore, be expounded in accordance with the canon of the Church—that is, the harmony of the Law and the Prophets with the covenant delivered at the advent of the Lord. The prophetic teaching, like the Incarnation itself, was a concession. The Lord possessed all virtue; and to lead man who had been nurtured in the world of sense up to the things of another world, He employed parables. Like all other languages, Hebrew has certain characteristics distinctive of the national genius. But prophecy is not marked by such features. It does not veil the truth for the sake of beauty of phrase, but because the truth does not belong to all. Even those to whom the science of interpretation specially belongs must advance gradually.[2]

The Greek philosophers name God, but do not know Him, for they do not worship God as God. They ascribe to God their own passions. They seek the probable, not the true. We are not to investigate truths in part, but truth itself. For the subject of God is not one thing but ten thousand things. There is a difference between seeking God and the things about God, between things and name, between the expression and the thing signified. Those

---

[1] vi. 14 [109-114].

[2] vi. 15 [115-138]. Here follows (vi. 16 [133-148]) a gnostic exposition of the decalogue. See pp. 199, 200.

who lay hold of the mere expression are like ravens who imitate the voices of men, but have no conception of what they say. Philosophy was given by God as a preparatory discipline. Its very existence shows its origin. Light cannot produce darkness, nor can vice do anything virtuous. As philosophy makes men virtuous, it must be the work of God, whose only work is to do good. Every benefit related to life proceeds in its ultimate ground from God the Father, who is ruler over all, and it is perfected through the Son.[1]

The gnostic is always engaged in the most essential matters If he has leisure he turns to Greek philosophy as a recreation or a dessert, though he does not direct his energy to superfluous or insignificant points For true science, such as the gnostic alone possesses, is a firm hold, leading up through true and sure reason to the knowledge of the cause. To philosophise is absolutely essential. The Greeks must be taught through the Law and the Prophets to worship the only God, who is truly Almighty, then to learn that nothing can be an image of God. From this he must advance through righteousness to knowledge. Those who boast their firm grasp of truth have been taught by men who cannot worthily declare the power of God. Even those taught by God require grace to attain such knowledge as they possess. Myriads of heralds prophesied of the time and place and signs of the advent of the Lord Greek philosophers are limited to a few scholars or adherents Christianity is in every race and country. Instead of being crushed by persecution, it grows and lives.[2]

Book VII. Now we show to the Greeks that the gnostic alone is truly pious. We shall use only arguments of a self-evident nature, and give only an outline of Christianity. The gnostic worships God in a manner worthy of God He honours the Son from whom he has learned to know the First Cause, the Father of the universe. He worships God by continuous cultivation of his soul and by training that which is divine in himself in the form of ceaseless love. Service of men is partly "meliorative," partly "ministerial." The truly devout man serves God in the affairs of men well and unblamably. He is a lover of God. For he who honours God loves God. He discharges a threefold function. He knows

[1] vi 17 149,161.   [2] vi 18 162,168

realities, he carries out the injunctions of the Word, he transmits the secret things of truth in a manner worthy of God.[1]

The first stage of faith is to know God, and then in harmony with this knowledge, in no way to commit wrong. The most excellent thing on earth is the most pious man; the most perfect and most royal is the nature of the Son. All men are His, some in the way of knowledge, some as friends, some as faithful servants, some as servants simply. He saves those who are willing. As befits the Lord of all, He cares for all. He is not touched by envy, nor ignorance, nor pleasure. In His love He clothed Himself with flesh for the common salvation of men, and can never neglect His own work. He governs all things from the greatest to the least. Without interfering with freewill, He made all things contribute to virtue, so that from age to age the Almighty was revealed through the Son. The one end of His saving righteousness is the bettering of each one.[2]

By fellowship with God through the great High Priest the gnostic becomes assimilated to the Lord, and then fashions himself and moulds those who hear him. The canons of the gnostic assimilation are gentleness, loving-kindness, and a splendid piety. Such virtues are an acceptable sacrifice with God. The Gospel and the Apostle agree as to the duty of putting ourselves to death. If we so sacrifice ourselves we need no other sacrifice. By such consecration we honour Him who was consecrated for us. God takes pleasure in our salvation alone He is in need of nothing and is not propitiated by sacrifices. He is revealed to the virtuous alone.[3] The gnostic masters all the causes of evil, and, like God, benefits all men, whatever his sphere be. His soul is a divine image of Him who is the express image of the Almighty Father. Thus master of himself, he gains a firm hold of divine science. He cultivates all forms of manliness. He belongs to this world and yet to a higher world. He is the true wrestler, with the universe for amphitheatre, God as the president, the Son of God as umpire, angels and gods as spectators. The terms are the same for all; the issue depends on our will and choice. For salvation through obedience we owe thanks to God. And our best thanks is to do what is well-pleasing to Him. He accepts our service of men as service of Himself;

[1] vii 1 [1-4].   [2] vii. 2 [5-12].   [3] vii. 3 [13-15].

and He regards the wrongs done to His believers as a dishonour to Himself.[1]

The Greeks represent their gods as human in passions as well as in form. Those who liken the divine nature to the worst of men are atheists. To represent men as injuring the gods implies that the gods are inferior. The ascription of wrath to the gods naturally begets superstition, and their devotees see portents everywhere. They have a dread of grains of salt, of squills, and brimstone. But the true God regards nothing holy but the character of the just man, and nothing accursed save what is unjust.[2]

Do we not rightly refrain from confining in temples made with hands that which contains all things? What work of mechanical art could be called holy? Better, surely, with others, to regard the whole universe as a fitting shrine for Him. Ridiculous that man, "the plaything of God," should make God, or that He should become the play of art. No work of art, however perfect, can be regarded sacred and divine. To localise God is an absurdity If we give the epithet " holy " to the building as well as to God Himself, why not rather to the church which is the congregation of saints? The soul of the gnostic is a shrine of God—that is, he is one in whom the knowledge of God is consecrated.[3]

God does not need the food of sacrifice as if He hungered. We honour Him by the sacrifice of prayer. The truly holy altar is the righteous soul, and the incense from it is holy prayer. We are to offer God the incense of united prayer.[4] We are commanded to honour the Son and Word whom we recognise as Saviour and Ruler, and through him the Father, not on select days, as feast-days and the like, but continuously throughout our whole life and in every way. If intercourse with a good man ennobles one, much more will fellowship with God. Hence all our life we keep festival. And this applies specially to the gnostic He is the truly kingly man, the holy priest of God. He does not approach the spectacles, touches not costly wines or wreaths that effeminate the soul. He enjoys all things as divine gifts. He believes that God knows all things and hears our thought. God has not to wait for any voice of ours. The gnostic prays for the things that are really good— the things of the soul , and, as he prays, he works, so that these good

[1] vii. 3 16.21.   [2] vii. 4 22.27.   [3] vii. 5 28.29.   [4] vii. 6 30, 34.

things may be no external ornaments, but that he himself may be good To pray aright we must pray with a knowledge of God. Prayer is converse with God. Though we open not our lips we cry in our inmost being from the heart. This cry God ever hears. Hence we lift up head and hands and feet at the closing prayer, as if to separate the body from the earth as we speak. Some pray at fixed hours, the gnostic prays all his life. As God can do all that He wills, the gnostic receives whatsoever he may ask Though God gives good things without asking, the petition is not superfluous. The faith that he will receive is a form of prayer stored up in a gnostic fashion The holiness of the gnostic is a responsive feeling of loyalty on the part of a friend of God True worship is characterised both by will and knowledge.[1] God answers our thoughts. Character in relation to duty is tested by prayer. We send up our prayers to God without a voice. As light arises out of the east, we pray towards the east. The gnostic is united to the Spirit by the bond of infinite love. He maintains contemplation without ceasing by self-discipline. He possesses boldness of utterance, and conceals nothing from fear or from a desire to please. He is incapable alike of giving way to corruption or temptation. He is untouched either by pleasure or pain. If reason calls, he is an inflexible judge and walks in the paths of justice. He is persuaded that all things are administered for the best. He has no anxiety about the necessaries of life. He prays that he may never fall away from virtue. His knowledge of God is a guarantee that his virtue will not be lost. Hence the gnostic alone is pious. He already possesses the future. As the physician co-operates with the patient for his health, God co-operates with the gnostic for knowledge and right action. Having done his part, like the athlete in the story, he can claim that God should do His. The whole world contributes to the salvation of the gnostic who has conscientiously fulfilled his duty. His whole life is a holy festival. His sacrifices are prayer and praise and the reading of the Scriptures by day and by night. He is one with the divine choir. He prays everywhere without ostentation, for his thought is a prayer.[2] Such an one need not take an oath; his life is a security against falsehood. By his actions he swears faithfully, so that the witness of

[1] vii 7 $^{35\text{-}42}$.　　　　　　　　　　　　[2] vii. 7 $^{43\text{-}49}$.

his tongue is a superfluity. He will die under torture rather than lie.[1] He thinks truly and speaks truly, though, when occasion demands it, as a physician to the sick, he may lie, stooping to accommodation for the sake of others. To him a lie is no idle word, but a force for wickedness. He witnesses to the truth both in word and deed. From this summary account of gnostic piety it is plain that the Christian is neither an atheist nor given to impiety.[2]

Knowledge is a perfection, as it were, of man as man, and by it truth is perfected. By faith the knowledge of God grows   This is the foundation of knowledge. Christ is both the foundation and the superstructure. Faith and love cannot be taught; knowledge can be transmitted and taught. Faith, knowledge, love, the heavenly inheritance, are the four ascending grades. By knowledge those fitted for it learn the nature of the life to be, and its purifications and honours, with everlasting contemplation of the Lord and fellow-ship with Him as its crown. Faith, then, is a summary knowledge of essentials, but knowledge is a firm demonstration of the things received through faith   As the gnostic has advanced from faith to knowledge, and from knowledge to love, so after having reached the highest stage in the flesh, he goes on advancing unto the Father's house[3]   The gnostic has a true conception of the universe. He has a unique understanding of the commandments. He never prefers the pleasant to the expedient. He has an unshaken conviction that whatever may befall him may be a means of salvation. He uses the creatures of God with thanksgiving. He does not dwell on his wrongs, but rather pities his fellows because of their ignorance. He looks to noble examples,—above all, to that of the Lord. Like the body of the athlete, his soul is in tiptop condition   It is an image of the divine power, and becomes a temple of the Holy Spirit. He fears no apparent or external danger. He is not irrationally brave   A true martyr, he does not rush into danger without cause, but taking care of himself in accordance with reason, he willingly surrenders himself at the call of God. He obeys the call of God from no low motive, but simply from love to Him. By love he grows to the " perfect man," and takes rank as a son of God. The vision of God face to face is his highest goal

[1] vii. 8 51.   [2] vii. 9 52.54.   [3] vii 10 55.59.

and attainment.[1] He is just in all his relations to others. He assists his brother, not giving to all equally but according to desert. He gives even to his enemies. As God is the enemy of no one, so is the gnostic. He is truly continent. He is not merely master of his passions but of what is good; for the scientific possession of good is "the science of things divine and human." He eats and drinks and marries, not as if such things were principal ends, but from necessity. By his knowledge the soul is separated from passion, so that it can say, "I live as thou willest." And he who pleases God is well-pleasing to good men. Only One is free from desire, the Lord who for us became man. We can only gain a like stamp by training. The gnostic gains life by knowledge; ignorance produces atrophy in the soul. All his life is prayer and fellowship with God. What is inexpedient he does not ask; what is expedient he receives at once with his thought. He prays for the repentance of those who hate him. The future is the real to him. He fasts always from the love of money and pleasure, from deeds condemned by the Law and thoughts alien to the Gospel. He honours the resurrection of the Lord in his inner life. He can look on beauty without carnal desire. His brethren are those who choose, learn, remember, hope for the same things as he does. Thought spent on food is to him a robbery of higher things. As a "stranger and pilgrim," he lives in the city as if it were a desert. His surroundings do not affect him. In brief, he makes up for the absence of the apostles by upright living, by accurate knowledge, by help of the deserving, by removing "mountains" from his neighbours. He impoverishes himself for the sake of others, for he has a grasp of realities. By knowledge he becomes, as it were, a partner of the divine will. He prays with angels, as equal to angels. He prays that he may live in the flesh as one free from flesh. In fellowship with Christ hereafter he hopes to become all light himself, and not luminous by sharing in fire. Day and night he rejoices exceedingly, speaking and doing the commandments of the Lord. He is patient under trial[2] He forgives those who have sinned against him, for he regards all men as the work of One Will. His prayer is a demand, not a request. He prays that the wants of the needy may be supplied, and thus assists them without ostentation or vain-

[1] vii. 11 [60].[63].   [2] vii. 12 [69].[80].

glory, as being only an instrument of the goodness of God.   He
is the temple of God, God-bearing and God-borne.   So much to
the Greeks about the gnostic.[1]

Of the apathy of the gnostic—I mean, his progression from faith
through love to the perfect man—I note but one scriptural passage,
out of many, from the divine apostle in the First Epistle to the
Corinthians.[2]   From this it is evident that the gnostic should suffer
wrong rather than inflict wrong in retaliation, for that were to do
wrong himself.   How could one "judge angels"—that is, the
apostate angels—if himself an apostate from the Gospel precept
as to the forgetfulness of wrong?   "Ye defraud your brethren."[3]
That is, by praying against them, ye defraud them of the goodness
of God.[4]   "Wrong-doers shall not inherit the kingdom of God"[5]
That is, those who seek revenge in deed or word or thought.   "Ye
washed yourselves."[6]   That is, with knowledge you flung aside the
passions of the soul.   "Ye were sanctified,"[7] as with a holiness
higher than this world.   "God shall destroy them."[8]   That is, those
who live as if they were born to eat.   "He that is joined to a
harlot (the activity contrary to the covenant) unto one flesh (unto a
heathenish life) becomes another body," which is not holy.   "He
that is joined to the Lord" is a spiritual body.[9]   That is, he is
wholly a son, passionless, gnostic, being formed by the teaching of
the Lord.   So much for those who have ears to hear.   We are to
be perfect as the Father in heaven, perfect in forgiving sins and
forgetting wrongs, perfect as He would have us be.   For it is not
possible for any one to be perfect as God is.[10]

"We ought not to believe," you say, "because of the variety and
dissonance of the sects."[11]   That is an idle pretext.   It cannot be
defended on any practical grounds, and is condemned by analogy.
It regards as false or unprovable what we regard as fundamental,
that there is truth, that it has its own criterion, that the Scriptures
are from God, and as such have a demonstration of their own.
This is ignored by the heretics who have broken away from the

---

[1] vii. 13 [81-83].   [2] 1 Cor. vi.   [3] Ib., vi. 3.   [4] Ib , vi. 8.
[5] Ib , vi 9.   [6] Ib , vi 11.   [7] Ib.   [8] Ib., vi. 13.
[9] Ib , vi 16, 17.   [10] vii 14 [84-88].
[11] For a fuller statement of Clement's discussion of the question, see Lecture II ,
pp 57-60.

authoritative possessor of truth, and in their conceit and muddiness of soul cannot see the light of truth.   Ignorance is the characteristic of the heathen, conceit of the heretics, knowledge of the Church. In their love of glory and slothfulness they close their ears to the truth.   They ignore the antiquity and unity of the Catholic Church.[1] With some remarks on the distinctive characteristics of Jews and heretics, and on the literary form of the Stromateis, the Seventh Book comes to a close.[2]

[1] vii. 15-17 [89-108].   [2] viii. 18 [109-111].

APPENDIX D.

As stated on page 10, the hypothesis that the works of Clement were not written in the order commonly held was first started by Wendland. It is supported by Heussi and Harnack, and accepted, without discussion, by Duchesne and Stahlin.[1] It is rejected by Bardenhewer, who accepts the view of Zahn.[2] It is ignored by Mayor. Now, it is plain that a hypothesis so supported is one which, on the face of it, it may seem presumptuous to doubt and an impertinence to criticise. But an examination of the reasons adduced, together with the presentation of some grounds that may be adduced to the contrary, may tend at least to cast doubt on the necessity of an unconditional acceptance of it.

In his 'Quæstiones Musonianæ,' published in 1886, in which he proved the dependence of Clement on Musonius, Wendland expressed the opinion that the reference by Clement to a treatise Περὶ ἐγκρατείας was due to the fact that the whole was a quotation from Musonius ; that Clement had written no work on that subject, but that he had with extraordinary negligence transcribed the passage from Musonius, "dormitans integrum hoc enunciatum ex Musonio transtulit," and thus had ascribed to himself a writing which was really a writing of Musonius. This incredible hypothesis is of interest as showing the attitude of the critic to Clement, but does not otherwise call for comment. In a review of the work of

[1] Duchesne, 'Histoire ancienne de l'Eglise,' p. 337 Stäh., vol. iii. p. lxiii.
[2] I have not been able to see the article of Zahn to which Harnack makes reference Op. cit., p. 9, note 5.

de Faye[1] he abandoned this hypothesis, and writes as follows :
" In Pæd. ii. 94, καθόλου μὲν οὖν εἰ γαμητέον ἢ γάμου εἰς
τὸ παντελὲς καθαρευτέον—ἔχεται γὰρ ζητήσεώς καὶ τοῦτο—
ἐν τῷ περὶ ἐγκρατείας ἡμῖν δεδήλωται.   Dies problem findet
sich nun Strom. ii. 137, ζητοῦμεν δὲ εἰ γαμητέον . . . aus-
fuhrlich behandelt innerhalb einer Erörterung uber ἐγκρατεία, die
von Strom. ii. 103 bis zum Ende von Buch III. reicht, aber auch
ins vierte ubergreift.   Und St. iii. 22 heist es ausdrucklich ὁ δὲ
περὶ ἐγκρατείας ἡμῖν προβαινέτο λόγος.   (Auf die Auseinander-
setzung mit gnostichen Enkratiten St. iii., passt weiter die verweisung Pæd. ii. 52 [2]).   Endlich beziehe ich auf diese Bucher der
St, besonders ii. 137-146 ; iv. 59-65, 125-129, die mit den
wörtern ἐν τῷ γαμικῷ διέξιμεν λόγῳ schliessende Aufzàhlung
Paed. iii. 41.   Wer die stellen vergleicht und die antike Citir-
methode kennt, kann gar nicht an der Beziehung zweifeln.   Beach-
tet man weiter die Praeterita an den beiden ersten, das Futurum
an der letzen Stelle, so ergiebt sich dass Clemens, als er den Paed.
schrieb, bereits einen theil der St. fertig hatte, deren Ausarbeitung
er durch den Paed. unterbrach.   Dazu stimmt, dass sich nur in
St. vi. und vii. je eine Ruckweisung auf Prot. und Paed. findet.
Man kann zweifeln, ob man den Paed. doch später ansetzen soll
als Neumann, 'Der rom. Staat und die Kirche,' i. 100, oder
ob die Stelle über die Verfolgungen, St. ii. 125, spaterer
Zusatz ist."
    Heussi puts the matter thus : "Clemens verweist namlich Pæd.
ii. 94 bei der Besprechung der Ehe auf seine ausfuhrliche Erörterung περὶ ἐγκρατείας . . . δεδήλωται.   Das mit diesen
Worten umschriebene Problem finden wir nun St. ii. 137,
ζητοῦμεν . . . behandelt, innerhalb einer langer Erörterung über
die ἐγκρατεία, die von St. ii. 103 bis ins IV. Buch hinein reicht.
Ebenso bezieht sich die Verweisung Pæd. ii. 52, δειλήφαμεν . . .
τάττεται auf St. iii.   Schliesslich finden wir Pæd. iii. 41, ἐν
τῷ γαμικῷ διέξιμεν λόγῳ einen Hinweis auf die Ausfuhrungen,
St., ii. 137, 146 ; iv. 59-65, 125-129.   Die antike Manier zu cit-

---

[1] Theol. Lit.-Zeit., 1898.
[2] διειλήφαμεν δὲ βαθυτέρῳ λόγῳ ὡς ἄρα οὔτε ἐν τοῖς ὀνόμασιν ̈οὔδε μὴν ἐν τοῖς
συνουσιαστικοῖς μορίοις καὶ τῇ κατὰ γάμον συμπλοκῇ, καθ' ὧν κεῖται τὰ ὀνόματα τὰ
περὶ τὴν συνήθειαν οὐ τετριμμένα, ἢ τοῦ ὄντος αἰσχροῦ προσηγορία τάττεται.

iren lasst es ausser Zweifel, dass Clemens an den gennanten Stellen im Paed. nicht auf selbstandige Werke περὶ ἐγκρατείας u s.w., verweist, sondern auf die betreffenden Darlegungen in den Str. Die Praeterita an den beiden ersten Stellen, δεδήλωται, διειλήφαμεν und das Futurum an den dritten Stelle διέξιμεν aber beweisen dass Clemens einen Teil der Str. vor dem Paed. geschrieben haben muss "[1]

Harnack writes as follows : " Hier ist von der Entdeckung Wendlands ausgehen, die Heussi bestatigt hat, dass die 4 ersten Bucher der Stromateis vor dem Padagog geschrieben sind. Diese Entdeckung wirft nicht nur die bisherige Chronologie des Schriftstellers Clemens, sonder auch die wichtigsten der bisher geltenden Vorstellungen von seinem schriftstellerischen Absichten uber denn Haufen Die Entdeckung ist zuverlassig, denn liegt kein Grund vor, das Zitat in Paedag. ii. 10, 94 (καθόλου μὲν οὖν ἢ γαμητέον ἢ γαμου εἰς τὸ παντελὲς καθαρευτέον—ἔχεται γὰρ ζητήσεως καὶ τοῦτο—ἐν τῷ περὶ ἐγκρατείας ἡμῖν δεδήλωται), auf einen anderen Abschnitt zu beziehen als auf die grosse Ausfuhrung, die von Strom. ii. 20, 103, bis in das 4 Buch hineinreicht, s. bes. ii. 23, 137. Nicht anders ist uber das Zitat Paedag. ii. 6, 52, διειλήφαμεν, &c, zu urteilen, es ist das 3 Buch der Stromateis gemeint, und endlich ist der γαμικὸς λόγος auf den Paedag. iii. 8, 41, verwiesen wird, in denselben Ausfuhrungen, namlich Strom. ii. 23, 137, 146; iv. 8, 59-65; iv. 20, 125-129 zu suchen. Besondere Schriften des Clemens περὶ ἐγκρατείας (oder uber die Ehe) hat nie jemand genannt ; kein Zitat findet sich aus ihnen. Dagegen enthalten die betreffenden Abschnitte der Stromateis das im Padagog Vorausgesetzte. Nun aber beobachtet man weiter, dass der Protrepticus und Padagog nur in den spateren Buchern der Stromateis zitiert werden (Strom., vi. 1, 1, vii. 4, 22) Gerade aber in den fruheren Buchern musste man Verweisungen auf sie oder doch mindestens auf den Padagog erwarten, wenn sie fruher geschrieben waren und wenn die Stromateis den Zweck verfolgten, das im Padagog Ausgefuhrte nun in eine hohere Sphare zu heben. In diesen fruheren Buchern der Stromateis aber wird die Aufgabe so angefasst, dass sie in keinem sinne als Fortsetzung erscheint, vielmehr die Aufgaben mit umfasst, die

---

[1] Z. fur W. Th., 1902, p. 474.

im (Protrepticus und) Padagog behandelt sind. Als Clemens die Stromateis i.-iv. schrieb, hatte er also jene beiden Bucher weder schon geschrieben noch geplannt."[1]

From the similarity of the reasons brought forward, it may be assumed that no more cogent grounds can be submitted. As for the absence of reference in the earlier books of the Stromateis to the Pæd., that does not seem an argument of much weight by itself. It might be asked in reply, Why no reference in Strom. v. or in the Pæd. to the earlier books of the Strom.? Or, why no reference in the Pæd. to some of the subjects promised in the Strom , and never discussed?

The essential points in the passages quoted by Wendland, Heussi, and Harnack are these: (1) At the time that the Pæd. was written, Clement had already written on the subject of ἐγκράτεια, with special reference to marriage. (2) In that or a cognate treatise he had discussed somewhat elaborately the specific point noted in Pæd. ii. 52. (3) When he had finished the Pæd. he had still in contemplation a special work on the subject of marriage.

As to the last point. That διεξίμεν is to be taken in the ordinary future sense there can be no doubt. If this be so, how can the allusion to the γαμικὸς λόγος in Pæd. iii. 41 refer to sections in the Stromateis, when, ex hypothesi, they had preceded its composition? If we are to give the natural force to δεδήλωται, must we not do the same with διεξίμεν? It is plain from many indications that the subject had a special interest for Clement, alike on physiological, ethical, psychological, and exegetical grounds. But is it probable, after the detailed discussion in the Stromateis and the Pædagogus, that he should have thought of returning to the subject? Is it not more likely that the sections in the Strom. are the fulfilment of the proposed γαμικὸς λογός, and that accordingly the Pæd preceded the Stromateis? Harnack, it will be noted, while adopting the other arguments, passes by the distinction of tenses.

As to the second point. In Pæd. ii. 52 he states that he had touched at length on the points there noted. But in none of the

[1] Die Chronologie des alt. Lit., vol. ii. pp. 9, 10.

passages referred to by Heussi does he touch directly on the specific points indicated, even where such a discussion might naturally have taken place.[1] The points are referred to definitely and specifically in some sections of the Pæd.,[2] but not in the Strom. Does not this suggest that the matters alluded to were discussed in another treatise of which we have no further knowledge?

As to the first point. This is the only argument of importance, and it is weighty. That Clement could refer to a section of another work as a separate treatise is, of course, undoubted. That the questions there discussed cover precisely the same ground as that indicated in Pæd. ii. 94 is equally undoubted; so that, if no other explanation of the phenomena were possible, and no evidence could be adduced to the contrary, the hypothesis might be accepted unconditionally. But some general grounds as well as some special considerations may be adduced to the contrary. To begin with, it is certain that Clement conceived of a threefold and progressive activity of the Logos, and that the three works as they stand correspond generally to that conception.[3] He had a clear distinction in his own mind between the Pædagogic and the Didactic function, and in the Pæd. sometimes checks his tendency to digress. Again, in Strom. vii. 27, he says that it was his method to begin with the uprooting of evil opinions as a preliminary to the mention of the more important principles, and he seems to ground this on the practices of those who are initiated into the mysteries. The analogy between the three stages represented by the Prot., the Pæd., and the Strom., and the three grades of initiation into the mysteries, has often been noted. If that was his principle, is it not probable that he adopted it in his writings? That the Pædagogus was designed to be of the nature of a preliminary discipline, he himself expressly states.[4] Further, at the beginning of Strom. iv. he sketches with some detail the plan of work which he proposes to follow, and he carries it out, or at least some stages of it, substantially as he

---

[1] Cf. Str., iii. 4[34].   [2] Cf. Pæd., ii. 10[92], [93].
[3] τῇ καλῇ συγχρῆται οἰκονομίᾳ ὁ πάντα φιλάνθρωπος λόγος, προτρέπων ἄνωθεν, ἔπειτα παιδαγωγῶν, ἐπὶ πᾶσιν ἐκδιδάσκων. Pæd., i. 1[3].
[4] Str., vi. 1[1].

had planned it. Is it probable that he interrupted his design by so long an interval as the writing of the Pæd. must have involved? Moreover, does not the reference in Pæd. ii. 94 imply on this hypothesis that Strom. 1-iv. had been published separately? Clement repeatedly refers to works which he had in contemplation, and which in all probability he never wrote nor published; but what point was there in referring to a work which had been written but not published? And in that case is it not improbable that he should have delayed the plan which he had sketched for an indefinite period, and entered upon Strom. v. without any reference to the previous sections of the work?

As against the hypothesis, the following points may be urged. The manner in which the gnostic is referred to in the Pæd., as contrasted with the manner in which he is referred to in the Strom., is difficult to account for on the hypothesis under consideration. In each of the first four books of the Strom. the word "gnostic" is a technical term, introduced now as a noun, now as an adjective, now as an adverb, without any qualification or explanation.[1] He is delineated at length in relation to God, to his own body, and to his ethical ideals and motives.[2] Clement draws a distinction between simple and gnostic martyrdom,[3] between the reward promised to the simple believer and the gnostic,[4] interprets Psalm viii 6 of "the perfect man and the gnostic,"[5] and speaks of the apostles as truly gnostic and perfect,[6] and represents Clement of Rome as well as St Paul as delineating the character of the gnostic.[7] In the Pæd. there are only two allusions, but neither in letter nor in spirit are they in harmony with these conceptions. In Pæd. i. 31 he says, with reference to Valentinus, that there "are not, then, some who are gnostics and others who are psychical, but that all are equal and spiritual before the Lord," quoting in proof the words of St Paul in Galatians.[8] In Pæd. i. 52 he speaks of the audacity of those who dare to call themselves "perfect and gnostic" thinking more highly of themselves than Paul. In view of the dis-

---

[1] Cf. Str., i. 10⁴⁹; iii. 6⁵³; ii. 18⁸⁰, &c.
[2] Ib., iv. 22¹³⁷, 22¹⁴⁰, 25¹⁶⁰, &c. [3] Ib., iv. 4¹⁵ [4] Ib., iv. 18¹¹⁴.
[5] Ib., iv. 3⁸. [6] Ib., iv. 9⁷⁵. [7] Ib., iv. 17¹⁰⁵; 16¹⁰⁰, ¹⁰¹.
[8] Gal. iii. 26, 27.

cussion and the usage in the Strom., is it sufficient explanation to say that the passage is controversial? If the allusions elsewhere had been incidental, that had been sufficient explanation, but not in view of their detailed character. And, moreover, should we not have expected in that case, not a contrast with the modesty of St Paul, but with those who possessed the true gnosis as opposed "to the gnosis falsely so-called," such as we find more than once in the Strom.? In view of the prominence given to the delineation of the gnostic in Strom. iv., it is hard to understand how such statements could have been made in the Pæd. without some qualification such as Clement was fond of adding.

In Pæd i 35-52, Clement gives an altogether fanciful exegesis of 1 Cor iii. 2, seeking to show with quaint lore that the "milk" to which the apostle referred did not mark a lower stage than "meat," but that they represented the same thing. As it is of the nature of a digression, and its elaborate exegesis is not in harmony with the general trend of the Pæd., it may be held all the more certainly to illustrate his thought at the time. But in Strom. 1. 179, v. 26, and v. 66, he interprets the words in their natural sense. Is it not more probable that the former marks the earlier stage? And would it not be strange if, after having given the natural interpretation in Strom. i and the like in Strom. v., he should in the interval have given the unnatural interpretation to be found in Pæd. i. 33-52?

There is a difficulty, no doubt, in accounting for the disappearance of the treatise on ἐγκρατεία, on the supposition that it was a separate work. Yet, in view of the loss of other writings of Clement, this objection has less weight than it seems. Of the works named by Eusebius, for example, nothing survives of the 'Discussions on Fasting'; of the 'Ecclesiastical Canon,' only one passage has been preserved. Heussi asks, "Why did he not refer to the work on ἐγκρατεία, instead of transcribing it?" Plainly that assumes the point at issue — the identity of the two   But the question suggests a possible solution. If incorporated in a later work, may not that account for its disappearance? Have not "Q" and the "Logia" disappeared as separate works, because incorporated in the Synoptic Gospels? Moreover, on the assumption that διέξιμεν is a future, a like difficulty arises in connection with the disappearance of the γαμικὸς λόγος. If, on the other hand, the Pæd. was written before the Strom., it may be regarded as embedded in the relative sections of the Strom., ii.-iv. 1. There are difficulties on either hypothesis; but I venture to submit that the case for reversing the traditional view as to the relation between the Pæd. and the earlier books of the Strom. has not been incontrovertibly demonstrated.

According to de Faye, the Stromateis is not to be regarded as representing the last stage of the plan of work intended by Clement. The crown of the work was to be a treatise designated "The Teacher" (ὁ διδάσκαλος), which has hitherto been confounded with the Stromateis. The hypothesis is approved by Mayor (pp. xvi, xvii). It received an exhaustive and adverse criticism from Heussi (Z. f. W. Th., 1902), and his conclusions are accepted and regarded as decisive by Harnack (pp. 13-15).

APPENDIX E.

LOST WRITINGS OF CLEMENT.

I. EUSEBIUS (H. E., vi. 13, 14), in his account of the writings of Clement, names, in addition to the Stromateis, the Protrepticus, the Pædagogus, and the Quis Dives, the following —

    (1) Αἱ Ὑποτυπώσεις. See pp. 23-25. (Fragments in Stahlin, vol. iii. pp. 195-215)

    (2) Περὶ τοῦ πάσχα. (Fragments in Stahlin, vol. iii. pp. 216-218.

    (3) Διαλέξεις περὶ νηστείας καὶ περὶ καταλαλιᾶς (of this nothing survives).

    (4) Ὁ Προτρεπτικὸς εἰς ὑπομονὴν ἢ πρὸς τοὺς νεωστὶ βεβαπτισμένους. (Cambridge Texts and Studies, vol. v. pp. 47-49 (1897). Stahlin, vol. iii. pp. 221-223.) See Lecture V.

    (5) Κανὼν ἐκκλησιαστικὸς ἤ πρὸς τοὺς Ἰουδαίζοντας. (Fragment in Stahlin, vol. iii. p. 218.) The Judaisers, in the opinion of Harnack, were such as objected to the allegorical interpretation of the Old Testament. 'History of Dogma,' vol. i. p 292.

II. Not mentioned by Eusebius are:—

    (a) Περὶ προνοίας. (Fragments in Stahlin, vol. iii. pp. 219-221.)

    (b) Εἰς τὸν προφήτην Ἀμώς. (Stahlin, vol. iii. p. lxiii.) It is doubtful whether this was a separate work.

III. Writings referred to by Clement himself:—

    (1) Περὶ ἐγκρατείας. See Appendix D.

    (2) Ὁ λόγος γαμικός. See Appendix D.

    (3) Περὶ ἀρχῶν καὶ θεολογίας (Q. D. 26. Cf. Str., iii. 2^13; v. 14^140, &c.) From a comparison of the terms which

he employs in speaking of this work with those employed in speaking of writings that were contemplated, it seems most natural to infer that the work had been completed.

(4) Περὶ ἀναστάσεως. (Pæd , i. 6 [47], ii. 10 [104].)

(5) Περὶ προφητείας. (Str., iv. 1 [2], v. 13 [88].)

(6) Περὶ ψυχῆς. (Str., ii. 20 [113], v. 13 [58].)

(7) Περὶ τῆς ἀνθρώπου γενέσεως. (Str., iii. 14 [95].)

(8) Περὶ τοῦ διαβόλου. (Str., iv. 11 [85].)

(9) Περὶ τῆς εὐχῆς. (Str., iv. 26 [171].)

(10) Περὶ γενέσεως κόσμου. (Str., vi. 18 [168].)

In all probability the works enumerated 4-9 were intended to be sections of the Strom., and were never written. (Cf. Stah., vol. iii. pp. lxiv, lxv.)

APPENDIX F.

THE BIBLICAL TEXT IN CLEMENT.

THE Canon and Text of the Septuagint represented in the works of Clement are discussed by Stahlin in his 'Clemens Alexandrinus und die Septuaginta' (1901). With regard to the Text, his conclusions are — (1) That in many passages, particularly in the Prophets, the text used by Clement agrees with the revisers, especially with Theodotion; (2) that throughout there is a difference between his text and that of Codex B.

The text of Ecclesiasticus employed by Clement is shown by Hart to be akin to that of the Old Latin.[1] This accounts for many of the deviations from the current text.

The New Testament Text of the Gospels and Acts is the subject of an exhaustive study by Barnard in the Cambridge Series of Texts and Studies (vol. v., 1899). In an Introduction by Professor Burkitt, it is held that the study confirms the conclusion "that the earliest texts of the Gospels are fundamentally Western."

The following note is meant to set forth some of the more distinctive features of the text used by Clement in the Pauline Epistles. To this end it is important to classify the quotations. They may be divided into four classes : I. Quotations where the name of the Epistle is mentioned   II. Quotations where "The Apostle" or Paul is named. III. Quotations for which scriptural authority is alleged or implied. IV. Quotations introduced without reference. Speaking generally, for textual purposes that is the order of merit, but sometimes the fact that a quotation is made from memory may reduce the value of a quotation from a higher

---

[1] J. H. A. Hart, Ecclesiasticus, 1909, pp. 321-346.

to a lower rank, and sometimes from the fact that it occurs in a long passage or is quoted with a ἕως, a quotation in the lower rank may be raised to a higher rank. The importance of attending to such principles of classification may be seen from the following examples, where Clement may be quoted in support of different readings: Class I.—Rom. i. 17 (Str., ii. 6 [29]) δικαιοσύνη γάρ (WH.)   Class II. (Str., v. 1 [3]) δικαιοσύνη δέ.   I. Rom. vi. 22 (Str., ii. 22 [134]), νυνί (WH.)   II. (Str., iv. 3 [11]), νῦν.   I. 1 Cor. iv. 15 (Str., iii. 15 [99]), ἐν Χριστῷ (WH.)   II. (Str., v. 1 [15]) ἐν Χριστῷ Ἰησοῦ.   I. Eph. v. 28 (Str., iv. 8 [64]) ὡς τὰ ἑαυτῶν σώματα.   III. (Pæd., iii. 12 [94]) ὡς τὰ ἴδια σώματα.   I. Col. iii. 12 (Str., iv. 8 [66]) οἰκτιρμοῦ (WH.)   IV. (Str., iv. 7 [55]) οἰκτιρμῶν.

The general features of the text of Clement may be indicated under the following heads (a) The cases in which Clement supports the readings of WH. as against the Textus Receptus ; (b) the cases in which he supports the readings of the Textus Receptus as against WH. ; (c) The cases in which he supports ℵ when it differs from B , (d) the cases in which he supports B when it differs from ℵ; (e) the cases in which he supports the Neutral Text when it differs from the Western Text ; (f) The cases in which he supports the Western Text when it differs from the Neutral Text.   Preserving the classification of readings already suggested, I note the following :—

(a) *Romans*: (I.) 7 [23]; (II.) 1 [21], 2 [14], 2 [17] (twice), 3 [22], 3 [26], 3 [29], 6 [15], 8 [11], 8 [15], 8 [36], 10 [3], 10 [9], 10 [15], 10 [19], 12 [2], 13 [3], 13 [9], 13 [11], 15 [29]; (III) 12 [11], 15 [4], 15 [14]. 1 *Corinthians*: (I.) 4 [21], 6 [2], 6 [8], 13 [11], (II.) 1 [22], 2 [7], 2 [10] (twice), 2 [13], 2 [15], 3 [2], 3 [3], 3 [12], 4 [9], 4 [13], 5 [7] (twice), 6 [10], 7 [9], 7 [12], 7 [35], 7 [38] (twice), 7 [30], 8 [2] (five times), 8 [8], 8 [9], 8 [11] (twice), 10 [1], 10 [23], 10 [24], 10 [30], 11 [11], 11 [31], 11 [32], 12 [9], 12 [13], 13 [2] (twice), 13 [3], 14 [10] (twice); (III.) 7 [34], 9 [22], 10 [3]; (IV.) 7 [3], 7 [7] (twice), 11 [27] (twice), 15 [49]. 2 *Corinthians*: (I.) 3 [14], (II.) 1 [12], 2 [16], 5 [3], 6 [4], 6 [14], 7 [11] (twice), 8 [12], 11 [3] (twice); (III.) 4 [6]. *Galatians* . (II.) 4 [7], 5 [19], 5 [21]. *Ephesians*: (I.) 5 [22], 5 [23] (twice), 5 [25]; (II) 2 [21], 3 [3], 5 [4], 5 [5]; (III.) 5 [14], 6 [5], 6 [9], 6 [12]; (IV.) 3 [14], 4 [9]. *Philippians*: (I.) 2 [21]; (II.) 1 [14], 1 [23], 1 [24], 1 [30], 2 [1], 2 [15], 3 [14], 4 [12], 4 [13]. *Colossians*: (I.) 1 [10] (twice), 1 [26], 1 [27], 1 [28], 2 [2] (twice), 3 [11],

3^{12}, 3^{14}, 3^{15}, 3^{18}, 3^{22}, 3^{25}, 4^1; (II.) 3^5, 3^{16} (twice); (IV.) 2^{11}. *1 Thessalonians* · (II.) 4^8; (III) 5^5, 5^6; (IV.) 2^4. *Hebrews*: (I.) 5^{12}; (II.) 10^{34} (thrice), 10^{35}, 10^{38}, 11^3, 11^{26}, 11^{32} (thrice), 12^{15}; (III.) 8^{11}, 8^{12}. *1 Timothy*: (I.) 5^{21}, 6^{20}; (II.) 2^9 (twice), 6^5; (III) 4^{12}. *2 Timothy*: (I.) 3^{15}. *Titus*. (I.) 2^3; (II.) 3^5 (twice), (III.) 1^{10}.

(*b*) *Romans*: (I.) 7^{17}, 7^{20}, (II.) 8^2, 8^9, 8^{11}, 8^{14}, 8^{24}, 10^{14} (thrice), 10^{17}, 11^{22}, 12^2, 13^9. *1 Corinthians*: (I.) 6^9; (II.) 1^{20}, 1^{23}, 2^{10}, 3^8, 3^{10}, 4^{11}, 6^{10}, 7^6, 7^{10}, 7^{38}, 8^8 (twice), 9^4, 12^9, 13^3, 15^{50}; (III.) 7^{33}. *2 Corinthians*: (II.) 7^{11}, 8^{12}, 11^3; (IV.) 5^{10}, 6^{17}. *Galatians*: (I.) 4^{19}; (II.) 3^{23}, 5^{17}, 5^{20} (twice), 5^{21}, 5^{23}; (IV.) 6^{10}, 6^{14}. *Ephesians*: (I.) 4^{14}, 5^{24}; (II.) 5^5, (III.) 4^{26}; (IV.) 2^3. *Philippians*: (II.) 2^2, 3^{12}. *Colossians* · (I) 1^{10}, 3^{12}, 3^{20}, 3^{23}, 3^{24} (twice), 3^{25}; (II.) 2^3, 2^4, 3^{16}. *1 Thessalonians*: (II.) 2^7 (twice), 4^6, 4^8 (twice). *Hebrews*: (I.) 5^{12}; (II.) 10^{34} (twice), 10^{37}, 11^{32} (twice), 11^{37}, 11^{38}. *1 Timothy*: (II) 2^9, (IV.) 4^2, 4^3. *2 Timothy*: (I.) 3^{16}. *Titus*: (I.) 2^3, 2^5; (II.) 2^{12}.

(*c*) *Romans*: (I.) 3^8, 7^{20}, 8^{11}, 16^{19}; (II.) 1^{21}, 1^{27}, 3^{22}, 6^{21}, 8^{28}, 10^{15}. *1 Corinthians*: (I) 13^{11}; (II.) 6^{10}, 8^3, 8^8, 12^9, 12^{10}; (IV.) 2^9, 15^{49}. *2 Corinthians*: (II.) 1^{10}, 5^3, 7^{11}, 13^5; (III.) 6^{15}, 6^{16}. *Galatians*: (II.) 2^{20}, 4^2, 5^{20}, (III.) 6^2. *Ephesians*: (I.) 5^{24}; (III.) 4^{32}; (IV.) 6^{12}. *Philippians*: (I.) 2^{21}, (II.) 1^9, 1^{24} (twice), 3^{15}. *Colossians*: (I.) 1^9, 3^{11}, 3^{22} (twice), 3^{28}, 4^{37}; (II) 3^{16}, 3^{17}. *1 Thessalonians*: (II.) 4^7, 4^8; (III.) 5^{19}.

(*d*) *Romans*: (II.) 3^{29}, 8^{24}, 10^3, 10^9, 12^2, 13^9, 13^{12}, (III.) 15^4; (IV.) 3^5, 13^{13}. *1 Corinthians*: (I.) 4^{21}, (II.) 2^{10}, 6^{13} (ἕως), 8^6, 8^8, 12^{10}, 13^3, 13^5, 14^6 (twice); (IV.) 11^{27}. *2 Corinthians*: (II.) 1^{12}, (IV.) 5^{10}, 8^{12} (ἐξῆς). *Galatians* · (II.) 3^{24}, 3^{28} (twice), 4^3, 4^6, 5^{17}; (III.) 6^2. *Ephesians*: (II.) 4^{24}, 5^4; (III.) 4^{25}, 6^1, 6^5; (IV.) 2^4. *Philippians*: (II) 1^{10}, 1^{23}, 2^2, 3^{12}. *Colossians*: (I) 1^{27}, 3^{14}, 3^{21}, 3^{25}, 4^2; (II.) 2^7, 3^5, 3^6, 3^{16}, (IV.) 3^1, 3^{10}. *1 Thessalonians*: (II.) 2^5, 4^4; (III.) 5^{13}, 5^{15}, 5^{21}. *Hebrews*: (I) 5^{12}.

(*e*) *Romans*: (I.) 8^{13}, 8^{15}; (II.) 1^{26}, 3^{22}, 8^{37}, 8^{38}, 9^{14}, 13^{11}, 13^{14}, 14^2; (III.) 12^{11}, 12^{13}. *1 Corinthians*: (I) 6^1, 13^{11} (twice); (II.) 2^{10}, 3^2, 3^3 (twice), 4^{13}, 7^{10}, 7^{12}, 7^{14} (ἕως), 7^{28},

8 ^{2} (twice), 8 ^{13}, 10 ^{20}, 10 ^{31}, 11 ^{21}, 11 ^{32}, 12 ^{10}, 12 ^{11}, 14 ^{10}; (III.) 7 ^{34}; (IV.) 11 ^{28}, 15 ^{50} (twice). *2 Corinthians:* (I.) 3 ^{14}; (II.) 1 ^{12}, 2 ^{16}, 5 ^{1}, 5 ^{8}; (IV.) 6 ^{16}.   *Galatians:* (II.) 3 ^{24}, 5 ^{13}, 5 ^{19}, 5 ^{21}, 5 ^{23}; (III.) 5 ^{25}.   *Ephesians:* (II.) 4 ^{19} (twice), 4 ^{24}, 4 ^{29}, 5 ^{4}, 5 ^{14}; (III.) 6 ^{5}; (IV.) 2 ^{4}, 3 ^{14}.   *Philippians:* (II.) 1 ^{23}, 3 ^{12}; (IV.) 2 ^{11}, 4 ^{8}.   *Colossians* · (I.) 1 ^{27}, 3 ^{11}, 3 ^{18}, 3 ^{19}, 3 ^{21}, 4 ^{1}; (II.) 3 ^{6}, 3 ^{17}.   *1 Thessalonians:* (II.) 2 ^{6}; (III.) 5 ^{5}.

(*f*) *Romans:* (II.) 1 ^{27}, 5 ^{12}, 14 ^{16}.   *1 Corinthians:* (I.) 15 ^{32}; (II.) 2 ^{10}, 2 ^{15}, 7 ^{38}, 8 ^{8}, 12 ^{10}, 13 ^{3}, 14 ^{11}; (III.) 9 ^{22}; (IV.) 3 ^{19}. *Galatians:* (I.) 4 ^{19}; (II.) 3 ^{19}, 5 ^{28}.   *Ephesians:* (I.) 4 ^{13}, 5 ^{23}; (II.) 4 ^{18}, 4 ^{19}; (III.) 4 ^{26}, 4 ^{31}.   *Colossians:* (I.) 1 ^{28}; (II.) 3 ^{17}.

From these details it would appear that (*a*) The text of Clement agrees with that of WH. where it differs from the Textus Receptus ± 166 times; that it agrees with the Textus Receptus as against WH. ± 87 times; that it agrees with ℵ, where it differs from B ± 47 times; that it agrees with B as against ℵ ± 58 times; that it agrees with the Neutral Text as against the Western Text ± 70 times; that it agrees with the Western Text as against the Neutral Text ± 24 times. Further, it appears that there is a majority for WH. in each of the groups of passages; that there is a majority for B as against ℵ in all the groups save the first; that there is a majority for the Neutral Text as against the Western Text in all the groups; that in Galatians and 1 Thess. the Textus Receptus exceeds the text of WH., but the fewness of the references impairs the weight of such a comparison; and that the same may be said of the evidence of 2 Tim. and Titus.

How mixed the text of Clement is may be seen from the following illustration.   The following is his text of Col. iii. 16-iv. ¹ (verses 16, 17 are quoted as from "the Apostle"; vv. iii. 18-iv. 1 are quoted as from the Epistle to the Colossians, and from their length must have been transcribed):—

ὁ γὰρ λόγος ὁ τοῦ κυρίου ἐνοικείτω ἐν ὑμῖν πλουσίως, ἐν πάσῃ σοφίᾳ διδάσκοντες καὶ νουθετοῦντες ἑαυτοὺς ψαλμοῖς, ὕμνοις, ᾠδαῖς πνευματικαῖς ἐν τῇ χάριτι, ᾄδοντες ἐν τῇ καρδίᾳ ὑμῶν τῷ θεῷ· καὶ πᾶν ὅ τι ἂν ποιῆτε ἢ ἐν λόγῳ ἢ ἐν ἔργῳ, πάντα ἐν ὀνόματι κυρίου Ἰησοῦ, εὐχαριστοῦντες τῷ θεῷ καὶ πατρὶ

αὐτου (Pæd., ii. 4 ⁴⁸). αἱ γυναῖκες ὑποτάσσεσθε τοῖς ἀνδράσιν,
ὡς ἀνῆκει ἐν κυρίῳ. οἱ ἄνδρες, ἀγαπᾶτε τὰς γυναῖκας καὶ μὴ
πικραίνεσθε πρὸς αὐτάς· τὰ τέκνα ὑπακούετε τοῖς γονεῦσι
κατὰ πάντα. τοῦτο γαρ εὐάρεστον τῷ κυρίῳ. οἱ πατέρες,
μὴ ἐρεθίζετε τὰ τέκνα ὑμῶν ἵνα μὴ ἀθυμῶσιν. οἱ δοῦλοι,
ὑπακούετε κατὰ πάντα τοῖς κατὰ σάρκα κυρίοις, μὴ ἐν ὀφθαλ-
μοδουλείαις ὡς ἀνθρωπάρεσκοι, ἀλλ' ἐν ἁπλότητι καρδίας
φοβούμενοι τὸν κύριον. καὶ πᾶν ὁ ἐὰν ποιῆτε, ἐκ ψυχῆς
ἐργάζεσθε ὡς τῷ κυρίῳ δουλεύοντες καὶ οὐκ ἀνθρώποις, εἰδότες
ὅτι ἀπὸ κυρίου ἀπολήψεσθε τὴν ἀνταπόδοσιν τῆς κληρονομίας.
τῷ γὰρ κυρίῳ Χριστῷ δουλεύετε· ὁ γὰρ ἄδικος κομίσεται ὁ
ἠδίκησεν καὶ οὐκ ἔστι προσωποληψία. οἱ κύριοι τὸ δίκαιον
καὶ τὴν ἰσότητα τοῖς δούλοις παρέχετε, εἰδότες ὅτι καὶ ὑμεῖς
ἔχετε κύριον ἐν οὐρανῷ (Str, iv. 8 ⁶⁵).

The following points may be noted :—

(a) Clement agrees with WH. as against the Textus Receptus in
the following. He omits και before υμνοις and ωδαις,
and reads τω θεω for τω κυριω (v. 16) He omits
ιδιοις (v. 18), reads τον κυριον for τον θεον (v. 22),
o for o τι (v. 23), o γαρ for o δε (v. 25), εν ουρανω for
εν ουρανοις (ιv.¹).

(b) He agrees with the Textus Receptus as against WH. in the
following. He reads εν τη καρδια for εν ταις καρδιαις
(v. 16), και πατρι (v. 17), τω κυριω for εν κυριω (v. 20),
και παν (v. 23), απολη ψεσθε for ἀπολημψεσθε, inserts
γαρ after τω (v. 24), and has προσωποληψια for
προσωπολημψια (v. 25).

(c) He agrees with ℵ as against B in reading του κυριου for του
Χριστου (v. 16), αν for εαν (v. 17), εν οφθαλμοδου-
λειαις (ℵ οφθαλμοδουλιας) for εν οφθαλμοδουλεια,
αλλ' for αλλα (v. 22). Unlike B, he does not omit
και (v. 23).

(d) He agrees with B as against ℵ in reading εν τη χαριτι
for εν χαριτι (v. 16), ερεθιζετε for παροργιζετε (v. 21),
κομισεται for κομιειται (v. 25).

(e) He differs from the Western Text in the following. He puts
και before παν (v. 17). He does not insert υμων (v. 18).

He does not insert υμων after γυναικας (v. 19). He differs from it in reading ερεθιζετε (v. 21) and εν ουρανω (iv. 1).

(f) He agrees with the Western Text in putting και before πατρι (v. 17).

He differs from all three types of text in reading αυτου for δι' αυτου (v. 17), in omitting εστιν after ευαρεστον (v. 20), in reading αδικος for αδικων (v. 25), and παρεχετε for παρεχεσθε (iv. 1).[1]

---

[1] This note is based on Tischendorf, but with alterations in accordance with the text of Stahlin. V. Soden gives authorities for all the variants last noted, except αδικος.

APPENDIX G.

NON-CANONICAL SAYINGS IN THE WRITINGS OF CLEMENT.

THE following are the more important or interesting. They may be thus classified :—

I. Where the authority is cited.

    (a) Gospel according to the Hebrews.[1]

        1. He that wonders shall reign, and he that reigns shall rest.

        2. He that seeketh shall not stop until he finds, and when he has found he shall be astonished; and when he has been astonished he shall reign, and when he has reigned he shall rest.[2]

    (b) Gospel according to the Egyptians.

        1. When Salome inquired as to when the matters about which she asked should be known, the Lord said, When ye shall tread under foot the garment of shame, and when the two shall be made one, and the male with the female neither male nor female.[3]

        2. To the inquiry of Salome, How long shall death reign? the Lord said, As long as ye women bear children.[4]

        3. (Elsewhere this saying is quoted in the form, How

---

[1] ᾗ κἂν τῷ καθ' Ἑβραίους εὐαγγελίῳ, ὁ θαυμάσας βασιλεύσει, γέγραπται, καὶ ὁ βασιλεύσας ἀναπαήσεται (Str., ii. 9 ⁴⁸).

[2] οὐ παύσεται ὁ ζητῶν ἕως ἂν εὕρῃ· εὑρὼν δὲ θαμβηθήσεται, θαμβηθεὶς δὲ βασιλεύσει, βασιλεύσας δὲ ἐπαναπαήσεται (Str., v. 14 ⁹⁶). This saying is found in an imperfect form in the Oxyrhyncus Papyri, vol. iv. p. 4.

[3] πυνθανομένης τῆς Σαλώμης πότε γνωσθήσεται τὰ περὶ ὧν ἤρετο, ἔφη ὁ κύριος· ὅταν τὸ τῆς αἰσχύνης ἔνδυμα πατήσητε καὶ ὅταν γένηται τὰ δύο ἓν καὶ τὸ ἄρρεν μετὰ τῆς θηλείας οὔτε ἄρρεν οὔτε θῆλυ (Str., iii 13 ⁹²).

[4] τῇ Σαλώμῃ ὁ κύριος πυνθανομένῃ, μέχρι πότε θάνατος ἰσχύσει· . . . μέχρις ἂν, εἶπεν, ὑμεῖς αἱ γυναῖκες τίκτητε (Str., iii. 6 ⁴⁵). Cf. Ex. Theod., 67).

long shall men die? and with the addition.)
Then when she said, I did well, therefore,
in that I have not borne children, the Lord
answered, saying, Eat every herb, but that
which has bitterness, do not eat.[1]

4. (The heretics say that) the Saviour Himself said, I
came to destroy the works of the female.[2]

(c) The Preaching of Peter.[3]

1. Wherefore Peter says that the Lord said to
His disciples, If, then, any one of Israel
wills to repent and to believe in God through
My name, his sins shall be forgiven to him.
But after twelve years go ye forth into the
world, that no one may say we have not heard.[4]

2. Accordingly, in the Preaching of Peter the Lord
says to the disciples after the resurrection, I
chose you twelve, having judged you to be
disciples worthy of Me.[5]

II. Where the authority is not designated.

1. Not enviously did the Lord announce in a certain
Gospel, My mystery is for Me and the sons
of My house.[6]

2. Moses said, I am smoke from an earthen pot.[7]

---

[1] φαμένης γὰρ αὐτῆς, καλῶς οὖν ἐποίησα μὴ τεκοῦσα, ἀμείβεται λέγων ὁ κύριος· πᾶσαν φάγε βοτάνην, τὴν δὲ πικρίαν ἔχουσαν μὴ φάγῃς (Str., iii. 9 ⁶⁶).

[2] αὐτὸς εἶπεν ὁ σωτήρ· ἦλθον καταλῦσαι τὰ ἔργα τῆς θηλείας (Str , iii. 9 ⁶³).

[3] For the Preaching of Peter, see Dobschutz, ʿDas Kerugma Petri,ʾ (T. u U.), vol xi. 1894.

[4] διὰ τοῦτό φησιν ὁ Πέτρος εἰρηκέναι τὸν κύριον τοῖς ἀποστόλοις· ἐὰν μὲν οὖν τις θελήσῃ τοῦ ᾽Ισραὴλ μετανοήσας, διὰ τοῦ ὀνόματός μου πιστεύειν ἐπὶ τὸν θεόν, ἀφεθήσονται αὐτῷ αἱ ἁμαρτίαι μετὰ δὲ δώδεκα ἔτη ἐξέλθετε εἰς τὸν κόσμον, μή τις εἴπῃ· οὐκ ἠκούσαμεν (Str., vi. 6 ⁴³)

[5] αὐτίκα ἐν τῷ Πέτρου κηρύγματι ὁ κύριός φησι πρὸς τοὺς μαθητὰς μετὰ τὴν ἀνάστασιν· ἐξελεξάμεν ὑμᾶς δώδεκα, μαθητὰς κρίνας ἀξίους ἐμοῦ (Str., vi. 6 ⁴⁸). This is the form in which the saying is quoted by Potter and Resch, p. 393. Dobschutz, pp. 22, 23, and Stahlin include some lines that follow.

[6] οὐ γὰρ φθονῶν, φησί, παρήγγειλεν ὁ κύριος ἐν τινι εὐαγγελίῳ· μυστήριον ἐμὸν ἐμοὶ καὶ τοῖς υἱοῖς τοῦ οἴκου μου (Str., v. 10 ⁶³). See Resch, ʿAgrapha,ʾ pp. 167-169; Ropes, ʿDie Spruche Jesu,ʾ pp. 94-96. They compare Isa. xxiv. 16 (LXX., Symmachus and Theodotion).

[7] ἐγὼ δὲ εἰμι ἀτμὶς ἀπὸ χύτρας (Str., iv. 16 ¹⁰⁶). From Clem , ʿI Epis.,ʾ c. 17. See note in Lightfoot.

III. Passages quoted as Scripture.

    1. There are those who stretch the looms and weave nothing, says the Scripture.[1]

    2. Naturally, then, the Scripture exhorts us, Be ye approved money-changers.[2]

    3. Ask, says the Scripture, and I will do; think, and I will give.[3]

    4. She has brought forth, and she has not brought forth, says the Scripture.[4]

IV. Passages quoted as from a prophet or prophecy.

    1. They are fighters, strikers with their tails, according to the Prophet.[5]

    2. A certain prophecy says, For, then, affairs here turn out ill when men put their trust in images.[6]

    3. The land of Jacob was praised above the whole land, says the Prophet.[7]

V. Passages quoted with φησί.

    1. Thou hast seen thy brother, it is said, thou hast seen thy God.[8]

    2. Ask, it is said, the great things, and the small shall be added unto you.[9]

[1] οὗτοι οἱ τὰ κατάρτια κατασπῶντες καὶ μηθὲν ὑφαίνοντες, φησὶν ἡ γραφή (Str., i. 8 41). Resch, *op. cit.*, pp. 226, 227; Ropes, *op. cit.*, pp. 31, 32.

[2] εἰκότως ἄρα καὶ ἡ γραφή . . . παραινεῖ· γίνεσθε δὲ δόκιμοι τραπεζῖται (Str., i. 28 177. Cf. ii. 4 15; vi 10 81; vii. 15 90). Cf. Resch, pp. 233-239; Ropes, pp. 141-143; Westcott, 'Introduction to the Study of the Gospels,' 8 p. 458.

[3] αἴτησαι, φησὶν ἡ γραφή, καὶ ποιήσω· ἐννοήθητι καὶ δώσω (Str., vi. 12 101. Cf. vi. 9 78; vii. 7 41; vii. 12 73).

[4] τέτοκεν καὶ οὐ τέτοκεν, φησὶν ἡ γραφή (Str., vii. 16 84). The saying is quoted as from Ezekiel by Tertullian, 'De Carne Christ,' c. 23. Stählin compares Job xxi. 10

[5] πολεμισταί, πλῆκται ταῖς οὐραῖς αὐτῶν (Str., iii. 18 106. Cf. Rev. ix. 10).

[6] τότε γὰρ φησί τις προφητεία δυστυχήσεω τὰ τῇδε πράγματα, ὅταν ἀνδριάσι πιστεύσωσιν (Prot., x. 98).

[7] ἦν ἡ γῆ τοῦ Ἰακὼβ ἐπαινουμένη παρὰ πᾶσαν τὴν γῆν, φησὶν ὁ προφήτης (Str., iii. 12 88). 'Potter refers to Zeph. iii. 19.

[8] εἶδες γάρ, φησί, τὸν ἀδελφόν σου, εἶδες τὸν θεόν σου (Str., i. 19 94; ii. 15 70). Resch, p. 296; Ropes, p. 49. Cf. Gen. xxxiii. 10.

[9] αἰτεῖσθε γάρ, φησί, τὰ μεγάλα, καὶ τὰ μικρὰ ὑμῖν προστεθήσεται (Str., i. 24 188). Resch, p. 230; Ropes, p. 140. Cf. Matt vi. 33

3. In whatsoever things, it is said, I may find you, in those will I also judge you.[1]

VI. Sayings of the Lord.

1. Again the Lord says, He that is married, let him not cast away (his wife), and he that is not married, let him not marry.[2]

2. Wherefore the Saviour says, Be saved, thou and thy soul.[3]

VII. Of uncertain origin.

1. For those that cleave to them (the saints) shall be sanctified.[4]

2. Behold a man and his works before his face. For behold God and his works.[5]

VIII. From the Traditions of Matthias

1. Wonder at that which is before you.[6]

2. They say in the Traditions that Matthias the Apostle used to say, as opportunity offered, If the neighbour of an elect man sin, the elect man sinned ; for if he had conducted himself as the Word dictates, his neighbour would have so revered his life that he would not have sinned.[7]

IX. Additions to the Canonical Text.

1. The Apostle of the Lord, exhorting the Macedonians, becomes interpreter of the divine

---

[1] 'εφ' οἶς γὰρ ἂν εὕρω ὑμᾶς, φησίν, ἐπὶ τούτοις καὶ κρινῶ (Q. D., 40). Ropes, p. 141.

[2] πάλιν ὁ κύριός φησιν ὁ γήμας μὴ ἐκβαλλέτω καὶ ὁ μὴ γαμήσας μὴ γαμείτω (Str., iii. 14[98]). Resch, p. 429; "perhaps from the Gospel according to the Egyptians" (Stahlin). Cf. 1 Cor. vii. 21.

[3] διὰ τοῦτο λέγει ὁ σωτήρ· σῴζου σὺ καὶ ἡ ψυχή σου (Ex. Theod , 2, from Theodotus).

[4] ὅτι οἱ κολλώμενοι αὐτοῖς ἁγιασθήσονται (Str., v. 8[52]). Cf. note in Lightfoot, 'Clement of Rome,' c 46 ; Resch, p. 169 ; Ropes, p. 22.

[5] ἰδοὺ ἄνθρωπος καὶ τὰ ἔργα αὐτοῦ πρὸ προσώπου αὐτοῦ· ἰδοὺ γὰρ ὁ θεὸς καὶ τὰ ἔργα αὐτοῦ (Str., iv. 26[171]). Resch, p. 265; Ropes, p. 45. Cf. Tert., 'De Idolatria,' c. 20, Rev. xxii 12.

[6] θαύμασον τὰ παρόντα (Str , ii. 9[45]).

[7] ἐὰν ἐκλεκτοῦ γείτων ἁμαρτήσῃ, ἥμαρτεν ὁ ἐκλεκτός· εἰ γὰρ οὕτως ἑαυτὸν ἦγεν ὡς ὁ λόγος ὑπαγορεύει, κατῃδέσθη ἂν αὐτοῦ τὸν βίον καὶ ὁ γείτων εἰς τὸ μὴ ἁμαρτεῖν (Str., vii. 13[82]).

voice, saying, The Lord is at hand. *take care lest we should be found empty.*[1]

2. The saints of the Lord shall inherit the glory of the Lord and His power. What glory, O blessed one, tell me? That glory which eye hath not seen, nor ear heard, and hath not entered into the heart of man. *And they shall rejoice in the kingdom of their Lord for ever.*[2] Amen.

[1] ὁ κύριος ἤγγικεν, λέγων, εὐλαβεῖσθε μὴ καταληφθῶμεν κενοί (Prot., ix.⁸⁷). Cf. Zahn, 'Gesch. d. ntl Kan ,' vol. i. p. 174.

[2] καὶ χαρήσονται ἐπὶ τῇ βασιλείᾳ τοῦ κυρίου αὐτῶν εἰς τοὺς αἰῶνας, ἀμήν (Prot., x. ⁹⁴). Resch, p. 166; Ropes, p. 19. Cf. 1 Cor ii. 9. "From the Apocalypse of Elias " (Stahlin)

APPENDIX H.

BIBLIOGRAPHY.

THE fullest account known to me, in English, is that in Richardson, 'Bibliographical Synopsis,' Buffalo, 1887, pp. 38-42. Bardenhewer, 'Geschichte d. altkirk. Litt.,' vol. ii. pp. 15-66, gives a full list under the various questions discussed. A critical estimate of the literature from 1884 to 1900 is given by Ehrhard, 'Die altchrist. Litt. und ihre Erforschung,' vol. i. pp. 293-320. The more important works are noted in Kruger, 'Early Christian Literature,' pp. 162-173 (English translation).

Of editions of the text may be named. Potter, Oxford, 1715, 2 vols. (the standard edition before that of Stählin), Dindorf, Oxford, 1869, 4 vols. ("In every way disappointing, hastily put together," Westcott); Stahlin, 1905, 1906, 1909; Hort and Mayor, Strom., vii, 1902 (notes by Hort and Mayor, valuable introduction and appendices by Mayor); Barnard, 'Quis Dives Salvetur,' "Cambridge Texts and Studies," 1897.

Clement: His Writings and Teaching generally.—Of the older literature on the subject the most valuable is the 'Dissertationes...' of Le Nourry. 1703 (of which extensive use was made by Lumper, 1784). This is reprinted in Migne, 'Patrolog. Graec.,' vol. ix., and in excerpts in Dindorf, vol. iv. Of the literature that appeared in the nineteenth and twentieth centuries, the following may be noted: Guerike, 'De Schola quae floruit Alexandriae Catechetica,' 1824, 1825, Kaye, 'Some Account of the Writings and Opinions of Clement of Alexandria,' 1835; Reinkens, 'De Clemente Presbytero Alexandrino,' 1851; Cognat, 'Clément d'Alexandrie, sa doctrine et sa polémique,' 1859; Freppel, 'Clément d'Alexandrie,' 1865, &c; Bigg, 'The Christian Platonists of Alexandria,' 1886, Lehmann, 'Die Katechetenschule zu Alexandria,' 1896; E. de Faye, 'Clément

d'Alexandrie,' &c., 1898. The relative sections in the Histories of
Doctrine, of Harnack, Seeberg, Schwane, Tixeront, Bethune-Baker.
The articles in the Dictionary of Christian Biography (Westcott);
Herzog, R.E.[2] (Jacobi), R.E.[3] (Bonwetsch); Vacant-Dictionnaire de
Theologie Catholique (A. de la Barre); Pauly-Wissowa (Julicher);
'Encyclopædia Britannica' (Donaldson); Hastings' 'Encyclop. of
Religion and Ethics' (Inge); The Patrologies of Möhler, 1840, pp
430-485; Bardenhewer, 1898, pp. 141-149; Kihn, 1904, pp. 290-
307; Presensé, 'The Early Years of Christianity,' vol. ii. pp 540-566,
iii. pp. 256-295; Allen, 'The Continuity of Christian Thought,' 1895,
pp. 38-70; Hort, 'Ante-Nicene Lectures,' 1895, pp. 82-92, Chase,
'Norwich Cathedral Lectures,' 1896, pp. 257-290, Hitchcock,
'Clement' (Fathers for English Readers), 1899; Kling, 'Studien
und Kritiken,' 1841; Bratke, 'Studien und Kritiken,' 1894;
Overbeck, 'Über die Aufänge der patris. Litt.,' Hist. Zeitschrift,
1882; Courdaveaux, 'Rev. de l'histoire des Religions,' 1892;
Thomas, 'Revue de Theologie et Philosophie,' 1899; 'Church
Quarterly Review,' 1904. On the literary questions see the works
noted on p. 22 et seq.; Zahn, 'Supplementum Clementinum,' 1884;
Harnack, 'Die Chronologie der altchr. Litt.,' vol. ii. pp. 3-23.

Theology and Philosophy.—Ritter, 'Geschichte der Christ. Philosophie,' 1841, vol. i. pp. 421-464; Redepenning, 'Origenes,' vol. i.
pp. 83-163; Hébert-Duperron, 'Essai sur le polemique et la philosophie de St Clém. d'Al.,' 1855; Huber, 'Philosophie der Kir-
chenvater,' 1859, pp. 120-149; Schürmann, 'Die Hellenische
Bildung und ihr Verhaltniss zur Christlich.,' &c., 1859; Möller,
'Geschichte der Kosmologie in der griechischen Kirche,' 1860,
pp. 506-535; Müller, 'Idees dogmatiques de Cl. Al.,' 1861; Merk,
'C. A. in seiner Abhängigkeit von der griech. Philosophie,' 1879;
Denis, 'La philosophie d'Origène,' 1884; Pascal, 'La Foi et la
Raison dans Cl. d'Al.,' 1901; Wagner, 'Wert und Verwertung
der griechischen Bildung im Urteil des C. v. A.,' 1902; Daskolakis,
'Die eklektischen Anschauungen des C. A.,' 1908.

Person and Work of Christ.—Dorner, 'Doctrine of the Person
of Christ,' vol. i. pp. 285-303; Vacherot, 'Histoire Critique de
l'École d'Alex.,' 1846, vol. i. pp. 247-260; Lämmer, 'Cl. Al. de
λογῷ doctrina,' 1855; Ziegler, 'Die Logoschristologie des C. A.,'
1894; Aal, 'Gesch der Logosidee in der Griech. Philos.,' 1899,

vol. ii. pp 393-427; Kattenbusch, 'Das apostol. Symbol,' 1900,
vol. ii. pp. 102-134; Windisch, 'Taufe und Sunde im altesten
Christentum,' 1908, pp. 437-470; Caspari, 'Zeit f. k. W. u. K.
Leben,' 1886, Zahn, 'Glaubensregel,' Herzog, R. E.[3]; Hofling,
'Die Lehre d. Cl von Al. von Opfer im Leben und Cultus,' 1842;
Probst, 'Liturgie der drei ersten christlichen Jahrhunderte,' pp.
130-141; Struckmann, 'Die Gegenwart Christi in d. hl Euchar
n d. schriftlich. Quellen d. vornizan. Zeit,' 1905, pp. 115-139
Batiffol, 'L'Eucharistie,'[5] 1913, pp. 248-261; Love, 'Bibliotheca
Sacra,' 1888; Atzberger, 'Gesch. d. Christl. Eschatologie,' 1896,
pp. 335-363; Anrich, 'Klem und Orig. als Begrunder der Lehre
von Fegfeuer,' 1902

The Ethical Teaching.—The Histories of Christian Ethics,
Luthardt, Gass, and Ziegler; Reuter, 'Clem. Alex. theolog. moral,'
1853; Winter, 'Die Ethik d. Cl. v. Alex.,' 1882, Basilakes,
'Κλήμεντος τοῦ Ἀλεξανδρέως ἡ ἐθικὴ διδασκαλία,' 1892;
Ernesti, 'Die Ethik d. T. F. Clem. v. Al.,' 1900, Capitaine, 'Die
Moral d. Cl v. Al.,' 1903; Funk, 'Tüb. Quar.,' 1871; Markgraf,
'Zeit. f. Kirchengesch.,' 1901; Wagner, 'Der Christ und die
Welt nach Cl. v. Al.,' 1903.

Faith and Gnosis—Dahne, 'De γνώσει,' 1831; Lentzen, 'Er-
kennen und Glauben,' 1848, pp 68-92, 136 *et seq.*, Preische, 'De
γνώσει,' 1871; Knittel, "Pistis und Gnosis," 'Tübing Quartal-
schrift,' 1873; Ziegler, 'Die Psychol d C A,' 1894; Scherer,
'Klemens v. Al. und seine Erkentnissprincipien,' 1907, Inge,
'Faith and its Psychology,' 1910, pp 24-30

Scripture : The Canon of Scripture.—Stahlin, 'Cl. Al. und die
Septuag.,' 1901; Siegfried, 'Philo v. Alex.,' 1875, p 343 *et seq.*;
Heinisch, 'Der Einfluss Philos auf die alteste Christ. Exegese,'
1908; Charteris, 'Canonicity,' 1880; Zahn, 'Gesch. d. ntl.
Kanon,' 1888, vol 1; Harnack, 'Das neue Test. um das Jahr
200,' 1889; Leipoldt, 'Enstehung d. ntl. Kan.,' 1907; Jacquier,
'Le Nouveau Test. dans l'Eglise Chretienne,' 1911, Sanday,
'Inspiration,' 1893, p. 65 *et seq.*; Barnard, 'Clement of Alex-
andria's Biblical Text,' 1899, Hillen, 'Clem. Alex. quid de libris
sacris novi testamenti sibi persuasum habuerit,' 1867, Eickhoff,
'Cl. Al und d. N. T.,' 1890; Dausch, 'Der ntl. Schriftcanons
und Cl. v. Al,' 1894; Kutter, 'Cl. Al u das N. T.,' 1897.

INDEX.

THE END.

PRINTED BY WILLIAM BLACKWOOD AND SONS

Lightning Source UK Ltd.
Milton Keynes UK
UKOW051046141012

200547UK00013B/23/A